MASTERING

AUTOCAD 2000
OBJECTS

MASTERING™

AUTOCAD® 2000 OBJECTS

Dietmar Rudolph

SYBEX®

San Francisco • Paris • Düsseldorf • Soest • London

Associate Publisher: Harry Helms
Contracts and Licensing Manager: Kristine O'Callaghan
Acquisitions & Developmental Editor: Melanie Spiller
Editor: Pat Coleman
Project Editor: Colleen Wheeler Strand
Technical Editor: Mike Gunderloy
Book Designers: Patrick Dintino, Catalin Dulfu,
Franz Baumhackl
Graphic Illustrator: Tony Jonick
Electronic Publishing Specialist: Grey Magauran
Project Team Leader: Lisa Reardon
Proofreader: Jennifer Campbell
Indexer: Nancy Guenther
Cover Designer: Design Site
Cover Illustrator/Photographer: Sergie Loobkoof

Library of Congress Card Number: 99-67014
ISBN: 0-7821-2562-X

Manufactured in the United States of America

10 9 8 7 6 5 4 3 2 1

ACKNOWLEDGMENTS

This book is the result of a 17-year effort by Autodesk to define the AutoCAD drawing database and a 12-year effort by me to try to understand and document it. My part of this effort started in 1987 with AutoCAD version 2.6 when I created and later updated a German language version of *The Auto-CAD Database Book*, by Frederik H. Jones and Lloyd Martin. This was the first book to present a more detailed look into DXF (which is one view of the AutoCAD drawing database) than the meager documentation provided by Autodesk.

A couple of years and AutoCAD versions later, Thomas Stürznickel, Leo Weissenberger, and I wrote *Der DXF-Standard*. The German version was published in 1993 and documented the complete contents of the AutoCAD Release 12 drawing database as it was visible in DXF.

Now, a few years and a few more versions of AutoCAD later, the AutoCAD drawing database has changed a lot, and, more important, DXF is no longer the only or even the preferred way to access it. So I wrote this book to once again document the Auto-CAD drawing database and how to use it.

I wrote this book, but the information in it has been provided by a number of people. I'd like to thank the complete staff at Sybex who took this work from my brain to a bound stack of printed paper. And I'd like to thank the following AutoCAD experts, each of whom contributed to this book from his or her own large bank of knowledge:

Bill Adkison, Andrew Bichard, Anne Brown, Dave Byrnes, James Carrington, Art Cooney, Martyn Day, Mike Dickason, Stefan Dorsch, Cyrille Fauvel, Beat Fehr, Roswitha Fehr, Riccardo de Filippo, Jon Fleming, Rusty Gesner, Josh Gordon, Ralph Grabowski, Cynde Hargrave, Bob Henderson, Phil Holcombe, Bob Holt, Christian Immler, Steve Johnson, Frederik Jones, KC Jones, Markus Kraus, Sascha Krüning, Duff Kurland, Scott van der Linden, Jonathan Linowes, Michael Mackel, Joe MacRae, David Madsen, Lloyd Martin, Mark Middlebrook, Robert Müller, Randall Newton, Jeffrey Pike, Kate Pike, Matt Richards, Robert Rottermann, Susanne Rudolph, Ted Schaefer, Dieter Schlaepfer, Terence Shumaker, Kern Sibbald, Andrew Stein, Pit Steinlin, Thomas Stürznickel, Jeremy Tammik, Tony Tanzillo, Bill Townsend, Reini Urban, Serge Volkov, John Walker, Dave Weber, Leo Weissenberger, Owen Wengerd, Stephanie Yoder, Brad Zehring, and many more. Thank you!

And a special thanks goes to the people at Autodesk Developer Support who always sigh at my e-mail because I once again don't follow the rules or want to know the strangest things. Let's hope the publication of this book reduces your workload.

CONTENTS AT A GLANCE

	Introduction . . . . *xvii*
1	Understanding the AutoCAD Database	1
2	Accessing the Drawing Database	17
3	Data Types in a Drawing Database	53
4	Drawing-Specific Settings	75
5	Properties Common to All Objects	119
6	Objects without a Visual Representation—Part I	131
7	Objects without a Visual Representation—Part II	159
8	Organization of Drawing Entities	177
9	Common Properties for Entities	191
10	Curves and Other Simple Drawing Entities	211
11	Annotation Objects	231
12	Dimensioning Objects	251
13	Line and Face Collections	275
14	Hatches and Fills	299
15	Bitmap Images	313
16	Block Insertion and Attribute Objects	323
17	Layout Objects	337
18	Custom Objects	365
19	Embedded Objects	383

APPENDICES

A	The Drawing Preview Image	395
B	Additional Sources	399
	Index *406*

TABLE OF CONTENTS

Introduction . . . .*xvii*

1 Understanding the AutoCAD Database   1

What's in a Drawing? 2
   AutoCAD Drawings or AutoCAD Models? 3
Of Objects and Containers 3
   Symbol Tables 4
   Understanding Dictionaries 5
   Combining Entities into Blocks 6
   Non-objects in the Drawing Database 7
Identifying Objects 7
   Linking Objects 8
   Implicit Links 9
   Embedding Objects 9
About Classes and Hierarchies 9
Object Properties 11
   Defined versus Calculated Properties 12
   Missing Properties 12
Does This Book Completely Document the AutoCAD Drawing Database? 13
   Which Objects Are Covered? 14
   Summary 14

2 Accessing the Drawing Database   17

The Serialized Way—DXF 18
   Some Myths about DXF 19
   Some Criticisms of DXF 20
   Serializing Drawing Data 21
   ASCII and Binary DXF 22
   Differences between ASCII and Binary DXF 23
   The Structure of a DXF File 23
   Objects in DXF 25
AutoLISP—DXF by Another Name 26
   Database Access from AutoLISP 28
   Getting Entity Names 29
   Retrieving Entities with AutoLISP 30
   Dictionary Access in AutoLISP 32
   Modifying and Making Objects in AutoLISP 34
   Reading and Writing Drawing Settings 35
The Same Data with Names—ActiveX Automation 36
   Accessing the AutoCAD Database 37
   Of Collections, Objects, and Interfaces 38

Accessing Entities via ActiveX Automation 39
Creating Entities via ActiveX Automation 40
Working with Dictionaries in ActiveX Automation 41
Custom Objects in ActiveX Automation 41
Non-objects in ActiveX Automation 42
The Object-Oriented Way—ObjectARX 42
Accessing the AutoCAD Database 43
Opening and Closing Objects in a Database 44
Iterating through Containers 45
Entity Handling in ObjectDBX 47
Working with Dictionaries in ObjectDBX 49
Database Settings and Result Buffers 49
Other Ways to Access the Drawing Database 50
Summary 52

3 Data Types in a Drawing Database   53

Integers in the Drawing Database 54
Signed 16-Bit Integer 55
Signed 32-Bit Integer 56
Signed 8-Bit Integer 57
Disguised Integers 57
Enumerations As Integers 58
Group Codes 59
Colors and Lineweights 59
Booleans as Integers 60
Real Numbers in the Drawing Database 61
Length Units 63
Angle Units 63
Date and Time Values 63
Strings in the Drawing Database 64
Character Sets 64
Character Range 65
Handles in the Drawing Database 65
Object Pointers 66
Points in the Drawing Database 66
Points, Coordinates, and Point Lists 66
Points, Vectors, and Offsets 67
Coordinate Systems 68
Entity Coordinates 69
The Arbitrary Axis Algorithm 70
Binary Data in the Drawing Database 72
Summary 73

4 Drawing-Specific Settings   75

How to Access the Drawing Settings 77
Critical Settings 78
ACADVER (AutoCAD database version number) 79
ACADMAINTVER (AutoCAD database maintenance version number) 80

ATTMODE (attribute display mode) 80
DISPSILH (show silhouette lines for 3D solids) 80
DWGCODEPAGE (drawing character set) 81
FILLMODE (fill display mode) 82
LTSCALE (global linetype scale factor) 83
LWDISPLAY (linewidths display) 83
PDMODE (point display mode) 84
PDSIZE (point display size) 85
PSLTSCALE (paperspace linetype scaling) 86
QTEXTMODE (quick text display) 86
SPLFRAME (spline frame display) 87
TILEMODE (modelspace display) 87
VISRETAIN (retain visibility settings) 88
Additional Settings 89
Settings Sequence in DXF 115
Summary 118

5   Properties Common to All Objects   119
The Object Handle 120
Calculated Properties—Entity Name and ObjectID 120
The Object's Class 121
The Object's Owner 122
Reactor Links 123
Extension Dictionary Link 124
Other Pointers 125
Extended Object Data 126
Selecting Xdata 126
Reading and Writing Xdata 127
Xdata Group Codes and Values 128
Summary 129

6   Objects without a Visual Representation—Part I   131
Symbol Tables 132
The DXF Sequence for Symbol Tables 133
The Layers Table 134
Layer Table Sequence in DXF 134
The Layer Table Extension Dictionary 135
Layer Symbol Table Records in DXF 135
Layer 0 135
Layer Properties 135
External Layers 137
The Linetypes Table 138
Predefined Linetypes 138
Linetype Properties 139
Linetype Definitions 139
Text Styles 141
Text Style Properties 142
Dimension Styles 144

Dimension Style Families 145
Dimension Style Properties 145
User Coordinate Systems 151
UCS Properties 151
Named Views 152
View Properties 153
The Viewports Table 154
Viewport Properties 154
Registered Applications 158
Summary 158

7   Objects without a Visual Representation—Part II   **159**
Objects in DXF 161
Dictionaries Summarized 161
The Contents of a Dictionary 161
Merging Dictionaries 162
The Minimum Contents of the Root Dictionary .163
Dictionaries with Default 163
Placeholder Objects 164
Drawing Variables 164
Global Settings Saved As Variables 165
Locating the Dictionary Variables 165
DictionaryVariable Objects 166
Entity Groups 166
Locating a Group 166
AcDbGroup Objects 166
The Entity Order Index 167
Locating a Block's Entity Order Table 168
AcDbSortentsTable Objects 168
Spatial and Layer Indexes 169
The AcDbIndex Class 169
Spatial Indexes 170
Layer Indexes 170
Object Lists 170
Extension Records 171
Merging Extension Records 172
Drawing Properties 173
Layer Filters 174
Summary 175

8   Organization of Drawing Entities   **177**
Block Containers 178
The Block Table 178
Layout Blocks 182
External References 182
Block Begin and Block End Objects 183
The DXF Representation of Block Containers 184
The BLOCK_RECORD Table 184
BLOCK_RECORD Table Entries 185

The BLOCKS Section 186
The ENTITIES Section 188
Summary 188

9   Common Properties for Entities   **191**

The DXF Sequence for AcDbEntity 192
The Layer Property 193
The Color Property 193
    The AutoCAD Color Index 194
    By Block and By Layer Colors 202
The Linetype Property 203
    Linetype Mapping 203
The Linetype Scale Property 204
The Lineweight Property 205
The Plot Style Property 206
The Visibility Property 207
The Hyperlinks Property 208
The Paperspace Flag Property 208
Interactive-Only Properties 209
Summary 210

10   Curves and Other Simple Drawing Entities   **211**

The Properties of Curves 212
    Parametrical Representations of Curves 213
    Curve Properties 214
    Curves in DXF 215
Unbounded Straight Lines 215
Single-Bounded Straight Lines 216
Finite Straight Lines 216
    Lines That Have a Thickness 217
    Calculated Properties for Lines 218
Circular Curves 219
    A Circle's Local Coordinate System 219
    The Defining Properties of a Circle 219
    The Calculated Properties of a Circle 220
Circular Arcs 220
Ellipses and Elliptical Arcs 222
Spline Curves 224
    The Fit Data of a Spline 225
    NURBS Data 225
    The AcDbCurve Properties and Splines 226
    The DXF Sequence for Splines 227
3D Faces 227
Summary 229

11   Annotation Objects   **231**

Point Objects 232
Shape Symbols 234

Single Lines of Text 235
    Text Style and Characters 237
    Text Formatting 238
    Text Justification 238
Paragraph Text 240
    MText Location and Size 241
    MText Contents and Formatting 243
    DXF Representation of Paragraph Text 244
Feature Control Frames 245
    Dimension Style-Based Data 246
    Formatting Codes 247
Semi-Custom Annotation Objects 248
    Arc-Aligned Text 248
    Remote Text 249
Summary 250

12 Dimensioning Objects   251

Dimensions and Style 252
Dimension Scaling 253
Calculating the Dimension Text String 254
Adding Tolerances 256
Alternate Dimensioning 258
Dimension Text 259
Dimension Lines and Arrows 260
Positioning Dimension Text 263
AcDbDimension Properties 267
Aligned Linear Dimensions 269
Rotated Linear Dimensions 270
Angular Dimensions: Part I 270
Angular Dimensions: Part II 271
Diametrical Dimensions 272
Radial Dimensions 272
Coordinate Dimensions 273
Summary 274

13 Line and Face Collections   275

Leader Lines 276
Lightweight Polylines 279
    Arcs in Polylines 280
    Wide Polylines 281
Heavyweight Polylines 283
    Polyline Begin 284
    Vertex Objects 285
    Polyline End 285
    Curve-Fit Polylines 286
    Splined Polylines 286
Three-Dimensional Polylines 287

Polygon Meshes 288
   Splined Polymesh Surfaces 289
Polyface Meshes 290
   Polyface Mesh Vertices 290
   PolyFace Mesh Records 291
Multilines 292
   Multiline Styles 292
   Multiline Entities 294
   Multiline Breaks and Intersections 295
   Calculated Properties of Multilines 297
Summary 297

14 Hatches and Fills   **299**
The Elements of a Hatch Definition 300
Contours and Associativity 302
   Loop Types 302
   Polyline-like Loops 303
   Edge-Defined Loops 303
   Line Edges 304
   Circular Arc Edges 304
   Elliptical Arc Edges 305
   Spline Edges 305
   Associated Entities 306
Fills and Patterns 307
   Pattern Generation Parameters 307
   Pattern Line Families 308
AutoCAD's Boundary Tracer 309
Solids and Traces 310
Wipeouts 311
Summary 311

15 Bitmap Images   **313**
Image Definitions 314
   Finding an Image Definition 316
Image Entities 316
   Image Manipulation 317
   Image Clipping 318
   Images in DXF 318
Image Definition to Entity Link 319
Global Settings for Raster Images 319
Summary 321

16 Block Insertion and Attribute Objects   **323**
Block References 324
   Block Transformation 325
   Multiple Inserts 327
   Inherited Properties 327

Filtered Inserts 328
Spatial Filtering 328
Attribute Objects 331
Attribute Definitions 331
Constant Attributes 333
Variable Attributes 334
Finding Variable Attributes 335
Summary 335

17 Layout Objects   337

Plot Settings 338
Plot Devices 339
Plot Media 339
Plot Rotation 341
What to Plot 341
Plot Scales 343
Fine-Tuning the Plot 345
Plot Settings in DXF 346
Layout Objects 346
Layout Tabs 347
Layout-Specific Coordinates 347
Layout-Specific Settings 349
Layouts in DXF 350
Abstract Views 350
Defining an Abstract View 351
Clipping a View 352
Render Modes 353
View-Specific Coordinate Systems 354
Viewport-Specific Drawing Aids 355
Viewports to Modelspace 357
Viewport Scale 358
Clipped Viewports 359
Hiding Lines and Layers 360
Plot Styles within a Viewport 361
The Paperspace Viewport 361
Viewports in DXF and AutoLISP 361
Viewports in ModelSpace 363
Summary 363

18 Custom Objects   365

The Basic Problem 366
The Ideal Custom Object 368
Of Proxies and Zombies 368
Classes in DXF 370
DXF Sequence for the Class Definitions .370
Proxy Objects and Entities 371
Original Object Data 374
The DXF Sequence for Proxy Objects 374
Proxy Graphics 374

The Structure of Proxy Graphics 375
The Proxy Graphics Drawing Commands 376
Why Bother? 381
Summary 381

19 Embedded Objects   **383**
Bodies, Solids, and Regions 385
ACIS Data 386
Querying Volume and Area 387
OLE Data 389
The OLE Source and Type 390
Location, Orientation, and Size 391
OLE Data in DXF 391
VBA Projects 392
The Location of VBA Projects in a Drawing 392
VBA Project Data 392
And in the End... 393

APPENDICES

A The Drawing Preview Image   **395**
Previewing DWG 396
Previewing DXF 397
The Preview Bitmap 397

B Additional Sources   **399**
Computer Graphics Tutorials 400
Computer Graphics Reference Books and Material 400
AutoCAD Tutorials 400
AutoCAD Reference Books 401
AutoCAD Application Development 401
AutoCAD Programming 402
AutoLISP Programming 402
AutoCAD ActiveX Programming 403
ObjectARX and ObjectDBX 403
AutoCAD Database Objects 403
DWG 403
DXF 404
Spline Curves and Surfaces 404
ACIS 404
DIESEL 404
ActiveX Programming 405
Windows API 405

Index **406**

INTRODUCTION

AutoCAD is the world's most widely used software for Computer Aided Design and Drafting. According to Autodesk, more than 2 million people use AutoCAD in their daily work to define and document technical designs or to store maps, site plans, and other geometric data. This data is saved in AutoCAD drawing files. Again according to Autodesk, more than 2 billion AutoCAD drawing files are on the computers out there.

AutoCAD comes with a large set of commands and features to create, manipulate, and query the contents of a drawing file. But these built-in commands deal with only a few of the almost unlimited number of ways in which the contents of these files can be used. Some obvious uses of the embedded drawing data include statistics and report generation, NC program and plot file generation, and data exchange with other CAD or graphics products.

Consequently, there is a strong need to access a drawing file's internals. This need is best documented by the 1998 founding of the OpenDWG alliance, an association of Autodesk competitors formed to press for more access to AutoCAD drawing files.

This book covers many ways to read, write, evaluate, and manipulate the contents of AutoCAD drawing files. Some of these ways require no more than your being able to use a text editor or even a sheet of paper. Others require that you learn one of a dozen computer programming languages. Of course, this book cannot teach you all these languages. There are many other books available for that purpose.

However, no matter which *procedure* you use to access the data embedded in a drawing file, you are always faced with the same questions: What is the meaning of the data? Which objects can be found in a computer-generated drawing? Which properties are used to define these objects? What kinds of values are allowed, and how are they formatted?

The answer to these questions is what this book is about: the *contents* of an Auto-CAD drawing file. You will learn about all you may encounter when evaluating a drawing, which is usually called a *drawing database*. I will describe the various ways to find or manipulate objects, the items such as lines and circles that constitute the drawing database. My main goal, however, is to describe the *meaning* and *attributes* of each object.

Isn't It Obvious?

But do you really need an entire book to describe the contents of a drawing file? What's so complicated about the lines and circles that make up a drawing? Two things: First, there are many more objects embedded in a drawing file than lines and circles. Dimensions, spline curves, cubes, and even terrain models can be part of a drawing file, and you need to understand them in order to process and handle these objects. Second, even for objects that seem to be as simple as lines and circles, Auto-CAD saves and uses a large number of properties, many of them quite difficult to understand.

A good example is the point object. If you were to list all the things needed to define a point, how many properties would you need? And which? In 2D, that means on a sheet of paper, you would need two distances to describe the point: the distance from the left edge of the sheet (called X) and the distance from the bottom edge (called Y). In mathematical terms, these distances are called *coordinates*. In a three-dimensional space, for example, your office, you will need a set of three coordinates to define the point: its distance from the left wall, its distance from the back wall, and its height above the floor.

If you think more in terms of computer graphics than in terms of mathematical definitions, you will also add another property to your list: the color in which the point is displayed on the screen or on paper. In addition, most graphics programs use a layer property to group related objects.

But could you imagine giving your point a direction? Probably not. However, AutoCAD does. And it not only saves *one* direction with each point, it saves *two*! And to make things even more complicated, it even gives your point a height or a thickness. Now that's strange, isn't it? What is a *thick* point? As you will see, it's a certain arrangement of planar faces arranged in 3D. You wouldn't call this a point, but Auto-CAD does.

Some AutoCAD objects are easy to understand. For others you need detailed knowledge of how AutoCAD creates, manipulates, and saves drawing data. This is why I wrote this book, and in it you will find all you need to know about the contents of an AutoCAD drawing file, and maybe more.

Accessing AutoCAD Objects

Since the beginning of time, which was 1982 in the AutoCAD world, the programmers at Autodesk understood that they could not support each and every application that users might have for the data saved in a drawing file. Therefore, they added "openness" to the software. Even the very first version of AutoCAD allowed the user to access and manipulate a drawing's contents through means other than AutoCAD commands.

Over time, Autodesk added a broad set of methods that you can use to access Auto-CAD drawing data. And the developers at Autodesk continue to add more. However, no matter which method you choose, it has something in common with the rest: all methods allow you to read and write the internal drawing data. With only a few exceptions, you can access the complete contents of a drawing using any method. So it's up to you to select your preferred working environment.

Let's briefly take a look at the choices Autodesk gives you to read and write the contents of an AutoCAD drawing file, and let's also look at the advantages and disadvantages of each method.

AutoLISP and Visual LISP

You can access the complete contents of an AutoCAD drawing using AutoCAD's built-in programming language, AutoLISP. AutoLISP and its newer variant, Visual LISP, are LISP dialects. LISP is a programming language especially suited for handling the various data elements in a CAD drawing, such as coordinate lists, numbers, keys, and so on. AutoLISP includes some special language constructs to read and write data from the current drawing, including the *entget*, *entmod*, and *entmake* primitives.

AutoLISP and Visual LISP have almost complete access to the drawing database. One thing you cannot do with the two LISPs, however, is build arbitrary user-defined objects. Here are a couple of other drawbacks:

- AutoLISP and Visual LISP are only available inside an AutoCAD session.
- You can only access the drawing currently loaded in AutoCAD.

The big advantage associated with using AutoLISP and Visual LISP is that it takes only about five lines of code to make, extract, and manipulate a drawing object.

The ObjectARX Method

ObjectARX is the foundation on which AutoCAD itself is built. As a set of C++ libraries, ObjectARX is also available to any party interested in adding functionality to AutoCAD. The data access part of ObjectARX is called the AcDb library, which is short for *AutoCAD Database*. This library contains all the functions to create, evaluate, and manipulate objects in an AutoCAD drawing.

Using ObjectARX, a programmer can access every little detail of a drawing's contents. The library even allows simultaneous access to multiple drawings, regardless of whether they are currently open in AutoCAD. There is almost no functional restriction in what an ObjectARX program can do to an AutoCAD drawing. This includes creating totally new object classes. But some drawbacks are associated with using ObjectARX. First, it is limited to the AutoCAD environment. You can use ObjectARX programs only inside AutoCAD or with products based on the AutoCAD OEM kernel. The second drawback is programming effort. You are limited to C++, and you need a substantial amount of training and time to master this environment.

COM and ActiveX Automation

ActiveX Automation, formerly known as OLE Automation and now also referred to as COM Automation, is a Microsoft term for standardized interprocess communication. Different programs running concurrently under Microsoft Windows can export data and functionality to each other. Like many other programs, AutoCAD exposes most of a document's contents via ActiveX Automation, thus becoming an *automation server*. In AutoCAD, the document is usually called a drawing.

Any other program using this interface is called the *automation client*. It can query object data from AutoCAD. In addition, ActiveX Automation allows the client to create and manipulate objects. Like ObjectARX and the LISPs, ActiveX Automation is not limited to accessing the drawing data. You can use it to remotely control almost every function of AutoCAD.

ActiveX Automation is one segment of a larger picture, which is called DCOM (Distributed Component Object Model). One can see ActiveX Automation as a friendly package wrapped around a small segment of DCOM. A programmer may choose to access AutoCAD or other components through DCOM directly without using the ActiveX Automation layer. Usually, there's no need to do so because all the main programming environments also give you the friendlier ActiveX Automation interface to access AutoCAD drawing data. However, a few objects in a drawing can't be accessed through AutoCAD's ActiveX Automation interface, but are visible to DCOM directly. I will note DCOM only in these cases.

A big advantage is associated with ActiveX Automation: through its standardized interface, the programmer is free to choose whatever programming language or development environment he or she wants. The only requirement, of course, is that the language or development environment must support ActiveX Automation client programming. The most common environments for ActiveX client programming are Visual Basic and Delphi, as well as the Visual Basic for Applications (VBA) dialect embedded in many application programs such as Microsoft Excel, Microsoft Word, and even AutoCAD itself. However, ActiveX Automation clients can also be written in Java, C, or other languages. Drawbacks associated with using ActiveX Automation to evaluate or manipulate drawings include some limitations in object access and creation and its reliance on AutoCAD. Because the client program has no idea about the internals of the drawing, it needs AutoCAD running in order to open and talk to the drawing database.

The ObjectDBX Method

All the methods I've described so far need AutoCAD to load and evaluate the drawing. However, many people want to access a drawing file's contents without loading or even buying AutoCAD. From this need arose a market for drawing access libraries. Several companies developed and sold C libraries that read and write AutoCAD drawing files without AutoCAD.

All these companies had a big problem, though. Autodesk never documented the internal structure of a drawing file. All that Autodesk made available were the access methods described in this book. So the makers of DWG read/write libraries had to reverse-engineer the file format, literally guessing the meaning of each bit in a drawing file. Given the complexity of this task, the results were quite good, but not as good as if such a library were available from the basic source, Autodesk. Fortunately, such a toolkit is finally shipping from Autodesk, first called DWG Unplugged, and now called ObjectDBX.

Using ObjectDBX, a programmer can create programs that read and write Auto-CAD drawing files outside AutoCAD. ObjectDBX is a set of C++ libraries, which are identical to the AcDb libraries of ObjectARX. As with ObjectARX, you are limited to a specific environment to create programs that access a drawing's database. In this case, the environment is Microsoft Visual C++ and Microsoft Windows. If your program is supposed to run on a Sun workstation, you're out of luck.

The DXF File

What comes first also comes last. When AutoCAD was first released in 1982, there was no such thing as Microsoft Windows, AutoLISP, ObjectARX, or ActiveX Automation. But there was a way to read, write, and manipulate the contents of an AutoCAD drawing file. And you needed neither AutoCAD running nor a specific development platform. How did they do that?

The programmers at Autodesk had AutoCAD copy the complete contents of a drawing to a formatted text file. This file was called *Drawing Interchange File* or DXF for short. By definition, a DXF file contains the complete contents of an AutoCAD drawing file. It can be read by a simple computer program or even by a human being. Manipulating and creating a DXF file is extremely simple. Such a modified file can then be loaded into AutoCAD and thus constitute a new or changed drawing database.

Every AutoCAD version since 1982 is able to write and read DXF files. A DXF file and its corresponding DWG file are twins. They contain the exact same database, only formatted differently—unless there are some bugs, which happens now and then, of course. Unlike a DWG file, the database displayed in a DXF file is documented by Autodesk...well, at least kind of documented. The DXF documentation supplied with AutoCAD is historically known as incomplete, error-prone, and rarely understandable.

DXF can be read by almost every graphics program in the world and is even used to exchange drawings between parties that don't have AutoCAD. A big advantage associated with using DXF for drawing access and manipulation is its platform independence. Because DXF files are just plain text, they are accessible under Unix, MacOS, DOS, and Windows. Since the complete drawing database is available, there's almost no limitation on what you can do with it. Unlike the other methods I've discussed, DXF is also supported by AutoCAD LT. The big drawback associated with DXF is that it lacks error-handling. When manipulating a DXF file, you can introduce every possible error. Only when AutoCAD or another target program finally converts the DXF file back into a drawing database is the user notified that objects have been misdefined.

What Else?

In addition to using any of these five methods, you can extract objects from an AutoCAD drawing or import objects into a drawing in many other ways. However, only these five methods give you full and exact access to the drawing database. Every other method, such as WMF, DWF, IGES, STEP, SAT, 3DS, and so on, approximates the drawing contents. When you use one of these other methods, the contents are different from the contents of the original drawing. Sometimes objects are omitted, because the format simply doesn't support them. Most often objects are modified to fit into the target format. In any case, information is lost during the transfer process, and it cannot be retrieved. Only the five methods I've described allow you to get the complete contents of a drawing file and restore it later with exactly the same contents.

A Word about Versions

AutoCAD evolves. Every new version has additional functionality. In most cases, added functionality also means added contents to the drawing database. This is easy to understand: the added functionality needs some place to store related information, and the drawing database should be the only place to store drawing-related data.

NOTE A drawing database in AutoCAD does *not* contain the complete information needed to reconstruct a drawing from scratch. For instance, the shape of characters and/or symbols is not part of the DWG file. Instead, this information is located in separate computer files. The same goes for externally referenced drawing files or bitmap images.

When describing or using the AutoCAD drawing database, you therefore always need to add the version of the AutoCAD database and/or the corresponding version of AutoCAD. The following list includes the most important versions released since 1984.

AutoCAD Drawing Database Version	Belongs to AutoCAD Version	Release Date
AC1.50	AutoCAD Release 5, Version 2.0	1984
AC2.10	AutoCAD Release 6, Version 2.1	1985
AC1002	AutoCAD Release 7, Version 2.5	1986
AC1003	AutoCAD Release 8, Version 2.6	1987
AC1004	AutoCAD Release 9	1987
AC1006	AutoCAD Release 10	1988
AC1009	AutoCAD Release 11 and 12	1990
AC1012	AutoCAD Release 13	1994
AC1014	AutoCAD Release 14	1997
AC1015	AutoCAD Release 15, AutoCAD 2000	1999

This book describes version AC1015 of the AutoCAD drawing database. Although many of the concepts I discuss in this book also apply to other versions, many objects and properties are not available in older versions.

CHAPTER <u>1</u>

Understanding the AutoCAD Database

FEATURING

Understanding a drawing   2

Using objects and containers   3

Identifying objects   7

Understanding classes and hierarchies   9

Dealing with object properties   11

Before you start looking at specific objects in a drawing database, you need to understand the general concept of drawing data. This chapter provides basic information about the internals of AutoCAD's drawing database.

In the process of presenting this information, I will define a number of terms. Many of them, such as *containers* or *objects*, you already know from daily life. However, they have a special meaning when discussing computer-generated data. And they have an even more specific meaning when discussing a computer-generated drawing. Therefore, it's necessary to define these terms precisely.

 NOTE In books about computer graphics or programming, you'll often find various authors using different terms to describe the same thing. In this book I try to stay with the terminology used in the AutoCAD documentation. For a variety of reasons, mostly historic, this terminology does not always reflect the current industry standard. For example, in AutoCAD an *attribute* is a specific object type; usually, *attribute* is synonymous with the term *property*.

In this chapter, we'll take a look at the general structure of a computer-generated drawing. We'll look at the data elements saved in a drawing file and how to differentiate them. We'll also look at the internal composition of the drawing data and how the elements of the data correlate. In addition, you will see how objects are identified and linked.

An important question that concerns exchanging drawings between different programs is also a topic in this chapter: Is a drawing database a complete entity? In other words, does the information in an AutoCAD drawing file contain all the data necessary to construct an identical drawing in another program? And a second question arises: Is the documentation of an AutoCAD drawing file, for instance the one in this book, ever complete? This chapter will give you the answers to these questions.

What's in a Drawing?

Before I answer this question, let's start with the basic question: What *is* a drawing? In the pre-CAD era, a drawing was a sheet of paper, Mylar, or papyrus, containing lines in ink or color that formed a visual representation of a real-world or an imaginary object.

A computer-generated "drawing" still describes a real-world or an imaginary object, but it does so by using a mathematical model of the object. The CAD model of a car consists of multiple CAD models, including wheels, tires, and brakes. A tire has a geometrical description, but also has manufacturing properties such as materials and additional functional information such as maximum speed or inflation.

Although you still can output a CAD model onto a sheet of paper, the paper representation is only one of many uses for such a model. In addition, there may be many different visual representations of the model. The paper output may show a front or a side view, may show a detail of the braking system, or may demonstrate what a fully colored production model of the car looks like when caught in a traffic jam.

AutoCAD Drawings or AutoCAD Models?

You may want to say that these fully featured CAD models aren't here yet. Of all AutoCAD drawing files out there, 99.9 percent contain only lines and circles, as did the paper drawings of old.

Although you are correct about the contents of most drawing files, that a drafter used circles to draw a tire doesn't tell you anything about the relationship of lines on the page to the actual tires they represent. An AutoCAD drawing database can contain mathematical models of tires and brakes, just as it can contain lines.

And if you look closely, you'll see that there is no difference between a CAD tire and a CAD line. Both are abstract models of some real-world or abstract object. The CAD tire is an abstract model of a real-world tire. The CAD line is usually an abstract model of the edge of a real-world part.

Of Objects and Containers

An AutoCAD drawing is no more than a container for arbitrary abstract models or arbitrary *objects*. This collection of objects is called the *drawing database*.

In many aspects, the drawing database is similar to other databases you already know about or have worked with. Just like the database you use to organize your address book or CD collection, the drawing database contains tables that consist of rows (records) and columns (fields).

Records or objects in the drawing database can be ordinary lines or circles, but it is equally possible, and becoming increasingly probable, that some objects can be cars and tires, walls and doors, books and authors.

AutoCAD places almost no limit on what an object in a drawing database can be. Only if the object is supposed to have a visual representation must it follow a few rules; for instance, an AutoCAD object must have a color property.

The creator of an AutoCAD drawing database is free to add arbitrary objects to it. However, the creator is not free to add objects wherever he or she wants. Each object must be placed in one and only one of a number of containers that form the drawing database.

Symbol Tables

Objects that don't have a visual representation but belong to a certain predefined set of object types (or classes) must go into the Symbol Tables container. The Symbol Tables container is made from nine database tables. I'll discuss the following eight of them in detail in Chapter 6:

- The dimension style table (AcDbDimStyleTable, DIMSTYLE) defines a set of properties to be applied to dimensions, such as the arrow type or text justification.
- The layer table (AcDbLayerTable, LAYER) is for the layer objects that can be used to organize drawing entities.
- The linetype table (AcDbLinetypeTable, LTYPE) contains line styles that define how drawing entities will be displayed or plotted.
- The table of registered applications (AcDbRegAppTable, APPID) contains the names of third-party applications that save extended object data (xdata).
- The text style table (AcDbTextStyleTable, STYLE) defines a set of properties to be applied to text objects, such as the font and the character orientation.
- The user coordinate system table (AcDbUCSTable, UCS) lists Cartesian coordinate systems that a user might activate and work in.
- The viewport table (AcDbViewportTable, VPORT) defines named sets of tiled screen viewports.
- The view table (AcDbViewTable, VIEW) contains the definition of views into a drawing. A user can call such a view for display or plot.

In addition to these symbol tables, there is the special block table (AcDbBlockTable, BLOCK_RECORD), which consists of the block containers and all drawing entities. This table is covered in detail in Chapter 8.

Like a database table in dBase or Microsoft Access, each symbol table can contain only a specific type of object. The objects within a symbol table are called the *symbol table records*. Symbol table records in a symbol table are always objects of the same class. For example, all records in the layer table are layer record objects. Conversely, layer record objects aren't allowed anywhere outside the layer table.

All the records within a symbol table contain a *name* field that acts as an identifier or a key to the table record. Again this is similar to the primary key in a database table. The key value is a string and must be unique inside a symbol table to prevent duplicate data and to maintain data integrity. In this way, it is similar to a Social Security number in a corporation's employee records file. This key field identifier is unique only within one symbol table. Thus, both the layer and the linetype tables can include records whose key fields are STANDARD, but within one symbol table, two records cannot use the same key field value. There is one exception to this one record–one key rule: for reasons outlined in Chapter 6, the AcDbViewportTable is allowed to have duplicate keys.

The case of individual characters within a symbol table key does not matter. Thus, a symbol table can include a Standard key or a STANDARD key, but not both.

In addition to the key field, the records in a symbol table have several other fields. A layer table record, for instance, contains fields to store the color associated with this layer, its linetype, lock status, and many other properties. (See Chapter 6 for a complete discussion.)

Understanding Dictionaries

Symbol tables or any other database tables that use fixed records are inflexible. All records in a symbol table must look exactly the same. For example, you cannot mix linetype records with layer records in one table.

However, in a drawing database we have to deal with a number of different types of objects or records. We need to be able to put a circle object and a line object into a common container. Therefore, the drawing database contains a more flexible container for objects than the symbol tables. These containers are called *dictionaries*.

Every dictionary is a container for arbitrary objects, and each object in a dictionary is called a record. But unlike a symbol table, a dictionary can contain objects of different types, including other dictionaries. By putting complete dictionaries into another dictionary, you create a hierarchical structure of dictionaries that looks like a tree. At the bottom of this tree is a "root" dictionary, the one that is not contained in any other dictionary. In an AutoCAD drawing database, every dictionary is either contained in the "root" dictionary (directly or through a series of intermediate dictionaries), or it is linked to a specific drawing entity, for instance, a circle.

Like a symbol table, within each dictionary each record has a key value. This key value is unique within the dictionary, and, unlike symbol table records, the case of characters is significant. All objects that don't have a visual representation and aren't a symbol table record must go into a dictionary. There are no objects without visual representation outside of dictionaries or symbol tables.

You might be wondering why the distinction between symbol tables and dictionaries. There is no technical reason that a symbol table should not be just another dictionary. Symbol tables have been used in the drawing database much longer than dictionaries. Autodesk simply made the decision to differentiate between the two some time ago, however, and the distinction remains to this day.

Combining Entities into Blocks

Now you've learned where objects *without* a visual representation go. But where do you put those objects that *have* a graphical representation? These objects are called *entities* and are usually those in which most people are interested.

Again, entities go into containers. The containers for objects with graphical representation are called *blocks*. A drawing database can contain any number of blocks. Like dictionaries, there is a root container for blocks. No, it's not a root block, because blocks don't have a graphical representation and cannot belong to a block. And, no, the block container is not a dictionary either. It's a symbol table, the blocks table.

A block container can contain any number of entities, that is, objects that have a visual representation. A block can reference, but not contain, other block objects. By referencing another block, a block displays a transformed graphical representation of the complete contents of the referenced block.

Because each object in a block has a visual representation, a computer program such as AutoCAD can draw an image of the block contents to the screen or to a printout. This is called the *visualization* of the block.

Any block can be visualized. The AutoCAD drawing editor interacts directly with a block called **MODEL_SPACE*, adding entities to it, deleting entities, or modifying them. For this reason, the contents of the **MODEL_SPACE* block is what most people would call the "drawing."

In addition, the AutoCAD layout editor directly interacts with a block called **PAPER_SPACE*. This block references views of the **MODEL_SPACE* block and combines it with other entities. Because this block describes the layout of AutoCAD entities on a printout, other people would call *this* the "drawing."

 WARNING If your application works inside AutoCAD, be aware that activating a different layout *renames* the **PAPER_SPACE* block, exchanging its contents with that of another layout block, **PAPER_SPACE0*.

Technically there is no difference between these blocks and any other. Even in AutoCAD there are commands such as the contents explorer that can visualize other blocks, and even in AutoCAD there are commands such as Refedit that directly interact with other blocks.

Any block can contain any object that has a graphical representation. Such objects are lines, arcs, and circles, but likewise there may be cars and tires, walls and doors, books and authors. No key field is associated with the objects in a block container other than the database-global object identifier (see below). Thus, a block container is simply a list of objects.

Non-objects in the Drawing Database

So we have entities that have a graphical representation, and we have all the other objects that don't have a graphical representation. Can there be more than that?

Unfortunately, yes. An AutoCAD drawing file contains "things" that are not database objects. Again, there doesn't seem to be any functional reason for this. If you design a drawing database from scratch, the unspecified things get put into a dictionary, where they belong. And I'm sure Autodesk would put them there automatically as well if the developers had the opportunity to redesign the database from scratch.

The things I'm talking about are a number of settings that AutoCAD saves specifically for each drawing. These settings describe the state AutoCAD should go into after it loads a drawing. Most of these settings define how specific AutoCAD commands should work in each drawing or which defaults they should offer.

The overwhelming number of settings saved in a drawing file is completely irrelevant if you want to evaluate or manipulate an AutoCAD drawing. However, a few settings in a drawing file do have a meaning for the drawing contents. The most important setting is the AutoCAD database version number, because it determines which objects are to be expected in the drawing database. Other settings define if and how AutoCAD will display objects of a specific type, for instance, PDMODE and ATTDISP. Chapter 4 lists all settings in a drawing file and discusses in detail those settings that affect the visualization of a drawing. If an external program is to completely mimic how AutoCAD would display the drawing, it must be able to recognize these settings.

Identifying Objects

Every object in an AutoCAD drawing has a unique identifier (some objects, such as symbol table records or dictionary entries, additionally have a key string, which is unique inside the table or dictionary, but not throughout the whole database). This identifier is called the object's *handle*. Objects have a handle independent of whether they have a graphical representation. It's also irrelevant whether the object is included in a symbol table, a dictionary, or a block or whether it is one of these types of containers itself. Handles are unique within a drawing database, so no two objects in the database have the same handle.

For a couple of reasons, there may be additional identifiers, depending on the environment used to access the drawing database. One reason is that some environments, for instance, ObjectARX, allow your application program to access multiple drawings simultaneously, even drawings that are not opened in the AutoCAD drawing editor. You can, thus, end up with multiple objects from different drawings that share the same handle. Also, ObjectARX allows you to work with temporary, not database-resident, objects. These objects don't have a handle at all. In such environments, objects are usually referenced by an arbitrary, session-dependent *ObjectID*.

A second reason for the existence of additional identifiers is that unique object handles were introduced into the drawing database at a remarkably late stage of Auto-CAD's development. But, of course, the internal AutoCAD code knew how to distinguish one line from another, probably by means of pointers in the C programming language. But these were not written out to the database files. When AutoCAD introduced entity access through AutoLISP in 1986, AutoLISP needed a way to identify database objects. Because handles weren't invented yet, objects were identified by an additional *entity name*. Like an ObjectID, an entity name is session-dependent. It still exists as another identification for objects.

Linking Objects

The only object identification that survives database writes and loads (which means saving a drawing file and reopening it later) is the object handle. Therefore, handles are used to create links between database objects. For instance, if you want to link a brake object to a wheel object, you add the brake object's handle to the wheel object.

If you link the objects, you probably want this link to survive a number of operations. For instance, you might want to keep the link alive even if the brake object gets a new handle. This can happen during filing operations (for example, when you insert or block your design to a different database) or during database reorganization. To keep the link in these situations, you use a special kind of link called *soft pointer*. In this case, the old handle must be automatically replaced by the new handle.

In addition, you might want to lock the brake object. When you do so, the brake object can be changed, but it can't be deleted as long as the link is active. This kind of link is called a *hard pointer*.

In some sense, this makes the wheel object own the brake object. It forbids certain actions on the brake object. But the link is only one-directional: no matter what happens to the wheel object, the brake object is not affected. For certain types of links, though, you want the exact opposite. If the wheel object is deleted, you want to delete associated tire or rim objects automatically as well. In such a case, you use a link type called a *soft owner*. Unlike pointership, ownership is an exclusive property, which means that the tire object cannot have an owner other than the wheel object.

A fourth kind of link is called a *hard owner*. This link type combines a *hard pointer* with a *soft owner*. The owned object cannot be deleted as long as the link exists, but is deleted automatically when the owner is erased.

Implicit Links

These four types of links, along with a fifth nonintelligent pointer, allow you to express all the interobject relationships you can imagine. Unfortunately, nothing's ever that easy.

Links to the symbol table do not use handles like the links between containers do. When symbol tables were introduced and linked to drawing entities, handles had yet to be invented.

In most cases (but not all), links from database objects to symbol table records are made using the record's key field value (*symbol name*) instead of the record's handle. One example is the Layer property of drawing entities, which contains the corresponding layer name, that is, the value of the layer record's key string.

Compared with the various link methods listed earlier, links through a symbol name are always *hard pointer* links. You can't delete a symbol table record if even a single entity references it.

Embedding Objects

Even with close links such as hard pointers, a referencing object and a referenced object are still two objects on their own. Any link includes the risk of breaking. For custom objects, it is sometimes crucial to guarantee nonbreakable links.

For custom applications, it is possible to not only link two objects, but to directly embed one object in another. In this case, the embedded object becomes part of the referencing object, or, in other words, the outer object becomes a container for other objects.

About Classes and Hierarchies

Up to now you have seen that an AutoCAD drawing database consists of a series of containers, each of which contains a certain (usually unlimited) number of objects. And these objects can be containers for the objects embedded in them. But what are objects?

In object-oriented design and analysis, an *object* is an instance of a class. A *class* is an abstract definition or template for all the properties and methods owned by their objects. Translated to real life, this means that an object is always "some kind of something." A certain number of classes or object types can be used in a drawing database, for example, AcDbLine, which is the class for simple lines, and AcDbFcf, which is the class for feature control frames, also known as geometric tolerance annotations. Every object in the drawing database is an instance of the appropriate class that defines the object's structure and behavior.

Classes underlie a hierarchy in which objects of a class inherit the structure and behavior of all classes higher up in the hierarchy. Usually this hierarchy describes an "is a kind of" relationship between classes. The AcDbLine class, for instance, inherits properties from the AcDbCurve class (which means that every line is a curve and has curve properties, such as a length), which inherits from the AcDbEntity class (which means that every curve is an entity and has entity properties, such as a color), which finally inherits from the AcDbObject class (which means that each entity is an object and has object properties, such as a handle).

All objects in an AutoCAD drawing database are based on AcDbObject. Figure 1.1 shows the class hierarchy in an AutoCAD drawing database.

FIGURE 1.1A

*The AutoCAD data-
base class hierarchy*

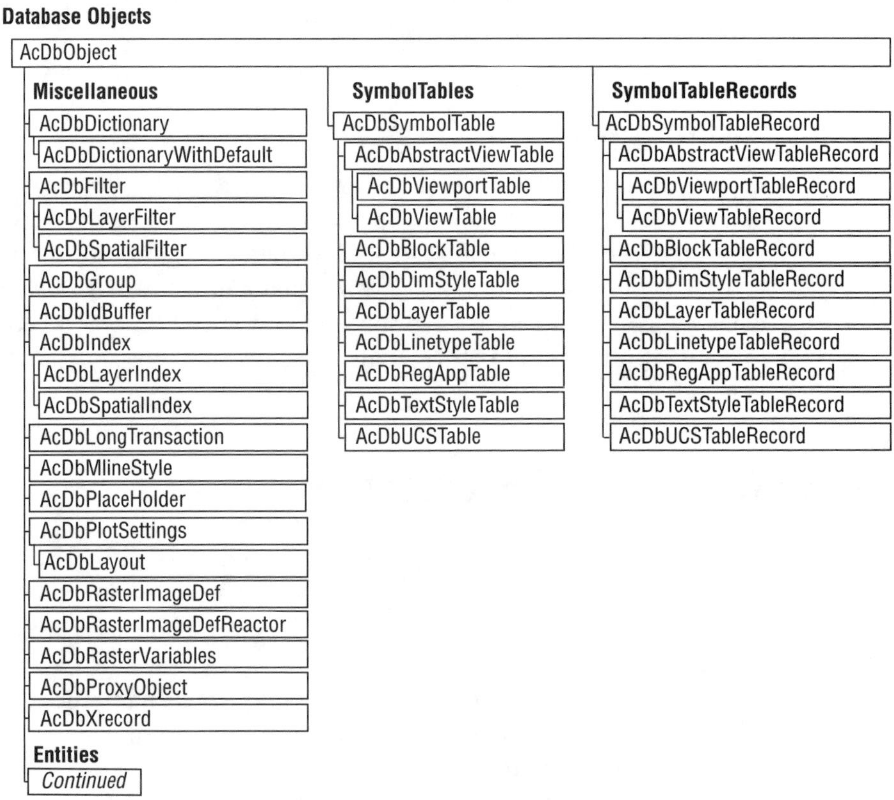

Database Objects

AcDbObject

Miscellaneous	SymbolTables	SymbolTableRecords
AcDbDictionary	AcDbSymbolTable	AcDbSymbolTableRecord
AcDbDictionaryWithDefault	AcDbAbstractViewTable	AcDbAbstractViewTableRecord
AcDbFilter	AcDbViewportTable	AcDbViewportTableRecord
AcDbLayerFilter	AcDbViewTable	AcDbViewTableRecord
AcDbSpatialFilter	AcDbBlockTable	AcDbBlockTableRecord
AcDbGroup	AcDbDimStyleTable	AcDbDimStyleTableRecord
AcDbIdBuffer	AcDbLayerTable	AcDbLayerTableRecord
AcDbIndex	AcDbLinetypeTable	AcDbLinetypeTableRecord
AcDbLayerIndex	AcDbRegAppTable	AcDbRegAppTableRecord
AcDbSpatialIndex	AcDbTextStyleTable	AcDbTextStyleTableRecord
AcDbLongTransaction	AcDbUCSTable	AcDbUCSTableRecord
AcDbMlineStyle		
AcDbPlaceHolder		
AcDbPlotSettings		
AcDbLayout		
AcDbRasterImageDef		
AcDbRasterImageDefReactor		
AcDbRasterVariables		
AcDbProxyObject		
AcDbXrecord		

Entities

Continued

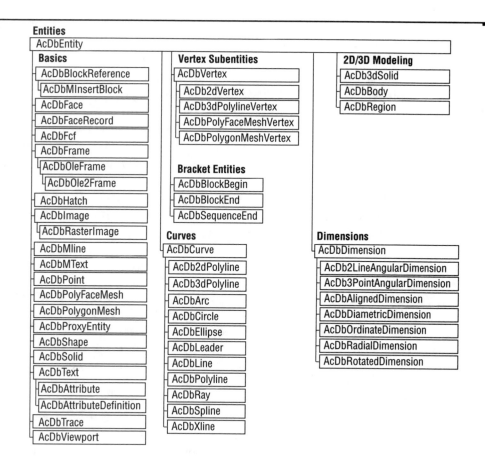

FIGURE 1.1B

Detail of the entities hierarchy of the AutoCAD database (Both Figures 1.1a and 1.1b ©1999 by Autodesk, Inc., reprinted with permission)

Entities
AcDbEntity

Basics
- AcDbBlockReference
- AcDbMInsertBlock
- AcDbFace
- AcDbFaceRecord
- AcDbFcf
- AcDbFrame
- AcDbOleFrame
- AcDbOle2Frame
- AcDbHatch
- AcDbImage
- AcDbRasterImage
- AcDbMline
- AcDbMText
- AcDbPoint
- AcDbPolyFaceMesh
- AcDbPolygonMesh
- AcDbProxyEntity
- AcDbShape
- AcDbSolid
- AcDbText
- AcDbAttribute
- AcDbAttributeDefinition
- AcDbTrace
- AcDbViewport

Vertex Subentities
- AcDbVertex
- AcDb2dVertex
- AcDb3dPolylineVertex
- AcDbPolyFaceMeshVertex
- AcDbPolygonMeshVertex

Bracket Entities
- AcDbBlockBegin
- AcDbBlockEnd
- AcDbSequenceEnd

Curves
- AcDbCurve
- AcDb2dPolyline
- AcDb3dPolyline
- AcDbArc
- AcDbCircle
- AcDbEllipse
- AcDbLeader
- AcDbLine
- AcDbPolyline
- AcDbRay
- AcDbSpline
- AcDbXline

2D/3D Modeling
- AcDb3dSolid
- AcDbBody
- AcDbRegion

Dimensions
- AcDbDimension
- AcDb2LineAngularDimension
- AcDb3PointAngularDimension
- AcDbAlignedDimension
- AcDbDiametricDimension
- AcDbOrdinateDimension
- AcDbRadialDimension
- AcDbRotatedDimension

Object Properties

Every object is an instance of its class and therefore has an identity. Each object has its own set of methods and properties, as defined by its class. An object's methods define the actions the object is able to perform. Using its methods, a database object changes over time; it copies, exports, or explodes itself. Although this evolution is an interesting and complex topic, it is not our topic here. In this book, we look at the drawing database as it appears at a fixed time. In other words, we look at the static picture of a drawing database.

Different objects of the same type (class) always differ in one or more properties. Even if two lines are completely identical, they have a different handle. Otherwise, they would not be two lines, only one.

Every class defines a certain set of properties, which describe this special instance of the class. Properties are often called attributes, but in the context of an AutoCAD drawing database, the term *attributes* is reserved for attribute objects, that is, objects of the class AcDbAttribute. The phrase *member variables* is also often used to describe properties available to objects within a class.

Most of this book deals with the object classes you will encounter in a drawing database and the associated properties. The properties of each object form a set of definitions that should define the object completely. I said "should" because not in all cases does the database contain all the information needed to describe an object completely. Some objects rely on data external to the drawing database.

Every object needs its own set of properties to describe its mathematical definition. It's up to the author of a class to decide which properties objects of each class need to completely define their appearance.

Defined versus Calculated Properties

The decision of which properties to choose as the properties needed to completely define an object is not necessarily obvious. Think of how you would define a circle's size. By its radius? Diameter? Area? All these are equivalent; in other words, if you know one, you can calculate the others.

Usually the drawing database stores only one of these equivalents. We call this the *defining property*. In some cases, the class author decided to store two or more of these equivalents in the drawing database even though they could be calculated easily. Such a redundancy is to be avoided! Not only does it create drawing files that consume more space than necessary, but more important, it creates the possibility of inconsistent drawing data. How do you expect a computer to handle a circle whose radius you define as 5 and whose diameter you define as 7?

Even though in most cases the AutoCAD drawing database contains only the minimum set of defining properties, some access methods automatically allow you to read or even write calculated properties as well. When using such an access method, you cannot tell which property is the defining property. However, by looking at the drawing database file itself, you can distinguish between the two. When there are useful calculated properties, I will list them as well.

Missing Properties

One would expect that the drawing database contains all the data needed to completely construct the drawing used to create the database. This is not the case. An AutoCAD drawing database is not complete.

Some information is missing from the drawing database, and some of this information is obvious, and some isn't. Among the more obvious missing details is font information. To display a line of text, you need to know which characters to draw and how these characters look. The drawing database contains the information about which characters to draw, but it does not contain the information about how these characters look.

Character definition is saved in a different file of type SHX or TTF. The drawing database contains only the name of this file. To completely generate a drawing, you need access to this secondary file as well. Like fonts, a drawing can also reference bitmap files, shape files, and, by use of externally referenced drawings, even other drawing databases. By embedding file names, database key fields, and other referencing information, any drawing object can point to a large number of additional properties that are known only to the creator of this object.

Does This Book Completely Document the AutoCAD Drawing Database?

Will you find an explanation in this book for every property of every object you might encounter in an AutoCAD drawing database? The simple answer is: No!

Until 1994, it was possible to document every class found in an AutoCAD drawing database, because there was a fixed set of classes only. But then came AutoCAD Release 13 and a completely redesigned drawing database.

One of the big advantages (or disadvantages, depending on your point of view) of this redesigned drawing database is that it now no longer contains only a fixed set of predefined classes. Instead, everyone is able to extend the AutoCAD database classes and create his or her own.

Since Release 13, you may find wheel objects in a drawing database, or you may find tires, walls, doors, or authors. How these objects are defined is totally up to the authors of the objects. And even worse, it's also totally up to the object's author to decide if and how these objects will be accessible through the various methods described in this book. Unfortunately, it's possible for a class author to make his object available only in ObjectARX while omitting DXF, AutoLISP, and ActiveX.

And finally, it's of course totally up to the author whether to document such custom objects. If you plan to implement custom objects, read this book carefully to see what others need to know to use the data that buyers of your application will put into their drawing files.

Which Objects Are Covered?

When writing this book, I had to answer a tough question: Which objects are important enough to be described here and to what level of detail? This question is much more difficult to answer than it seems, because you may encounter a large number of different objects in an AutoCAD drawing.

If a third-party sheet metal application saves its bending-tool objects in the drawing database, you'll probably want to know their definitions. But you won't be able to do so unless they have been documented by the objects' authors, and they can only be documented by the objects' authors. So I have to exclude all third-party objects from this book.

What about third-party objects made by Autodesk? Their architectural add-on creates a number of useful objects, including walls, doors, and windows. What's the difference between third-party add-ons written by Autodesk and those written by others? There is none.

So I'll concentrate on the so-called *core objects*. AutoCAD creates these without the help of third-party applications. Right? Wrong. Because even the core AutoCAD program is just a set of different add-ons (if you can call it that). With AutoCAD, "bonus" routines, such as Wipeout, create custom, undocumented objects, and an integrated application, such as a rendering module, creates its own custom, undocumented objects.

Because I had to decide about coverage from object to object, I selected those objects that I found most important and most often used, and I concentrated on the basic concepts of the drawing database. If you understand these concepts, you'll find it easy to read or evaluate other objects not listed here from your drawing's database—as long as you find them documented by their author, of course.

Summary

The AutoCAD drawing database consists of a huge number of objects. Some are well known such as lines and circles. Other objects such as layer table records are less known, and you will learn how to understand and use them throughout this book. In addition, a drawing database can contain specialized objects that are defined by add-on programs. To fully understand these, you need to check the add-on's documentation after reading this book.

This chapter introduced the general structure of the drawing database. You learned that the drawing database consists of four regions:

- Blocks, which are containers for graphical objects such as polylines or hatches.

- Symbol tables, which are containers for nongraphical objects such as layers or dimension styles. Each symbol table can contain only a specific object type (or record).

- Dictionaries, which are containers for nongraphical objects such as plot settings or embedded VBA macros. Dictionaries are able to contain more than one type of object.

- Drawing-specific settings, which are considered nonobjects.

The next chapter explains how you interact with the contents of a drawing database.

CHAPTER **2**

Accessing the Drawing Database

FEATURING

DXF	*18*
AutoLISP	*26*
ActiveX Automation	*36*
ObjectARX	*42*

I
n this chapter, you'll learn how to access the drawing database using various methods. You'll see a few code samples and follow a demonstration of the basic process to read a drawing's database. This overview is not intended to teach you programming. To use one of the methods presented here, you'll need additional information about the specific development environment you want to use.

The first access method I'll discuss is the oldest and most common way to access an AutoCAD drawing file: using the DXF® file format. I'll start with this method because you don't need to master any programming language to use it. You can read and edit a DXF file using almost any text editor. But DXF is based on a long line of versions, in which Autodesk always tried to minimize the changes from one version to the next. As a result, DXF is full of historic burdens and often successfully hides the almost clean database structure I described in Chapter 1.

The second access method involves using AutoLISP functions. You will see that the drawing database looks slightly different when reading it from AutoLISP, but you'll also see that the differences are minor. The contents of the drawing database are always the same, no matter how you look at it.

The third access method uses ActiveX Automation. ActiveX Automation is not directly linked to a specific programming language. Instead, it is a set of interfaces that programs written in different languages can use to access an automation server's methods and properties. These interfaces are defined in a *type library* (*.tlb*). You'll see a demonstration using the ActiveX Automation interface to the drawing database from a couple of programming environments.

The fourth access method uses ObjectARX/ObjectDBX. Because this is the foundation on which AutoCAD itself is built, it should provide the most useful way to access the drawing data. Unfortunately, it doesn't. In ObjectARX, the database access is hidden in a set of C++ libraries, which means that C++ is the only supported development environment for ObjectARX. Unfortunately, C++ is not necessarily a language that makes programming easy and reliable.

At the end of this chapter, I'll briefly discuss other ways to interact with an AutoCAD drawing database, such as DWG libraries.

This chapter concentrates on *reading* a drawing database. Everything said here also applies to *writing* drawing data. But writing a drawing database is usually a bit more complex than reading it, because writing also means to properly initialize all data and to correctly create all database links that the object is supposed to honor.

The Serialized Way—DXF

DXF is an abbreviation for Drawing Interchange Format. DXF is a registered trademark of Autodesk, which is now trying to replace the name with ObjectDXF. Despite this naming confusion, most people who deal with computer graphics claim to know what DXF is. And few really do.

The origins of DXF date from 1982 and the development of the first version of AutoCAD, at that time code-named MicroCAD. Autodesk founder and long-time president John Walker (at that time) set the specifications: "All versions of MicroCAD should be able to write an *entity interchange format* file. All versions of MicroCAD, regardless of internal file representation, will be able to interchange drawing[s] this way." (John Walker, *The Autodesk File*, New Riders Publishing, 1989, p. 474)

To understand this, you need to remember the microcomputer world of 1982. Hundreds of companies were developing custom microcomputers, all of them incompatible with one another and often using their own operating systems, file systems, and even different representations of floating-point numbers. MicroCAD was supposed to run on various machines, always using a drawing file format specifically optimized for the target computer. To transfer a drawing from one platform to another, Walker suggested copying the *complete* contents of the drawing database into a file that could be read on every computer, an ASCII text file. The recipient of the interchange file could then convert it back into a MicroCAD drawing file. Because the contents of the interchange file would completely represent the original drawing, the resulting drawing would resemble the original in every detail.

An *entity interchange file* is "a complete representation of the contents of an AutoCAD drawing database." Only the naming seemed to create problems. Walker's notes again: "Changed the extension and nomenclature for interchange files. Previously they were *entity interchange files, EIF*. Now they are *drawing interchange files, DIF*. There's a hundred people who know what a drawing is for every one who knows what an *entity* is." (*ibid.*, p. 480) So true, John. And how many know what an *object* is?

Finally on September 18, 1982, John Walker logged: "Mike Riddle points out that *.DIF* is used for VisiCalc interchange files. Changed drawing interchange file extension to *.DXF* to keep some gonzo from trying to load one into VisiCalc." (*ibid.*, p. 486) Thus, the DXF file was born. Anyone remember VisiCalc?

Because other users and third parties found the DXF file useful, Autodesk included a brief documentation of the file format with every release of AutoCAD. This led to an incredible number of applications based on DXF, including programs that automatically create or modify drawings, and import and export filters for almost every graphics program in the world.

Some Myths about DXF

Because of the way that DXF files are used in the industry, the origins and the initial meaning of the file format are often forgotten. Many people think of DXF as an international standard, because it's so common. But it's not! DXF was invented and is maintained by Autodesk, and the company changes the format at will.

Some people see DXF as a static format. But it's not! Because DXF is a complete representation of the AutoCAD drawing database, the specifications change as soon as the drawing database contents change. And this is the case with almost every release of a new AutoCAD version.

Some people think of DXF as a plot file format. In fact, when I wrote my first book on DXF, the desktop publisher wondered why I sent him HP/GL files for the illustrations. His publishing system was able to read DXF, so he expected the DXF images to display in his system just as I wanted them to display. But DXF is only the drawing database. It is not the visualization of the database on-screen or on paper. You can't tell from a DXF file whether an image of a 3D object is to be seen shaded, rendered, or with hidden lines removed.

A typical myth left over from older versions of the format is that a DXF file can define only a handful of geometric elements. But that is not the case! As you saw in Chapter 1, a drawing database can contain arbitrary objects. Consequently, a DXF file can hold arbitrary information. It's not difficult to create a DXF file representing an Excel spreadsheet. The only question is whether it makes sense.

Some Criticisms of DXF

More recent critics concentrate on the question of whether a DXF file is a *complete* representation of the drawing database. The myth is that DXF omits a huge amount of information contained in the AutoCAD drawing database as it would be saved in a DWG file. Again, this is not the case.

But there is a problem with DXF. The criticisms are valid. It is possible that a DXF file does not contain the complete drawing database. A drawing database can contain arbitrary objects, and, unfortunately, Autodesk left it to the authors of individual custom objects to decide whether they want their objects saved in DXF. If a developer was too lazy to implement the DXF output routines for his objects, they will be missing from the DXF file, and constructing the drawing database from the DXF file will create a different drawing. To try to control this inconsistency, Autodesk demands that applications qualified for the "Designed with ObjectARX" logo implement DXF filing functions that are logically equivalent in contents to their DWG filing counterparts.

A second, even more important criticism is the historic burden of DXF. Remember, a DXF file is a representation of the drawing database, and this changes with every version of AutoCAD. Therefore, it is to be expected that the most current DXF specification closely resembles the database structure, as explained in the previous section. But it doesn't.

Over the years of AutoCAD development, the programmers at Autodesk tried to minimize the changes in DXF. Although the goal was to break as few existing DXF applications as possible, the final result is a mess. The DXF file often successfully hides even an almost clean database structure.

Serializing Drawing Data

The AutoCAD drawing database is a multidimensional object: a container of containers of containers, and so on.

For filing purposes, that is, for writing the drawing database to a disk file, you need to flatten this multidimensional structure to a sequential structure. This procedure is called *serialization*. Reading a drawing file back into AutoCAD restores the hierarchical structure. This is true for both DXF and AutoCAD's own DWG file format.

You can serialize a multidimensional data structure in various ways. Within a DXF file, you'll find three serialization methods used:

- Bracketing
- Tagging
- Sequencing

Brackets in a DXF file indicate the beginning and end of containers, for example, SECTION/ENDSEC, TABLE/ENDTAB, and BLOCK/ENDBLK. When you read a DXF file, these brackets look like objects, but they don't belong to the database structure and are only inserted for filing purposes.

Within a DXF file, every bit of information saved is tagged with a group code. The group code is a 16-bit positive integer and indicates both the information's data type and its meaning in the current context. For example, a tag code of 40 indicates a single 64-bit floating-point number, usually a length or scale factor. In the context of an AcDbCircle entity (that is, a circle), the meaning of group 40's value is the circle radius. In the context of an AcDbText entity (that is, a single line of text), the meaning of group 40's value is the text height. Throughout the remaining chapters of this book, you will learn about the various object types and which group codes and values they use.

Sequencing is used to organize database data in the serialized file. This means that in certain areas of the DXF file the sequence of information bits is relevant for their interpretation. It is obvious that the placement of an object between brackets (that is, the sequence of brackets and objects) defines the container in which an object belongs. But also, within a single object, the sequence of information bits may or may not be relevant. In an AcDbLine (that is, a line), the endpoints are tagged differently, thus making the sequence in which they are stored irrelevant. In an AcDbSpline, all control points are tagged with the same group code, thus making the sequence very important.

ASCII and Binary DXF

A DXF file follows a very simple file structure. With one exception (the binary DXF sentinel string), all data in a DXF file come in pairs. The first part of the pair is the group code (tag) discussed earlier. The second part, immediately following the tag, is the corresponding information bit, the group value.

DXF files come in two variants: as ASCII text files or as binary files. ASCII DXF files consist of printable characters only. You can print them out or look at them with your favorite text editor. In an ASCII DXF file, all numbers are written as you would type them. The number 100, for instance, is written as three characters: a "1" and two "0"s.

In a binary DXF file, the number 100 is compressed to a single byte with the value 100. If you look at a binary DXF file with a text editor, you won't be able to recognize the "100" byte. Whenever I list the contents of a binary file, I use the hexadecimal representation of each byte. A byte consists of 8 bits; some are set, and some are not. The hexadecimal representation of the "100" byte is 64h (h is for hexadecimal, and 64 means 100 since 100 = 6 * 16 + 4), which means that the corresponding bit sequences are 0110 and 0100.

Again with one exception (comments are allowed only in ASCII DXF files), both the ASCII and the binary DXF versions of a drawing database contain identical information. ASCII DXF files are easier to read and edit, and binary DXF files are more compact and faster to process.

In an ASCII DXF file, group code and group value are separated by line feeds, which means that when you print the file, each appears on a separate line. Because the only supported platform for AutoCAD is some form of Microsoft Windows, DXF files use the Windows line feed sequence CR/LF (0D0Ah).

 NOTE Old DXF files may also use Macintosh, VMS, or Unix line separators (0Dh, 0A0Dh, 0Ah).

In a binary DXF file, group codes and group values don't need a separator because the group code is always 16 bit, that is, 2 bytes. Also, most group values have a fixed length and therefore don't need a termination. Group values that have differing lengths are strings and binary chunks.

String values in binary DXF are terminated with a zero byte (00h), that is, a byte in which all bits are zero. Binary chunks cannot be terminated by a zero byte because it may be part of the value and you don't want AutoCAD to stop reading the binary data simply because it contains a zero byte. Instead, binary chunks of data are preceded by an additional byte that contains the number of bytes in the chunk that follows. (For more information on how the different data types are saved in DXF and how they appear in the other environments, see Chapter 3.)

 NOTE In versions of AutoCAD prior to Release 13, binary DXF files used a group code value that consisted of either 1 or 3 bytes instead of the 2 bytes used today. Check the DXF file version to determine how to interpret group codes in binary DXF files; otherwise, your program may crash.

Differences between ASCII and Binary DXF

Even though they look very different, ASCII and binary DXF files carry the same amount of information taken from the AutoCAD drawing database used to create them. They also list the exact same data in the exact same sequence. There are only two differences in the contents of ASCII and binary DXF files:

- ASCII DXF files can contain comments, but binary DXF files cannot.
- A binary DXF file contains a sentinel string that is not in ASCII DXF files.

Comments are strings tagged with a 999 group code. AutoCAD does not add comment strings to a DXF file, but a user editing the file can use the 999 group to comment his changes. Because you are not expected to edit a binary DXF file by hand, there are no comments in a binary DXF file.

Binary DXF files contain a sentinel string of 22 bytes. This string opens the DXF file to indicate the file type. It is *not* tagged information (in other words, it is not preceded by a group code)! The sentinel string consists of the following:

- The string `"AutoCAD Binary DXF"`
- A line-feed sequence CR/LF (0D0Ah)
- An end-of-file character EOF (1Ah)
- A zero byte (00h)

The end-of-file character allows you to inadvertently print or output a binary DXF file without sending binary data to the screen or to the printer.

The Structure of a DXF File

As you already know, any information in a DXF file is a pair consisting of a group code and a group value. The only exception is the sentinel string that starts a binary DXF file.

A DXF file always ends with the end-of-file information, which is a group of code 0 and string *EOF*. In an ASCII DXF file, the last two lines are always the following:

```
0
EOF
```

In a binary DXF file, the last significant bytes are always the following:

```
00h 00h 69h 79h 70h 00h
```

The body of the DXF file is divided into seven sections, and each section is bracketed with a start-section bracket and an end-section bracket. The start-section bracket contains two groups: the first group is the string SECTION (group code 0), and the second group lists the section name string (group code 2). The end-section bracket is just the string ENDSEC (code 0). Let's look at what goes between the start and end brackets.

- The HEADER section contains drawing-specific settings saved with the database; I refer to these settings as the non-objects. The HEADER section is a sequential list of the setting name (a string in group 9) and the corresponding setting value (varying group codes).

- The CLASSES section provides auxiliary information regarding application-defined objects in the drawing database. It lists the class names in DXF and their corresponding C++ counterparts as well as printable information about the origin and use of the class. The information listed in this section does not represent database objects.

- The TABLES section contains the symbol tables and symbol table records. Each symbol table is enclosed between a start-table bracket and an end-table bracket. The start-table bracket contains various groups (covered in greater depth in Chapter 6). Most important are the string TABLE (code 0) and the table name string (code 2). The end-table bracket consists of only the string ENDTAB (code 0).

- The BLOCKS section contains entities, which are all objects with a graphical representation. To maintain compatibility with older DXF versions, entities of the *MODEL_SPACE* and *PAPER_SPACE* container blocks are *not* listed in the BLOCKS section. Instead, they appear in their own section titled ENTITIES. Following the same pattern as the sections themselves, each block is bracketed by a start-block bracket and an end-block bracket. The start-block bracket contains the string BLOCK (code 0), the block name (code 2), and a number of additional groups. The end-block bracket contains the string ENDBLK (code 0) and some other groups. I explain the additional group codes in Chapter 8.

- The ENTITIES section should logically be part of the BLOCKS section. Again, for compatibility reasons, the entities from the *MODEL_SPACE* and *PAPER_SPACE* blocks are listed in this special section. Entities that reside in the *PAPER_SPACE* block are listed in the ENTITIES section with a special group 67 code 1.

- The OBJECTS section contains all database objects that don't have a visual representation. This section does not use any bracketing. Instead, it's just a sequence of objects starting with the root directory.

- The THUMBNAILIMAGE section contains a small bitmap that can be used to provide a graphical visualization of the DXF file or the drawing as a whole.

The individual structures, group codes, and details associated with the various objects will be covered specifically in the discussion of these containers throughout the remaining chapters of this book.

Objects in DXF

Each object in a DXF file starts with the object's class DXF name. This is a string, and the associated group code is 0. The group code 0 is not used inside objects. Thus, whenever a program that is reading this DXF file encounters group code 0, it recognizes the mark as the beginning of a new object.

To parse a given container into individual objects, it is necessary to split the container's contents at every group 0. It is also possible to split the whole DXF file at every group 0. This provides the brackets used to represent the multidimensional structure of the database and auxiliary data, such as the thumbnail image bitmap.

If an object is directly embedded into another object, making the object itself into a container, the group code 0 cannot be used to indicate the embedded object's start. In such a case, the group code 101 is used to start an embedded object. The value of group code 101 is not the DXF class name of the embedded object; it is the string *Embedded Object*.

Following the object's start code (group 0 or 101) are the multiple data elements associated with this object, known as its properties. Here is a sample DXF excerpt defining an AcDbLine entity, that is, a straight line:

```
 0
LINE
 5
67
330
19
100
AcDbEntity
 8
```

```
  0
100
AcDbLine
 10
10.15197093840249
 20
5.593329978383998
 30
0.0
 11
19.86617617830376
 21
9.915398417065873
 31
0.0
```

You can see the various group pairs following the string LINE (code 0). The codes, number, and meaning of the groups describing the object are different from object type to object type. They result from the object's class definition. You will get a detailed look at these properties in the rest of this book.

A DXF file does not necessarily contain all the properties of a given object. To save file space, certain specific properties can be omitted and will default to standard values. In the previous example, you won't find a linetype (which would be tagged with group code 6) associated with the object, which means that the standard linetype is to be used. The standard linetype has the name *CONTINUOUS* and is a single continuous line without any gaps.

When you are writing a DXF file, I recommend that you don't rely solely on any defaults the reading program may use. Always fill in *all* the group codes. Unfortunately, AutoCAD itself does not follow this simple rule. When discussing the various object properties, I'll also list the default values to be used when a property is omitted from DXF if the default is not clear.

AutoLISP–DXF by Another Name

When AutoCAD introduced access to the drawing database through its built-in programming language AutoLISP, the developers reused the DXF file format. DXF already allowed access to all database objects, and this was documented.

Today, when you access a drawing database from AutoLISP, you get a very DXF-like result. It is not exactly DXF, but the differences are minimal.

NOTE Newer versions of AutoLISP, called Visual LISP, provide additional database access through ActiveX Automation, which I'll discuss in the next section.

If the DXF excerpt defining an AcDbLine entity from the previous section is to be evaluated in AutoLISP, the AutoLISP programmer will retrieve the following data list (formatted for clarity):

```
(
    (-1 . <Entity name: 2570520>)
    (0 . "LINE")
    (5 . "67")
    (330 . "19")
    (100 . "AcDbEntity")
    (67 . 0)
    (8 . "0")
    (100 . "AcDbLine")
    (10 10.1520 5.5933 0.0)
    (11 19.8662 9.9154 0.0)
    (210 0.0 0.0 1.0)
)
```

If you ignore the LISP-typical parentheses, you'll immediately recognize the familiar group code and value sequence. The main difference is that AutoLISP can work with coordinate lists such as this line's end points. So the group 10 in AutoLISP contains all three coordinates of the line's start point. In contrast, DXF can save only one coordinate per group. In DXF, group 10 contains only the start point's x coordinate; the y coordinate is in group 20, and the z coordinate is in group 30.

Another difference between DXF and AutoLISP is that AutoLISP returns *some* groups even if they have been given a default value. So you'll see the 67 and 210 groups listed in the AutoLISP files that were omitted from the DXF file, as they are standard (default) values. Other groups, such as the linetype (group 6), are still omitted if they have their default value.

Finally, you'll see the AutoLISP-internal *Entity name,* which is used to identify the object even if multiple databases are handled. The drawing-specific object handle is the string in group 5, by the way.

 NOTE Comparing the DXF and AutoLISP output of an entity seems to show a reduced precision in AutoLISP. This rounding occurs only in the printout of an AutoLISP expression. The internal values used in calculations are as exact as in the drawing database.

Database Access from AutoLISP

To extract any information about a database object, you use the AutoLISP *entget* function. The *entget* function takes one argument, which is the session-specific entity name. An optional second argument filters information belonging to specific add-ons (see the discussion of *xdata,* or application-specific data, in Chapter 5). To get the complete database contents associated with an object, you first get the object's entity name. You can do this in several ways, for instance, by using the AutoLISP functions *ssget* or *entsel.* Once you save the entity name to a variable (in this case, the symbol *AnEntity*), you can enter this AutoLISP expression at the command line:

```
(entget AnEntity '("*"))
=>
(
   (-1 . <Entity name: 2570520>)
   (0 . "LINE")
   (5 . "67")
   (330 . "19")
   (100 . "AcDbEntity")
   (67 . 0)
   (8 . "0")
   (100 . "AcDbLine")
   (10 10.1520 5.5933 0.0)
   (11 19.8662 9.9154 0.0)
   (210 0.0 0.0 1.0)
)
```

Although the AutoLISP term is *entity name* and although the database access function is called *entget,* the function works on all kinds of database objects, with or without a graphical representation.

The *entget* function always returns a list containing the corresponding object's database information. This list is often called the *entity association list.* Each element of this list is one database field or property. This sublist (that is, list within a list) is either a dotted pair (two atoms separated by a dot) or a complete list. If it's a dotted pair, the first atom is the group code integer, and the second atom is the group value. If it's a complete list, the group code is the first element. In any case, you can retrieve the group code of each sublist using the standard AutoLISP *car* function, which retrieves the first element from a dotted pair or a list. You'll get the group value using the standard AutoLISP *cdr* function, which returns the second element of a dotted pair or a list without its first element. Here are two examples that you can type at the command line:

```
(car '(5 . "67"))
=> 5
(cdr '(5 . "67"))
=> "67"
(car '(10 10.1520 5.5933 0.0))
=> 10
(cdr '(10 10.1520 5.5933 0.0))
=> (10.1520 5.5933 0.0)
```

If you look back at the return value of the *entget* function, you'll see among the various sublists a dotted pair starting with the code –1. The –1 group provides this object's entity name just like any other group. Keep in mind that this group is temporary and not part of the drawing database.

As long as a group code is unique within an object's properties, you can use the *assoc* function to directly retrieve one group by using its group code. If the group code is not unique, like the 100 code in our AcDbLine example, you need to traverse the groups using AutoLISP's standard list-processing functions *car* and *cdr, foreach* and *mapcar.*

If an object in a drawing database is deleted, the corresponding entity name is still valid until the database is written to a disk file (saved). Deleted objects that are requested using the *entget* function return the AutoLISP equivalent of "not available": *nil.*

Getting Entity Names

As you've already learned, the drawing database consists of three kinds of object containers (symbol tables, dictionaries, and block containers) plus the settings (or non-objects). The method you use to retrieve the entity names of all objects in a container depends on the container type.

If the container is a symbol table, you retrieve an object's entity name using the *tblobjname* function. This function takes two arguments: the DXF class name of the symbol table and the key value string of the symbol table record you're looking for. To look at the properties of layer "0", enter this expression at the command line:

```
(entget (tblobjname "LAYER" "0") '("*"))
=>
(
   (-1 . <Entity name: 2570478>)
   (0 . "LAYER")
```

```
(5 . "F")
(100 . "AcDbSymbolTableRecord")
(100 . "AcDbLayerTableRecord")
(2 . "0")
(70 . 0)
(62 . 7)
(6 . "CONTINUOUS")
)
```

To get the entity name, you need to know the symbol record's key string. There is no built-in function to extract all key strings from a symbol table, but you can use the following function inside your program:

```
(defun SymbolTableContents
       (SymbolTableDXFName / SymbolTableRecord ReturnValue)
   (while (setq SymbolTableRecord
           (tblnext SymbolTableDXFName (not ReturnValue))
          )
     (setq ReturnValue
       (cons (cdr (assoc 2 SymbolTableRecord)) ReturnValue)
     )
   )
   (reverse ReturnValue)
)
```

The *tblnext* function in the preceding routine steps through a symbol table and, with every call, returns some information about the next symbol table record. The data returned by *tblnext* is similar to the database information returned by *entget*, but the data is incomplete because several groups are missing. You should, therefore, always use *entget* to retrieve an object's properties.

The *tblobjname* function provides no access to symbol table records with duplicate keys. These types of records are allowed in the AcDbViewPortTable (VPORT). Therefore, it is not possible to retrieve the complete database information of viewport configurations using AutoLISP.

Retrieving Entities with AutoLISP

You will remember that entities (that is, objects that have a visual representation) are always contained in exactly one Block container. In the discussion on DXF sections at the beginning of this chapter, you also saw that the blocks *MODEL_SPACE* and *PAPER_SPACE* in a DXF file have undergone a special handling as they appear in a section on their own. When using AutoLISP, we have to keep both in mind: basically each entity goes to a single block container, except that the *MODEL_SPACE* and *PAPER_SPACE* blocks are mixed up.

To access a block container, you again use the *tblobjname* function, this time providing the string "BLOCK" and the block name. Assuming there is a block named "SOMEBLOCK" in your drawing, enter this expression at the command line:

```
(entget (tblobjname "BLOCK" "SOMEBLOCK") '("*"))
=>
(
    (-1 . <Entity name: 2570578>)
    (0 . "BLOCK")
    (5 . "57")
    (100 . "AcDbEntity")
    (67 . 0)
    (8 . "0")
    (100 . "AcDbBlockBegin")
    (70 . 0)
    (10 0.0 0.0 0.0)
    (-2 . <Entity name: 2570580>)
    (2 . "SOMEBLOCK")
    (3 . "")
)
```

In addition to the usual –1 group, which reports the block object's entity name, you will recognize a second entity name (group –2) in the preceding bit of code. This entity name points to the first entity in the corresponding block container.

You can now retrieve the entity name from the –2 group and then use *entget* to extract this object's database information. To access the second object in the block container, you use the *entnext* function. The entity name of the current object (in this case, the first object) is taken by the *entnext* as an argument and returns the entity name of the following object. At the end of the block container, *entnext* returns *nil*.

 WARNING If you use *entnext* to traverse the *MODEL_SPACE* block, it will not stop at the container's last entity. Instead, *entnext* continues with the contents of the *PAPER_SPACE* block.

The *tblnext* function omits the *MODEL_SPACE* and all *PAPER_SPACE* blocks when traversing the blocks in the database. The only way to get a list of *all* blocks in the drawing is to use the ActiveX Automation interface from AutoLISP. Here's a function you could incorporate into your program:

```
(defun AllBlocks (/ ReturnValue)
  (vlax-for b (vla-get-blocks
                    (vla-get-activedocument
                      (vlax-get-acad-object)))
    (setq ReturnValue (cons (vla-get-name b) ReturnValue))
  )
)
```

Dictionary Access in AutoLISP

Database objects that don't have a graphical representation and that aren't symbol tables or symbol table records go to the third kind of container, a dictionary.

Accessing dictionaries through AutoLISP is similar to accessing symbol tables. There are a few differences, however.

If you know the dictionary's entity name and the key string of the object, you use the *dictsearch* function. This function is similar to the *tblobjname* function, but differs in two areas. First, the *tblobjname* function needs the DXF name of the symbol table, and *dictsearch* needs the entity name of the parent dictionary. This is because there can be an unlimited number of dictionaries and because dictionaries can contain other dictionaries.

The second difference is that *dictsearch* directly returns the database information, and *tblobjname* returns only the entity name that is to be used in *entget*. To get the entity name of an object contained in a dictionary, you extract the –1 group value from the list returned by *dictsearch*. You will need this entity name to extract application-specific data (*xdata*) attached to the object. Suppose you are looking for the properties of the AcDbGroup object describing the AutoCAD group named "AGROUP," and suppose you already retrieved the entity name of the group dictionary. Typing the following expression at the command line returns the data you want:

```
(dictsearch EntityNameOfGroupDictionary "AGROUP")
=>
(
    (-1 . <Entity name: 2570560>)
    (0 . "GROUP")
    (5 . "54")
    (102 . "{ACAD_REACTORS")
    (330 . <Entity name: 2570468>)
    (102 . "}")
```

```
(100 . "AcDbGroup")
(300 . "Testgroup comment")
(70 . 0)
(71 . 1)
(340 . <Entity name: 2570530>)
(340 . <Entity name: 2570528>)
)
```

Like symbol tables, you need to know the key with which an object has been stored if you want to access it through *dictsearch*. As an alternative, you can use the *dictnext* function, which traverses all objects in a dictionary. The *dictnext* function is like *entnext* and *tblnext*, but returns the complete database information for each object.

To get a list of all keys used in a dictionary, you might integrate a routine similar to this in your program:

```
(defun DictionaryKeys (DictionaryEntityName)
 (mapcar 'cdr
    (vl-remove-if-not
     '(lambda (x) (= (car x) 3))
     (entget DictionaryEntityName)
    )
 )
)
```

A last question on dictionaries remains: How do you get the dictionary's entity name? This depends on which object owns the dictionary. A dictionary can be owned by any other non-dictionary object, or it can be included in another dictionary.

If a dictionary is owned by a non-dictionary object, it's called that object's *extension dictionary*. You'll find the extension dictionary's entity name in the object's group code list. Here's an example:

```
(
    (-1 . <Entity name: 2570578>)
    (0 . "BLOCK")
    (5 . "57")
    (102 . "{ACAD_XDICTIONARY")
    (-1 . <Entity name: 2579843>)
    (102 . "}")
    (100 . "AcDbEntity")
    (67 . 0)
...
```

All dictionaries other than extension dictionaries are nested and form a hierarchical tree structure, as explained in Chapter 1. Every dictionary by itself is included in a parent dictionary. Only one dictionary has no such parent, the "root" of the tree. It contains the top dictionaries, which may contain objects or other dictionaries. This root dictionary is called the *named objects dictionary*. Its entity name is returned by the *namedobjdict* function, which takes no arguments.

Modifying and Making Objects in AutoLISP

You can delete, alter, or create database objects using AutoLISP. To delete an object, you use the *entdel* function and pass the entity name as an argument.

To modify an object, you'll use the *entmod* function. This function needs one argument, which is an entity association list similar to the one returned by *entget*. This list must contain the –1 group with the entity name of the object to modify. And it must contain any groups you want to modify, for example:

```
(entmod
  '(
      (-1 . <Entity name: 2570520>)
      (10 10.0 5.0 0.0)
  )
)
```

To make an object from scratch, you pass the new object's entity association list to the *entmake* or *entmakex* command. The entity association list must not contain an entity name or a handle. You need to provide a minimum amount of information to create the entity; if you don't, your attempt will fail. For instance, to create a circle, you need to supply at least the object type, the radius, and the center point. Additional properties can be added during *entmake* or later. This input from the command line creates a circle:

```
(entmake
  '(
      (0 . "CIRCLE")
      (10 10.0 5.0 0.0)
      (40 . 5.0)
  )
)
```

Any group not included in the entity association list will be set to its default value.

The exact procedure that you use to create objects depends on the container in which they are supposed to land.

Symbol tables   You can make symbol table *records*, but you cannot create new symbol tables.

Blocks   You cannot create an individual entity and attach it to an arbitrary block container. You can create a new block container, which opens the container for writing; then all newly created entities are attached to this block. To close the block container, you need to use the *entmake* function to create an ENDBLK object. This is not a true object but the same pseudo-object used as the end-block bracket in a DXF file.

Layout blocks   If you create entities without opening a specific block container, they are automatically appended to the *MODEL_SPACE* block if their group 67 value is 0 or omitted. If the group 67 value is 1, entities go to the *PAPER_SPACE* block. In addition, you can provide a group 410 containing a layout name. In this case, the created object goes into the block container associated with the group 410 layout.

Dictionaries   .You can create dictionaries, but you cannot manipulate them directly using *entmod*. To add an object to a dictionary, you first create it with *entmakex* (not *entmake*!) and then use *dictadd* to connect the new object to its parent. The *dictadd* function takes three arguments: the dictionary's entity name, the new key string, and the new object's entity name. The function *dictrename* and *dictremove* modify a dictionary object. Using *entmod* you can attach and/or modify *xdata* to a dictionary object, but you cannot modify the object's primary groups.

Creation and modification of objects and entities will fail if the supplied entity association list contradicts certain rules. The main rules are that you need to include all mandatory groups and that you are not allowed to change critical groups such as the entity name or the handle. AutoLISP also checks that objects only go into a container in which they will fit. If you reference other objects implicitly or explicitly, AutoLISP verifies that the referenced object exists and is of the correct type.

Reading and Writing Drawing Settings

AutoLISP provides full support for reading and writing drawing-specific settings that are saved inside the drawing database.

Every setting has a name or a key string. You use the *getvar* function to read a setting, and you use the *setvar* function to write it. Try this at the command line to read and write the PDMODE setting, which controls the display of AcDbPoint objects:

```
(getvar "PDMODE")
=> 0
(setvar "PDMODE" 3)
=> 3
```

A number of settings, such as the database version ACADVER (which in AutoLISP is *not* the database version but the AutoCAD version you work in) cannot be modified through AutoLISP. (For more on global settings, see Chapter 4.)

In AutoLISP, you use the *getvar* and *setvar* functions not only for database-specific settings, but also to operate on a number of additional settings that are session specific or configuration specific. (See Chapter 4 for a list of drawing-specific header variables.)

The Same Data with Names—ActiveX Automation

As you have learned, all the methods described in this chapter access the same drawing database contents. Only the access methods differ. In DXF and AutoLISP, properties are referenced by group codes, that is, by numbers. Using ActiveX Automation, the same properties are referenced by a name.

ActiveX Automation (also known as COM Automation) is not directly linked with a specific programming language. Instead, it is a set of interfaces that programs written in different languages can use to access an automation server's methods and properties. These interfaces are defined in a *type library* (*.tlb*). You can use this type library from many programming environments.

Here's an example of how the same database access in a program's code looks when using different programming languages:

Visual Basic	`ADatabaseCircle.Radius = 3.0`
Visual LISP	`(vla-put-Radius AdatabaseCircle 3.0)`
Delphi	`ADatabaseCircle.Radius := 3.0;`
Java	`ADatabaseCircle.Radius(3.0);`

ActiveX Automation or, more precisely, the dispatch interface to AutoCAD's COM objects as declared in the type library, defines *Circle* objects that have a *Radius* property that can be changed. How this change is performed is internal to the automation server, in this case AutoCAD. How the communication takes place is defined in COM (Microsoft's Component Object Model), the underlying architecture of ActiveX Automation. How you access the interface in a certain environment depends on the programming language and its syntax rules. Describing these rules is beyond the scope of this book since there are a large number of programming languages to choose from. See the documentation for your favorite development platform to learn how ActiveX Automation works within that specific environment.

Most people use Visual Basic to write programs using ActiveX Automation. This can be done through the Visual Basic (VB) development system that creates stand-alone executables or through the Visual Basic for Applications (VBA) dialect included in products such as Microsoft Word, Microsoft Excel, or AutoCAD. Because VB(A) is the environment preferred for use with ActiveX Automation, I'll demonstrate this variant of drawing database access using VB(A) code. Please translate the examples to your favorite programming language.

NOTE If you use Visual LISP to access AutoCAD's ActiveX Automation objects, you need to initialize the COM interface using the *vl-load-com* function.

Accessing the AutoCAD Database

An ActiveX Automation client (that is, the software you are writing to access Auto-CAD objects) and an ActiveX Automation server (that is, AutoCAD) are two unrelated programs. They don't have to share the same address space and can even run on different computers. They communicate by means of a set of standard interfaces.

To open an ActiveX communication with AutoCAD, you need to *get* the AutoCAD object running in memory, or you need to *create* a new AutoCAD object. In a Visual Basic program this segment looks like this:

```
Dim AutoCADObject As AcadApplication
Set AutoCADObject = GetObject(, "AutoCAD.Application")
If Err.Number Then
  Set AutoCADObject = CreateObject("AutoCAD.Application")
End If
```

Once you connect your application to AutoCAD, you can access the drawings already opened by AutoCAD, or you can create or open another.

One service that the AutoCAD ActiveX Automation server provides to your application program is the *Documents* collection. The *Documents* collection contains all documents (which is the name ActiveX Automation uses for drawing databases) currently open in the AutoCAD to which you're connected. *AutoCADObject.Documents .Item(0)* is the first available database, if any are available. *AutoCADObject.Documents .New* creates a new drawing database from a template drawing, and *AutoCADObject .Documents.Open* opens another drawing file.

Using *AutoCADObject.Documents.Item(Index),* you can select the drawing database with which you want your program to work. Alternatively, *AutoCADObject.Active-Document* is the drawing database currently active in AutoCAD.

Each of these calls returns an object of the type *AcadDocument.* By traversing this document object, you can access all segments of the drawing database. There is often a bit of confusion about the difference between a document and a database in Auto-CAD's ActiveX interfaces. A document is a database loaded into the current AutoCAD session for editing. In addition to the database resident information, the document object also contains temporary information, such as selection sets, and methods to plot or interactively query information.

 TIP   An *AcadDocument* is a database loaded into the current AutoCAD session for editing through the ActiveX Automation interface.

The next section describes how to use ActiveX Automation to retrieve and modify information from the database portion of the document.

Of Collections, Objects, and Interfaces

You already know that the objects in a drawing database follow a strict hierarchy. Every object is contained in exactly one container, which in turn may be a member of another container, and so on.

In Visual Basic, the equivalent of a container is a *collection*. If you query the symbol table containing all layers, you use the *.Layers* property of the document object. The *.Layers* property returns a collection containing all layers from the drawing database.

Collections have a *.Count* property that returns the number of objects in the collection. Using the *.Item* method, you can access every object in the collection. Collection indices start from zero:

```
With Collection
  For Index = 0 To .Count - 1
    DoSomethingWith .Item(Index)
  Next Index
End With
```

As I discussed in Chapter 1, symbol table records in the AutoCAD drawing database always have a unique key within the symbol table. This key can be used to directly access a member of a symbol table collection, for example:

```
TheDrawingDocument.Layers("ALAYERNAME")
```

The document object provides collections for every symbol table in the drawing database: *.DimStyles, .Layers, .Linetypes, .RegisteredApplications, .TextStyles, .UserCoordinateSystems, .Viewports,* and *.Views.* In addition, the document object provides other collections that do not correspond to symbol tables.

Once you reach a symbol table record, you can access all related database fields using the object's properties. For instance, *ALayerObject.Handle* returns the layer's handle, and you can retrieve the layer's name using *ALayerObject.Name.* This series of properties and methods (as well as events) forms the *automation interface* to the layer object. Every database object has its own interface available through ActiveX Automation.

Accessing Entities via ActiveX Automation

As you remember, within the drawing database, entities (objects that have a graphical representation) belong to exactly one block container. Access to these containers and their contents is quite easy and logical if you work with ActiveX Automation.

The drawing database (the document object) contains a *.Blocks* collection. This collection contains all block containers. You can iterate through them using the collection index or by directly using the block name, for example, TheDrawingDatabase .Blocks("SOMEBLOCK").

Unlike in AutoLISP, access to the *MODEL_SPACE* and *PAPER_SPACE* blocks is the same as access to any other block using ActiveX Automation. As a shortcut, you can also use the *.ModelSpace* and *.PaperSpace* properties of the document object to access these blocks. These properties are just aliases for the longer forms.

Any block container is a collection of the entities contained in the block. You can easily iterate through them using a routine such as this:

```
With TheDrawingDatabase.Blocks("SOMEBLOCK")
  For Index = 0 To .Count - 1
    DoSomethingWith .Item(Index)
  Next Index
End With
```

Because entities don't have key strings, you need to iterate sequentially through the block container. Of course, there are other ways to find an item, such as by means of links from other objects, or you can find an item interactively. For more information, see the "VBA and ActiveX Automation" topic in AutoCAD's help system.

As soon as you reach an entity (an item in the block container), you can retrieve its database contents by simply using the corresponding properties. If you know that the entity is an AcDbLine, you can, for instance, query the start and end point using the *.StartPoint* and *.EndPoint* properties.

To access a property, you don't need the group code used in AutoLISP and DXF. You simply use the property name. Which property names are available depends on the type of object. For instance, a circle has a radius, and a line doesn't. Before using a property, it is wise to check the exact object type or to otherwise ensure that the property is available for the object in question. You'll find the object type using the *.ObjectName* property, which is the AutoCAD class name string, for example, "AcDbLine".

AutoLISP and DXF deliver only raw database contents; ActiveX Automation provides calculated properties that are not saved in the drawing database. Typical examples are the length of a line or the start point of an arc. Although you can modify defining properties, calculated properties are usually read-only.

Some complex database items are not available as properties of the object. This is the case when the property itself is not a simple data structure, such as a point, or a string. If the data structure is a collection or even a more complex object, in order to retrieve the data, you need to call a method of the object that returns the information. This is true, for instance, for application-defined add-on information (*xdata*) or for the list of objects that make a hatch boundary. Therefore, you cannot write *The-DatabaseItem.XData* to retrieve or modify the object's data. Instead, you use:

```
Dim TheItemsXdataTypes As Variant
Dim TheItemsXdataValues As Variant
TheDatabaseItem.GetXData "", _
    TheItemsXdataTypes, TheItemsXdataValues
```

The two variants in this method call will be filled by AutoCAD with the corresponding database contents. You need to use similar methods when writing complex data structures.

In contrast to AutoLISP and DXF, ActiveX Automation sometimes provides only a limited view of the drawing entities. One example is the DXF class name of an object, which is available through DXF, AutoLISP, and ObjectDBX, but not available through the ActiveX Automation interface.

Creating Entities via ActiveX Automation

The ActiveX Automation interface does not provide a general entity creation method such as AutoLISP's *entmake*. Instead, there is a separate creation method for each entity type.

As in AutoLISP, you need to supply an entity-specific set of minimum properties to create a valid object. Thus, to create a circle you need to supply a radius and a center point. Unlike in AutoLISP, you cannot supply additional properties when creating the object. Properties such as layer and color must be set later.

Because block containers are just collections in ActiveX Automation, you create a new object by simply adding it to the collection using the correct *add* method. The collection you add the object to may be any block. Unlike in AutoLISP, you can easily add objects to existing blocks.

The various *add* methods are named according to the object they generate, for example, *.AddLine, .AddCircle,* or *.AddArc.* Note that not every database object has an *add* method. For instance, to add an arbitrary solid model, you can't use an *.Add3dSolid* method. In contrast, some *add* methods do not correspond directly to a database object. For instance, *.AddBox* and *.AddCone* both create an AcDb3dSolid object, but from different parameters.

Working with Dictionaries in ActiveX Automation

The document object's *.Dictionaries* collection in ActiveX Automation corresponds to the *namedobjdict* in AutoLISP. This collection is the root dictionary that contains the top dictionaries of the database container for objects without a graphical representation. In addition, any object's *.GetExtensionDictionary* method returns this object's extension dictionary.

Every object in the *.Dictionaries* collection is a dictionary object, but not all dictionaries are members of the *.Dictionaries* collection. The *.Dictionaries* collection contains only the top-level dictionaries. If a dictionary is contained within another dictionary, it won't appear in the *.Dictionaries* collection. Instead, you will find it by traversing the hierarchical dictionary tree.

Any object in a dictionary is either another dictionary or an arbitrary object. The dictionary object provides methods to retrieve, rename, or delete a certain member object. Because every dictionary is a table of (similar or not) database objects, the dictionary owns methods for adding arbitrary objects to the collection.

Like AutoLISP, ActiveX Automation provides no functionality to define your own object classes, but you can use objects defined by AutoCAD or by add-ons written in ObjectARX as long as the objects themselves provide an ActiveX Automation interface. To add a custom object to a dictionary, you call the dictionary's *.AddObject* method with the new key string and the class name of the object to add.

AutoCAD's ActiveX Automation interface offers a number of shortcuts for AutoCAD-defined objects. For instance, you'll find the *ACAD_GROUP* dictionary as a separate *Groups* collection. But this is only an alias to simplify your code. It doesn't tell you anything about the database structure or contents. Other such shortcuts are the *PlotConfigurations* collection (the *ACAD_PLOTSETTINGS* dictionary, see Chapter 17) and *ADictionary.AddXRecord* (to concurrently create an AcDbXrecord object and add it to the directory; see Chapter 7).

Custom Objects in ActiveX Automation

An AcDbLine object is an AutoCAD entity. Thus, the AcDbLine class is derived from the AcDbEntity class, and every entity is an AutoCAD object or, in other words, is derived from AcDbObject. Translated to ActiveX Automation and COM, this means that the AcadLine object not only supports its own interface (*IAcadLine*) but also the *IACADEntity* and *IAcadObject* interfaces. Although the line's start point comes from the *IAcadLine* interface, its layer comes from the *IAcadEntity* interface, and its handle comes from the *IAcadObject* interface.

For standard AutoCAD objects, it does not matter which interface delivers the properties and methods you want to use. You're transparently calling the appropriate function, and the underlying interfaces are hidden.

However, non-standard (that is, custom) objects may not expose an automation interface if the object's author was too lazy to implement one.

 NOTE For ObjectARX logo compliance, a basic ActiveX implementation for every custom object is required.

If an object omits a complete interface, the hidden interfaces are still there and can be used. Because every custom object is derived from AcDbObject, you can still use some property, such as the *.Handle* property, of the object. If the custom object has a visual representation (that is, if it is derived from AcDbEntity), it automatically has a *.Layer* property and more. Also, the *.AddCustomObject* method creates a custom object if the corresponding class definition is available.

Non-objects in ActiveX Automation

Like AutoLISP, in ActiveX Automation, you can query the current value of certain settings saved in the drawing. In ActiveX Automation, you'll find these settings are part of the document object, not part of the database object.

The method to retrieve a setting is called *GetVariable* and needs one argument: the setting's name. The counterpart is the *SetVariable* method, which takes the name and the new value as arguments.

As in AutoLISP, you can query all settings from the drawing database plus many more.

The Object-Oriented Way—ObjectARX

In ActiveX Automation, you deal with objects that have properties, methods, and, in some cases, events. Within the scope of this book, all we're interested in are the properties (although you have to use methods to get more complex properties as we did in the *xdata* discussion earlier).

Using ObjectARX and ObjectDBX, you get access to these same properties, but you access them using member functions of predefined C++ classes. Because we are still dealing with the same data, the differences are much less than one could expect.

ObjectDBX is the database part of ObjectARX. Because ObjectDBX is the foundation on which AutoCAD itself is built, it provides the most complete way to access a drawing's database. There can't be anything in an AutoCAD database that you cannot access using ObjectDBX. ObjectDBX is extensible (in fact, the X is for *extensions*). You can load additional modules into ObjectDBX that define additional objects in the database. Thus, in a given database you may not be able to understand certain objects if the corresponding extension module is not available.

The only supported environment for ObjectDBX is Microsoft Visual C++. The complete functionality for database access is hidden in a set of C++ libraries, which you need to link to your application code. I won't go into the complex technical details of writing, compiling, and linking a complete ObjectDBX application, but I will describe how the AutoCAD database looks when you access it from within an ObjectDBX application. And compared with the three access methods I've already discussed (DXF, AutoLISP, and ActiveX Automation), this is remarkably simple to understand.

Accessing the AutoCAD Database

In any C++ program, if you want to use an object of a certain class, you *instantiate* it. You do so by calling the class's constructor, which then returns a pointer to the new object. In C++ code, this looks like the following:

```
AcDbDatabase *pDatabase = new AcDbDatabase(Adesk::kFalse);
```

The constructor for an AcDbDatabase object takes one argument, *buildDefaultDatabase,* which is Boolean, that is, of type *Adesk::Boolean*, and can be either *Adesk::kTrue* or *Adesk::kFalse*. This parameter defines how AutoCAD creates the drawing database. It must be *Adesk::kTrue* if you want to start with a plain blank database, and it must be *Adesk::kFalse* if you want to load an existing drawing file into this database.

Once you create the database object, you can use all associated member functions, for instance, *readDwgFile()*. In code, this is similar to ActiveX Automation. Depending on whether you work with references or pointers, you write either a dot or a pointing arrow:

```
pDatabase->readDwgFile("aDrawing.dwg");
aDatabase.readDwgFile("aDrawing.dwg");
```

You can create as many database objects as you like, and you can use them concurrently. Before using any database-related code, you need to have at least one drawing database to work on.

Although you can interact with all database objects you opened, there is always one *current* drawing database. If your application is running inside AutoCAD, you can access the database current to AutoCAD using the *acdbHostApplicationServices()->workingDatabase()* function.

Because instantiating a new database allocates all the memory needed to interact with the database object, you need to explicitly *delete* any object you created when you're done with it. (And, of course, you should file out, that is, write to a disk file, any changes before deleting the object.)

Opening and Closing Objects in a Database

ObjectDBX is the foundation that AutoCAD itself uses. When working in AutoLISP and ActiveX Automation, you use a friendly wrapper around the low-level AutoCAD functions. But when you work with ObjectDBX, you have to deal with the raw Auto-CAD core functionality. This becomes most obvious when opening and closing objects in a database.

Up to now, you assumed that your application was the only one to access a drawing database at a particular time, but this is not necessarily the case. Applications running inside AutoCAD share a drawing database with AutoCAD and among themselves. In almost all cases, ActiveX Automation and AutoLISP make you believe you are the only one working with the database by shielding the necessary actions to take for multiple access.

ObjectDBX operates differently. As you do when working with disk files in a multi-tasking environment, you need to explicitly open and close the objects you want to work with. And you need to tell AutoCAD how you are going to use the object. You can open an object for read-only or for write. (You can also open an object for notification, which means that your program is notified whenever the object changes. In this book, we look at the properties of AutoCAD objects, not at their ability to change over time. Therefore, I won't discuss notification.) As you will expect, an object can be opened for read-only by multiple applications. Only one application at a time, however, can open an object for write.

To open an object, you pass four parameters to the *acdbOpenObject()* function:

- The memory address of a pointer to the object's location in memory
- The object's identification
- The open mode
- A flag indicating if you want to open erased objects as well

The function template looks like this:

```
extern Acad::ErrorStatus
acdbOpenObject(
  AcDbObject*& pObj,
  AcDbObjectId objId,
  AcDb::OpenMode mode,
  Adesk::Boolean openErasedObject = Adesk::kFalse);
```

The open mode is one of the following: *AcDb::kForRead*, *AcDb::kForWrite*, and *AcDb::kForNotify*. Open an object for read-only if you only want to extract information, and open it for write if you want to change information. As I said earlier, opening an object for notification is beyond the scope of this book.

 NOTE The *acdbOpenObject* function is just a shortcut to either *acdbOpenAcDbObject()* or *acdbOpenAcDbEntity()*, depending on the type of object that is to be opened. If the *acdbOpenObject()* function does not exist for a certain class, you need to call *acdbOpenAcDbObject()* directly (or *acdbOpenAcDbEntity()*, if the object is an entity).

Every object you open must be closed as soon as access to it is no longer needed. Don't delay closing an object; other applications may need it. To close an object, you call the *close()* method of the opened object like this:

```
pointerToOpenedObject->close();
```

ObjectARX and ObjectDBX provide hundreds of functions to access the drawing database. Many of them open objects implicitly. For instance, the *getBlockTable()* function not only returns a pointer to the block table, it also opens the block table object. This is why you have to provide an open mode for *getBlockTable()* as well. Consequently, you need to explicitly close the block table object as soon as you finish using it. Many *get* functions implicitly open objects, as do all object constructors. Thus, if you create a new AcDbLine object, don't forget to close it.

All ObjectDBX functions return an error code, which you should check, of course. After both *acdbOpenObject()* and *close()*, you have to look at the returned error code. If everything went smoothly, you will get *Acad::eOk*. See the ObjectDBX documentation for other error codes that a specific function can return.

Iterating through Containers

If you already know an object's key field string, perhaps a linetype's name, you can directly access the corresponding symbol table record by using the *getAt()* function:

```
Acad::ErrorStatus
AcDbLinetypeTable::getAt(
  const char* entryName,
  AcDbLinetypeTableRecord*& pRecord,
  AcDb::OpenMode openMode,
  Adesk::Boolean openErasedRecord = Adesk::kFalse) const;
```

You pass the object's key field string and the open mode. In return, you'll get a pointer to the corresponding symbol table record. The object will be opened, and you are responsible for closing it later.

If you don't want to open the symbol table record, you can use a variant of the *getAt()* function. It returns only the object's identification, which can be used in a later call to *acdbOpenObject()*.

```
Acad::ErrorStatus
AcDbLinetypeTable::getAt(
  const char* entryName,
  AcDbObjectId& recordId,
  Adesk::Boolean getErasedRecord = Adesk::kFalse) const;
```

The error code returned by *getAt()* indicates whether the symbol table record was found (*Adesk::eOk*). If no object is using the specified key, you'll receive an error code of *Adesk::eKeyNotFound*.

If you don't know a symbol table record's key field string, you need to iterate through the symbol table to find the records contained therein. To do this, each symbol table object provides a *newIterator()* function that creates an iterator object for the symbol table. The function returns a pointer to the newly created iterator. Two optional arguments allow you to position the iterator at the container's beginning or end and to skip or include deleted objects:

```
Acad::ErrorStatus
newIterator(
  AcDbLinetypeTableIterator*& pIterator,
  Adesk::Boolean atBeginning = Adesk::kTrue,
  Adesk::Boolean skipDeleted = Adesk::kTrue) const;
```

You can use the iterator's *step()* function to step through the container's contents, or you can use the iterator's *seek()* function to position the iterator at a specific record. If you use *step()*, you need to call the iterator's *done()* function to recognize the end of the container.

At any time, you can use the iterator's *getRecord()* function to open the corresponding symbol table record object. As soon as the iterator is no longer needed, you must delete it. Here is a code segment showing how to iterate through the linetype table:

```
AcDbLinetypeTableIterator *pointerToIterator;
pointerToLinetypeTable->newIterator(pointerToIterator)
for (; !pointerToIterator->done(); pointerToIterator->step())
  {
  pointerToIterator->getRecord(pointerToRecord, AcDb::kForRead);
  doSomething(pointerToRecord);
```

```
    pointerToRecord->close();
 }
delete pointerToIterator;
```

To add additional records to a symbol table, you first create the corresponding object and then add it to the symbol table. If you don't add it to the container object, the newly created record will not become part of the database. The *add()* function for symbol tables comes in two variants depending on whether you want the object identification back:

```
Acad::ErrorStatus
add(
   AcDbLinetypeTableRecord* pRecord);
```

or

```
Acad::ErrorStatus
add(
   AcDbObjectId& recordId,
   AcDbLinetypeTableRecord* pRecord);
```

Entity Handling in ObjectDBX

Using entities in ObjectDBX is similar to symbol record handling as discussed earlier. Every entity is a member of exactly one block container (unless it's a temporary object without an owner). You access the block containers using the block table records, which you get just like you get any other symbol table record.

Every block table record is a container for entities. Once you receive a pointer to the corresponding block table record (for example, by using the block table's *getAt()* function), you can iterate through the block contents. To do this, you once again use the *newIterator()* function. But this time you call the *newIterator()* function of the AcDbBlockTableRecord object, not the function of the block table.

 NOTE   Do not confuse *AcDbBlockTableRecord::newIterator()* with *AcDbBlockTable-Record::newBlockReferenceIdIterator()*. The first function iterates through the contents of a block container referenced by the block table record. The second function iterates through all references to this block throughout the complete database.

While iterating through the contents of a block container, you will not get to the AcDbBlockBegin and AcDbBlockEnd objects of the block. These objects are supplied for compatibility reasons only. They exist in ObjectDBX only because old applications might have attached application-specific data (*xdata*) to them and there needs to be an access route to this data. If you ever need to access the two objects, use the block table record's *openBlockBegin()* and *openBlockEnd()* functions.

Because entities in a block container do not have a key string, there is no *getAt()* function to directly access one object without iteration. But because every database object (entity or not) has a unique handle, you can use this function to directly access a specific object no matter where it resides:

```
Acad::ErrorStatus
AcDbDatabase::getAcDbObjectId(
  AcDbObjectId& retId,
  Adesk::Boolean createIfNotFound,
  const AcDbHandle& objHandle,
  Adesk::UInt32 xRefId = 0);
```

If the object you find is an entity, you can use its *blockId()* function to find the block table record of the container to which it belongs.

Once you have a pointer to a specific entity, you can use all its member functions to set and retrieve the individual data associated with it. Typical member functions for retrieval are *color()* and *linetype()*. Typical member functions for setting are *setColor()* and *setLinetype()*.

You can use an entity's member functions to access all database-resident data associated with the object. In addition, you can use many member functions that simplify object handling (such as transformations).

Finally, ObjectDBX provides you with access to data elements not saved in the drawing database but taken directly from the class definition. One example is the location of grip points that AutoCAD displays for an object of a certain class. In ObjectDBX, you can query an object's grip points using the *getGripPoints()* function. This type of information is not available to ActiveX Automation, AutoLISP, or DXF.

To add another object to a block container, you use the block table record's *appendAcDbEntity()* function. Like the *add()* function for symbol tables, this function comes in two variants, depending on whether you want the database-internal identification of the object returned:

```
Acad::ErrorStatus
AcDbBlockTableRecord::appendAcDbEntity(
  AcDbObjectId& outputId,
  AcDbEntity* pEntity);
```

or

```
Acad::ErrorStatus
AcDbBlockTableRecord::appendAcDbEntity(
  AcDbEntity* pEntity);
```

Working with Dictionaries in ObjectDBX

As you know, dictionaries either belong to a specific object or form a hierarchical tree with a root dictionary containing other dictionaries. To get a pointer to this root dictionary, you use the *getNamedObjectsDictionary()* function of the database.

To retrieve an object's extension dictionary, you use the *extensionDictionary()* function. Check the return value against *isNull()* to see if there is no extension dictionary for the object.

Once you get to this or any other dictionary, you can iterate through its objects using the *newIterator()* function discussed in the previous section. But the *newIterator()* function for dictionaries needs an additional parameter that defines the iterating sequence. If you supply *AcRx::kDictSorted*, you'll get the dictionary objects according to the alphabetic sequence of their keys. If you supply *AcRx::kDictCollated*, you'll iterate according to the sequence in which the objects were inserted in the dictionary.

Every object you'll find during iteration is either an object or another dictionary, through which you can also iterate.

If you know an entry's key field string, you can directly retrieve it using the dictionary's *getAt()* function.

Dictionaries don't have an *add()* or an *append()* function as symbol tables or block containers do, because they don't support simple adding of objects. Every object you add to a dictionary must have a search key string that will be used to retrieve the object later. Therefore, the corresponding function is called *setAt()*:

```
Acad::ErrorStatus
AcDbDictionary::setAt(
  const char* srchKey,
  AcDbObject* newValue,
  AcDbObjectId& retObjId);
```

To add an object to a dictionary, both the dictionary and the object must be opened for write.

As is the case with ActiveX Automation, a couple of shortcuts are defined for the AutoCAD-specific dictionaries in ObjectARX. An example is *getGroupDictionary()*, which is short for a *getAt()* of the ACAD_GROUP dictionary in the root dictionary.

Database Settings and Result Buffers

ObjectDBX also contains shortcuts to the database settings. For example, the CECOLOR setting defines the default color for newly created database entities. You can access this setting using the *AcDbDatabase::cecolor()* and *AcDbDatabase::setCecolor()* functions.

For every setting there is a function that retrieves the current value of the setting, and there is a correspondent set function to modify the value.

In addition, there is a generic function to read and write system variables, and it can access both the database settings and other temporary or configuration-dependent settings like those you get through the AutoLISP and ActiveX Automation functions. These functions are called *acedGetVar()* and *acedSetVar()*. As the *aced* prefix demonstrates, these are not database functions but editor functions.

Using the *acedGetVar()* function is quite complicated, because it uses a special structure to return the setting's value. This value may be an integer, a real number, a point, or a string. Therefore, the result buffer (*resbuf*) structure contains a type field indicating the data type returned along with the true value. And to allow really complex return values, result buffers include a pointer to another result buffer. This allows result buffers to be linked and to return large lists of points, numbers, or strings.

Other Ways to Access the Drawing Database

DXF, AutoLISP, ActiveX Automation, and ObjectDBX/ObjectARX are four methods you can use to access the contents of an AutoCAD drawing database. Each has some disadvantages.

DXF is not AutoCAD's native file format, and although AutoCAD reads and writes DXF files transparently, users most often save their drawings in AutoCAD's DWG file format, which needs an additional user action to create a copy in DXF format.

AutoLISP and ActiveX Automation both rely on the presence of AutoCAD when evaluating or modifying a drawing. Without AutoCAD, they can't be used to access drawings.

Routines based on ObjectDBX can run both inside AutoCAD and inside other programs. This allows you to create external programs that use native AutoCAD drawing files to save drawing databases. However, ObjectDBX is limited to one specific platform (Microsoft's 32-bit Windows) and to one specific development environment (Microsoft Visual C++). Although Visual C++ is the language of connection for Auto-CAD programmers using ObjectDBX, Delphi and other object-oriented programs have occasionally broken through the barrier. Visual C++ is the only supported and tested environment to create ObjectDBX applications for the current version of AutoCAD.

A final problem with ObjectDBX is that you need to license its use from Autodesk. This licensing not only involves royalties, but also restrictions on marketing and use of your ObjectDBX-based programs. For instance, Autodesk does not allow you to create a program that directly competes with AutoCAD.

Due to these disadvantages, there are a number of alternatives to read and write a drawing's database. The most obvious alternative is to directly read an AutoCAD DWG drawing file without going through ObjectDBX. By doing this, you are free to select your development and target platforms as you are for DXF, but your users don't have to remember to use DXF instead of DWG.

Because Autodesk considers the DWG file format a trade secret and will not disclose it, you'll need to decipher the bits and pieces of a DWG file by yourself. But you're not alone. An organization called the OpenDWG Alliance was formed in 1998. Its goal is to force Autodesk to document the structure and contents of AutoCAD drawing files. Until this happens, the alliance provides its members with tools and documents that help them to read and write DWG files directly. The Web page you'll find at http://www.opendwg.org documents the file format as the alliance has succeeded in reengineering it so far.

Before the formation of OpenDWG, some developers found out how DWG files are made up and sold their knowledge in the form of programming libraries. The three most important developers were Jonathan Linowes of Sirlin, Gary Rohrabaugh of SoftSource, and Matt Richards of MarComp. Sirlin was acquired by Autodesk, and MarComp was acquired by Visio Corp. The MarComp libraries became the foundation of the OpenDWG libraries. The SoftSource libraries are called "Drawing eXchange Engine" (DXE), and at the time I am writing this book they are still available at http://www.softsource.com/dxe.html.

Using the DWG file format directly or using the OpenDWG libraries (or other, similar libraries) also has disadvantages, as you might suspect. One disadvantage is that it's a lot like trying to hit a moving target. During the AutoCAD Release 14 lifetime (and after the formation of OpenDWG), Autodesk introduced a slight change in the file format. You wouldn't have noticed this while using any of the methods described in this chapter, but programs based on third-party libraries suddenly didn't accept these files. You might wonder *why* Autodesk introduced this change other than to demonstrate the imperfection of the strategy to rely on reengineered libraries, but I'll leave the conclusions to you.

A second, even more severe disadvantage is the delay span. As soon as Autodesk releases a new version of AutoCAD and its accompanying new database format, you can be sure that the four main access methods discussed in this chapter will be updated. This means you can start adjusting your applications to the new database format immediately (or even earlier if you have access to alpha or beta versions). If you use a third-party library or your own direct-access routines, it will take some time until the changed file format has been reengineered and you can start porting your applications.

Summary

The drawing database is the collection of all the information that AutoCAD saves in a drawing file. You can use this information in many ways. Besides working interactively in AutoCAD and looking at database objects using the LIST command or the Properties window, you can programmatically retrieve, manipulate, and even create database objects.

Autodesk provides four main methods to access the drawing database: stand-alone programs can use the DXF file format or the ObjectDBX libraries; add-ons to AutoCAD can use AutoLISP, ActiveX Automation, or ObjectDBX as well. No matter which method you use, you will find the AutoCAD objects as documented in this book.

The next chapter concentrates on how the data you'll find is formatted.

CHAPTER **3**

Data Types in a Drawing Database

FEATURING

Integers	54
Disguised integers	57
Real numbers	61
Strings	64
Handles	65
Object pointers	66
Points	66
Binary data	72

So far, you have seen the drawing database as a series of objects collected into different containers. An object in this context is typically a line, an arc, or a circle. As you've learned, each object has its own set of properties that define this special instance of its class. For example, the defining properties of a circle are its center point and its radius.

Within the drawing database, only the defining properties are saved and filed out (saved to a disk file). All other aspects of the object, such as its graphical appearance or any calculated properties, are not part of the drawing database. These aspects are subject to the program that is evaluating the database, which could be AutoCAD itself, a third-party application running inside AutoCAD, or a stand-alone program talking to AutoCAD or directly accessing a drawing database saved to a DXF or a DWG file.

If you look at the defining properties of any database object, you'll see that you need only a small number of data types to describe them. In the case of a circle, it's clear that the radius is a positive real number and that the center is a point in 3D. (The AutoCAD drawing database is 3D. Even if you draw a simple circle in 2D, the center point has three coordinates, as the LIST command in AutoCAD will tell you.)

This chapter discusses the basic data types used in the database objects, which we'll inspect throughout the remaining chapters of this book. Let's start with simple numbers and look at how simple numbers appear in the various access methods. You will also see some typical properties that are saved as simple numbers to the drawing database.

Integers in the Drawing Database

An integer stores a whole number in the drawing database, that is, a number that doesn't have a decimal part or a fraction. The most common integer is the *signed 16-bit integer* (an integer that takes up 16 bits [which equals two bytes] of storage space and contains a sign to indicate either a positive or negative number).

Many properties of objects in the drawing database are saved as signed 16-bit integers. One example is the number of faces in a polyface mesh object (AcDbPolyFaceMesh, see Chapter 13), which, for instance, may have 18 faces. How your program sees the number of faces depends on how you access the drawing database (using DXF, AutoLISP, ActiveX Automation, or ObjectDBX). This is also true for other types of integers, for real numbers, for strings, and for every other type of information in the drawing database.

This chapter explains how the same data (such as the 18 saved as the polyface object's number of faces) appears in different environments. Within the application program you write to extract or modify a property, you need to declare your variables accordingly. In some cases, you even need to perform certain conversions to correctly work with the data that the drawing database returns to you.

Signed 16-Bit Integer

A signed 16-bit integer (*AcDb::kDwgInt16*) is a whole number in the range −32768 through 32767. Where do these odd numbers come from? Using 16 bits, you can set individual bits in 65536 different combinations. This means that using a 16-bit integer you can store exactly one of 65536 numbers. Because our integer is signed, we need one bit to indicate whether the value is positive or negative. If the sign bit is not set, the number is positive. With 15 bits left, we can store 32768 different positive numbers ranging from 0 (no bit set) through 32767 (all 15 bits set). The remaining 32768 bit combinations are used to express negative numbers (from −1 through −32768).

In ASCII DXF, AutoCAD saves a signed 16-bit integer by writing the individual digits of the number to the DXF file (see Chapter 2). ASCII, the American Standard Code for Information Interchange, defines which combination of bits is to be used to represent a certain digit or character. For instance, the numeral 1 is represented by the bit code 0011 0001. In ASCII DXF, a signed 16-bit integer is right-justified to the sixth column and padded with leading spaces. Thus, integer 18 is saved to an ASCII DXF file with four leading spaces.

····18

(For clarity, nonprinting characters have been shown to indicate spaces.)

If you look at the individual bytes of the DXF file, you will see 4 space characters (whose hexadecimal representation is 20h), the numeral 1 (31h), and the numeral 8 (38h). (If you are not familiar with hexadecimal representation of bytes, turn back to Chapter 2.) The program you write to evaluate the ASCII DXF file needs to read the individual characters and translate them back to the number 18 that you want to use in your code. Fortunately, in most programming languages, built-in functions do this conversion for you.

From Chapter 2, you will remember that there are two flavors of DXF: ASCII DXF, in which all numbers are saved digit by digit, and binary DXF, in which numbers are saved in their compressed binary form. When writing a 16-bit (or 2-byte) integer to a binary DXF file, AutoCAD simply writes the 2 bytes of which the number is made.

When evaluating a DXF file from within your program, you need to read the 2 bytes and convert them back to a 16-bit integer. To do so, you need to know the order in which the bytes appear in the file. For instance, if the first byte you read is 12h (0001 0010) and the second byte is 00h (0000 0000), is the resulting integer calculated from the sequence 0001 0010 0000 0000 or from the sequence 0000 0000 0001 0010? The first sequence gives you the number 4608 (4096 + 512), and the second sequence gives you the number 18 (16 + 2). In binary DXF, 16-bit integers are always saved with their least-significant byte (the lower-value bits) first. Thus, the DXF sequence 12h 00h indeed means the number 18. You need to take this into account if your DXF reading program is supposed to run on a computer that uses a different byte order.

Negative numbers are saved using their binary complement. Thus, when converting the 2 bytes back to an integer, you need to first check whether the number is negative. You do so by looking at the sign (highest-value) bit. Since 16-bit integers are saved with the least-significant byte first, the sign bit is the first bit in the second byte! If the sign bit is set, you calculate the resulting number by first complementing each bit (that is, if it's 0, make it 1 and vice versa), add 1, and take the result as negative. Again, in most programming languages, standard functions do all this for you.

If you are not reading a drawing database byte by byte as you do when working with DXF, you don't have to worry about the internal formatting of a 16-bit integer. If you are working in AutoLISP, ActiveX Automation, or ObjectDBX, to retrieve the value of any property of an object in the drawing database, all you have to do is declare your variable so that it fits the data type that AutoCAD will return to you. If the data type does not fit, your program will probably crash or display unexpected results.

In AutoLISP, you don't declare variables. Instead, AutoLISP automatically creates an atom of a correct type. If you query an AutoCAD database object using *entget*, any property whose value is a 16-bit integer is returned as an atom of type *integer*.

If you query the value of a database object's property in ActiveX Automation, signed 16-bit integers are returned as numbers of type *long*. You need to declare your internal variables accordingly. When writing to a property, be aware that the ActiveX Automation data type *long* allows you to use numbers larger than 32767. Since the drawing database will only take a 16-bit portion of the number you pass, results may be different from what you expect.

In ObjectDBX, the corresponding data type is *Adesk::Int16*. Thus, whenever your program asks ObjectDBX to give you the value of a database object's property that is documented as a 16-bit integer throughout the remaining chapters of this book, you need to declare the return value as *Adesk::Int16*.

Signed 32-Bit Integer

A signed 32-bit integer (*AcDb::kDwgInt32*) is a whole number in the range –2147483648 through 2147483647. Again, this comes from the maximum number of combinations (numbers) that can be expressed using 32 bits, one of them used as a sign bit. AutoCAD uses 32-bit integers when it needs to save to the drawing database those integers whose values exceed the 16-bit range. Only a few properties save their value as a 32-bit integer.

In ASCII DXF, you'll find a left-justified, signed 32-bit integer. Thus, the integer 18 is saved to an ASCII DXF file as 31h 38h.

NOTE   With 32-bit integers, there is no padding with space characters as there is with 16-bit integers.

In binary DXF, a signed 32-bit integer is saved within 4 bytes, with the least significant byte first. Thus, the integer 18 is saved as 12h 00h 00h 00h. Negative numbers are saved using their binary complement.

In AutoLISP, you receive an atom of type *integer*. In ActiveX Automation, signed 32-bit integers are returned as numbers of type *long*. In ObjectDBX, the corresponding data type is *Adesk::Int32*. You see that, in AutoLISP and ActiveX Automation, 16-bit integers and 32-bit integers are handled identically.

Signed 8-Bit Integer

A signed 8-bit integer (*AcDb::kDwgInt8*) is a whole number in the range –128 through 127, which is what combinations of 8 bits allow. Until Release 13 of AutoCAD, 8-bit integers were not used in the drawing database, and even today very few properties use 8-bit values.

In ASCII DXF, a signed 8-bit integer is left-justified. Thus, the integer 18 is saved to an ASCII DXF file as 31h 38h. You can't tell whether a number you see is supposed to be an 8-bit integer or a 32-bit integer (or even a string) just by looking at a DXF file. You need to know which data type is associated with the group code for the specific object. The discussion of the various objects in the drawing database throughout the remaining chapters of this book will provide you with this information.

In binary DXF, a signed 8-bit integer is saved as a single byte. Thus, the integer 18 is saved as 12h. Negative numbers are saved using their binary complement.

As is the case with 16-bit and 32-bit integers, neither AutoLISP nor ActiveX Automation distinguishes precision between 8-bit integers and 16-bit integers. Again you'll receive an atom of type *integer* in AutoLISP or a number of type *long* in ActiveX Automation. In ObjectDBX, the corresponding data type is *Adesk::Int8*.

Disguised Integers

Signed integers of 16-bit length are used to store many of the properties of objects in the drawing database. You would expect that the value of such a property could be any number in the range –32768 through 32767, but this is not always the case.

Take, for instance, the property of a dimension style that specifies whether the first extension line is to be suppressed. This property is allowed to have only two values: yes and no. In most programming languages, you would use the Boolean data type, or yes/no, for such a setting.

In the drawing database, there is no such data type. Instead, AutoCAD uses a signed 16-bit integer to save the setting to the drawing database. It simply declares that if the 16-bit integer is zero (0), the setting is "no", and if it's one (1), the setting is "yes". Other values are invalid.

In this property, the signed 16-bit integer type is abused to represent a completely different data type, the Boolean type. Depending on the object and property and depending on the programming environment, AutoCAD is sometimes friendly enough to convert the integer into the correct data type for you. In other cases, you need to do this conversion within the program you write.

In many places in the drawing database, integers represent a different, more specialized data type. If the environment you work in is friendly enough, you are working with database integers without knowing that they are integers. This section discusses these integers in disguise.

Enumerations As Integers

A typical example of data elements saved as an integer in a drawing database are *enumerations*. If a data type is an enumeration, it carries exactly one of a very limited set of values. The Boolean data type listed above, for instance, is an enumeration with only two possible values: yes (or true) and no (or false).

Let's look at the *LUNITS* database setting, which defines how to display linear units. In the drawing database, this setting is saved as a signed 16-bit integer and, as such, could take any value up to 32767. But if you look at the AutoCAD documentation (or in Chapter 4 of this book), you will see that the only possible values for this setting are 1, 2, 3, 4, and 5. In DXF, AutoLISP, and ObjectDBX, the LUNITS setting looks like any other signed 16-bit integer, so you really can't tell that it is limited to the values 1 through 5. In ActiveX Automation, you can use the integer 1 if you want exponential (scientific) format, but you probably won't. Usually, you use the predefined constant *acScientific* to set the LUNITS value.

Predefined constants for the values of an integer are used when the value range is very small, as in the LUNITS example in which only five values are possible. I will list integer *enumerations* for small value ranges with the relevant properties when I discuss the various object types throughout the remaining chapters of this book. It is wise to use predefined constants instead of the corresponding numbers in your code because your code is then more readable. Using predefined constants also allows a value of a constant to change with a new database version without breaking your code, although it is unlikely that constants change in this way from AutoCAD version to AutoCAD version.

Group Codes

Of the disguised integers that represent enumerations you may use in a program to access the AutoCAD drawing database, the DXF group code needs special consideration. In Chapter 2, you learned that the group code is invisible to ActiveX Automation and will be filled in by AutoCAD automatically when you create new objects or change the value of properties.

In ObjectDBX, you can use the many predefined constants of the enumerated type *AcDb::DxfCode* to fill in a DXF group code when writing certain properties of an object or to compare information you retrieved from the drawing database with a certain group code. In binary DXF, the group code is handled exactly the same as a signed 16-bit integer, but in ASCII DXF, the group code is saved right-justified to the third column (and not the sixth, as is usual) with leading spaces. Group codes larger than 999 are left-justified.

 WARNING Older specifications of binary DXF used a combination of 1-byte and 3-byte group codes. Therefore, do not assume that the group code is 2-byte (16-bit) in every DXF file your program may need to read. If you do, your program will probably crash on old-style DXF files. Always check the second byte of the very first group code in the file. If this byte is zero (00h), it's a DXF file with all group codes saved as 16-bit integers. If the second byte is not zero, it's an old-style DXF file with 1-byte and 3-byte group codes.

Colors and Lineweights

A number of database fields define a color or lineweight property. In the drawing database, this information is stored as an ordinary signed 16-bit integer. Depending on the environment used to talk to the database, the value of a color or lineweight property may be automatically converted to a much friendlier data type and look quite different from an integer.

Colors in DXF and AutoLISP are integers associated with group code 62. In ActiveX Automation, a color is an object of type ACAD_COLOR with predefined constants for the most often used colors. In ObjectDBX, a color is an object of type AcCmColor with a lot of member functions.

Lineweights in DXF and AutoLISP are integers associated with group code 370. In ActiveX Automation, you'll get an object of type ACAD_LWEIGHT with predefined constants for the lineweights allowed. In ObjectDBX, the lineweight is a member of the enumeration *AcDb::LineWeight*, for example, *kAcLnWt005*.

Booleans as Integers

Even though a drawing database contains many settings of data type Boolean, there is no such type in the drawing database. A Boolean property (also known as a *flag*) can take only two values: yes or no; or true or false. Ordinarily, you would need only a single bit to save the value of such a property. Instead, even a simple flag such as *Visibility* is saved to the drawing database as a signed 16-bit integer and takes up 16 bits of storage space instead of only 1 bit.

When looking for the *Visibility* property of an object in either DXF or AutoLISP, you will find only the 16-bit integer. You then need to check whether this integer is 0 (*visible*) or 1 (*invisible*). In ObjectDBX, you can use an enumerated type called *AcDb::Visibility* to check whether the corresponding object is visible. The property value is either *AcDb::kVisible* or *AcDb::kInvisible*. (This is an exception. In ObjectDBX, most other Booleans are of type *Adesk::Boolean*.)

In ActiveX Automation, this data element is a true Boolean entity, as it should be. You can simply use true and false to set the *Visibility* property.

To save space in the database, you will find database objects to which several independent Boolean flags have been saved for what looks like a single property. If you look at the AcDbAttribute object in ActiveX Automation (*AcadAttribute*), you will find the following four Boolean flags:

- Constant
- Invisible
- Preset
- Verify

Similarly, in ObjectDBX you will find four member functions of AcDbAttribute, each to set or query the four flags of type *Adesk::Boolean*, for example, *isConstant()*, *isInvisible()*, and so on.

In both DXF and AutoLISP, you will get *one* single integer describing all four flags. Each flag has a numeric value of 0 (false) or 1 (true). These numeric values are combined into a single integer by factoring with 2, that is, by packing each value into one bit of the resulting integer.

Thus, if in the program you write to interact with the drawing database you want to verify that an attribute is preset, you need to extract the corresponding bit from the integer. This extraction is usually done through a logical *and* function (*logand* in AutoLISP). In this case, the *preset* property is saved in the fourth bit of the attribute's group 70 value. This means you need to *and* the integer with $2^{(4-1)}$ and then check the result against zero to find out whether the property is set.

Real Numbers in the Drawing Database

A *real number* (or simply *real*) is a number that has a decimal part. Most numeric values in an AutoCAD drawing database are not integers. All coordinates, lengths, or angle values are real numbers. (And even if they accidentally have no decimal or fractional part, they are still real numbers.)

In theory, a real number can have an indefinite number of significant digits. However, in data processing we're used to limiting real numbers to a finite range and precision because we don't really care what the 356th digit of a calculated number is and because we don't have the time to wait until the computer calculates such a precise result.

The AutoCAD drawing database uses 64-bit floating-point numbers to store real values (*AcDb::kDwgReal*). Of these numbers, 52 bits make up the mantissa, and the remaining 12 bits are used for the exponent.

 NOTE A mantissa, if you'll remember your high school math, is the part of a logarithm to the right of the decimal point. Real numbers in a computer are logarithms based on the number 2.

The mantissa defines the maximum precision of numbers. Using 52 bits, the precision is limited to approximately 4,500,000,000,000,000 numbers. This is precise enough to locate every object of the solar system within a single centimeter and should be sufficient for all technical drawings in the near future.

The 12-bit exponent defines the range in which the real numbers you will work with lie. Using different exponents, you can place the numbers in the range $\pm10^{-308}$ through $\pm10^{308}$, which should be sufficient. (Although the AutoCAD drawing editor does not allow you to input values that exceed $\pm10^{-99}$ to $\pm10^{99}$, the calculated numbers inside the drawing database may be larger or smaller than that.)

In AutoLISP, whenever you query the value of an object's property, you'll get real numbers as atoms of type *real*. In ActiveX Automation, this data type is called *double*. ObjectDBX defines a type called *ads_real*.

In binary DXF, a real number is saved as an 8-byte double-float, according to IEEE Standard 754-1985, with the least significant byte first. Thus, the real number 10.0 is saved to binary DXF as the following sequence of bytes: 00h 00h 00h 00h 00h 00h 24h 40h.

NOTE   The IEEE (Institute of Electrical and Electronics Engineers) is an organization that coordinates computing and communications standards. For more information on the IEEE, go to its Web site at www.ieee.org.

In ASCII DXF, saving a real number is both simple and complicated. It's simple because you write the number digit by digit just as you would in any programming language. It's complicated because you need to follow a few rules to create valid numbers:

- Any real number in ASCII DXF must have at least one digit before and one digit after the decimal delimiter.

- The decimal delimiter is always a decimal point, regardless of the local standard, which may be a comma in some geographic areas.

- The maximum number of digits is 16 because this is the maximum precision of a 52-bit mantissa. Thus, if you have 10 digits in front of the decimal point, you can't have more than 6 digits following it.

- You can append an exponent to the number if necessary. The exponent always starts with the letter E, followed by the sign of the exponent (+ or –), followed by a maximum of three digits.

Examples of properly formatted reals are 1.0, 0.56, and 0.7E+2. The following examples are not valid, and AutoCAD or another DXF-reading program may refuse to load the drawing file: 25., .12, 1 3/4, or 0.9E2.

TIP   When writing an ASCII DXF file in AutoCAD, you can set the precision. In fact, you set the number of digits to follow the decimal point. If you keep the default of 16 digits, the accuracy of numbers in the DXF file equals the accuracy within the database. Rounding errors are in the range you normally expect with finite-length real numbers.

WARNING   If you select fewer than 16 digits when setting the precision during DXF creation, you alter the database contents! The database in DXF now differs from the original database. Under extreme circumstances (using 0 digits), this may render the database information invalid, perhaps by introducing scale factors of zero.

Length Units

Although integers often define quantities (and are therefore considered unit-less), real numbers in a technical drawing usually have an associated unit. Most real numbers define lengths. To define a length completely, you need to add a unit of measurement.

Unfortunately, the AutoCAD drawing database is unit-less. The eye of the user of a drawing interprets its lengths. You can't tell just from looking at the coordinates in a drawing database whether the drawing uses millimeters, inches, or parsecs.

There is a unit of measurement associated with blocks, which means that you can tell whether a block is designed to use millimeters or inches. However, AutoCAD itself does not honor these units. Only the DesignCenter application, which is shipped with AutoCAD, honors them. The unit assigned to blocks can be found as *xdata* attached to the block's symbol table record. For the *MODEL_SPACE* block, such information is saved in the INSUNITS drawing setting.

Angle Units

Unlike length units, which are nonexistent, the unit of measurement for angles and directions in a drawing database is implicit. Unfortunately, the angle unit that is used depends on how you look at the drawing database.

In DXF (ASCII and binary), angles are measured in decimal degrees and are between but excluding –360° and 360°. In AutoLISP, ActiveX Automation, and ObjectDBX, angles are measured in radians and range from $-\pi$ to π.

Date and Time Values

In addition to lengths, angles, and just plain simple real numbers (such as scale factors), the drawing database uses real numbers to save date and time values.

The value of a couple of timers represents the number of days since the timer started. The fractional part of the real number is the fractional part of a day. An example of this is the cumulative editing time you can retrieve from the TDINDWG setting (see Chapter 4).

Date and time values, like the last save, are also saved within a real number. The AutoCAD drawing database uses Julian dates, which are calculated by the number of days since January 1, 4713 B.C. Again, the fractional part defines the hours, minutes, and so on.

In ObjectDBX, you'll get dates as instances of AcDbDate, a class containing several member functions that provide a more comfortable access to date values.

Strings in the Drawing Database

Besides numbers, a drawing database also contains several text strings, that is, combinations of text characters such as annotations, layer names, and so on. These strings fall into two categories: strings that will be displayed as part of the drawing (for example, text, multiline text, attributes, and so on) and strings that work as references (for example, layer names, filenames, and hyperlinks).

Database strings (*AcDb::kDwgText*) can be of any length. When working with properties of database objects that have string values, in AutoLISP and ActiveX Automation, you'll see the strings as *string* type objects. In ObjectDBX, the correspondent type is *char**. In ASCII DXF, a string is simply a line of characters. In binary DXF, a string is also a sequence of characters, but terminated by a zero byte (00h).

Character Sets

Until recently, computers, operating systems, and application programs were limited in the number of different characters they could display and use. Some systems, such as Windows 95/98, are still limited in this way. On such systems, the user must select (typically during installation of the operating system) a certain set of characters to work with. For example, if your system is set to use Latin characters, you won't be able to type Japanese or Greek characters.

The AutoCAD drawing database is independent of the character set that a specific machine uses. The database supports the Unicode character set, which is a superset of all national character sets. Character sets are also called *code pages*.

Depending on the platform used to run the database access program, the full Unicode character set may not be available. For instance, although Windows NT allows you to work with the full Unicode range of characters, Windows 95/98 allows you to use only a small 256-character set.

If the full Unicode character set is not available, you will see database strings translated to the local character set. All characters in the local code page will be seen as is, while all Unicode characters not in the local set will be translated into a control code sequence. This sequence consists of a Unicode escape sequence followed by a 4-digit hexadecimal representation of the Unicode character. Whenever the program you write to access the drawing database retrieves a string from an object's property, you should expect that it may contain Unicode control codes, at least if you cannot guarantee that your program runs only on systems that support the full Unicode range of characters.

For example, look at the string *This is angle α*. Because the alpha character is usually not part of a Windows 95/98 code page, you will see this text represented as *This is angle \U+03b1*. Depending on your programming language, you might also see the backslash doubled.

If your program runs inside AutoCAD, you can query the non–database-resident global setting *SYSCODEPAGE* for the local code page name. (As explained in Chapter 2, the AutoLISP, ActiveX Automation, and ObjectDBX functions for retrieving the drawing settings that I'll discuss in Chapter 4 also allow you to retrieve temporary and configuration-dependent settings from AutoCAD that are not saved to a drawing database. See the AutoCAD documentation on system variables for a complete list of the settings not listed in Chapter 4.) If your program runs on its own using ObjectDBX, it must ask the operating system about the current code page.

If you are working with DXF, you need to use the code page that was active when the DXF file was written. You'll find the name of this code page in the *HEADER* section under the heading *DWGCODEPAGE*.

Character Range

Depending on what a string is going to represent in the drawing database, the number and range of characters that can be used may be limited. For example, symbol table record keys are not allowed to use the following characters:

<>/\":?*,='

Characters in the range 00h through 1Fh are unprintable control characters and are not allowed in any string in a drawing database.

Handles in the Drawing Database

The database-unique object handle (*AcDb::kDwgHandle*) is a 64-bit integer value. However, it is never seen as such.

In ObjectDBX, the handle is represented by its own class, *AcDbHandle*. In DXF, AutoLISP, and ActiveX Automation, the handle is shown to any program requesting it as a string containing the hexadecimal representation of the 64-bit integer. Thus, the handle 18 is represented by the string "12" (18 = 1 * 16 + 2).

If you're working in ObjectDBX, you can get the string representation of a handle using the function *AcDbHandle::getIntoAsciiBuffer()*.

Object Pointers

During the discussion of links between objects in Chapter 2, you learned that there are four different types of inter-object links:

- AcDb::kDwgHardOwnershipId
- AcDb::kDwgSoftOwnershipId
- AcDb::kDwgHardPointerId
- AcDb::kDwgSoftPointerId

Object links require that one object point to the other object to which it is linked. How you see the other object's reference in the database depends on the method you use to evaluate it.

In DXF, you will find the referenced object's handle (again, in its string representation). When working with AutoLISP, the reference is the other object's *Entity name*. In ObjectDBX you will get an *ObjectID*.

In ActiveX Automation, you will not get a pointer to the referenced object at all. Instead, you will transparently get the object itself, which you can use directly.

Points in the Drawing Database

Every entity in a DXF file has at least one set of coordinates that define the object's position within the model. Depending on the object type, you need one or more points (*AcDb::kDwg3Real*) to describe the location and size of the entity. A point is an exact location in space defined by its x, y, and z coordinates.

Points in an AutoCAD drawing database always have three coordinates (except for a few exceptions that I will point out in later chapters during the discussion of the objects by which they are used). Every model in the database is three-dimensional. Even a simple 2D draft has z coordinates; they're just all the same (0.0).

Even though coordinates are lengths that should each have a unit of measurement, the AutoCAD drawing database is unit-less. Each coordinate is just a unit-less 64-bit real number.

Points, Coordinates, and Point Lists

How object properties that are points are returned to your application program depends on the access method you use to read the drawing database.

ObjectDBX uses a special data type called *AcGePoint3d* to pass points as parameters to and from routines. The *AcGePoint3d* is an array of *ads_real* indexed by 0, 1, and 2.

Predefined constants x, y, and z allow you to query a point's x coordinate by *Some-Point[X]*.

In AutoLISP, a point is handled as a list of three real numbers. You can extract the three coordinates using the standard AutoLISP functions *car*, *cadr*, and *caddr* respectively.

In ActiveX Automation, there is no predefined data type suited for points. Therefore, you use *variants* to read and write points. A single point is passed as an array of *double* indexed by 0, 1, and 2. Several objects are defined by a list of points. In this case, you also use an array of *double*, but it now needs to have more components (three doubles per point).

In DXF, the storage of points is a bit strange. For some reason, a point was not considered as a separate data type to fit into a single group value. Instead, the three coordinates making the point are three individual groups. To read a point's coordinates, you need to read three group values. With every point, the group code for the y coordinate is calculated from the x coordinate's group code by adding 10, and for the z coordinate, by adding 20. Thus, if a point's group code in AutoLISP is 14, in DXF you'll find the x coordinate in group 14, the y coordinate in group 24, and the z coordinate in group 34.

Points, Vectors, and Offsets

A *point* exactly defines a location in 3D space, for example, the point with the x coordinate 10.0, the y coordinate 20.0, and the z coordinate 30.0. A *vector* exactly defines a bearing in 3D space, like from *here* 15.0 units along *this* direction. Another way to express a vector is to say: from *here* 5.0 units parallel to the x-axis, then 10.0 units parallel to the y-axis, and finally 10.0 units parallel to the z-axis. Both variants describe the exact same vector. Vectors are independent of their starting point (the *here* in the previous sentences). Wherever you move the vector around in space, it is always the same vector (because the vector is just the direction and the distance, not the location of *here*.)

Both points and vectors have three coordinates, and so, both mathematically and in the AutoCAD database, there is no apparent difference between the two. Whether you see a coordinate set as a point or as a vector depends on the context in which you use it.

What I just explained and what is known mathematically as a vector is called an offset in all Autodesk documentation. Whenever the documentation uses the term *vector*, it is referring to a (mathematical) vector that has an additional special property: a length (distance) of one (1.0). Such a vector is usually called a *unit vector* or a *normalized* vector. Since the distance part of a normalized vector is always 1.0, an (Autodesk) vector just expresses a direction in 3D space.

When accessing a drawing database using ObjectDBX, you retrieve (Autodesk) vectors as objects of class AcGeVector3d, which is a structure (not an array!) of three real numbers. You access a vector's y coordinate by writing *SomeVector.y,* in which *SomeVector* represents the vector you would name in your bit of code

If an object contains point, vector, and offset type properties, you will also notice a difference in the way these properties change while the object is modified. No matter whether the object is moved, scaled, rotated, stretched, or mirrored, point properties of this object usually change accordingly. Vector properties change only when the object is rotated or mirrored—they are independent of move, scale, or stretch operations. Offset properties work the same as vectors as they change with rotations and mirroring operations, but also change their length if the object is scaled.

Coordinate Systems

AutoCAD uses only three-dimensional, Cartesian coordinate systems. A Cartesian coordinate system is defined by its origin point and three axes. The three axes are perpendicular to one another and right-oriented, which means that they follow the right-hand rule:

> If the thumb, the index finger, and the middle finger of your right hand build 90° angles to one another and if the thumb points along the x-axis and the index finger points along the y-axis, the middle finger points along the z-axis.

Coordinate systems differ in their origin points and in the direction of their axes. When working with the AutoCAD drawing database, you will have to use various coordinate systems.

The complete drawing database is based on a global, arbitrary coordinate system called the *World Coordinate System (WCS).* The WCS "origin" is the point (0,0,0), where the x-axis goes from the WCS origin through the point (1,0,0), the y-axis through the point (0,1,0), and the z-axis through (0,0,1). A model or drawing can be oriented arbitrarily within the WCS, which means that there is nothing special about the WCS. If your model is a house, you don't say that the elevation is parallel to the WCS z-axis. Nothing will hinder you from drawing the house with the elevation parallel to the WCS x-axis. Thus, in relationship to the model, the WCS is just one arbitrary coordinate system.

While working in AutoCAD, a user can create his or her own Cartesian coordinate systems. These *User Coordinate Systems (UCS)* have their own origin and axis orientation. Although the database objects do not reflect in which UCS they were drawn, the drawing database contains a list of named UCS definitions that a user can recall. The UCS symbol table (discussed in detail in Chapter 6) is the list of all named UCS definitions within the drawing database. When working interactively in AutoCAD, the drawing editor transparently converts an object's coordinates to the current coordinate system and vice versa. When working with the drawing database directly, your program eventually needs to do these conversions.

Another coordinate system you will encounter in the drawing database is the *Screen Coordinate System (SCS)*, which is used to define window locations on the Auto-CAD graphical user interface. The SCS defines coordinates starting from the lower left corner of the screen's drawing display area, with the x-axis pointing to the right. The SCS is a two-dimensional coordinate system with the point (1,1) located at the upper right corner of the screen's drawing display area. Thus, any point within the drawing display area has an x and/or y coordinate between 0.0 and 1.0.

Entity Coordinates

Every entity in the drawing database has an associated *Entity Coordinate System (ECS)*, which may or may not be equal to the WCS. The Autodesk documentation has introduced the term *Object Coordinate System (OCS)* as an alternative to ECS. Because only entities (that is, objects with a graphical representation) have an ECS, this change in terminology does not represent a functional change. Since the term *Entity Coordinate System* is both more known and more correct, I'll stay with the abbreviation ECS throughout this book.

For most entities, the ECS corresponds to the WCS, especially when you think of three-dimensional objects. But it makes sense to give two-dimensional planar (that is, flat) objects their own coordinate system. For example, consider a circular arc. Because the arc can be arbitrarily oriented in 3D space, you must first define a coordinate system (ECS) with its x/y plane parallel to the plane on which the arc is drawn. All points on the arc curve have the same z coordinate in ECS. Also this coordinate system simplifies the storage of the arc's start and end parameters. Instead of using points or vectors, you can simply store the start and end angles relative to the x-axis of the ECS.

When accessing the drawing database, some point properties will be WCS points, and others will be ECS points. Whether a returned point is in WCS or ECS sometimes depends on the access method. The arc center, for instance, will be returned in WCS coordinates by ObjectDBX and the ActiveX Automation interface, but the same point property will be returned in ECS coordinates by AutoLISP and DXF.

Even though multiple coordinate systems are in use, the arc center point is still the arc center point; however, its coordinate values depend on the coordinate system in which you locate it. It's often necessary to translate an object's coordinates into another coordinate system. Because ObjectDBX returns points in WCS, you may want to know the coordinate values of a point if you used the ECS instead. To do this translation, ObjectDBX contains the *acdbWcs2Ecs()* transformation function, which takes a WCS point and returns the coordinate values within the ECS.

On the other hand, many point properties of objects are returned to AutoLISP in ECS coordinates. There is no built-in function to translate such an ECS point into the WCS, but you can easily create your own, for instance, by copying these lines to your program's code:

```
(defun PointInWCS (Entity PointInECS)
  (trans PointInECS Entity 0)
)
```

The Arbitrary Axis Algorithm

If you work with a DXF file, there is no predefined function to transform coordinates because there is only a data file in this format. And when working in ActiveX Automation, there's also no predefined function.

Thus, for these two applications, you need to know how an object's ECS is defined and how you can calculate the ECS definition from the data you find in the drawing database.

To define a plane in space, you usually need a point and two vectors. At the time the drawing database was enhanced to 3D memory, disk space was still very expensive. Consequently, the AutoCAD drawing database uses only a single vector to fully define the ECS. How does this work?

The ECS is valid for planar entities only. A *planar entity* is any entity that has a two-dimensional nature, for example, a circle, an arc, an annotation object, or a hatch pattern. Even though you can orient such a planar entity anywhere in 3D space, you always need to first define the plane on which you draw the object (like placing a sheet of paper onto your drawing board and then moving, tilting, and rotating the drawing board). The sheet of paper on the drawing board defines the plane in space where the object should appear. The direction perpendicular to the drawing board's surface is called the *normal* (also known as *normal vector*) of the plane on which the object is drawn (or simply the normal of the object).

Since the normal is just a direction (and, if you remember the earlier discussion on vectors, therefore expressed as a normalized or unit vector, that is, a vector of length 1.0), it does not matter at which point we place our normal vector. It is always the same. When calculating the ECS of a planar entity, you start with this normal vector and go back to the plane (or sheet) on which the object was drawn.

When Normals Differ

In the drawing board example, I said that the normal is the direction perpendicular to the drawing board surface. If you think about this for a moment, you will recognize that there are *two* directions perpendicular to the plane: one pointing toward you and the other pointing toward the drawing board. This is the reason for a typical problem in AutoCAD.

It is possible to draw two planar objects, maybe arcs, next to each other that have the same radius and, therefore, generate a similar outline. But one of these arcs may have its normal pointing "up," and the other may have its normal pointing "down." You will not notice the different normals during most AutoCAD operations. But if you try to fillet the two arcs, you'll get an error message because AutoCAD only fillets objects whose normals are parallel. Or if you add a thickness to the arcs, they will extrude in different directions. The normal direction is also important during the generation of rendered images, since computer programs usually render only one side of a surface, the one to which the normal vector points.

The normal vector of a planar entity defines the ECS z direction, but the direction alone defines only the orientation of the drawing board surface, not its location. An unlimited number of parallel planes still share the same normal. As an arbitrary but valid prerequisite, the ECS origin is therefore set so that it is always equal to the WCS origin. We, therefore, eliminate all the parallel planes and are left with only one of them. It may not necessarily pass through our drawing board's surface, but the z coordinate of any point of our planar object tells us the location of the "drawing board surface."

Now, all that is left to find out is the direction of the remaining axes, x and y, within the plane we just calculated. And because the three axes are perpendicular to one another, you can easily calculate the ECS y-axis once you identify the ECS x-axis.

But how do you calculate the ECS x-axis? AutoCAD uses a trick called the *arbitrary axis algorithm*. This is not an arbitrary *algorithm*, but an algorithm to calculate an arbitrary axis. Because the sole input is the ECS z direction (the normal), it doesn't really matter which x-axis AutoCAD calculates; it is only important to always calculate the *same* x-axis from a given normal. Thus, your axis may be arbitrary, and you'll use this calculation:

```
ECS_X = WCS_Z × ECS_Z
```

In this formula, WCS_Z is the z-axis of the WCS, (0,0,1). But there is a small problem: what if the normal (ECS_Z) is equal or very close to the WCS z-axis (WCS_Z)? Because this proximity gives an undefined result, you must add one more check and one alternative, in which WCS_Y is (0,1,0):

```
if ECS_Z is close to WCS_Z
  then
    ECS_X = WCS_Y × ECS_Z
  else
    ECS_X = WCS_Z × ECS_Z
```

Now you only have to define what is meant by *is close to*. The arbitrary axis algorithm defines this as follows:

$$(-\varepsilon < ECS\_Z[x] < \varepsilon) \Delta (-\varepsilon < ECS\_Z[y] < \varepsilon)$$

which means that we call the axes *close* if both the normal's x and y components are smaller than ε, a threshold value. The value of ε is defined as 0.015625 = 1.0/64.0, a value you can display exactly in both decimal and binary forms, thus giving you a fast and exact calculation no matter type the of computer on which the algorithm is supposed to run.

Once you know the axes and origin, you can easily translate coordinates between the two coordinate systems. Most development environments come with routines that use transformation matrices to translate coordinates between coordinate systems.

Binary Data in the Drawing Database

All the information in a drawing database should consist of numbers and/or strings, but there are exceptions. It is possible to store other sorts of information inside a drawing database, such as a true-color animation of the designed part or the sound an engine is supposed to make.

Although you could divide the information into numbers and strings, it makes sense to keep this information in its binary form. Therefore, the drawing database allows another data type called a *binary chunk* (*AcDb::kDwgBChunk*). This chunk of binary data can hold everything that does not easily fit into numbers or strings. Any object in the drawing database can have one or more properties that hold binary data.

If you retrieve a binary chunk of data from the drawing database using AutoLISP or if you look into an ASCII DXF file, a binary chunk is seen as a string containing the hexadecimal representation of the binary data. To use it, you need to convert the hexadecimal codes back to binary data. In binary DXF, you'll simply see the binary data. But, because there is no end-of-data character, as is the case with strings (since in a binary chunk, any character might be a valid data byte), the binary chunk is preceded by length information.

The length information is a single unsigned 8-bit integer. Because the maximum number you can represent using 8 bits (without a sign bit) is 255, the maximum length of a binary chunk is 255 bytes (plus the 1 length byte). If you read a group value from a binary DXF file and the group value is supposed to be a binary chunk, you read the first byte (the length information), and then you read as many data bytes as this length of byte indicates.

In ObjectDBX, a binary chunk is seen as data of type *ads_binary*. This structure (struct) consists of length information called *.clen* and a pointer to the binary data. Even though the length information *.clen* is defined as a short, remember that the maximum length for binary chunks is 255 bytes.

In ActiveX Automation, a binary chunk is returned as a *safearray*, which is an array in which all elements are of the same type. In the case of binary chunks, the individual array elements are bytes.

Summary

This concludes the discussion of data types you may encounter in an AutoCAD drawing database. Even though a drawing can have many different objects, the objects' individual properties are made from only a few basic primitives. If the program you write to access the drawing database knows how to handle the three types of integers, real numbers, points and vectors, handles, pointers, strings, and binary chunks, all that is left to do is to read the individual objects from the drawing database and decode their properties.

Chapters 1, 2, and 3 have given you basic information about the AutoCAD drawing database: its internal organization, the various ways to access it, and the data elements used to describe the objects in the database. In the remaining chapters of this book, I'll concentrate on the individual segments (containers) of the drawing database and on the objects located in them. The following chapter discusses the part of the drawing database that contains the drawing-specific settings.

CHAPTER **4**

Drawing-Specific Settings

FEATURING

Accessing the drawing settings   **77**

Understanding the critical settings   **78**

*Understanding the settings sequence
in DXF*   **115**

One part of the AutoCAD drawing database does not deal with what a drafter would call a drawing, which are the lines, arcs, and circles that constitute a design. This separate part contains a number of settings that AutoCAD saves specifically for a drawing. These settings describe the state into which AutoCAD should go after it loads the drawing. Most of these settings define how specific AutoCAD commands should work in this drawing or which defaults they should offer.

Most of the settings saved in a drawing file are completely irrelevant if you want to evaluate or manipulate an AutoCAD drawing. Therefore, when you are reading a drawing file, you can safely ignore all the settings intended only for the AutoCAD commands. If the program you write to access the drawing database runs inside AutoCAD (or with ActiveX Automation parallel to AutoCAD), you will probably use some of these settings to ensure that your program works the same as an AutoCAD command. In this case, you also need to take a look at the temporary and configuration-specific settings in AutoCAD that also affect how AutoCAD commands work. You'll find documentation of all temporary, configuration-specific, and drawing-specific settings in the AutoCAD help files.

When writing a drawing file (in DXF) directly or when your program runs inside AutoCAD and creates a new drawing database from scratch, it's wise to supply a set of standard values to the settings so that AutoCAD can go into a state that is fitting for the drawing's contents and task. If you do so, everyone using your program or loading your DXF files will find AutoCAD acting as expected. These standard values depend on the type of drawing you create. A mechanical design needs settings that are different from those of a floor plan or a street map. The easiest way to determine the preferred values is to start AutoCAD and interactively create a drawing similar to those your program will produce. Then look at all the settings by using the SYSVAR command or by printing out the HEADER section of the corresponding DXF file. Make a note of these settings, and be sure that your program uses them as defaults.

A few settings in a drawing file have an effect on how AutoCAD displays or prints the drawing or on how other programs will read and interpret the drawing database file (in DXF or DWG).

The most important setting within the drawing database is the AutoCAD database version number. This version number determines which objects will be allowed in the drawing database. Other settings define if and how AutoCAD will display objects of a specific type. For example, the PDMODE setting affects the display of AcDbPoint objects, and the ATTDISP setting changes the way AutoCAD displays AcDbAttribute objects. If an external program, such as a desktop publishing application or another CAD application, that reads an AutoCAD drawing database (in DXF or DWG) is to completely mimic the AutoCAD display of the drawing, it must recognize these settings.

I talked about how to access a drawing's settings using the various programming environments in Chapter 2, but I will summarize that information briefly in this chapter. Then you'll take a close look at those settings that affect a drawing's appearance or that are important in other ways for both creating and evaluating drawings. Finally, I will discuss the rest of the settings that are used less frequently.

How to Access the Drawing Settings

The drawing settings are not considered database objects. Therefore, you cannot access them using the typical methods. Instead, each environment has its own functions to read and write a setting.

Let's look at a setting called UCSORG and compare how the access works in the environments introduced in Chapter 2. The UCSORG setting specifies that the origin (ORG) of the User-defined Coordinate System (UCS) be current after the drawing loads into AutoCAD.

The simplest way to retrieve this setting is probably in ObjectDBX. You simply ask the database to return *AcDbDatabase::ucsorg()*, which gives you the origin in the form of an AcGePoint3d (see Chapter 3 for a discussion on data types used in the drawing database). The *AcDbDatabase::setUcsorg()* function stores a new origin point.

In ActiveX Automation, you need to query the setting from the document object by writing *TheDocumentObject.GetVariable("UCSORG")*; *TheDocumentObject* is an object variable that refers to the document you're interested in. The returned value is a *variant*, in this case, an array of three *doubles*. The complementary function is *SetVariable*.

In AutoLISP, it's equally simple. You write *(getvar "UCSORG")* to query the UCS origin. AutoLISP returns an S-expression (which is a list or a single atom) of the proper type: an integer, a real number, or a string or a list of real numbers. In the UCSORG case, AutoLISP returns a list of three real numbers containing the coordinates of the point. The complementary function in AutoLISP is called *setvar*.

In DXF, you'll find the drawing settings in the HEADER section of the file. Within this HEADER section are the settings' names as groups of code 9 followed by the settings' values as one or more groups. Here's an excerpt from an ASCII DXF file containing the UCSORG setting:

```
  9
$UCSORG
 10
0.0
 20
0.0
```

```
30
0.0
```

Please note two things: First, in DXF, the setting's name (group 9 value) is preceded by a dollar sign ($). You don't write this character when you access a setting from any of the other environments. Second, as with every point in DXF, the three coordinates come in three different groups with their numbers in steps of 10. Here, the three *groups* 10, 20, and 30 together contain the location of the origin.

The group code(s) used to describe a setting's value in DXF are determined by the value's type:

- Group codes 1 and 3 describe strings.
- Group codes 2, 6, and 7 refer to symbol table or dictionary record keys.
- Group code 5 is a handle.
- Group code 10 (and consequently 20 and 30) describes a point.
- Group code 40 is for real numbers describing lengths.
- Group code 50 is used for real numbers describing angles.
- Group code 62 describes a color.
- Group code 70 describes a signed 16-bit integer (or a Boolean).
- Group code 370 describes lineweight information.

Critical Settings

Although most of the drawing settings affect only the future defaults and actions of AutoCAD commands, a few settings directly affect the appearance of the drawing in AutoCAD or are otherwise critical for evaluating the database. If you're creating a drawing for import into AutoCAD or if you want your application to exactly mimic the AutoCAD display, you need to take these settings into account.

The critical settings are:

ACADVER

ACADMAINTVER

ATTMOD

DISPSILH

DWGCODEPAGE

FILLMODE

LTSCALE

LWDISPLAY

PDMODE

PDSIZE

PSLTSCALE

QTEXTMODE

SPLFRAME

TILEMODE

VISRETAIN

I'll cover these in detail in the next sections.

ACADVER (AutoCAD database version number)

When using AutoLISP, ActiveX Automation, or ObjectDBX, the database you work with is always current with the AutoCAD/ObjectDBX software you use. You don't have to worry if the drawing loaded in AutoCAD is from an older database version. AutoCAD transparently translates each drawing into the current database version when it loads a drawing file.

If you are working with stand-alone database files (DXF or DWG), it is important to know which version the drawing database adheres to. The information contained in this book is valid only for drawing databases of version number (ACADVER setting) AC1015. This is the version number AutoCAD 2000 uses (and not AC1500 as the DXF documentation incorrectly states). Most of the information in this book can also be used if you're working with an older database version, but I can't predict how much will be valid for future database versions.

When you are using DXF, the *ACADVER* setting is the very first setting in the HEADER section. The version number is a string associated with group code 1 as shown in this example:

```
9
$ACADVER
1
AC1015
```

If you're working with DWG files directly, the version number is the first six characters in the file.

 NOTE   When you are using AutoLISP or ActiveX Automation, the ACADVER setting returns the version of AutoCAD your application is running under, *not* the database version!

ACADMAINTVER (AutoCAD database maintenance version number)

The ACADMAINTVER setting is only relevant when you are working with DXF or DWG files directly. It defines a subversion number of the AutoCAD database. The initial release version of AutoCAD 2000 uses subversion 6.

When you are using DXF, the *ACADMAINTVER* setting is the second setting in the HEADER section. The subversion number is a signed 16-bit integer associated with group code 70. If you're working with DWG files directly, the subversion number is in bytes 11 and 12 of the file.

ATTMODE (attribute display mode)

The AcDbAttribute is a variable text object associated with a block insertion. As you know from working in AutoCAD, you can insert the same block multiple times into a drawing. In AutoCAD drawing database terminology, we say that the same block container can be referenced multiple times by another block container (in this case, the modelspace block). Except for scaling and rotation, the elements of the inserted block display identically with each reference. But if the block has associated attributes, the text values of each attribute insertion can be different. This allows multiple references to the same block labeled with different text strings.

An attribute's text string can be visible or invisible in the drawing. The visibility is set during the definition of the AcDbAttributeDefinition object, and from there, the AcDbAttribute objects associated with the various block references inherit the visibility.

The *ATTMODE* setting overwrites the attribute visibility for all AcDbAttributes in a drawing database. Depending on the setting, attributes may be visible even though individually declared as invisible and vice versa.

The *ATTMODE* value is a signed 16-bit integer (see Chapter 3 for information about how this data type is handled in a specific environment). In DXF files, the value of the *ATTMODE* setting is associated with group code 70. Possible values are:

Value	Meaning
0	All AcDbAttribute objects are invisible, regardless of their definition.
1	The default setting: AcDbAttribute objects are visible or invisible depending on their definition.
2	All AcDbAttribute objects are visible, regardless of their definition.

DISPSILH (show silhouette lines for 3D solids)

Curved 3D solids, such as a cylinder, can display an abbreviated image that consists of only a few defining curves (the so-called wire frame), or they can display these defining curves plus their actual outline as seen from the current view. This outline is named *silhouette,* and the *DISPLSILH* setting determines whether it is displayed.

In addition, if the *DISPSILH* is true, or turned on, hidden line views of 3D solid objects (for example, AcDb3dSolid, not AcDbSolid) display only their silhouette. If the setting is false, hidden line views of solid objects in AutoCAD display a tessellated surface.

The *DISPSILH* value is Boolean. If you look back at Chapter 3, you'll see that how Boolean values from the drawing database look depends on the environment in which you are working. If you are working with ObjectDBX (note that the access function is spelled *dispSilh()*), the DISPSILH value is of type *Adesk::Boolean,* which means that the return value is *Adesk::kTrue* if DISPSILH is turned on and *Adesk::kFalse* if it's turned off.

In AutoLISP, the value of DISPSILH is of type *integer*. If the silhouette display is turned on, this integer is 1; if it's turned off, the value is 0. When working with ActiveX Automation, you'll see Boolean values as type *Boolean* (as you learned in Chapter 3). However, with the drawing settings, there is an exception: Boolean settings (such as DISPSILH) are returned to an ActiveX Automation program as integers (*long*) and not as Booleans. As in AutoLISP, you'll get either 0 (DISPSILH turned off) or 1 (DISPSILH turned on).

Within a DXF file, the DISPSILH value is saved using group code 70. As with all Boolean values, this is a signed 16-bit integer, which is either 0 or 1 depending on whether DISPSILH is turned off or on. The following list displays the return value in the various environments and the associated meaning. You'll see similar lists as we look at the other critical settings in this section of the chapter.

Value		Meaning
Adesk::kFalse	0	In hidden line views, do not display the silhouette; show faces triangulated.
Adesk::kTrue	1	Display the silhouette of solid objects.

DWGCODEPAGE (drawing character set)

The *DWGCODEPAGE* setting defines the character set to use when reading strings from the drawing database. A code page is a table within the operating system that tells the computer, for example, that a byte of value 61h is to be interpreted as a lowercase a and not as the digit 8, a comma, or an accented character.

The drawing code page is only relevant if you look at a drawing database *file* (DXF or DWG). Once the drawing is loaded into AutoCAD, it is transparently translated to whatever character set the computer uses. In fact, DWGCODEPAGE is not available at all once the drawing is read into AutoCAD. As I mentioned in Chapter 3, some operating systems, such as Windows 95/98, use only a limited character set instead of the full Unicode set. If your program works within such an environment, characters not defined in the current character set are seen as Unicode control codes.

As long as the drawing resides on its own either as a DXF or a DWG file, the DWG-CODEPAGE setting defines the character set to use when reading strings from the drawing database. The program that is reading the file needs to translate each character from the drawing code page to the code page of the operating system. If you encounter Unicode control codes (as discussed in Chapter 3), you also need to translate them accordingly.

The DWGCODEPAGE setting is a string. A typical value is "ANSI_1252", which is the name of the code page used by Windows 95/98 in most of the Western world (defined in ISO Standard 8859-1 and also known as Latin I). In a DXF file, the DWG-CODEPAGE setting uses group code 3.

NOTE The ISO is an international standards-making body that establishes global standards for communications and information interchange. Its official English-language name is International Organization for Standardization. ISO is not an abbreviation, but a derivation of the Greek word *isos,* which means equal. –

FILLMODE (fill display mode)

Several database entities display hatched or filled areas: the AcDbHatch, AcDbSolid, and AcDbTrace objects as well as the AcDbMline object when filling the multiline area, and AcDbPolyline and AcDb2dPolyline objects when drawing wide lines. AcDbSolid, AcDbTrace, AcDbPolyline, and AcDb2dPolyline objects will display their fill only if the current view direction is parallel to the object's normal. (See Chapter 3 for further discussion of normals.)

The *FILLMODE* setting globally defines whether objects will display their fills/hatching and affects all objects in the current drawing database. If filling is off, the objects display only their outlines (if any). Curved, wide polylines also display a radial division when the fill display is off.

The *FILLMODE* value is a Boolean. In AutoLISP and ActiveX Automation, you'll see it as a signed 16-bit integer. In DXF, it uses the group code 70.

Value		Meaning
Adesk::kFalse	0	Fills and hatches are invisible.
Adesk::kTrue	1	Fills and hatches display if the other conditions are fulfilled.

LTSCALE (global linetype scale factor)

Every noncontinuous linetype consists of dashes and/or dots, and gaps. The linetype symbol table record (AcDbLinetypeSymbolRecord) of a particular linetype as saved in the linetype table (LTYPE) defines the length of dashes and gaps. It uses drawing units as the unit of measurement.

Depending on the drawing scale, the lengths of dashes and gaps need to be scaled as well. If a line is 100 units long, using dashes of size 0.5 makes as little sense as using the same size dashes on lines that are 0.1 units long. In the first case, you would see too many, very little dashes and gaps, and the result would look like a continuous line. In the second case, you would get too few very large dashes or gaps (in the example here, only one dash that is as large as the line itself); again, the result would look like a solid line. The size of dashes and gaps must be proportional to the overall size of the drawing.

The global linetype scale factor (*LTSCALE*) is applied to the linetype definition prior to displaying any lines. Thus, if the value of *LTSCALE* is 10.0, any dash or gap length will be multiplied by 10 and will then be used to display the lines in the drawing (see Figure 4.1).

FIGURE 4.1

The same line at different LTSCALE values

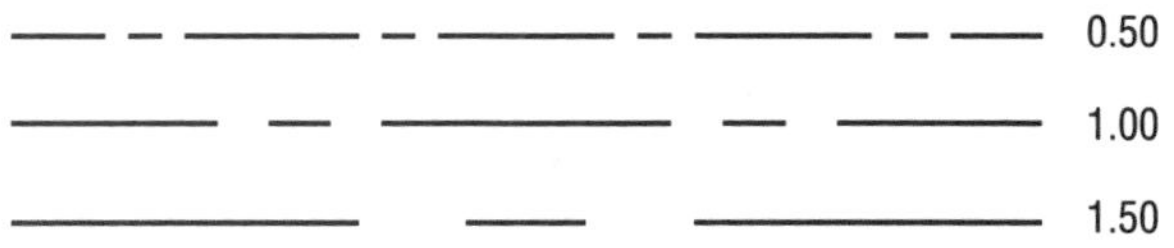

An additional entity-specific linetype scale factor is also applied to the dash and gap length on an individual basis. For example, if a line has an entity-specific linetype scale of 2.0 and if the value of *LTSCALE* is 10.0, every dash and gap length *for this specific line* will be multiplied by 2.0*10.0 = 20.0.

Another setting, *PSLTSCALE*, also affects the scaling of linetypes prior to their display. You'll see more on this setting in the section on *PSLTSCALE* later in this chapter.

The value of *LTSCALE* is a 64-bit real number and uses the group code 40 in DXF.

LWDISPLAY (linewidths display)

As is the case with *FILLMODE*, the owner of a drawing is free to choose whether to display objects in their associated linewidth using LWDISPLAY. If *LWDISPLAY* is false, all objects except for wide polylines are displayed by hairlines only. (A hairline is a line of the smallest width that the monitor can display; it's one pixel wide.)

The *LWDISPLAY* value is a Boolean. In AutoLISP and ActiveX Automation, you'll see it as a signed 16-bit integer. In DXF, it uses the group code 290. Note that the corresponding function in ObjectDBX is called *lineWeightDisplay()*.

Value		Meaning
Adesk::kFalse	0	Linewidth is not shown.
Adesk::kTrue	1	Linewidth is shown.

PDMODE (point display mode)

The AcDbPoint object defines a location in 3D space (see Chapter 11). Depending on the drawing contents, such a location may or may not be visible to the drafter. If it is to be visible, you may want to use a simple dot, a tick mark, a small x, or a circle to display the point's location by using the point display mode—*PDMODE*.

The AcDbPoint object itself does not contain any information about how it is to display. The display type of points is a global setting valid for the complete database. Thus, you cannot have two points in a single drawing that display differently. The global size of point symbols is set by the *PDSIZE* setting (see further discussion of PDSIZE below).

The value of *PDMODE* is a signed 16-bit integer and uses group code 70 in DXF. The following list shows how its value is calculated.

Value	Meaning
0	A single pixel or dot.
1	No display.
2	A plus sign (+).
3	A cross (X).
4	A tick mark (').
+32	One of the symbols listed above surrounded by a circle. Thus, a *PDMODE* value of, for instance, 35 (3+32) displays crosses surrounded by circles.
+64	One of the symbols listed above surrounded by a square

You, therefore, can have 20 different values for *PDMODE,* which means that 20 different symbols can display a point. Figure 4.2 shows them all.

FIGURE 4.2

The AutoCAD point
symbols

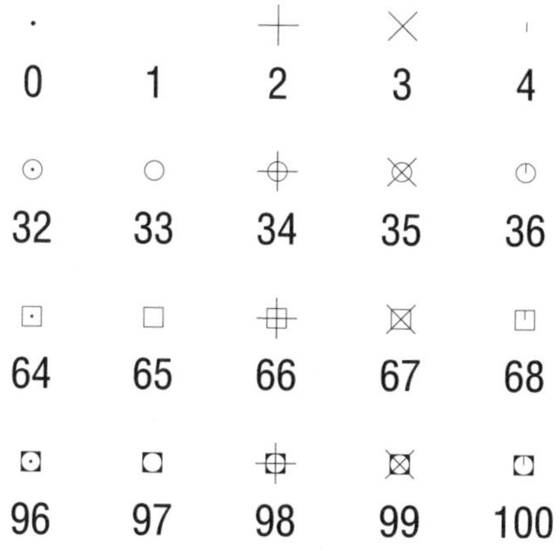

.		+	×	ı
0	1	2	3	4

⊙	○	⊕	⊠	◔
32	33	34	35	36

⊡	□	⊞	⊠	◱
64	65	66	67	68

⊡	▢	⊕	⊠	◰
96	97	98	99	100

PDSIZE (point display size)

The *PDSIZE* setting is a companion to *PDMODE*. Like *PDMODE*, this setting defines how AcDbPoint entities will display and print in AutoCAD. *PDMODE* defines the symbol used to display a point, and *PDSIZE* defines the size in which the symbol is to appear. Of course, *PDSIZE* is irrelevant if you use a single pixel (*PDMODE* = 0) or nothing (*PDMODE* = 1) to display points.

The value of *PDSIZE* is a 64-bit real number and may be either positive or negative. In DXF, PDSIZE uses the group code 40.

If the value of *PDSIZE* is positive, it defines the size of point symbols in absolute drawing units. For example, if *PDSIZE* is 0.5, the value G in Figure 4.3 equals 0.5.

If the value of *PDSIZE* is negative, it defines the size of point symbols as a percentage of the current view height. Thus, if *PDSIZE* is –10.0 and the current view is 150 drawing units high, the value G in Figure 4.3 equals 15.0 (10%).

If *PDSIZE* is zero, points display at 5% of the current view height.

FIGURE 4.3

The size of point
symbols

2	3	4

34	64	96

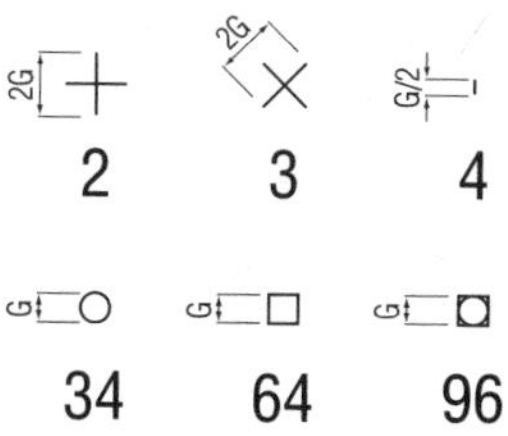

PSLTSCALE (paperspace linetype scaling)

Despite its name, *PSLTSCALE* is *not* another scale factor for linetypes. Instead, it is a flag indicating whether an additional scaling is to be applied to linetypes.

PSLTSCALE affects only noncontinuous lines in *MODEL_SPACE*, or referenced by *MODEL_SPACE*, and seen through a paperspace viewport (see the discussion on AcDb-Viewport in Chapter 17). Each paperspace viewport applies one more scaling to all objects. A one-unit modelspace circle seen through a paperspace viewport that has a view scale of 1:2 will look the same size as a one-half unit circle drawn directly in paperspace or a one-half unit circle seen through a 1:1 scale viewport. The same scaling also applies to the length of dashes and gaps in a noncontinuous line.

The *PSLTSCALE* setting defines whether you want to apply this viewport-specific scaling to dashes and gaps. If it is false (this means Adesk::kFalse or 0 depending on the environment you work in), paperspace is not taken into account, and viewport-specific linetype scaling is applied. Thus, dashes in a noncontinuous line may have different lengths when seen through two viewports of different scale.

If *PSLTSCALE* is true (Adesk::kTrue, 1), paperspace is taken into account, and noncontinuous lines show the same length dashes and gaps no matter which scale is used to display them. The dash length relative to paperspace is then calculated from the global and entity-specific linetype scales only.

The *PSLTSCALE* value is a Boolean. In AutoLISP and ActiveX Automation, you'll see it as a signed 16-bit integer; in DXF it uses the group code 70.

Value		Meaning
Adesk::kFalse	0	Paperspace is not taken into account, and viewport-specific scaling is applied to dash and gap lengths.
Adesk::kTrue	1	Paperspace is taken into account, and dashes and gaps have the same length, independent of their viewport scale

QTEXTMODE (quick text display)

QTEXTMODE is a global flag that indicates whether text objects (AcDbText, AcDbMText, AcDbAttributeDefinition, and AcDbAttribute) will display themselves on a drawing.

If *QTEXTMODE* is false (Adesk::kFalse, 0), text objects display normally as readable text. If it is true (Adesk::kTrue, 1), text objects do not display as readable text. Instead, the location of a text object is represented by a simple rectangle (or by a parallelogram if the text is slanted) of the size of the text outline.

QTEXTMODE is primarily intended to speed up drawing display and will be false in most cases. To create a correct AutoCAD drawing or to display/print a drawing just like AutoCAD does, this setting should not be ignored.

The value of *QTEXTMODE* is a Boolean, but looks like a signed 16-bit integer in AutoLISP and ActiveX Automation. The DXF group code is 70.

Value		Meaning
Adesk::kFalse	0	No quick text; text displays normally.
Adesk::kTrue	1	Quick text display: text is represented by rectangles/parallelograms.

SPLFRAME (spline frame display)

The *SPLFRAME* setting affects the display of splines (AcDbSpline), splined polylines (AcDb2dPolyline, AcDb3dPolyline), splined surfaces (AcDbPolygonMesh), and 3D faces (AcDbFace).

If *SPLFRAME* is true (Adesk::kTrue, 1), these objects display additional information not usually seen in a drawing:

- Splines display their control polygon in addition to the spline curve.
- Splined polylines display their control polygon (the original polyline) in addition to the generated spline curve.
- Splined surfaces display their control polygon mesh (the original mesh) in addition to the generated splined surface.
- 3D faces display any edges made invisible in addition to the visible edges.

The *SPLFRAME* value is a Boolean. In AutoLISP and ActiveX Automation, you'll see it as a signed 16-bit integer. In DXF, it uses the group code 70.

Value		Meaning
Adesk::kFalse	0	Do not display spline frames and invisible edges of 3D faces.
Adesk::kTrue	1	Display spline control polygons and invisible edges of 3D faces.

TILEMODE (modelspace display)

The *TILEMODE* setting defines whether the drawing should display and print its *MODEL_SPACE* block or its *PAPER_SPACE* block.

The name *TILEMODE* is a bit confusing and results from the origins of the paperspace concept. When the concept of a drawing layout was introduced to AutoCAD, the term *viewport* already had a meaning—a portion of the drawing editor's screen space in which you can select points and manipulate data. With tiled viewports you could (and still can) divide the modelspace display into different views. These viewports must be *tiled*, that is, they cannot overlap and must fill the entire display area. In paperspace, viewports are *floating*, that is, they can appear anywhere on the layout—even on top of other viewports.

If *TILEMODE* is true (Adesk::kTrue, 1), the AutoCAD editor uses tiled viewports only; it displays the **MODEL_SPACE* block. If *TILEMODE* is false (Adesk::kFalse, 0), the AutoCAD editor uses floating viewports; it displays the active layout (**PAPER_SPACE*).

Like all flags, the *TILEMODE* value is a Boolean. In AutoLISP and ActiveX Automation, you'll see it as a signed 16-bit integer. In DXF, it uses the group code 70.

Value		Meaning
Adesk::kFalse	0	Display the **PAPER_SPACE* block.
Adesk::kTrue	1	Display the **MODEL_SPACE* block.

VISRETAIN (retain visibility settings)

Since version 11, AutoCAD has been able to reference the modelspace of external drawings. The command to reference a different drawing (database) from within the current drawing is XREF. As soon as external drawings are involved, the symbol tables of these external drawings are merged with the symbol tables of the current drawing's database. This is done so that the user can modify the visibility or color of any layer whether it is in the current drawing's database or in the referenced database. Making changes to the visibility or color of a layer modifies only the local symbol table. It does not modify the referenced database. Other users referencing the same external drawing will not notice the change.

To allow the user to save the modifications for later reuse, symbol table records referencing symbol tables in an external database are saved with the current database. When the drawing is next loaded, the external database is read, and its modelspace is displayed again. Now you have a problem: there are two symbol table records describing the same object. If the external database changes or if you modified the settings in your local symbol table, you could end up with two colors for one layer or with one layer that ought to be both visible and invisible.

Here's where *VISRETAIN* steps in. This flag simply indicates whether to use the symbol table record saved in the local database or whether to use the symbol table record from the external database.

If *VISRETAIN* is true (Adesk::kTrue, 1), you choose to retain the saved settings from the local copy of the symbol table record. If *VISRETAIN* is false (Adesk::kFalse, 0), you choose to use the current settings from the external database.

The value of *VISRETAIN* is a Boolean. In AutoLISP and ActiveX Automation, you'll see it as a signed 16-bit integer. In DXF, it uses the group code 70.

Value		Meaning
Adesk::kFalse	0	Use layer settings from the external drawing database.
Adesk::kTrue	1	Use layer settings from the local copy of the external symbol table record.

Additional Settings

In addition to the settings critical for a correct display and evaluation of a drawing database, a large number of settings are not relevant for drawing database query and modification. These settings simply provide defaults for various functions of the AutoCAD editor. Although it makes sense for AutoCAD to remember these settings and provide users with reasonable defaults the next time they open the drawing, an external application will not necessarily care much about AutoCAD defaults.

As I mentioned in the introduction to this chapter, only the settings I've discussed so far are critical in that they affect the ways in which AutoCAD displays or interprets the drawing database. All other settings can be easily ignored when reading an Auto-CAD drawing database. Or you can use them if the program you write to use a drawing database also allows the user to interact with the drawing using AutoCAD-like functionality.

When writing a drawing database, you should use reasonable settings so that Auto-CAD will act quite naturally when your drawing is loaded. These reasonable settings vary, depending on the drawing's contents. The easiest way to get these settings is to draw a similar drawing in AutoCAD, export the settings as DXF, look at the DXF file, and note the settings to be used by your program.

Here is a list of the additional settings in alphabetic order. You use them exactly as the settings I discussed earlier. At the end of the list, you'll find some notes with valuable information about certain settings. All settings listed as "integer" are signed 16-bit integers unless otherwise noted.

 NOTE Many of the elements in the following table require further discussion. In order to simplify the listing, notes are provided immediately following the table.

Name	Type	Meaning
ANGBASE	angle (DXF: 50)	Defines the direction of the 0° angle relative to the x-axis of the current user coordinate system—which direction you want when you enter 0°. This setting does not effect the angles saved in the drawing database.
ANGDIR	Boolean (DXF: 70)	Defines the direction in which positive angles are drawn relative to ANGBASE. If true (*Adesk::kTrue*, 1), angles are measured clockwise; if false, counterclockwise.
AUNITS	integer (DXF: 70)	Defines the format in which AutoCAD reports angles on the command line. In applications written in ActiveX Automation or ObjectDBX, angles are always passed as radians; applications written in AutoLISP or for DXF will get angles in decimal degrees. See note 1 for a list of possible values.
AUPREC	integer (DXF: 70)	Defines the precision AutoCAD uses when reporting angles. See note 2 for a list of possible values and their meaning.
CECOLOR	color (DXF: 62)	Defines the entity color to be used for the next entity created. See Chapter 5 for a discussion of color values. Note that AutoLISP returns the strings "BYLAYER" and "BYBLOCK" for these two special colors.
CELTSCALE	real (DXF: 40)	Defines the entity-specific linetype scale to be used for the next entity created.
CELTYPE	symbol table record (DXF: 6)	Defines the linetype to be used for the next entity created. ObjectDBX returns the AcDbObjectId of the corresponding symbol table record, and DXF, AutoLISP, and ActiveX Automation return the key string.
CELWEIGHT	lineweight (DXF: 370)	Defines the lineweight to be used for the next entity created. See Chapter 5 for a discussion of lineweight values.
CEPSNTYPE	plot style (DXF: 380)	Defines the plot style to be used for the next entity created. This is a reference to an ACDBPLACEHOLDER object. You can get the plot style name by looking at the corresponding entry in the placeholder's owner dictionary. For more on plot styles, see Chapter 5.

Name	Type	Meaning
CHAMFERA	length (DXF: 40)	Defines a default for the next chamfer operation, in this case the chamfer distance from the corner along the first line.
CHAMFERB	length (DXF: 40)	Defines a second default for the next chamfer operation, that is, the chamfer distance from the corner along the second line.
CHAMFERC	length (DXF: 40)	Defines a third default for the next chamfer operation, the chamfer length.
CHAMFERD	angle (DXF: 40)	Defines a forth and final default for the next chamfer operation, the chamfer angle measured against the first line. Caution: this is an angle. Although all other angle type settings use group code 50 in DXF, this one doesn't.
CLAYER	symbol table record (DXF: 8)	Defines the layer to be used for the next entity created. ObjectDBX returns the AcDbObjectId of the corresponding symbol table record, and DXF, AutoLISP, and ActiveX Automation return the key string.
CMLJUST	integer (DXF: 70)	Defines the default justification for newly created multilines. See Chapter 13 for possible values.
CMLSCALE	real (DXF: 40)	Defines the default width scale for newly created multilines.
CMLSTYLE	dictionary record (DXF: 2)	Defines the multiline style to be used for newly created multilines. ObjectDBX (*AcDbDatabase::cmlstyleID*) returns the AcDbObjectId of the corresponding dictionary record, and DXF, AutoLISP, and ActiveX Automation return the key string.
DIMADEC	integer (DXF: 70)	Defines the display precision for newly created angular dimensions. Possible values and their meaning are like those in AUPREC. See note 3.
DIMALT	Boolean (DXF: 70)	Defines whether alternate units (e.g., inches in addition to millimeters) are to be included in dimension labels for linear dimension. See note 3.
DIMALTD	integer (DXF: 70)	Defines the display precision for alternate units in newly created linear dimensions. Possible values and their meaning are like those in LUPREC. See note 3.

Name	Type	Meaning
DIMALTF	real (DXF: 40)	Defines the multiplier from dimension text in drawing units to the dimension text in alternate units. See note 3.
DIMALTRND	real (DXF: 40)	Defines a rounding value for alternate units. See note 3.
DIMALTTD	integer (DXF: 70)	Defines the display precision for tolerance values in alternate units of newly created linear dimensions. Possible values and their meaning are like those in LUPREC. See note 3.
DIMALTTZ	integer (DXF: 70)	Defines how zeros in tolerance values for alternate units are to be handled. Different values allow suppression of zero feet and/or zero inches, zeros preceding and/or following the decimal delimiter. Possible values and their meaning are like those in DIMZIN. See note 3.
DIMALTU	integer (DXF: 70)	Defines the display format of alternate units for newly created linear dimensions. Possible values and their meaning are like those in DIMUNIT. See note 3.
DIMALTZ	integer (DXF: 70)	Defines how zeros in alternate units are to be handled. Different values allow suppression of zero feet and/or zero inches, zeros preceding and/or following the decimal delimiter. Possible values and their meaning are like those in DIMZIN. See note 3.
DIMAPOST	string (DXF: 1)	Defines a template for the dimension text in alternate units. Open and closed brackets ([ ]) are replaced by the measured value in alternate units. If the placeholder for the measured value is not included, the DIMAPOST string is appended to the alternate units' string. See note 3.
DIMASO	Boolean (DXF: 70)	Defines whether AutoCAD dimensioning commands are to draw dimension objects or just simple blocks containing an image of the dimension. If true (*Adesk::kTrue*, 1), associative dimension objects are drawn.
DIMASZ	real (DXF: 40)	Defines the size of arrowheads and leader line hooks. See note 3.

Name	Type	Meaning
DIMATFIT	integer (DXF: 70)	Defines how AutoCAD will move dimension arrows and dimension text when the dimension length does not allow placing both inside extension lines. See note 4 for a list of possible values. Also see note 3.
DIMAUNIT	integer (DXF: 70)	Defines the display format for newly created angular dimensions. Possible values and their meaning are like those in AUNITS. See note 3.
DIMAZIN	integer (DXF: 70)	Defines how zeros in angular dimensions are to be handled. This is a combination of Boolean flags, which allows you to suppress zeros preceding and/or following the decimal delimiter. See note 5 and note 3.
DIMBLK	symbol table record (DXF: 1)	Defines the arrowhead block to be used. Note that ObjectDBX returns the AcDbObjectId of the corresponding symbol table record and DXF, AutoLISP and ActiveX Automation return the key string. See note 6 for a list of predefined arrow blocks and note 3.
DIMBLK1	symbol table record (DXF: 1)	Defines the first (or left) arrowhead to be used when arrowheads differ. See DIMBLK and note 3.
DIMBLK2	symbol table record (DXF: 1)	Defines the second (or right) arrowhead to be used when arrowheads differ. See DIMBLK and note 3.
DIMCEN	real (DXF: 40)	Defines the size and outlook of center marks drawn with radial and diagonal dimensions. The center mark is an axis-parallel cross at the arc center. If the value of DIMCEN is positive, it controls the length of the cross' arms; if it is negative, its absolute value controls the length of the cross's arms, the length of a gap following the arm, and the length that the additional line extends the arc outline. See note 3.
DIMCLRD	color (DXF: 70)	Defines the color of dimension lines, arrows, and leader lines. This is a color even though the DXF group code suggests an integer. See note 3.

Name	Type	Meaning
DIMCLRE	color (DXF: 70)	Defines the color of dimension extension lines. This is a color even though the DXF group code suggests an integer. See note 3.
DIMCLRT	color (DXF: 70)	Defines the color of dimension text. This is a color even though the DXF group code suggests an integer. See note 3.
DIMDEC	integer (DXF: 70)	Defines the display precision for the measured value in linear dimensions. Possible values and their meaning are like those in LUPREC. See note 3.
DIMDLE	length (DXF: 40)	Defines how far the dimension line should extend beyond the extension lines. This is only relevant if the selected arrowhead is either "_ArchTick", "_Oblique", "_None", or "_Integral". See note 3.
DIMDLI	length (DXF: 40)	Defines the spacing of baseline dimensions as well as the offset used for dimension chains if dimensions would otherwise overlap. See note 3.
DIMDSEP	single character (DXF: 70)	Defines the decimal delimiter used for dimensions. This is a single character in ObjectDBX, a string in ActiveX Automation and AutoLISP, but an integer (ASCII code of the character) in DXF. See note 3.
DIMEXE	length (DXF: 40)	Defines how far an extension line should extend beyond the dimension line. See note 3.
DIMEXO	length (DXF: 40)	Defines the gap between the dimensioned location and the start of the extension line. See note 3.
DIMFRAC	integer (DXF: 70)	Defines how to display fractions inside dimension text. For a list of possible values, see note 7. See also note 3.
DIMGAP	real (DXF: 40)	If positive, defines the minimum gap between dimension text and dimension line; if negative, defines the offset from a dimension text to a surrounding frame box (and draws this box). See note 3.
DIMJUST	integer (DXF: 70)	Defines where to place the dimension text along the dimension line. See note 8 for a list of possible values. See also note 3.

Name	Type	Meaning
DIMLDRBLK	symbol table record (DXF: 1)	Defines the arrowhead to be used with leader lines. See DIMBLK. See also note 3.
DIMLFAC	real (DXF: 40)	Defines a global scale factor applied to all linear measurements, thus scaling the value shown as dimension text. The value of DIMLFAC can be positive or negative. A positive value is applied to all linear dimensions. If the value is negative, its absolute is applied to linear dimensions drawn in paperspace, and dimensions drawn in modelspace will not be scaled.
DIMLIM	Boolean (DXF: 70)	Defines whether the dimension text displays a single value (*Adesk::kFalse*, 0) or minimum and maximum measurements. If true, the maximum value is stacked on top of the minimum value. DIMTP and DIMTM are used to calculate those values. See note 3.
DIMLUNIT	integer (DXF: 70)	Defines the display format for newly created linear dimensions. For possible values and their meaning, see note 9. See also note 3.
DIMLWD	lineweight (DXF: 70)	Defines the lineweight to be used for dimension lines. See Chapter 5 for a discussion of lineweight values. This is a lineweight even though the DXF group code indicates an integer. See note 3.
DIMLWE	lineweight (DXF: 70)	Defines the lineweight to be used for extension lines. See Chapter 5 for a discussion of lineweight values. This is a lineweight even though the DXF group code indicates an integer. See note 3.
DIMPOST	string (DXF: 1)	Defines a template for the dimension text. The less than and greater than characters (< >) are replaced by the measured value. If the placeholder for the measured value is not included, the DIMPOST string is appended to the dimension text. See note 3.
DIMRND	real (DXF: 40)	Defines a rounding factor for linear units. The measured value is rounded according to this setting's value. See note 3.

Name	Type	Meaning
DIMSAH	Boolean (DXF: 70)	Specifies whether different arrowheads should be used. If true (*Adesk::kTrue*, 1), AutoCAD uses the arrowheads defined by DIMBLK1 and DIMBLK2; if false, AutoCAD uses DIMBLK for both arrowheads. See note 3.
DIMSCALE	real (DXF: 40)	Specifies an overall scale factor to be applied to all lengths used during dimension generation. This does not change the measured value or dimension text. Instead it modifies the overall size of the dimension or leader object. If the value of DIMSCALE is 0.0, the inverse of the view scale is used instead. See note 3.
DIMSD1	Boolean (DXF: 70)	if true (*Adesk::kTrue*, 1), suppresses the half of the dimension line next to the first extension line. See note 3.
DIMSD2	Boolean (DXF: 70)	if true (*Adesk::kTrue*, 1), suppresses the half of the dimension line next to the second extension line. See note 3.
DIMSE1	Boolean (DXF: 70)	If true (*Adesk::kTrue*, 1), suppresses the first extension line. See note 3.
DIMSE2	Boolean (DXF: 70)	If true (*Adesk::kTrue*, 1), suppresses the second extension line. See note 3.
DIMSHO	Boolean (DXF: 70)	Specifies whether associative dimensions always show their actual value when being dragged (*Adesk::kTrue*, 1).
DIMSOXD	Boolean (DXF: 70)	if true (*Adesk::kTrue*, 1), suppresses arrowheads if they do not fit between the extension lines. See note 3.
DIMSTYLE	symbol table record (DXF: 2)	Defines the dimension style to be used for newly created dimension, leader, and feature control frame objects. ObjectDBX returns the AcDbObjectId of the corresponding symbol table record, and DXF, AutoLISP, and ActiveX Automation return the key string.
DIMTAD	integer (DXF: 70)	Specifies where to place the dimension text vertical against the dimension line. See note 10 for a list of possible values. See also note 3.

Name	Type	Meaning
DIMTDEC	integer (DXF: 70)	Defines the display precision for tolerance values of newly created linear dimensions. Possible values and their meaning are like those in LUPREC. See note 3.
DIMTFAC	real (DXF: 40)	Defines the text size of tolerance values in relation to the dimension text size. See note 3.
DIMTIH	Boolean(DXF: 70)	Specifies whether the dimension text is horizontal (*Adesk::kTrue*, 1) or parallel to the dimension line. DIMTIH is recognized only if the text fits between the extension lines. See note 3.
DIMTIX	Boolean (DXF: 70)	Defines whether the dimension text is to be forced inside between the extension lines (*Adesk::kTrue*, 1), even if AutoCAD would normally place text and arrows outside. See note 3.
DIMTM	real (DXF: 40)	Defines the lower tolerance (tolerated value is up to true dimension minus DIMTM). See note 3.
DIMTMOVE	integer (DXF: 70)	Specifies whether to add a leader arrow if the dimension text is moved away from the dimension line. See note 11 for a list of possible values. See also note 3.
DIMTOFL	Boolean (DXF: 70)	Defines whether a dimension line between the extension lines will be drawn (*Adesk::kTrue*, 1) even when text and arrows are placed outside. See note 3.
DIMTOH	Boolean (DXF: 70)	Specifies whether the dimension text is horizontal (*Adesk::kTrue*, 1) or parallel to the dimension line. DIMTOH is recognized only if the text is placed outside. See note 3.
DIMTOL	Boolean (DXF: 70)	Specifies whether dimension tolerances are to be shown. If true (Adesk::kTrue, 1), AutoCAD adds the upper and lower tolerance to the dimension text. See note 3.
DIMTOLJ	signed 8-bit integer (DXF: 70)	Specifies where to place the tolerance values. This is an 8-bit integer. See note 12 for a list of possible values. See also note 3.
DIMTP	real (DXF: 40)	Defines the lower tolerance (tolerated value is up to true dimension plus DIMTP). See note 3.

Name	Type	Meaning
DIMTSZ	length (DXF: 40)	Defines the size of the slash at the end of the dimension line when using an arrow-head of `"_ArchTick"`, `"_Oblique"`, or `"_Integral"`. See note 3.
DIMTVP	length (DXF: 40)	Defines the vertical distance between dimension text center and dimension line center when DIMTAD is set to *acVertCenter* (0). See note 3.
DIMTXSTY	symbol table record (DXF: 7)	Defines the text style to be used with dimension text. ObjectDBX returns the AcDb-ObjectId of the corresponding symbol table record, and DXF, AutoLISP, and ActiveX Automation return the key string. See note 3.
DIMTXT	length (DXF: 40)	Defines the size of the dimension text. See note 3.
DIMTZIN	integer (DXF: 70)	Specifies how zeros in tolerances are to be handled. Different values allow suppression of zero feet and/or zero inches, zeros preceding and/or following the decimal delimiter. Possible values and their meaning are like those in DIMZIN. See note 3.
DIMUPT	Boolean (DXF: 70)	Defines whether the user's pick places only the dimension line (*Adesk::kFalse*, 0) or both the dimension line and the dimension text. See note 3.
DIMZIN	integer (DXF: 70)	Specifies how zeros in dimension text are to be handled. Different values allow suppression of zero feet and/or zero inches, zeros preceding and/or following the decimal delimiter. For a list of possible values and their meaning see note 13. See also note 3.
ELEVATION	real (DXF: 40)	Defines the default Z coordinate for all objects newly added to the *MODEL_SPACE* block.
ENDCAPS	8-bit integer (DXF: 280)	According to the DXF documentation this defines the line ends of newly created objects (round = 1, angle = 2, square = 3), but there is no way in AutoCAD to change or use this setting.

Name	Type	Meaning
EXTMAX	point (DXF: 10/20/30)	Defines the upper right corner of the *MODEL_SPACE block's bounding box, that is, the maximum X, Y, and Z coordinates used by this block.
EXTMIN	point (DXF: 10/20/30)	Defines the lower left corner of the *MODEL_SPACE block's bounding box, that is, the minimum X, Y, and Z coordinates used by this block.
EXTNAMES	Boolean (DXF: 290)	Specifies whether the user is allowed to use long (extended) symbol names. If false (*Adesk::kFalse*, 0), symbol names are limited to AutoCAD Release 14 format: max. 32 characters, no spaces or special characters. If true, symbol names can be a maximum of 255 characters and use special characters.
FILLETRAD	length (DXF: 40)	Defines the radius to use with subsequent fillets.
FINGERPRINTGUID	string (DXF: 2)	A globally unique identifier (GUID) of this particular drawing. Will be generated the first time the drawing is saved by AutoCAD. This setting is only available to ObjectDBX and DXF.
HANDSEED	handle (DXF: 5)	Defines the next free handle in the drawing database.
HYPERLINKBASE	string (DXF: 1)	Defines the path for all relative hyperlinks in the drawing database.
INSBASE	point (DXF: 10/20/30)	Defines the anchor point for the *MODEL_SPACE block when this block is inserted into another drawing.
INSUNITS	integer (DXF: 70)	Defines the units of measurements used by the *MODEL_SPACE block. For a list of possible values, see note 14.
JOINSTYLE	8-bit integer (DXF: 280)	According to the DXF documentation, this setting defines the line joins of newly created objects (round = 1, angle = 2, flat = 3), but there is no way in AutoCAD to change or use this setting.
LIMCHECK	Boolean (DXF: 70)	Defines whether AutoCAD should check the user-defined limits when interacting with the *MODEL_SPACE block.

Name	Type	Meaning
LIMMAX	2D point (DXF: 10/20)	Defines the upper right corner of the user-defined limits when interacting with the *MODEL_SPACE* block. This is a 2D point only. In DXF, there is no corresponding group 30. In ObjectDBX, the function returns an object of class AcGePoint2d.
LIMMIN	2D point (DXF: 10/20)	Defines the lower left corner of the user-defined limits when interacting with the *MODEL_SPACE* block. See LIMMAX.
LUNITS	integer (DXF: 70)	Defines the format in which AutoCAD reports lengths and coordinates with a user. Applications always see only real numbers. See note 15 for a list of possible values.
LUPREC	integer (DXF: 70)	Defines the precision used by AutoCAD to display lengths and coordinates. If the format selected by LUNITS contains fractions, the value of LUPREC defines the lowest dominator (2^{LUPREC}) to be used. If no fractions are involved, the value of LUPREC sets the number of decimal places behind the delimiter.
MAXACTVP	integer (DXF: 70)	Specifies the maximum number of active viewports the user selected to show concurrently.
MEASUREMENT	integer (DXF: 70)	Specifies whether AutoCAD is to use metric or American support files with this drawing database. For a list of possible values, see note 17.
MENUNAME	string (DXF: 1)	Defines the full path and name of the menu file that AutoCAD is to load along with this drawing database. In DXF, this setting is called *MENU*. In ObjectDBX, use the getMenu() function.
MIRRTEXT	Boolean (DXF: 70)	Specifies whether AutoCAD should mirror text during editing. If false (*Adesk::kFalse*, 0), mirrored text will move to the mirrored location but still display readable (i.e., unmirrored) on the screen or print-out.
OLESTARTUP	Boolean (DXF: 290)	Specifies whether AutoCAD should try to launch the parent OLE application when printing embedded objects.

Name	Type	Meaning
ORTHOMODE	Boolean (DXF: 70)	Specifies whether cursor movement in AutoCAD should be restricted to horizontal and vertical movements only.
PELEVATION	real (DXF: 40)	Defines the default Z coordinate for all objects newly added to the current *PAPER_SPACE* block.
PEXTMAX	point (DXF: 10/20/30)	Defines the upper right corner of the current *PAPER_SPACE* block's bounding box, that is, the maximum X, Y, and Z coordinates used by this block.
PEXTMIN	point (DXF: 10/20/30)	Defines the lower left corner of the current *PAPER_SPACE* block's bounding box, that is, the minimum X, Y, and Z coordinates used by this block.
PINSBASE	point (DXF: 10/20/30)	Defines the anchor point for the current *PAPER_SPACE* block when this block is inserted into another drawing.
PLIMCHECK	Boolean (DXF: 70)	Defines whether AutoCAD should check the user-defined limits when interacting with the current *PAPER_SPACE* block.
PLIMMAX	2D point (DXF: 10/20)	Defines the upper right corner of the user-defined limits when interacting with the current *PAPER_SPACE* block. See LIMMAX.
PLIMMIN	2D point (DXF: 10/20)	Defines the lower left corner of the user-defined limits when interacting with the current *PAPER_SPACE* block. See LIMMAX.
PLINEGEN	Boolean (DXF: 70)	Defines how AutoCAD should distribute dashes and gaps of noncontinuous linetypes on newly created 2D polylines. If true (*Adesk::kTrue*, 1), the linetype bends along the complete curve, allowing gaps at corners or short segments. If false, the linetype is applied on every single segment, thus guaranteeing dash segments at all corners.
PLINEWID	length (DXF: 40)	Defines the default width for newly created polylines.
PROXYGRAPHICS	Boolean (DXF: 70)	Defines whether AutoCAD should save the most current graphical image of each custom object along with the drawing database. If false (*Adesk::kFalse*, 0), custom objects are graphically seen by their bounding box only. The corresponding function in ObjectDBX is called *saveproxygraphics()*.

Name	Type	Meaning
PSVPSCALE	real (DXF: 40)	Defines the viewport scale for newly created viewports. A scale of 0.0 lets AutoCAD calculate the scale to maximize the view scale while still showing all objects.
PUCSBASE	symbol table record (DXF: 2)	Defines the name of the User Coordinate System (UCS) that defines the orthogonal set of coordinate systems for the current *PAPER_SPACE block. ObjectDBX returns the AcDbObjectId of the corresponding symbol table record, and DXF, AutoLISP, and ActiveX Automation return the key string.
PUCSNAME	symbol table record (DXF: 2)	Defines the name of the active User Coordinate System (UCS) for the current *PAPER-_SPACE block. ObjectDBX returns the AcDb-ObjectId of the corresponding symbol table record, and DXF, AutoLISP, and ActiveX Automation return the key string. See note 16.
PUCSORG	point (DXF: 10/20/30)	According to the DXF documentation, this setting defines the origin of the active user coordinate system for the current *PAPER_SPACE block. It is always 0,0,0, however. See note 16.
PUCSORGBACK	point (DXF: 10/20/30)	According to the DXF documentation, this setting defines the origin of the back workplane coordinate system for the current *PAPER_SPACE block. It is always 0,0,0, however. See note 16.
PUCSORGBOTTOM	point (DXF: 10/20/30)	According to the DXF documentation, this setting defines the origin of the bottom workplane coordinate system for the current *PAPER_SPACE block. It is always 0,0,0, however. See note 16.
PUCSORGFRONT	point (DXF: 10/20/30)	According to the DXF documentation, this setting defines the origin of the front workplane coordinate system for the current *PAPER_SPACE block. It is always 0,0,0, however. See note 16.
PUCSORGLEFT	point (DXF: 10/20/30)	According to the DXF documentation, this setting defines the origin of the left workplane coordinate system for the current *PAPER_SPACE block. It is always 0,0,0, however. See note 16.

Name	Type	Meaning
PUCSORGRIGHT	point (DXF: 10/20/30)	According to the DXF documentation, this setting defines the origin of the right workplane coordinate system for the current *PAPER_SPACE* block. It is always 0,0,0, however. See note 16.
PUCSORGTOP	point (DXF: 10/20/30)	According to the DXF documentation, this setting defines the origin of the top workplane coordinate system for the current *PAPER_SPACE* block. It is always 0,0,0, however. See note 16.
PUCSORTHOREF	symbol table record (DXF: 2)	According to the DXF documentation, this setting refers to the named coordinate system, to which the coordinate system of the current *PAPER_SPACE* block is orthogonal. It is always an empty string, however.
PUCSORTHOVIEW	Booleaninteger (DXF: 70)	Defines the orthogonal projection used to generate the actual coordinate system of the current *PAPER_SPACE* block from the named coordinate system listed in PUCSBASE. See note 16.
PUCSXDIR	normalized vector (DXF: 10/20/30)	Defines the X direction for the active user coordinate system of the current *PAPER_SPACE* block. See note 16.
PUCSYDIR	normalized vector (DXF: 10/20/30)	Defines the Y direction for the active user coordinate system of the current *PAPER_SPACE* block. See note 16.
REGENMODE	Boolean (DXF: 70)	Specifies whether AutoCAD should automatically regenerate the drawing if it finds it necessary.
SHADEDGE	integer (DXF: 70)	Defines how AutoCAD's shade command is to display faces and edges. See note 18 for a list of possible values.
SHADEDIF	integer (DXF: 70)	Defines the level of ambient or diffuse light in a shaded rendering. The ambient light is (100 - SHADEDIF) percent of the main light.
SKETCHINC	length (DXF: 40)	Defines the increment or minimum length of strokes used when sketching an image.
SKPOLY	Boolean (DXF: 70)	Specifies whether AutoCAD's sketch command is to generate 2D polylines (*Adesk::kTrue*, 1) or ordinary lines (*Adesk::kFalse*, 0).

Name	Type	Meaning
SPLINESEGS	integer (DXF: 70)	Defines the number of line segments used to approximate each segment of a polyline-based spline curve. If the value is negative, a corresponding number of arc segments is used. This value is recognized only for newly approximated curves.
SPLINETYPE	integer (DXF: 70)	Defines the type of spline to generate when converting polylines to splines. Possible values are 5 (creates a quadratic B-Spline, order=3) and 6 (creates a cubic B-Spline, order=4).
STYLESHEET	string (DXF: 1)	Always an empty string. Probably intended to contain the plot style table (style sheet) associated with the current layout.
SURFTAB1	integer (DXF: 70)	Defines the density in M direction for newly created polygon meshes.
SURFTAB2	integer (DXF: 70)	Defines the density in N direction for newly created polygon meshes.
SURFTYPE	integer (DXF: 70)	Defines the type of surface to generate when converting polygon meshes to surfaces. Possible values are 5 (creates a quadratic B-Spline surface, order=3), 6 (creates a cubic B-Spline surface, order=4), and 8 (creates a Bézier surface).
SURFU	integer (DXF: 70)	Defines the density in M direction of polygon segments used to approximate each segment of a spline surface. This value is recognized only for newly approximated surfaces.
SURFV	integer (DXF: 70)	Defines the density in N direction of polygon segments used to approximate each segment of a spline surface. This value is recognized only for newly approximated surfaces.
TDCREATE	date & time (DXF: 40)	Indicates the date and time that this drawing database was created; in local time of the creation place.
TDINDWG	elapsed time (DXF: 40)	Indicates the total editing time for this drawing database.
TDUCREATE	date & time (DXF: 40)	Indicates the date and time of the creation of this drawing database in GMT.

Name	Type	Meaning
TDUPDATE	date & time (DXF: 40)	Indicates the date and time that this drawing database was last saved; in local time of the editing place.
TDUSRTIMER	elapsed time (DXF: 40)	Indicates the last state of the user-defined timer.
TDUUPDATE	date & time (DXF: 40)	Indicates the date and time that this drawing database was last saved; in GMT.
TEXTSIZE	length (DXF: 40)	Defines the height of newly created text objects.
TEXTSTYLE	symbol table record (DXF: 7)	Defines the text style to be used with newly created text objects. ObjectDBX returns the AcDbObjectId of the corresponding symbol table record, and DXF, AutoLISP, and ActiveX Automation return the key string.
THICKNESS	length (DXF: 40)	Defines the thickness or extrusion for newly created planar entities.
TRACEWID	length (DXF: 40)	Defines the width for newly created AcDbTrace objects.
TREEDEPTH	integer (DXF: 70)	Defines the size of a spatial index tree that AutoCAD uses internally to improve object selection. The value of TREEDEPTH is a four-digit number, of which the first two digits define the maximum tree depth when editing the *MODEL_SPACE block. The remaining two digits define the maximum tree depth when editing a *PAPER_SPACE block. If the value is negative, Z coordinates are excluded from the spatial index.
UCSBASE	symbol table record (DXF: 2)	Defines the name of the User Coordinate System (UCS) that defines the orthogonal set of coordinate systems for the *MODEL_SPACE block. ObjectDBX returns the AcDbObjectId of the corresponding symbol table record, and DXF, AutoLISP, and ActiveX Automation return the key string. See note 16.
UCSNAME	symbol table record (DXF: 2)	Defines the name of the active user coordinate system for the *MODEL_SPACE block. ObjectDBX returns the AcDbObjectId of the corresponding symbol table record, and DXF, AutoLISP, and ActiveX Automation return the key string. See note 16.

Name	Type	Meaning
UCSORG	point (DXF: 10/20/30)	Defines the origin of the active User Coordinate System (UCS) for the *MODEL_SPACE* block. See note 16.
UCSORGBACK	point (DXF: 10/20/30)	According to the DXF documentation, this setting defines the origin of the back workplane coordinate system for the *MODEL_SPACE* block. It is always 0,0,0, however. See note 16.
UCSORGBOTTOM	point (DXF: 10/20/30)	According to the DXF documentation, this setting defines the origin of the bottom workplane coordinate system for the *MODEL_SPACE* block. It is always 0,0,0, however. See note 16.
UCSORGFRONT	point (DXF: 10/20/30)	According to the DXF documentation, this Defines the origin of the front workplane coordinate system for the *MODEL_SPACE* block. It is always 0,0,0, however. See note 16.
UCSORGLEFT	point (DXF: 10/20/30)	According to the DXF documentation, this setting defines the origin of the left workplane coordinate system for the *MODEL-_SPACE* block. It is always 0,0,0, however. See note 16.
UCSORGRIGHT	point (DXF: 10/20/30)	According to the DXF documentation, this setting defines the origin of the right workplane coordinate system for the *MODEL-_SPACE* block. It is always 0,0,0, however. See note 16.
UCSORGTOP	point (DXF: 10/20/30)	According to the DXF documentation, this setting defines the origin of the top workplane coordinate system for the *MODEL-_SPACE* block. It is always 0,0,0, however. See note 16.
UCSORTHOREF	symbol table record (DXF: 2)	According to the DXF documentation, this setting refers to the named coordinate system to which the coordinate system of the current *MODEL_SPACE* block is orthogonal. It is always an empty string, however.
UCSORTHOVIEW	Booleaninteger (DXF: 70)	Defines the orthogonal projection used to generate the actual coordinate system of the current *MODEL_SPACE* block from the named coordinate system listed in UCSBASE. In

Name	Type	Meaning
		ObjectDBX, AutoLISP, and ActiveX Automation, this setting is called *UCSORTHO*. See note 16.
UCSXDIR	normalized vector (DXF: 10/20/30)	Defines the X direction for the active user coordinate system of the *MODEL_SPACE* block. See note 16.
UCSYDIR	normalized vector (DXF: 10/20/30)	Defines the Y direction for the active user coordinate system of the *MODEL_SPACE* block. See note 16.
UNITMODE	integer (DXF: 70)	Specifies whether AutoCAD is to display lengths in a user-friendly format (0) or in the same format needed to input lengths (1). This is especially important for feet, inches, and fractional inches, when the space character for separations is not a valid input character.
USERI1 - USERI5	integer (DXF: 70)	Indicates a set of five integer variables that allow a user to store arbitrary numbers inside the drawing database.
USERR1 - USERR5	real (DXF: 40)	Indicates a set of five real variables that allow a user to store arbitrary numbers inside the drawing database. Many AutoCAD releases ago, this was the only way to keep some non-AutoCAD data in a drawing file.
USRTIMER	Boolean (DXF: 70)	Specifies whether the user timer (see TDUSRTIMER) is currently on (*Adesk::kTrue*, 1) or off (*Adesk::kFalse*, 0).
VERSIONGUID	string (DXF: 2)	Indicates a globally unique identifier (GUID) of this version of the drawing. Will be generated every time AutoCAD saves the drawing. This setting is available only to ObjectDBX and DXF.
WORLDVIEW	integer (DXF: 70)	Defines the coordinate system in which a user expresses view changes. Possible values are 0 (the current UCS; see UCSNAME), 1 (the world coordinate system), and 2 (the coordinate system set in UCSBASE).
XEDIT	Boolean (DXF: 70)	Specifies whether AutoCAD is allowed to edit this drawing database while it is referenced from another database.

Note 1—AUNITS

The value of *AUNITS* is one of the values listed in the following table. The named constants are available only in ActiveX Automation. There you can use either the constants or the values in your code (see Chapter 3). No named constant is associated with value 4.

Value		Meaning
acDegrees	0	Decimal degrees (e.g., 49.434)
acDegreesMinutesSeconds	1	degrees with minutes and seconds (e.g., 49d26'3")
acGrads	2	Decimal gradians (e.g., 54.927g), 360° = 400g
acRadians	3	Radians (e.g., 0.863r)
	4	Surveyor's units (e.g., N 40d33'57" O)

Note 2-AUPREC

The value of *AUPREC* defines the number of decimal places to use when reporting angles. If *AUNITS* is set to 1 or 4, the value of *AUPREC* specifies whether minutes, seconds, and fractional seconds will be shown. Figure 4.4 displays all combinations of *AUNITS* and *AUPREC* with the same angle.

FIGURE 4.4

AUNITS and AUPREC

$AUPREC	\\ $AUNITS → 0	1	2	3	4
0	49	49d	55g	1r	N 41d O
1	49.4	49d26'	54.9g	0.9r	N 40d34' O
2	49.43	49d26'	54.93g	0.86r	N 40d34' O
3	49.434	49d26'3	54.927g	0.863r	N 40d33'57" O
4	49.4341	49d26'3"	54.9269g	0.8628r	N 40d33'57" O
5	49.43417	49d26'3.0"	54.92687g	0.86279r	N 40d33'57.0" O
6	49.434179	49d26'3.05"	54.926866g	0.862789r	N 40d33'56.95" O
7	49.4341792	49d26'3.045"	54.9268658g	0.8627892r	N 40d33'56.955" O
8	49.43417923	49d26'3.0452"	54.92686581g	0.86278919r	N 40d33'56.9548" O

Note 3-Dimension Settings in General

A complete discussion of dimension-related settings and their actions is in Chapter 12. The global settings for dimensions do not affect any dimension object in the drawing database. They are, rather, defaults for any dimension subsequently created in Auto-CAD. If settings differ from their definition in the current dimension style (*DIMSTYLE*), they will be used as dimension style overrides, that is, they will take precedence over the corresponding dimension style setting.

Note 4-DIMATFIT

The value of *DIMATFIT* is one of the settings in the following list. The named constants are available only in ActiveX Automation.

Value		Meaning
acTextAndArrows	0	Move text and arrows if space between extension lines is insufficient.
acArrowsOnly	1	Try to move the arrows outside first. If they still don't fit, also move the text.
acTextOnly	2	Try to move the text outside first. If it still doesn't fit, also move the arrows.
acBestFit	3	Move either text or arrows or both—whatever fits best.

Note 5-DIMAZIN

The value of *DIMAZIN* is a combination of Boolean flags. The following list shows how it is calculated.

Value	Meaning
+1	Suppress zeros preceding the decimal delimiter (e.g., 0.123 becomes .123)
+2	Suppress zeros following the decimal delimiter (e.g., 1.100 becomes 1.1)

Note 6-DIMBLK

The value of *DIMBLK* refers to a block symbol table record. AutoCAD automatically creates corresponding blocks if the user selects one from the dialog box. In addition, the user can provide his or her own block. The following list contains the predefined block names used by AutoCAD's dimensioning feature. When working with ActiveX Automation, there is an associated *AcDimArrowheadType* enumeration, listed here for completeness. The enumeration for a user-defined block is *acArrowUserDefined*.

Value	Enum	Meaning
`" "`	acArrowDefault	Filled triangle
`"_ArchTick"`	acArrowArchTick	Architectural tick, a thick slash
`"_BoxBlank"`	acArrowBoxBlank	Unfilled square
`"_BoxFilled"`	acArrowBoxFilled	Filled square
`"_Closed"`	acArrowClosed	Unfilled triangle, dimension line ends at top
`"_ClosedBlank"`	acArrowClosedBlank	Unfilled triangle, dimension line ends at base
`"_DatumBlank"`	acArrowDatumBlank	Datum triangle unfilled
`"_DatumFilled"`	acArrowDatumFilled	Datum triangle filled
`"_Dot"`	acArrowDot	Filled circle
`"_DotBlank"`	acArrowDotBlank	Unfilled circle, dimension line ends at outline
`"_DotSmall"`	acArrowDotSmall	Small filled circle
`"_Integral"`	acArrowIntegral	Integral-like curve
`"_None"`	acArrowNone	No arrowhead
`"_Oblique"`	acArrowOblique	Thin slash
`"_Open"`	acArrowOpen	Two lines opening approximately 20°
`"_Open30"`	acArrowOpen30	Two lines opening 30°
`"_Open90"`	acArrowOpen90	Two lines opening 90°
`"_Origin"`	acArrowOrigin	Unfilled circle, dimension line ends at center
`"_Origin2"`	acArrowOrigin2	Two concentric circles
`"_Small"`	acArrowSmall	Small unfilled circle

Note 7-DIMFRAC

The value of *DIMFRAC* is one of the following. The constants are available only in ActiveX Automation.

Value		Meaning
acHorizontal	0	Use a horizontal fraction bar.
acDiagonal	1	Use a diagonal fraction bar.
acNotStacked	2	Use a simple slash character.

Note 8-DIMJUST

The value of *DIMJUST* is one of the following. The constants are available only in ActiveX Automation.

Value		Meaning
acHorzCentered	0	Dimension text will be centered between extension lines.
acFirstExtensionLine	1	Dimension text will be placed next to the first extension line.
acSecondExtensionLine	2	Dimension text will be placed next to the second extension line.
acOverFirstExtension	3	Dimension text will be rotated and placed in extension of the first extension line.
acOverSecondExtension	4	Dimension text will be rotated and placed in extension of the second extension line.

Note 9-DIMLUNIT

The value of *DIMLUNIT* is one of the following. The constants are available only in ActiveX Automation.

Value		Meaning
acDimLScientific	1	Exponential format (e.g., 1.56E+10)
acDimLDecimal	2	Decimal format (e.g., 54.927)
acDimLEngineering	3	American engineering format; uses feet, inches, and decimal inches (e.g., 3'-0.61")
acDimLArchitectural	4	American architectural format; uses feet, inches, and fractions (e.g., 3'-0 5/8")
acDimLFractional	5	Fractional format (e.g., 38 5/8)
acDimLWindowsDesktop	6	Decimal format using Windows Desktop local country settings (e.g., 54,927)

Note 10-DIMTAD

The value of *DIMTAD* is one of the following. The constants are available only in ActiveX Automation.

Value		Meaning
acVertCentered	0	Dimension text will be centered with the dimension line, which is usually broken to display the text (see also DIMTVP).

Value		Meaning
acAbove	1	Dimension text will be placed above the dimension line.
acOutside	2	Dimension text will be placed on the outer side of the dimension.
acJIS	3	Dimension text will be placed according to Japanese Industrial Standards (JIS).

Note 11-DIMTMOVE

The value of *DIMTMOVE* is one of the following. The constants are available only in ActiveX Automation.

Value		Meaning
acDimLineWithText	0	Moves the dimension line to follow the dimension text after it was moved.
acMoveTextAddLeader	1	Moves the dimension text and connects it to the dimension line with a leader line.
acMoveTextNoLeader	2	Moves the dimension text freely without adding a connection line.

Note 12-DIMTOLJ

The value of *DIMTOLJ* is one of the following. The constants are available only in ActiveX Automation.

Value		Meaning
acTolBottom	0	Align the bottom of dimension text and tolerance text.
acTolMiddle	1	Align the center of dimension text and tolerance text.
acTolTop	2	Align the top of dimension text and tolerance text.

Note 13-DIMZIN

The value of *DIMZIN* is a combination of an integer and Boolean flags. It is calculated like this.

Value		Meaning
	0	Suppress zeros in both feet and inches (e.g., 0' - 6" becomes 6" and 6' - 0" becomes 6').

Value	Meaning
1	Do not suppress zeros in either feet or inches (e.g., both 0' - 6" and 6' - 0" display unchanged).
2	Suppress zeros in inches only (e.g., 6' - 0" becomes 6').
3	Suppress zeros in feet only (e.g., 0' - 6" becomes 6").
+4	Suppress zeros preceding the decimal delimiter (e.g., 0.123 becomes .123).
+8	Suppress zeros following the decimal delimiter (e.g., 1.100 becomes 1.1).

Note 14-INSUNITS

The value of *INSUNITS* is one of the following. The constants are available only in ActiveX Automation.

Value		Meaning
acInsertUnitsUnitless	0	No unit of measurement specified
acInsertUnitsInches	1	Inches (i.e., $2.54*10^{-2}$m)
acInsertUnitsFeet	2	Feet (i.e., $3.048*10^{-1}$m)
acInsertUnitsMiles	3	Statute miles (i.e., $1.609344*10^{3}$m)
acInsertUnitsMillimeters	4	Millimeters (i.e., $1.0*10^{-3}$m)
acInsertUnitsCentimeters	5	Centimeters (i.e., $1.0*10^{-2}$m)
acInsertUnitsMeters	6	Meters (i.e., $1.0*10^{0}$m)
acInsertUnitsKilometers	7	Kilometers (i.e., $1.0*10^{3}$m)
acInsertUnitsMicroinches	8	Microinches (i.e. $2.54*10^{-8}$m)
acInsertUnitsMils	9	Mils (i.e., $2.54*10^{-5}$m)
acInsertUnitsYards	10	Yards (i.e ,$9.144*10^{-1}$m)
acInsertUnitsAngstroms	11	Angstrom (i.e., $1.0*10^{-10}$m)
acInsertUnitsNanometers	12	Nanometers (i.e., $1.0*10^{-9}$m)
acInsertUnitsMicrons	13	Microns (i.e., $1.0*10^{-6}$m)
acInsertUnitsDecimeters	14	Decimeters (i.e., $1.0*10^{-1}$m)
acInsertUnitsDecameters	15	Decameters (i.e., $1.0*10^{1}$m)
acInsertUnitsHectometers	16	Hectometers (i.e., $1.0*10^{2}$m)
acInsertUnitsGiagmeters	17	Gigameters (i.e., $1.0*10^{9}$m)

Value		Meaning
acInsertUnits-AstronomicalUnits	18	Astronomical units (i.e., $1.4959787*10^{11}$m)
acInsertUnitsLightYears	19	Light years (i.e., $9.46053*10^{15}$m)
acInsertUnitsParsecs	20	Parsecs (i.e., $3.085677*10^{16}$m)

Note 15-LUNITS

The value of *LUNITS* is one of the following. The constants are available only in ActiveX Automation.

Value		Meaning
acScientific	1	Exponential format (e.g., 1.56E+10)
acDecimal	2	Decimal format (e.g., 54.927)
acEngineering	3	American engineering format, uses feet, inches, and decimal inches (e.g., 3'-0.61")
acArchitectural	4	American architectural format, uses feet, inches and fractions (e.g., 3'-0 5/8")
acFractional	5	Fractional format (e.g., 38 5/8)

Note 16-UCS settings

The actual coordinate systems for the current *MODEL_SPACE* and *PAPER_SPACE* blocks are saved separately to DXF and DWG files. While working interactively in AutoCAD using AutoLISP or ActiveX Automation, there is only a single setting for both. Depending on which block is visualized currently, the UCS-related settings report the value of the *MODEL_SPACE* block or the value of the *PAPER_SPACE* block. The settings affected by this are UCSBASE, UCSORG, UCSORTHOVIEW (UCSVIEW), UCSXDIR, and UCSYDIR.

The UCSORTHOVIEW setting is named USCORTHO in ObjectDBX, AutoLISP, and ActiveX Automation. The following values are possible.

Workplane	ObjectDBX	DXF	X-axis	Y-axis
top	kTopView	1	UCS X	UCS Y
bottom	kBottomView	2	UCS –X	UCS Y
front	kFrontView	3	UCS X	UCS Y
back	kBackView	4	UCS –X	UCS Y
left	kLeftView	5	UCS –Y	UCS Z
right	kRightView	6	UCS Y	UCS Z

The various other origins saved to DXF, such as UCSORGBOTTOM, are always 0,0,0 and meaningless, because the *current* coordinate system does not contain any information about eventual orthogonal coordinate systems. If predefined orthogonal coordinate systems are related to a coordinate system, this is always a named coordinate system, and you'll find the corresponding settings in the AcDbUCSTableRecord object. The origin settings (other than UCSORG) are not available in environments other than DXF.

Note 17-MEASUREMENT

The value of *MEASUREMENT* is one of the following. The *ac* constants are available only in ActiveX Automation, and the *k* constants are available only in ObjectDBX.

Value		Meaning
acEnglish/kEnglish	0	Use American (inch-based) support files.
acMetric/kMetric	1	Use metric (millimeter-based) support files.

Note 18-SHADEDGE

The value of *SHADEDGE* is one of the following.

Value		Meaning
	0	Shade edges and faces.
	1	Shade faces; edges display in the background color.
	2	Shade edges; faces display in the background color.
	3	Fill faces; edges display in the background color.

Settings Sequence in DXF

If you're working with AutoLISP, ActiveX Automation, or ObjectDBX to access the drawing settings, you don't have to worry about the sequence in which they are saved in the drawing database. This is why the settings are listed in alphabetic order. However, when working with a serialized database (that is, DXF), the sequence may matter. Here's the sequence in which drawing settings are saved to a DXF file:

1 ACADVER	2 ACADMAINTVER	3 DWGCODEPAGE
4 INSBASE	5 EXTMIN	6 EXTMAX

7 LIMMIN	8 LIMMAX	9 ORTHOMODE
10 REGENMODE	11 FILLMODE	12 QTEXTMODE
13 MIRRTEXT	14 LTSCALE	15 ATTMODE
16 TEXTSIZE	17 TRACEWID	18 TEXTSTYLE
19 CLAYER	20 CELTYPE	21 CECOLOR
22 CELTSCALE	23 DISPSILH	24 DIMSCALE
25 DIMASZ	26 DIMEXO	27 DIMDLI
28 DIMRND	29 DIMDLE	30 DIMEXE
31 DIMTP	32 DIMTM	33 DIMTXT
34 DIMCEN	35 DIMTSZ	36 DIMTOL
37 DIMLIM	38 DIMTIH	39 DIMTOH
40 DIMSE1	41 DIMSE2	42 DIMTAD
43 DIMZIN	44 DIMBLK	45 DIMASO
46 DIMSHO	47 DIMPOST	48 DIMAPOST
49 DIMALT	50 DIMALTD	51 DIMALTF
52 DIMLFAC	53 DIMTOFL	54 DIMTVP
55 DIMTIX	56 DIMSOXD	57 DIMSAH
58 DIMBLK1	59 DIMBLK2	60 DIMSTYLE
61 DIMCLRD	62 DIMCLRE	63 DIMCLRT
64 DIMTFAC	65 DIMGAP	66 DIMJUST
67 DIMSD1	68 DIMSD2	69 DIMTOLJ
70 DIMTZIN	71 DIMALTZ	72 DIMALTTZ
73 DIMUPT	74 DIMDEC	75 DIMTDEC
76 DIMALTU	77 DIMALTTD	78 DIMTXSTY
79 DIMAUNIT	80 DIMADEC	81 DIMALTRND
82 DIMAZIN	83 DIMDSEP	84 DIMATFIT
85 DIMFRAC	86 DIMLDRBLK	87 DIMLUNIT
88 DIMLWD	89 DIMLWE	90 DIMTMOVE
91 LUNITS	92 LUPREC	93 SKETCHINC
94 FILLETRAD	95 AUNITS	96 AUPREC
97 MENU	98 ELEVATION	99 PELEVATION
100 THICKNESS	101 LIMCHECK	102 CHAMFERA

103 CHAMFERB	104 CHAMFERC	105 CHAMFERD
106 SKPOLY	107 TDCREATE	108 TDUCREATE
109 TDUPDATE	110 TDUUPDATE	111 TDINDWG
112 TDUSRTIMER	113 USRTIMER	114 ANGBASE
115 ANGDIR	116 PDMODE	117 PDSIZE
118 PLINEWID	119 SPLFRAME	120 SPLINETYPE
121 SPLINESEGS	122 HANDSEED	123 SURFTAB1
124 SURFTAB2	125 SURFTYPE	126 SURFU
127 SURFV	128 UCSBASE	129 UCSNAME
130 UCSORG	131 UCSXDIR	132 UCSYDIR
133 UCSORTHOREF	134 UCSORTHOVIEW	135 UCSORGTOP
136 UCSORGBOTTOM	137 UCSORGLEFT	138 UCSORGRIGHT
139 UCSORGFRONT	140 UCSORGBACK	141 PUCSBASE
142 PUCSNAME	143 PUCSORG	144 PUCSXDIR
145 PUCSYDIR	146 PUCSORTHOREF	147 PUCSORTHOVIEW
148 PUCSORGTOP	149 PUCSORGBOTTOM	150 PUCSORGLEFT
151 PUCSORGRIGHT	152 PUCSORGFRONT	153 PUCSORGBACK
154 USERI1	155 USERI2	156 USERI3
157 USERI4	158 USERI5	159 USERR1
160 USERR2	161 USERR3	162 USERR4
163 USERR5	164 WORLDVIEW	165 SHADEDGE
166 SHADEDIF	167 TILEMODE	168 MAXACTVP
169 PINSBASE	170 PLIMCHECK	171 PEXTMIN
172 PEXTMAX	173 PLIMMIN	174 PLIMMAX
175 UNITMODE	176 VISRETAIN	177 PLINEGEN
178 PSLTSCALE	179 TREEDEPTH	180 CMLSTYLE
181 CMLJUST	182 CMLSCALE	183 PROXYGRAPHICS
184 MEASUREMENT	185 CELWEIGHT	186 ENDCAPS
187 JOINSTYLE	188 LWDISPLAY	189 INSUNITS
190 HYPERLINKBASE	191 STYLESHEET	192 XEDIT
193 CEPSNTYPE	194 FINGERPRINTGUID	195 VERSIONGUID
196 EXTNAMES	197 PSVPSCALE	198 OLESTARTUP

Summary

This chapter has been a discussion on the global settings saved in an AutoCAD drawing database. It did not cover the various objects that make up the database, such as lines, arcs, and circles, but it provides a good starting point for the following chapters, which concentrate on the individual object types (or "classes") used in an AutoCAD drawing. As you've seen, interpreting and understanding the drawing settings is rather easy. In the next chapters, you will learn about much more complicated objects that each have many settings (which we call properties).

Keep in mind that although most settings are of value only to AutoCAD's own drawing editor, a few settings directly affect how AutoCAD will display and print the drawing database. If you want AutoCAD to interpret your drawing database exactly as you intend, fill at least the critical settings with reasonable values. And if you want to write an application that is to mimic AutoCAD's display behavior exactly, you also need to take these settings into account. You will use the tables provided in this chapter often as you set up your own drawing databases.

CHAPTER 5

Properties Common to All Objects

FEATURING

The object handle   120

The object's class   121

The object's owner   122

Reactor links   123

The extension dictionary link   124

Other pointers   125

Extended object data   126

The AutoCAD drawing database is a container for a wide variety of objects. It can contain simple objects such as lines and circles, complex objects such as nuts and bolts, or even abstract objects such as books and authors. Some objects have a visual representation (and are named *entities*), and some don't have associated graphics.

Depending on the class to which an object belongs, the drawing database contains a different number of properties that define this special instance of the class. Throughout the rest of this book, we will look at the most important classes you will encounter in a drawing database, and I will list and explain their associated properties.

A very small number of properties is common to all objects in an AutoCAD drawing database. They are independent of the individual object's class because all objects in an AutoCAD drawing database are derived from (based on) a generic class called *AcDbObject*.

This chapter covers the properties of *AcDbObject*, that is, the properties associated with every object in the database.

The Object Handle

You already learned that *every* object in an AutoCAD drawing database has a unique identifier, its *handle*. The handle is a data type on its own and is available to the various programming environments as follows:

ObjectDBX	ActiveX Automation	DXF/AutoLISP
getAcDbHandle()	Handle	Group 5

 NOTE One object in the drawing database uses a different group code for its handle property! This is the *AcDbDimStyleTableRecord* (DIMSTYLE), which for historic reasons uses group code 105.

Calculated Properties—Entity Name and ObjectID

Calculated from the object's handle, which is unique inside a drawing database, are the entity name and the ObjectID, both of which are unique across all drawing databases currently in use.

The entity name is of class *ads_name* in ObjectDBX. In AutoLISP, it is a symbol type on its own. The entity name is available only to ObjectDBX and AutoLISP. To translate between an entity name and the corresponding ObjectID in ObjectDBX, use the *acdb-GetAdsName()* and *acdbGetObjectID()* functions.

The ObjectID is of class AcDbObjectId. In ActiveX Automation, this is a signed 32-bit integer. The ObjectID is available to ObjectDBX and ActiveX Automation only.

ObjectDBX	ActiveX Automation
AcDbObjectId()	ObjectID

The Object's Class

Every object in a drawing database is an instance of a specific class. In a large number of applications, finding out the class to which an object belongs is essential. The route you follow to do so depends on the environment. Finding the class is easiest in ActiveX Automation. You use the object's *ObjectName* property. This returns the ObjectDBX class name as a string, for example, `"AcDbCircle"`.

In ObjectDBX itself, you use an object's *isA()* function. This returns a pointer to an AcRxClass object, which in turn you can query by its *Name()* function. This process finally gives you the class name string.

The AcRxClass object, however, has a second naming function. In addition to the ObjectDBX class name, each class also has a DXF class name, returned by the class's *dxfName()* function. The DXF name of an AcDbCircle is `"CIRCLE"`.

The DXF name of an object is not unique, contrary to its class name. Two classes may share the same DXF class name. For example, `"POLYLINE"` is used by AcDbPolygonMesh, AcDbPolyFaceMesh, and others.

The difference between the class name and the DXF name becomes clear if you remember that objects have a hierarchy. An AcDbCircle is not an object on its own; it's a specialized AcDbEntity that in turn is inherited from AcDbObject. Each stage of this hierarchy has its own set of properties.

If you look at a serialized variant of the database, for example, a DXF file, you'll see that the group code number is not sufficient to completely define a property. Both a class at a lower level of the hierarchy and a class at a higher level can use the same group code 99 to contain some completely different information.

Therefore, the serialized file contains all subclass names (using group code 100), which separate the various information bits. To simplify access to an object in DXF, the base class name AcDbObject (which is common to all objects in the database anyway) is replaced by the final class DXF name and the group code 0. Here's an example:

```
    0
CIRCLE
<AcDbObject-related groups>
```

```
100
AcDbEntity
<AcDbEntity-related groups>
100
AcDbCircle
<AcDbCircle-related groups>
```

This entire section of the DXF file describes a single circle. The first part of the section includes the properties common to all objects derived from AcDbObject, the second part includes properties common to all objects derived from AcDbEntity, and the third part includes properties that are unique to objects of the AcDbCircle class.

Since AutoLISP uses the exact same group code structure as DXF, you'll find the subclass marker strings (group 100) as well as the DXF name string (group 0) with each object.

ObjectDBX	ActiveX Automation	DXF/AutoLISP
Name(isA())	ObjectName	Group 100
dxfName(isA())	n/a	Group 0

The Object's Owner

Except for the root directory and the symbol tables, every object in the drawing database is owned by another object. For instance, every entity is owned by one symbol table record, the corresponding AcDbBlockTableRecord.

You can query an object's owner in all environments. As is the case with all pointers, you'll see the object's owner as an ObjectID in ObjectDBX and ActiveX Automation and as an entity name in AutoLISP, and you'll see the object's handle in DXF.

The root dictionary and all symbol tables don't have an owner. They return *kNull* in ObjectDBX and list a null handle (0) in DXF.

ObjectDBX	ActiveX Automation	DXF/AutoLISP
ownerId()	OwnerID	Group 330

The Owner information is redundant because it creates a bottom-up relationship in addition to the top-down relationship already created through the ownership hierarchy. Therefore, it would be better if AutoCAD would not file the owner information out to DXF or DWG because it creates the potential problem of inconsistency. This information was not filed out in older versions of DXF and DWG.

Reactor Links

In addition to being linked to its owner, any object can have links to any number of database objects. AutoCAD uses these pointers in a number of ways, as do many other applications that work with AutoCAD data.

One example of such a link is the persistent object reactor. (There are also nonpersistent object reactors, which only exist during the current AutoCAD editing session.) Persistent links are filed out to DXF and DWG files and remain intact when the drawing is saved and opened again.

A reactor does not react. In the drawing database, it is simply a link between two objects. Inside AutoCAD, this link is used to create an active link between the two objects. Whenever one object is modified, all its reactor-linked objects are notified by AutoCAD. It's up to application programs to handle this notification and, therefore, react to the other object's modification. The implementation of this reaction is not part of the drawing database.

In ObjectARX, the *AcDbObject::reactors()* function returns a list of reactor objects associated with this object. You can then iterate through this list and determine whether the reactor is persistent and to which object it points. In ActiveX Automation, there is no way to access an object's reactor links.

In DXF and AutoLISP, several groups are used to list the various objects that may react to an object's modifications. The listing starts with a 102 group that contains the string "{ACAD_REACTORS", followed by one or more 330 groups that contain soft pointers to the reacting objects (see Chapter 2 for details about the *soft pointer* link). The list ends with a second 102 group containing the string "}". Here's an example. Whenever this circle is modified, the object with the handle "32" (which is an AcDbGroup object in this case) receives a notification:

```
 0
CIRCLE
 5
2B
102
{ACAD_REACTORS
330
32
102
}
330
```

```
1F
100
AcDbEntity
   8
0
100
AcDbCircle
  10
125.0
  20
165.0
  30
0.0
  40
95.0
```

Although in DXF, you'll see the reacting object's handle, in AutoLISP, you'll see the corresponding entity name as you do with all interobject pointers.

Reactor links are used with every AcDbDictionary. Any dictionary content contains a reactor link to its parent dictionary, which is also its owner.

Extension Dictionary Link

Another common link used in AutoCAD is the link between an object and the object-specific dictionary. The object-specific dictionary can contain any number of objects. Usually, these objects are AcDbXrecord objects, which can contain any type of data. This structure allows an application developer to extend an object's properties and to include any application-specific data the developer may need. Therefore, this dictionary is called the object's *extension dictionary*.

In ObjectDBX, the *AcDbObject::extensionDictionary()* function returns the ObjectID of the extension dictionary, if any (*AcDbObjectId::kNull* otherwise).

In ActiveX Automation, the *.GetExtensionDictionary* method returns the dictionary object. However, this method also creates an extension dictionary if none exists and returns the newly created dictionary. To determine only whether an extension dictionary exists, use the *.HasExtensionDictionary* property.

In DXF and AutoLISP, the extension dictionary link is similar to a reactor link. Again, it starts with a 102 group, this time containing the string "{ACAD_XDICTIONARY", followed by exactly one 360 group that contains a hard owner link to the extension dictionary object (see Chapter 2 for details about the *hard owner* link). The link uses a handle in DXF and an entity name in AutoLISP. The list ends with a second 102 group containing the string "}". Here is an example:

```
((-1 . <Entity name: 159ad60>)
 (0 . "CIRCLE")
 (5 . "2C")
 (102 . "{ACAD_XDICTIONARY")
 (360 . <Entity name: 159ada0>)
 (102 . "}")
 (330 . <Entity name: 159acf8>)
 (100 . "AcDbEntity")
 (67 . 0)
 (410 . "Model")
 (8 . "0")
 (100 . "AcDbCircle")
 (10 338.611 148.211 0.0)
 (40 . 94.7276)
 (210 0.0 0.0 1.0)
)
```

 NOTE An object can have one extension dictionary or none. It cannot have more than one extension dictionary.

Other Pointers

AutoCAD applications created by third parties or by Autodesk can use the same structure that reactors and extension dictionaries use to create other interobject links.

Neither ObjectDBX nor ActiveX Automation nor DXF/AutoLISP provide any access to these application-specific links unless the application provides corresponding access routines or outputs the corresponding data.

If an application outputs these links in DXF or AutoLISP, it should follow the outline that is used for reactors and extension dictionaries. The list of linked objects should start with a 102 group that contains a string consisting of a curly bracket "{" and an application-specific identifier.

Next should follow the list of objects to which this object is linked. Depending on the link type, the following group codes must be used:

Soft pointer	Group codes 330 through 339
Hard pointer	Group codes 340 through 349
Soft owner	Group codes 350 through 359
Hard owner	Group codes 360 through 369
Arbitrary link	Group code 320 through 329

For a detailed discussion of the various link types, see Chapter 2. Arbitrary links are simply pointers to other objects. AutoCAD does not check or alter them.

Extended Object Data

Before the introduction of extension dictionaries, AutoCAD provided a different way to add arbitrary, application-specific data to any object—*Extended Entity Data* or *xdata,* for short. Since nonentities such as dictionary entries or symbol table records may also have *xdata,* the term *Extended Object Data* is probably more correct.

The additional data was saved in a specific memory segment that AutoCAD reserved for each object. Consequently, an object's xdata is limited to 16383 bytes. Xdata is considered a historic relict, as you will see when looking at the access methods for xdata. It is recommended that application developers use extension dictionaries instead.

Selecting Xdata

Multiple applications can add xdata to an object; however, they share the upper limit of 16383 bytes of total xdata. When writing xdata, you always need to include the application name whose xdata you want to modify. This name must correspond to the key of an AcDbAppTableRecord.

When reading xdata, you can select the application whose xdata you want. The corresponding name is passed as an argument to *AcDbObject::xData()* in ObjectDBX or to *.GetXData* in ActiveX Automation. If you pass a null string, you'll get all xdata from all applications.

In AutoLISP, you also pass the application name to the *entget* function. However, *entget* allows you to pass a list of several application names, including wild cards. If you want all xdata from all applications, pass a list containing the string "*". In DXF, you'll always see all xdata.

Reading and Writing Xdata

Extended object data consists of strings, numbers, points, vectors, binary data, and more. Such a heterogeneous data structure is difficult to handle in most programming languages. Therefore, how you read and write xdata depends on the environment.

The simplest way to access xdata is in DXF. An object's xdata *follows* all other groups of this object. Even though xdata belongs to the AcDbObject level, the corresponding groups do not appear between the AcDbObject data! Thus, our example should correctly read:

```
0
CIRCLE
<AcDbObject-related groups>
100
AcDbEntity
<AcDbEntity-related groups>
100
AcDbCircle
<AcDbCircle-related groups>
<AcDbObject-related xdata>
```

An object can contain xdata for multiple applications. Every segment of xdata belongs to one application and starts with a 1001 group. The group value is the key string of the application's AcDbRegAppTableRecord. Following this 1001 group are the application's xdata groups. Another 1001 group begins another application's xdata, and so on.

```
1001
<Application 1 key string>
<Application 1 xdata groups>
1001
<Application 2 key string>
<Application 2 xdata groups>
```

In AutoLISP, an object's xdata is returned as *one* additional group of code –3. The group's value is a list of xdata lists. Each list starts with the application's key string, followed by this application's xdata in group code/value pairs as usual:

```
(-3
 (<Application 1 key string> <Application 1 xdata groups>)
 (<Application 2 key string> <Application 2 xdata groups>)
)
```

In ActiveX Automation, you use the *.GetXData* method to retrieve xdata group codes and values. You have to supply two variables of the variant data type, which will be filled by AutoCAD. AutoCAD fills the first of these variants with an array of integers and fills the second with an array of variants. The first variable is filled with the xdata group codes, and the second variable is filled with the xdata group values. It is then your task to associate group codes and values correctly by their index, that is, the first group value belongs to the first group code and so on. A group 1001 containing the application key string is used to separate xdata from multiple applications.

In ObjectDBX, you'll get the xdata groups and values as a linked list of result buffers (*resbuf*). The result buffer structure contains a type field indicating the data type returned along with the true value. The first result buffer will have the type code RTSHORT, the value 1001, and a pointer to the next result buffer. The second result buffer will have the type code RTSTR, the application's key string as its value, and a pointer to the next result buffer.

To create or modify xdata, you need to pass the same structure back to AutoCAD, that is, a *resbuf* list, two arrays of group codes and values, or the –3 group in AutoLISP.

Xdata Group Codes and Values

Xdata may contain arbitrary information that makes sense only for the application that generated it. Unless the application developer decided to document xdata usage, you have no way to evaluate or manipulate the data contained in xdata.

Xdata uses the group codes 1000 through 1071 to save arbitrary information. The group code defines the type of information stored, and the group sequence defines the group's meaning to the application.

AutoCAD checks and automatically modifies xdata according to their group code, as shown in Table 5.1.

TABLE 5.1: GROUP CODES AND THEIR MEANINGS

Group Code	Meaning
1000	An arbitrary string; is not checked or modified.
1001	Parent application key string; must exist in the symbol table for registered applications.
1002	The string " { " or " } "; can be used to group xdata. Brackets must be balanced; i.e., any opening bracket must be followed by a closing bracket prior to the end of this application's xdata. Brackets can be nested, however.

Continued ▶

TABLE 5.1: GROUP CODES AND THEIR MEANINGS (CONTINUED)	
Group Code	**Meaning**
1003	A string containing a layer name. This must be one of the key strings used in AcDbLayerTable. AutoCAD automatically modifies this group if the layer is renamed. All environments return the layer string, not the corresponding AcDbLayerTableRecord object.
1004	A chunk of binary data; is not checked or modified.
1005	An object handle; corresponds to a soft pointer link. In other words, if the associated object's handle changes, this group is modified accordingly. AutoCAD's drawing audit will detect and delete 1005 groups that point to objects that don't exist.
1010	An arbitrary point; is not checked or modified. As with every point, in DXF the corresponding groups 1020 and 1030 are used to add the remaining coordinates.
1011	An object-related point in WCS. AutoCAD modifies this group if the object moves, rotates, scales, or mirrors or if the area of the object containing this point is stretched.
1012	An object-related vector. AutoCAD modifies this group if the object rotates, scales, or mirrors. Vectors don't change during move or stretch operations.
1013	An object-related direction, usually a unified vector. AutoCAD modifies this group if the object rotates or mirrors. Directions don't change during move, scale, or stretch operations.
1040	An arbitrary real number; is not checked or modified.
1041	An object-related distance. AutoCAD modifies this group if the object is scaled.
1042	An object-related scale factor. This factor is modified during scale operations. There is no technical difference between groups 1041 and 1042.
1070	An arbitrary 16-bit signed integer; is not checked or modified.
1071	An arbitrary 32-bit signed integer; is not checked or modified.

Summary

Except for the drawing-specific settings discussed in Chapter 4, everything in the AutoCAD drawing database is an AutoCAD database object, that is, an instance of the class AcDbObject.

This chapter described the properties of an AcDbObject: handle, class name, DXF class name, links, and xdata. You will find these properties along with more specialized properties with every object in the drawing database, for example, with every symbol table and symbol table record, which I'll discuss in the next chapter.

CHAPTER <u>6</u>

Objects without a Visual Representation– Part I

FEATURING

Symbol tables	**132**
Linetypes	**138**
Text styles	**141**
Dimension styles	**144**
User Coordinate Systems	**151**
Views	**152**
Viewports	**154**
Registered applications	**158**

As you know by now, a drawing database is a set of structured containers for arbitrary objects. You also know that a drawing database consists of three kinds of containers: symbol tables, dictionaries, and blocks. Only objects in the block containers have a visual representation that AutoCAD can display or plot. These objects are called *entities*.

Both the symbol tables and the dictionaries contain only objects that don't have a visual representation. In this chapter we'll look at the symbol tables, and in the following chapter we'll look at the dictionaries.

Even though the objects in symbol tables and dictionaries don't have a visual representation, they are nevertheless important. These invisible objects define the internal structure of the drawing data. They define if and how entities will display or plot. If you ignore the information contained in these objects, you may still be able to evaluate or display database entities. However, you will probably display incorrect entities or display entities incorrectly.

Symbol Tables

AutoCAD manages eight symbol tables:

AcDbDimStyleTable   Contains objects of type AcDbDimStyleTableRecord (DXF class name: DIMSTYLE), which define a set of properties to be applied to dimensions, for example, the arrow type or text justification. Records of this table are referenced by dimension objects such as AcDbAlignedDimension, AcDbLeader, or AcDbFcf.

AcDbLayerTable   Contains objects of type AcDbLayerTableRecord (DXF class name: LAYER), which can be used to organize drawing entities. Each entity references exactly one layer record.

AcDbLinetypeTable   Contains objects of type AcDbLinetypeTableRecord (DXF class name: LTYPE), which define how drawing entities will be displayed or plotted. Each entity references exactly one linetype record. Several entities, however, ignore their linetype setting and use continuous lines to display.

AcDbRegAppTable   Contains objects of type AcDbRegAppTableRecord (DXF class name: APPID). Any application that saves extended object data (xdata) with any object must register itself in this table. There are no other uses for these symbol table records.

AcDbTextStyleTable   Contains objects of type AcDbTextStyleTableRecord (DXF class name: STYLE), which define a set of properties to be applied to text objects, for example, the font and the character orientation. Records of this table are referenced by text objects such as AcDbAttribute and AcDbMText.

AcDbUCSTable   Contains objects of type AcDbUCSTableRecord (DXF class name: UCS), which define arbitrary Cartesian coordinate systems that a user might activate and work in. The records of this table are not referenced except for the UCSNAME global setting.

AcDbViewportTable   Contains objects of type AcDbViewportTableRecord (DXF class name: VPORT), which define named sets of tiled-screen viewports. Multiple table records share the same key string value. Records of this table are not referenced anywhere in the database.

AcDbViewTable   Contains objects of type AcDbViewTableRecord (DXF class name: VIEW), which define views in a drawing. A user can display or plot such a view. This table's records are not referenced anywhere in the database.

In addition to these symbol tables, there is the special block table, which consists of the block containers and all entities. This table is covered in detail in Chapter 8.

The DXF Sequence for Symbol Tables

As you know, the serialized version of the drawing database (DXF) uses brackets to create containers. The symbol tables section of a DXF file starts with

```
  0
SECTION
  2
TABLES
```

and ends with

```
  0
ENDSEC
```

Within this section are the symbol tables. Although the sequence of tables should be arbitrary, AutoCAD-generated DXF files always contain symbol tables in this order:

1. VPORT (AcDbViewportTable)
2. LTYPE (AcDbLinetypeTable)
3. LAYER (AcDbLayerTable)
4. STYLE (AcDbTextstyleTable)
5. VIEW (AcDbViewTable)
6. DIMSTYLE (AcDbDimStyleTable)
7. UCS (AcDbUCSTable)
8. APPID (AcDbRegAppTable)
9. BLOCK_RECORD (which is a placeholder for the block containers and will be discussed in Chapter 8)

We will now look at every symbol table and its records in order of importance.

The Layers Table

Layers are a grouping tool for entities (that is, objects that have a visual representation). Every entity is associated with one and only one layer; however, the layer table can contain layers other than those being referenced by the database entities.

The main purpose of layers is to hide a group of objects. Every layer can be visible or invisible and can thus create different sets of drawings. In layouts, multiple views of an object may show certain layers visible in one view and invisible in another.

In addition to visibility, layers in AutoCAD also define the default appearance of entities associated with them. Unless an entity has an individual color or linetype assignment, it uses the default values that are set in the corresponding layer symbol table record.

Layer Table Sequence in DXF

In the serialized database (DXF), the layer table is enclosed in brackets. The layer table starts with

```
0
TABLE
2
LAYER
```

which is followed by the remaining AcDbObject groups.

The symbol table itself is of subclass AcDbSymbolTable and lists only one additional property:

```
70
<symbol table records count>
```

The value associated with group 70 is the number of layer records included in this table. In ActiveX Automation, you can use the *Count* property to get the number of records.

 NOTE   The record count value in symbol tables is unreliable. Iterate through the table until you find the corresponding end bracket.

The layer table ends with

```
0
ENDTAB
```

The Layer Table Extension Dictionary

Like any other object in the AutoCAD drawing database, the AcDbLayerTable object can own an extension dictionary. AutoCAD uses this extension dictionary to store user-defined layer filters.

These layer filters are used to simplify the display of long layer lists within Auto-CAD's user interface. Using layer lists, a user can choose to list, for example, only those layers whose names start with *Floor1*, only red layers, or all layers that have been turned off. See the next chapter for more information about layer filters.

Layer Symbol Table Records in DXF

The DXF class name for Layer records is `"LAYER"`. Following the standard AcDbObject groups are a subclass marker for AcDbSymbolTableRecord with no properties and a subclass marker for AcDbLayerTableRecord, followed by the layer properties.

The DXF sequence of the AcDbLayerTableRecord groups is 2, 70, 62, 6, 290, 370, 390. The significance of these group records is discussed in the following sections.

Layer 0

Every drawing database has a layer record using the key string `"0"`. In DXF, this record is always the very first record in the layer table.

Layer `"0"` is mandatory and has one more special property: if a block is referenced by another block, all entities from this block that are associated with layer `"0"` will act as if they were drawn on the block reference's layer. For details, see Chapter 16.

Layer Properties

A layer record has several properties. Some define the appearance of the layer, and others define defaults for entity properties.

The primary property of a layer is its *Name* or key string.

ObjectDBX	ActiveX Automation	DXF/AutoLISP
getName()	Name	Group 2

The layer's visibility is controlled by the *Frozen* and *Off* properties. There is a small but important difference between frozen and off layers. Entities on frozen layers are temporarily excluded from the drawing database in all calculations, including display. Entities on off layers are part of the drawing database but invisible.

This means that a 3D object on an off layer still hides other objects, and that the same object on a frozen layer does not. If a block reference is on an off layer, all block entities that are on visible layers are displayed. However, if the same block reference entity is on a frozen layer, no block entity is displayed, even if it is associated with a visible layer. Finally, AutoCAD ignores entities on frozen layers while calculating the current drawing extents; entities on off layers still enlarge the drawing area.

The *Frozen* property is a Boolean value.

ObjectDBX	ActiveX Automation	DXF/AutoLISP
isFrozen()	Freeze	First bit (1) of group 70

The *Off* property is also a Boolean value. However, in DXF this information is hidden in the group 62 color property. Yes, this is historic. If the color property is negative, the layer is off. If it is positive, the layer is on. ActiveX Automation uses the *LayerOn* property, which tells whether a layer is *On*, but in ObjectDXB, you can see whether the layer is *Off*.

ObjectDBX	ActiveX Automation	DXF/AutoLISP
isOff()	LayerOn	On if group 62 is positive; off if group 62 is negative

A layer can be locked or unlocked. AutoCAD refuses to edit entities that reside on a locked layer. The *Locked* property is a Boolean value.

ObjectDBX	ActiveX Automation	DXF/AutoLISP
isLocked()	Lock	Third bit (4) of group 70

A layer can be set to unplottable. In this case, entities associated with this layer will not plot even if they are visible. The *Plottable* property is a Boolean value.

ObjectDBX	ActiveX Automation	DXF/AutoLISP
isPlottable()	Plottable	Group 290 (if omitted, true)

A final Boolean value defines whether the layer should be frozen by default in any newly created layout viewport.

ObjectDBX	ActiveX Automation	DXF/AutoLISP
VPDFLT()	ViewportDefault	Second bit (2) of group 70

NOTE The seventh bit (64) of group 70 in DXF and AutoLISP is supposed to indicate whether any object in the database references this symbol table record. However, this bit is unreliable.

Additional properties of a layer are *Color, Linetype, Lineweight,* and *Plotstyle*. Each of these properties sets the default for any entity associated with this layer that misses an individual setting of this property.

The color is of type AcCmColor. Colors in AutoCAD are referenced by their *Auto-CAD Color Index* (ACI). (See Chapter 9 for details about the ACI.) In DXF and AutoLISP, the sign bit of the color integer is used to represent the *Off* property and must be excluded to get the color value.

ObjectDBX	ActiveX Automation	DXF/AutoLISP
color()	Color	Absolute value of group 62

The layer linetype is an ObjectID in ObjectDBX and points to the corresponding AcDbLinetypeTableRecord. In ActiveX Automation, AutoLISP, and DXF, you'll see the Linetype record's key string instead.

ObjectDBX	ActiveX Automation	DXF/AutoLISP
linetypeObjectId()	Linetype	Group 6

The layer's default lineweight is of type AcDb::LineWeight. For more on the value of the lineweight property, see Chapter 9.

ObjectDBX	ActiveX Automation	DXF/AutoLISP
lineWeight()	LineWeight	Group 370

The fourth layer property that creates a default for entities associated with this layer is the default plot style. In ObjectDBX, you will get either the plot style's name or the AcDbObjectID of the corresponding AcDbPlaceHolder object. In DXF, you'll get the plot style's handle.

ObjectDBX	ActiveX Automation	DXF/AutoLISP
plotStyleName(), plotStyleNameId()	PlotStyleName	Group 390

External Layers

The AcDbLayerTable contains all layers defined in the current drawing database, regardless of whether they are referenced by other entities. In addition, the symbol table also contains all layers from any external database (XREF) that is referenced by this drawing.

This copy of the external database's symbol table records is used to save any layer settings that the user might want to see when viewing the external database. These local settings are independent of the external settings for this layer. Thus, a user can turn off an xref-dependent layer even though it is on in the external database. (See the discussion on the VISRETAIN global setting in Chapter 4 for information about the preference for the local settings versus the external settings.)

An external layer uses a special name that is derived from the external database reference name (see the discussion of the block table in Chapter 8 for details), a vertical bar, and the external layer name. Thus, `"ExternalDatabase|ExternalLayer"` references the layer `"ExternalLayer"` from the `"ExternalDatabase"`.

ObjectDBX, DXF, and AutoLISP supply two additional Boolean values for external layers: *Dependent* is true if the layer is located in an external database; *Resolved* is true if the external layer was found the last time AutoCAD tried to load it.

ObjectDBX	ActiveX Automation	DXF/AutoLISP
isDependent()	n/a	Fifth bit (16) of group 70
isResolved()	n/a	Sixth bit (32) of group 70

NOTE In ObjectDBX, these two properties belong to the AcDbSymbolTableRecord subclass.

The Linetypes Table

Linetypes are a visualization tool for entities. A linetype is a series of dashes, gaps, dots, and shapes that will be mapped onto an entity's geometry when it is output to the screen or to a printer.

The drawing database supports an arbitrary number of arbitrarily defined linetypes. This is different from the behavior of most other programs. The AutoCAD user maintains a series of files that contain the linetype definitions. However, the drawing database does not reference these files (as it does fonts). Instead, the definitions for all referenced linetypes and even some nonreferenced linetypes are saved with the drawing database.

The AcDbLinetypeTable contains these definitions. The table is similar to the layer table, which is why I'll describe only the differences here.

The DXF class name of AcDbLinetypeTableRecord is `"LTYPE"`. The sequence of groups is 2, 70, 3, 72, 73, 40, 49, 74, 75, 340, 46, 50, 44, 45, 9 (repeats from 49).

Linetypes may be externally dependent; thus, the *Dependent* and *Resolved* properties exist.

Predefined Linetypes

Every drawing database contains at least three predefined linetypes:

- `"ByBlock"`
- `"ByLayer"`
- `"Continuous"`

`"Continuous"` is the plain, simple, solid line without gaps. `"ByLayer"` and `"ByBlock"` are placeholders only and allow entities to reference these two virtual linetypes. (See Chapter 9 for more about these special linetypes.)

The predefined linetypes are defined as follows.

Property	Continuous	ByBlock/ByLayer
Description	`"Solid line"`	None
Alignment	65	65
Length	0.0	0.0
Segments	0	0

Linetype Properties

Linetypes have the same *Name* property as layers. In addition, linetypes have a description string.

ObjectDBX	ActiveX Automation	DXF/AutoLISP
asciiDescription()	Description	Group 3

This is the only information about linetype definitions accessible through ActiveX Automation.

A linetype consists of a number of segments that make up the linetype definition. Segments can be a dash, a gap, a dot, a shape symbol, or a text string. Both the number of segments (an integer) and the combined length (a length) can be queried. The maximum number of segments is 12.

ObjectDBX	ActiveX Automation	DXF/AutoLISP
numDashes()	n/a	Group 73
patternLength()	n/a	Group 40

A linetype will be either stretched at its ends in such a way so that there are no gaps at the beginning or end of an entity's geometry, or it will be scaled to fit exactly onto the entity's geometry. (For the exact procedure, see Chapter 9.) The *ScaledToFit* property indicates whether a linetype is stretched or scaled. This property is a Boolean in ObjectDBX and an integer in DXF/AutoLISP (65 for false, 83 for true).

ObjectDBX	ActiveX Automation	DXF/AutoLISP
isScaledToFit()	n/a	Group 72

Linetype Definitions

A linetype is defined by a series of segments: dashes, gaps, dots, text strings, or shapes. The definition uses true measurements, which are later scaled three times until they can be mapped on an entity's geometry: first by the entity-specific linetype scale, then by the global linetype scale (see the LTSCALE global setting), and eventually by the view scale (see the PSLTSCALE global setting).

The linetype definition contains all the segments and a series of properties for each segment. In ObjectARX, you access a segment's properties using this segment's index. In DXF and AutoLISP, you'll get the first segment's properties first, then the second segment's properties, and so on.

Each segment has a length, which can be positive, negative, or zero. If the length is positive, there will be a dash of appropriate length; if the length is zero, there will be a dot. If the length is negative, there will be a gap of appropriate length.

ObjectDBX	ActiveX Automation	DXF/AutoLISP
dashLengthAt()	n/a	Group 49

In any case, the gap or the dash length can be filled with a text string or a shape symbol. In DXF and AutoLISP, the second bit (2) of group 74 is set if a text string is embedded; the third bit (4) of group 74 is set if a shape symbol is embedded. In ObjectDBX, you can use the *shapeNumberAt()* function, which returns 0 for text strings, and the *textAt()* function, which returns *isNull()* if there's no text to get the same information.

Alternatively, you can use the *shapeStyleAt()* function, which returns the AcDb-ObjectID of the corresponding Textstyle symbol table record. You can then check the symbol table record type to see if it's a shape library or a text style. This pointer to the Textstyle table is also returned by DXF and AutoLISP. As are all pointers, it is seen as a handle or an entity name.

ObjectDBX	ActiveX Automation	DXF/AutoLISP
shapeStyleAt()	n/a	Group 340

The *Shape Number* property indicates which shape symbol is to be used. If the embedded object is a text string, the value 0 is returned. If it's a symbol shape, the number (an integer) points to the corresponding entry in the symbol library.

ObjectDBX	ActiveX Automation	DXF/AutoLISP
shapeNumberAt()	n/a	Group 75

If the embedded object is a text string, the *Text* property contains the value to be used.

ObjectDBX	ActiveX Automation	DXF/AutoLISP
textAt()	n/a	Group 9

The shape or text string can be scaled, offset, and rotated. The scale of a shape symbol is relative to its definition in the shape file; the scale of a text string is relative to the text height defined in the associated text style (supply 1.0 if 0.0).

ObjectDBX	ActiveX Automation	DXF/AutoLISP
shapeScaleAt()	n/a	Group 46

The shape offset is a 2D vector (AcGeVector2d) that describes the offset of the shape starting point relative to the end of the previous linetype segment. In DXF and Auto-LISP, the X displacement is in group 44, and the Y displacement is in group 45.

ObjectDBX	ActiveX Automation	DXF/AutoLISP
shapeOffsetAt()	n/a	Groups 44 and 45

The shape rotation is an angle (and thus in degrees in DXF; in radians elsewhere). This rotation may be absolute (relative to the x-axis of the coordinate system in which the entity is drawn) or relative (which is relative to the line direction). A Boolean value is true for an absolute rotation.

ObjectDBX	ActiveX Automation	DXF/AutoLISP
shapeRotationAt()	n/a	Group 50
shapeIsUcsOrientedAt()	n/a	First bit (1) of group 74

Text Styles

The text style symbol table has a history. Knowing it makes understanding some of its concepts easier.

Early versions of AutoCAD had their own definition for fonts. Such an AutoCAD-specific vector font included the vector strokes that make up each character in the font. These vector fonts of file type SHX are still in use in AutoCAD.

Because there is no fundamental difference between text characters and any other small symbol, the exact same vector definition and the exact same SHX files were also used to define libraries of symbol shapes. AutoCAD had (and still has) no knowledge of how the character in a font or the shape in a symbol library looks. Therefore, the entire drawing database contains only references to the corresponding entries in external files.

When AutoCAD was able to recognize Windows fonts (True Type fonts), nothing changed. Characters were and are still referenced by their position in a font file, not by a font name and attributes.

The AcDbTextStyleTable, therefore, contains AcDbTextStyleTableRecord objects that define three completely different things:

- References to SHX font files
- References to SHX shape libraries
- References to Windows font files

Text styles referring to font files are more than just font references. A text style defines the complete appearance of a text string, which is composed of the font, the text height, the slant, the running direction, and the text compression. We'll look at these issues shortly.

Again, this table is similar to the layer table, which is why I'll describe only the differences here.

The DXF class name of AcDbTextStyleTableRecord is "STYLE". The sequence of groups is 2, 70, 40, 41, 50, 71, 42, 3, 4.

Text styles are always local to the current database. Every drawing database contains at least one predefined text style named "Standard". Its definition may vary.

Text Style Properties

Text styles have the same *Name* property as layers, but only if they refer to a font file. Text style table entries referring to a shape library have a blank name ("").

In ActiveX Automation, check the *Name* property to see whether the symbol table record describes a font reference or a shape library reference. The other environments additionally provide a Boolean flag.

ObjectDBX	ActiveX Automation	DXF/AutoLISP
isShapeFile()	n/a	First bit (1) of group 70

The main information in a text style table record is the filename of the font or symbol file.

ObjectDBX	ActiveX Automation	DXF/AutoLISP
fileName()	FontFile	Group 3

Even though SHX font files can include any Unicode character definition, they are limited to 256 characters. Therefore, AutoCAD supports so-called Big Fonts, which you can use if you need SHX fonts and more than 256 characters to create a text style. As is the case with SHX fonts, the definition of Big Fonts is not documented by Autodesk, and space constraints prevent documenting it here.

ObjectDBX	ActiveX Automation	DXF AutoLISP
bigFontFileName()	BigFontFile	Group 4

NOTE Both properties contain a filename string that can include drive and/or directory references. Ensure that these filenames are in accordance with the specification of the target operating system.

Under Windows, a font file defines a specific member of a font family. Attributes of this member are italic, bold, pitch, and character set. In ObjectDBX, you can query this information using the *font()* function.

Some SHX fonts can be used in two orientations: horizontal or vertical. The *Vertical* property is a Boolean that can be queried in ObjectDBX, DXF, and AutoLISP. If the *Vertical* property is set, AutoCAD draws the characters of a text string below one another. Only certain SHX files allow vertical text.

ObjectDBX	ActiveX Automation	DXF/AutoLISP
isVertical()	n/a	Third bit (4) of group 70

The remaining properties of a text style do not directly affect all text-based objects in the drawing database. For AcDbText objects, these properties are simply defaults for any subsequently drawn text. Every text object has its own set of properties similar to these. Other objects, such as AcDbMText, do not contain their own properties but use those of the associated AcDbTextStyleTableRecord.

The *Backwards* and *Upside Down* properties are Boolean flags; however, they are not shown as such. Backward text is mirrored along the y-axis, and upside-down text is mirrored along the x-axis. In all the environments described here, these two Boolean flags are merged into a single integer:

ObjectDBX	ActiveX Automation	DXF/AutoLISP
flagBits()	TextGenerationFlag	Group 71

ActiveX Automation provides two constants for the flags:

Value	Corresponding Bit	Meaning
acTextFlagBackward	Second bit (2)	Draw text from right to left.
acTextFlagUpsideDown	Third bit (4)	Draw characters upside-down.

The *Height* property defines the (default) height for text drawn using this text style. Remember that AcDbText objects already in the drawing database have their own *Height* property. Even though the text height should be a length (that is, a positive real), the value 0.0 is valid. This indicates no default height, meaning that AutoCAD will ask the user to supply a text height when using this style.

ObjectDBX	ActiveX Automation	DXF/AutoLISP
textSize()	Height	Group 40

In addition, the text style table record is used to save the last height used to draw a text in this style or to draw a symbol from this shape library.

ObjectDBX	ActiveX Automation	DXF/AutoLISP
priorSize()	LastHeight	Group 42

The obliquing angle defines the (default) slant for text objects. This angle is used to create italic text. An angle of zero draws the characters as they are defined in the font file. A positive value slants them to the right; a negative, to the left.

ObjectDBX	ActiveX Automation	DXF/AutoLISP
obliquingAngle()	ObliqueAngle	Group 50

The last property for text styles is the (default) compression value, or X scale. A value of 1.0 draws the characters as defined in the font file. A larger value stretches each character by this factor, and a smaller value compresses it. The scale must not be zero or less and must not exceed 100.0.

ObjectDBX	ActiveX Automation	DXF/AutoLISP
xScale()	Width	Group 41

Dimension Styles

Just as text styles define the appearance of textlike objects in a drawing, dimension styles define the appearance of dimensionlike objects, including leaders and feature control frames.

To define the appearance of a dimension, you need many more properties than you need to define a text style. Consequently, a dimensionlike object does not contain a copy of the dimension style settings. Therefore, these are not defaults, but true settings. And changing a dimension style automatically changes all dimension objects that reference it. However, a dimension may override settings from its associated dimension style.

Again, this table is similar to the other tables, and I'll describe only the differences.

The DXF class name of AcDbDimStyleTableRecord is "DIMSTYLE". The sequence of groups is 2, 70, 3, 4, 5, 6, 7, 40, 41, 42, 43, 44, 45, 46, 47, 48, 71, 72, 73, 74, 75, 76, 77,

78, 79, 140, 141, 142, 143, 144, 145, 146, 147, 148, 170, 171, 172, 173, 174, 175, 176, 177, 178, 179, 270, 271, 272, 273, 274, 275, 276, 277, 278, 279, 280, 281, 282, 283, 284, 285, 286, 287, 288, 289, 340, 341, 342, 343, 344, 371, 372.

 NOTE Remember that AcDbDimStyleTableRecord is the only class that uses group 105 for its handle!

Dimension styles are always local to the current database.

Dimension Style Families

Dimension styles can exist in so-called families. This has no consequence for any dimensionlike object already in the database. It affects only dimensions created interactively in AutoCAD after this drawing database was loaded into the AutoCAD editor.

Dimension style families share the same base name. The dimension family parent has only the base name. A postfix of $0 defines a dimension family child for linear dimensions. If the parent style is current and an AutoCAD user draws a linear dimension, the program checks to see if a $0 child exists. If it does, AutoCAD uses the style settings from the dimension family child's symbol table record. If it doesn't, the parent's settings are used.

Other valid child styles use the postfix $2 for angular dimensions, $3 for diameter dimensions, $4 for radius dimensions, $6 for ordinate dimensions, and $7 for leaders and feature control frames.

ObjectDBX contains two functions, *getDimstyleChildId()* and *getDimstyleParentId()*, that allow you to find family members without using the postfix of the name.

Dimension Style Properties

As is the case with layers, dimension styles, even child styles, have a *Name* property. The remaining properties all correspond to the global setting of the same name. Table 6.1 includes a brief explanation of each property along with its type and information about how to access it. (See Chapter 12 for a detailed discussion of dimension settings and their effects.)

In ActiveX Automation, you cannot access the individual properties of a dimension style. To read them, you need to activate the style and then query the various global settings.

TABLE 6.1: THE DIMENSION STYLE PROPERTIES

ObjectDBX	DXF/AutoLISP	Type	Meaning
dimadec()	179	Integer	Display precision for angular dimensions.
dimalt()	170	Boolean	Defines whether alternate units (e.g., inches in addition to millimeters) are to be included in dimension labels for linear dimensions.
dimaltd()	171	Integer	Display precision for alternate units' linear dimensions.
dimaltf()	143	Real	Specifies the multiplier from dimension text in drawing units to the dimension text in alternate units.
dimaltrnd()	148	Real	Specifies the rounding value for alternate units.
dimalttd()	274	Integer	Display precision for tolerance values in alternate units of linear dimensions.
dimalttz()	286	Integer	Defines how zeros in tolerance values for alternate units are to be handled. Different values allow suppression of zero feet and/or zero inches, as well as zeros preceding and/or following the decimal delimiter.
dimaltu()	273	Integer	Display format of alternate units for linear dimensions.
dimaltz()	285	Integer	Defines how zeros in alternate units are to be handled.
dimapost()	4	String	The template for the dimension text in alternate units. Open and closed brackets ([ ]) will be replaced by the measured value in alternate units. If the placeholder for the measured value is not included, the DIMAPOST string is appended to the alternate units string.
dimasz()	41	Real	Specifies the size of arrowheads and leader line hooks.
dimatfit()	289	Integer	Defines how AutoCAD will move dimension arrows and dimension text when the dimension length does not allow placing both inside extension lines.
dimaunit()	275	Integer	Defines the display format for newly created angular dimensions. Possible values and their meaning are like those in AUNITS.
dimazin()	79	Integer	Defines how zeros in angular dimensions are to be handled. This is a combination of Boolean flags that allow you to suppress zeros preceding and/or following the decimal delimiter.

Continued

TABLE 6.1: THE DIMENSION STYLE PROPERTIES (CONTINUED)

ObjectDBX	DXF/AutoLISP	Type	Meaning
dimblk()	342, 5	Symbol table record, string	Specifies the arrowhead block to be used. ObjectDBX returns the AcDbObjectId type of the corresponding symbol table record, and DXF and AutoLISP return both the handle/entity name and the key string.
dimblk1()	343, 6	Symbol table record, string	Specifies the first (or left) arrowhead to be used when arrowheads are different. See dimblk().
dimblk2()	344, 7	Symbol table record, string	Specifies the second (or right) arrowhead to be used when arrowheads are different. See dimblk().
dimcen()	141	Real	Specifies the size and outlook of center marks drawn with radial and diagonal dimensions. The center mark is an axis-parallel cross at the arc center. If the value of dimcen() is positive, it controls the length of the cross's arms; if it is negative, its absolute value controls the length of the cross's arms, the length of a gap following the arm, and the length that the additional line extends the arc outline.
dimclrd()	176	Color	Specifies the color of dimension lines, arrows, and leader lines.
dimclre()	177	Color	Specifies the color of dimension extension lines.
dimclrt()	178	Color	Specifies the color of dimension text.
dimdec()	271	Integer	Specifies the display precision for the measured value in linear dimensions.
dimdle()	46	Length	Defines how far the dimension line should extend beyond the extension lines. This is only relevant if the selected arrowhead is either "_ArchTick", "_Oblique", "_None", or "_Integral".
dimdli()	43	Length	Specifies the spacing of baseline dimensions as well as the offset used for dimension chains if dimensions would otherwise overlap.
dimdsep()	278	Single character	Specifies the decimal delimiter used for dimensions. This is a single character in ObjectDBX, but an integer (ASCII code of the character) in DXF!
dimexe()	44	Length	Defines how far an extension line should extend beyond the dimension line.

Continued ▶

TABLE 6.1: THE DIMENSION STYLE PROPERTIES (CONTINUED)

ObjectDBX	DXF/AutoLISP	Type	Meaning
dimexo()	42	Length	Specifies the gap between the dimensioned location and the start of the extension line.
dimfrac()	276	Integer	Defines how to display fractions inside dimension text.
dimgap()	147	Real	If positive, defines the minimum gap between dimension text and dimension line; if negative, defines the offset from a dimension text to a surrounding frame box (and draws this box).
dimjust()	280	Integer	Specifies where to place the dimension text along the dimension line.
dimldrblk()	341	Symbol table record	Specifies the arrowhead to be used with leader lines. Depending on the environment, you'll get an AcDbObjectId, a handle, or an entity name.
dimlfac()	144	Real	Defines the global scale factor applied to all linear measurements, thus scaling the value shown as dimension text. The value of dimlfac() can be positive or negative. A positive value is applied to all linear dimensions. If the value is negative, the absolute of it will be applied to linear dimensions drawn in paperspace, and dimensions drawn in model space will not be scaled.
dimlim()	72	Boolean	Specifies whether the dimension text will display a single value (Adesk::kFalse, 0) or minimum and maximum measurements. If true, the maximum value will be stacked on top of the minimum value. The *dimtp()* and *dimtm()* properties are used to calculate those values.
dimlunit()	277	Integer	Defines the display format for linear dimensions.
dimlwd()	371	Lineweight	The line weight to be used for dimension lines. (See Chapter 9 for a discussion of lineweight values.)
dimlwe()	372	Lineweight	Defines the line weight to be used for extension lines.
dimpost()	3	String	Defines the template for the dimension text. The less-than and greater-than characters (< >) will be replaced by the measured value. If the placeholder for the measured value is not included, the dimpost() string will be appended to the dimension text.

Continued ▶

TABLE 6.1: THE DIMENSION STYLE PROPERTIES (CONTINUED)

ObjectDBX	DXF/AutoLISP	Type	Meaning
dimrnd()	45	Real	Defines the rounding factor for linear units. The measured value will be rounded according to this setting's value.
dimsah()	173	Boolean	Specifies whether different arrowheads should be used or not. If true (Adesk::kTrue, 1), AutoCAD uses the arrowheads defined by dimblk1() and dimblk2(); if false, AutoCAD uses dimblk() for both arrowheads.
dimscale()	40	Real	Defines the overall scale factor to be applied to all lengths used during dimension generation. This does not change the measured value or dimension text. Instead, it modifies the overall size of the dimension or leader object. If the value of dimscale() is 0.0, the inverse of the view scale is used instead.
dimsd1()	281	Boolean	If true (Adesk::kTrue, 1), suppresses the half of the dimension line next to the first extension line.
dimsd2()	282	Boolean	If true (Adesk::kTrue, 1), suppresses the half of the dimension line next to the second extension line.
dimse1()	75	Boolean	If true (Adesk::kTrue, 1), suppresses the first extension line.
dimse2()	76	Boolean	If true (Adesk::kTrue, 1), suppresses the second extension line.
dimsoxd()	175	Boolean	If true (Adesk::kTrue, 1), suppresses arrowheads if they do not fit between the extension lines.
dimtad()	77	Integer	Specifies where to place the dimension text vertical against the dimension line.
dimtdec()	272	Integer	Specifies whether to display precision for the tolerance values of linear dimensions.
dimtfac()	146	Real	Specifies the text size of tolerance values in relationship to the dimension text size.
dimtih()	73	Boolean	Specifies whether the dimension text will be horizontal (Adesk::kTrue, 1) or parallel to the dimension line. The *dimtih()* property is recognized only if the text fits between the extension lines.

Continued ▶

	TABLE 6.1: THE DIMENSION STYLE PROPERTIES (CONTINUED)		
ObjectDBX	**DXF/AutoLISP**	**Type**	**Meaning**
dimtix()	174	Boolean	Defines whether the dimension text will be forced inside the extension lines (Adesk::kTrue, 1), even if AutoCAD would normally place text and arrows outside.
dimtm()	48	Real	Defines the lower tolerance (tolerated value is up to true dimension minus dimtm() value).
dimtmove()	289	Integer	Specifies whether to add a leader arrow if the dimension text is moved away from the dimension line.
dimtofl()	172	Boolean	Specifies whether a dimension line between the extension lines will be drawn (Adesk::kTrue, 1) even when text and arrows are placed outside.
dimtoh()	74	Boolean	Specifies whether the dimension text will be horizontal (Adesk::kTrue, 1) or parallel to the dimension line. The *dimtoh()* property is recognized only if the text is placed outside.
dimtol()	71	Boolean	Specifies whether dimension tolerances are to be shown. If true (Adesk::kTrue, 1), AutoCAD adds the upper and lower tolerance to the dimension text.
dimtolj()	283	Integer	Specifies where to place the tolerance values.
dimtp()	47	Real	Defines the lower tolerance (tolerated value is up to true dimension plus dimtp() value).
dimtsz()	142	Length	Defines the size of the slash at the end of the dimension line when using an arrowhead of "_ArchTick", "_Oblique", or "_Integral".
dimtvp()	145	Length	Defines the vertical distance between dimension text center and dimension line center when *dimtad()* is zero.
dimtxsty()	340	Symbol table record	Defines the text style to be used with dimension text. As with every pointer, depending on the environment, this is an AcDbObjectId, an entity name, or a handle.
dimtxt()	140	Length	Defines the size of the dimension text.
dimtzin()	284	Integer	Defines how zeros in tolerances are to be handled.
dimzin()	78	Integer	Defines how zeros in dimension text are to be handled.

Group codes 270 (dimunit) and 287 (dimfit) are obsolete and not to be used.

User Coordinate Systems

User Coordinate Systems (UCSs) have no direct effect on any database item. They help the AutoCAD user save and restore workplanes and coordinate systems.

The AcDbUCSTable is simply a list of named coordinate systems. In AutoCAD, the user can restore any of these using its name. The AcDbViewTableRecord and AcDb-ViewportTableRecord objects refer to entries in this table to define an associated UCS to be activated with the view.

All previous comments on symbol tables apply for the UCS table as well. A named UCS is always local to a database.

The DXF class name of AcDbUCSTableRecord is "UCS". The sequence of groups is 2, 70, 10, 11, 12, 79 (constant 0), 146 (constant 0.0), 71, 13 (repeat from 71).

UCS Properties

User Coordinate Systems have the same *Name* property as layers. To define a Cartesian (that is, orthogonal) coordinate systems, you need three points/vectors:

- The origin
- The direction of the x-axis
- The direction of the y-axis

The z-axis direction is calculated as the cross-product of the two, since it is orthogonal to both.

Origin and axes are defined in world coordinates, of course. In UCS coordinates, they would always be (0,0,0), (1,0,0), and (0,1,0). The origin is a point, and the two axes are normalized vectors (of length 1).

ObjectDBX	ActiveX Automation	DXF/AutoLISP
origin()	Origin	Group 10
xAxis()	XVector	Group 11
yAxis()	YVector	Group 12

In most applications, a UCS is used to define a workspace within a larger model. Within this workspace, it is common to work in orthogonal workplanes. The *top* workplane uses the same x-, y-, and z-axes as the base coordinate system. It may, however, use a different origin. The other five workplanes are orthogonally rotated against the base UCS.

Workplane	ObjectDBX	DXF	X-axis	Y-axis
Top	kTopView	1	UCS X	UCS Y
Bottom	kBottomView	2	UCS −X	UCS Y
Front	kFrontView	3	UCS X	UCS Y
Back	kBackView	4	UCS −X	UCS Y
Left	kLeftView	5	UCS −Y	UCS Z
Right	kRightView	6	UCS Y	UCS Z

Each of these workplanes may have its own origin, thus defining the elevation above the X/Y plane in which the user is going to work and the reference point he or she will use to enter coordinates.

You can query the six workplanes' origins in ObjectDBX and DXF. In ObjectDBX, you use the *ucsBaseOrigin()* function and supply the workplane constant as a parameter. In DXF, the workplanes are listed in group 71/group 13 pairs. Group 71 contains the workplane integer, and group 13 (and its associated groups 23 and 33) contains the origin point. Groups 71 and 13 are omitted for workplanes that have the same origin as the base UCS.

Named Views

Like named coordinate systems, named views do not affect any database objects. A view defines various aspects of how the model will display on the screen or on paper.

For two-dimensional drawings, a view usually defines the view center and the view area. For three-dimensional drawings, a view defines the view direction, a perspective, the clipping planes, and more. Remember that an AutoCAD drawing database is always three-dimensional. We will look at the details of a view definition in the discussion of the AcDbViewport entity, which defines a view on a layout sheet. (See Chapter 17.)

The AcDbViewTable is simply a list of named views. In AutoCAD, the user can restore any of these using its name. All previous comments on symbol tables also apply to the view table. Named views are always local to a database.

In ObjectDBX, an AcDbViewTableRecord is subclassed from AcDbAbstractViewTableRecord. This is not visible in the other environments.

The DXF class name of AcDbViewTableRecord is "VIEW". The sequence of groups is 2, 70, 40, 10, 41, 11, 12, 42, 43, 44, 50, 71, 281, 72, 110, 111, 112, 346, 79, 146.

View Properties

Views have the same *Name* property as layers. AutoCAD remembers if a named view is supposed to display a view of the model or a view of a layout sheet. There is no technical difference between the two other than that AutoCAD switches to the corresponding space before showing the view.

ObjectDBX	ActiveX Automation	DXF/AutoLISP
isPaperspaceView()	n/a	First bit (1) of group 70

A view table record primarily defines an abstract view into the model, which is a 2D projection of drawing entities. (See Chapter 17 for information on how to define an abstract view.) With each named view, you'll find the following view parameters.

ObjectDBX	ActiveX Automation	DXF/AutoLISP
target()	Target	Group 12
viewDirection()	Direction	Group 11
perspectiveEnabled()	n/a	First bit (1) of group 71
centerPoint()	Center	Group 10
height()	Height	Group 40
width()	Width	Group 41
viewTwist()	n/a	Group 50
lensLength()	n/a	Group 42
frontClipDistance()	n/a	Group 43
frontClipEnabled()	n/a	Second bit (2) of group 71
frontClipAtEye()	n/a	Inverse of fifth bit (16) of group 71
backClipDistance()	n/a	Group 44
backClipEnabled()	n/a	Third bit (3) of group 71
renderMode()	n/a	Group 281
isUcsAssociatedToView()	n/a	First bit (1) of group 72
UcsName()	n/a	Group 346
IsUcsOrthographic()	n/a	Group 79
getUcs(), origin	n/a	Group 110
getUcs(), xAxis	n/a	Group 111
getUcs(), yAxis	n/a	Group 112
elevation()	n/a	Group 146

The Viewports Table

AcDbViewportTableRecord objects are similar to named views. They should not be confused with AcDbViewport entities, even though AutoCAD calls both of them viewports.

Just like an AcDbViewTableRecord, a viewport table record defines an abstract view. In addition, the viewport table record defines some visual aids, such as grid and snaps, that become available to the AutoCAD user as soon as he or she activates the viewport.

The AcDbViewportTable is the only symbol table with non-unique key strings. Several viewport table records can share the same key string and, therefore, form a so-called *viewport configuration*.

If an AutoCAD user recalls a viewport configuration, the program divides the drawing's modelspace view into the corresponding number of *viewports*. Each viewport acts like a small screen on its own, displaying a different view to the model and different visual aids.

The viewports in a viewport configuration must be *tiled*. This means that they must cover the whole modelspace view area and must not overlap. This is the main difference between viewports and the AcDbViewport entities discussed in Chapter 17, which are located on a layout sheet, may be separated from each other, and may overlap.

A viewport configuration can consist of as many as 16 viewport table records. Every drawing database must have at least one viewport configuration called "*ACTIVE*", which, in turn, must contain at least one viewport table record.

Again, I'll cover the details of the abstract view definition in the discussion of the AcDbViewport entity in Chapter 17.

Named views are always local to a database. In ObjectDBX, an AcDbViewport-TableRecord is subclassed from AcDbAbstractViewTableRecord. This is not visible in the other environments.

The DXF class name of AcDbViewportTableRecord is "VPORT". The sequence of groups is 2, 70, 10, 11, 12, 13, 14, 15, 16, 17, 40, 41, 42, 43, 44, 50, 51, 71, 72, 73, 74, 75, 76, 77, 78, 281, 65, 110, 111, 112, 346, 79, 146.

Viewport Properties

Although viewports also have a *Name* property, it is not unique. Viewports that share the same name form a viewport configuration. You need to iterate through the viewport table to find all viewports that make one configuration. The name "*ACTIVE*" exists at least once.

Like a named view, a viewport table record defines an abstract view into the model. (See Chapter 17 for information on how to define an abstract view.) With each named view, you'll find the following view parameters.

NOTE Some parameters and many group numbers differ from an AcDbViewTable-Record definition.

ObjectDBX	ActiveX Automation	DXF/AutoLISP
target()	Target	Group 17
viewDirection()	Direction	Group 16
perspectiveEnabled()	n/a	First bit (1) of group 71
centerPoint()	Center	Group 12
height()	Height	Group 40
width()	Width	Group 41. See the note following this list.
viewTwist()	n/a	Group 51
lensLength()	n/a	Group 42
frontClipDistance()	n/a	Group 43
frontClipEnabled()	n/a	Second bit (2) of group 71
frontClipAtEye()	n/a	Inverse of fifth bit (16) of group 71
backClipDistance()	n/a	Group 44
backClipEnabled()	n/a	Third bit (3) of group 71
renderMode()	n/a	Group 281
isUcsSavedWithViewport()	n/a	First bit (1) of group 65
UcsName()	n/a	Group 346
IsUcsOrthographic()	n/a	Group 79
getUcs(), origin	n/a	Group 110
getUcs(), xAxis	n/a	Group 111
getUcs(), yAxis	n/a	Group 112
elevation()	n/a	Group 146

 NOTE A viewport's *Width* property does *not* contain the viewport width. Instead, it contains the proportion of viewport height and width.

In addition to these view parameters, a viewport table record also has several other properties.

A viewport is located on the screen. Each viewport covers a fixed rectangular screen area. Lower-left and upper-right corners of this rectangle are expressed in screen coordinates. The lower-left corner of the available screen area (in AutoCAD 2000, this is the Model tab) has the coordinates 0,0. The upper-right corner has the coordinates 1,1.

Therefore, both coordinates of the viewport's screen location are between 0.0 and 1.0. Remember that all viewports in a viewport configuration together must completely use the area 0,0 to 1,1. Both viewport corners are 2D points (AcGePoint2d).

ObjectDBX	ActiveX Automation	DXF/AutoLISP
lowerLeftCorner()	LowerLeftCorner	Group 10
upperRightCorner()	UpperRightCorner	Group 11

A viewport can be set to automatically follow any UCS changes applied. If this flag is set, the viewport always display the plan (or top) view of the current UCS.

ObjectDBX	ActiveX Automation	DXF/AutoLISP
ucsFollowMode()	n/a	Fourth bit (8) of group 71

The following two properties are from the era when computers were too slow to even display a small drawing fast enough. Fast zooms are always enabled today, which is why this flag is always set in any database created by AutoCAD 2000. The *Detailing* property defines at which level small gaps, for example, in linetypes, should be ignored. It also defines how many straight vectors are used to approximate circles and other curves on the screen.

This integer is a percentage. At 100 (percent), AutoCAD displays circles perfectly round at the current view scale. A value of 200 creates more vectors so that even at a 200% magnification the circle still looks perfectly round. This property's value is in the range 1 through 20.000.

ObjectDBX	ActiveX Automation	DXF/AutoLISP
fastZoomsEnabled()	n/a	First bit (1) of group 73
circleSides()	ArcSmoothness	Group 72

Each viewport can display the UCS icon, which helps the user to understand the current orientation for the coordinate system. As an additional aid, this UCS icon can be set to display itself at the UCS origin, as long as the origin is within the viewport.

ObjectDBX	ActiveX Automation	DXF/AutoLISP
iconEnabled()	UCSIconOn	First bit (1) of group 74
iconAtOrigin()	UCSIconAtOrigin	Second bit (2) of group 74

Another visual construction aid is the drawing grid, which is an array of dots with different spacing in X and Y directions. The grid spacing is a 2D point in ObjectDBX and DXF/AutoLISP. The grid can be turned on and off.

The grid is always shown in the current X/Y plane; however, it does not cover the entire plane. The grid is limited to the rectangle bounded by the LIMMIN and LIMMAX global settings (in layouts, the PLIMMIN and PLIMMAX settings). The grid rows follow the orientation set by the snap angle and start at the snap origin (see below).

ObjectDBX	ActiveX Automation	DXF/AutoLISP
gridEnabled()	GridOn	First bit (1) of group 76
gridIncrements()	GetGridSpacing	Group 15

The grid dots are simply a visual aid. They don't affect any coordinate input. A second setting, called *snap,* is used to limit coordinate input. If a snap grid is active, coordinate input with the mouse is only possible in specific increments.

The snap grid starts at the snap origin, a 2D point relative to the current UCS. Snap rows follow the orientation set by the snap angle. The *Snap Spacing* property contains the spacing of snap points along the rows and columns of the snap grid.

Snap grids can be orthographic or isometric. In this case, the horizontal rows and vertical columns (or snap pairs) follow certain orientations that allow the user to draw easily within the specified isometric plane. The following planes exist.

Isometric Plane	Code	Horizontal	Vertical
Left	0	30°	90°
Top	1	30°	150°
Right	2	150°	90°

Both ObjectDBX and DXF/AutoLISP use these codes.

ObjectDBX	ActiveX Automation	DXF/AutoLISP
snapEnabled()	SnapOn	First bit (1) of group 75
snapIncrements()	GetSnapSpacing	Group 14
snapBase()	SnapBasePoint	Group 13
snapAngle()	SnapRotationAngle	Group 50
isometricSnapEnabled()	n/a	First bit (1) of group 77
snapPair()	n/a	Group 78

Registered Applications

This last symbol table is easy to understand. The AcDbRegAppTable is simply a list of names. It contains the application shortcuts used to associate an object's xdata with a specific owner.

If any object contains xdata, the corresponding shortcut must be listed in an AcDbRegAppTableRecord.

All previous comments about symbol tables apply to the RegApp table as well. Application names are always local to a database.

The DXF class name of AcDbRegAppTableRecord is "APPID". The sequence of groups is 2, 70.

In addition to the unreliable seventh bit of group 70, the only property of interest is the *Name* or key string.

ObjectDBX	ActiveX Automation	DXF/AutoLISP
getName()	Name	Group 2

Every AutoCAD drawing database contains at least one RegApp table record with the name "ACAD".

Summary

The symbol tables of an AutoCAD drawing database and the record objects contained therein do not define any visible part of the drawing; however, they define if and how the visible parts display. Understanding and implementing symbol table records correctly is, therefore, essential for a correct display and plot of a drawing entity.

The layer table defines whether an entity is to display and, in some cases, which properties it is to use. The linetype table defines how center lines, hidden lines, and broken lines should display. The textstyle and dimension style tables define, to a great extent, how annotations will appear on the screen and on paper. Other tables, such as the UCS, view, and viewport tables, simply provide settings that an AutoCAD user can restore later. They do not affect the actual drawing display. The last table is only a list of third-party applications that have saved custom data with one or more database objects.

The next chapter covers additional objects without a visual representation.

CHAPTER 7

Objects without a Visual Representation— Part II

FEATURING

Objects in DXF   *161*

Dictionaries   *161*

Placeholders   *164*

Variables   *164*

Groups   *166*

The entity order index   *167*

Spatial and layer indexes   *169*

Extension records   *171*

I n addition to symbol tables, the AutoCAD drawing database consists of entities (which have a visual representation) and non-entities (which don't have a visual representation). Non-entities are usually called *objects*, which is a bit strange since all other database items are objects as well.

AutoCAD itself is highly oriented to visual representation. Therefore, a plain Auto-CAD drawing database contains few non-entities. Even those few that exist are usually closely related to a specific type of entity, which is why I'll describe them in later chapters together with their parent entities:

- AcDbPlotStyles along with other properties common to all entities
- AcDbMlineStyle objects along with AcDbMline entities
- AcDbPlotSettings and AcDbLayout objects along with other layout-related entities
- AcDbRasterImageDef, AcDbRasterVariables, and AcDbRasterImageDefReactor objects along with bitmap images
- AcDbFilter (AcDbLayerFilter and AcDbSpatialFilter) objects along with block insertions

This reduces the list of AutoCAD-generated non-entities to the following, which I'll cover in this chapter:

- AcDbDictionary
- AcDbDictionaryWithDefault
- DictionaryVariables
- AcDbGroup
- AcDbIndex (AcDbLayerIndex, AcDbIdBuffer, and AcDbSpatialIndex)
- AcDbSortentsTable, AcDbXrecord, and a strange thing called AcDbPlaceHolder

I'll discuss one more non-graphics object in Chapter 19. An AutoCAD drawing file may contain embedded VBA macros. Since everything in an AutoCAD database file is an AcDbObject, so are embedded VBA projects. The corresponding class is called AcDb-VbaProject.

Keep in mind that an AutoCAD drawing database may contain many more object classes. Every developer of AutoCAD add-ons and, in fact, every AutoCAD user is allowed to create their own objects and add them to a database.

Objects in DXF

As you already know, the serialized version of the drawing database (DXF) uses brackets to create containers. All non-entities in a drawing database are in their own container. The objects section of a DXF file starts with

```
0
SECTION
2
OBJECTS
```

and ends with

```
0
ENDSEC
```

Within this section and only in this section will you find non-entities. The first entry in this section is the root dictionary, also called the named object dictionary.

Dictionaries Summarized

Since I discussed dictionaries in the first part of this book, I'll just summarize the topic here. A dictionary is an AcDbObject like any other and, therefore, has all AcDbObject properties such as handle, owner, and xdata.

 NOTE The root dictionary has no owner; however, you will find a null value (0) in DXF.

The DXF class name for dictionaries is "DICTIONARY", and the subclass name is "AcDb-Dictionary". The sequence of DXF groups is 280, 281, 3, 350/360 (repeat from 3).

The Contents of a Dictionary

A dictionary is a list of pairs, and each pair consists of a key string (*Name*) and an object reference. A dictionary always owns the objects it references, which means that you cannot delete the dictionary without deleting the referenced objects.

This ownership can be hard or soft. If ownership is hard, you cannot delete the referenced object unless you first remove the reference from the dictionary. In most cases, objects should not exist without a corresponding entry in a dictionary, except for objects owned by other objects. Therefore, dictionary references are usually hard ownership references.

In DXF, hard ownership references in dictionaries use group code 360; soft ownership references use group code 350. But even soft ownership references may sometimes need the same treatment as hard ownership references. This is necessary in some cases when a dictionary is cloned into another database and should take its entries with it, even those to which it has only soft ownership references. Therefore, a separate flag indicates whether the entries in a dictionary should be treated as being hard-owned even though they are not.

Depending on the environment you work in, you'll find this flag in group 280 or by using the *isTreatElementsAsHard()* function. This property is not available to ActiveX Automation.

ObjectDBX	ActiveX Automation	DXF/AutoLISP
isTreatElementsAsHard()	n/a	Group 280

To read a dictionary's contents, you iterate through the dictionary as described in Chapter 2. In DXF, for instance, you read the key string in group 3 and then the following reference.

In ObjectDBX and ActiveX Automation, you can directly query the object associated with a specific key string using the *getAt()* function in ObjectDBX or the *GetObject* method in ActiveX Automation. Both environments also provide the number of entries in a dictionary as a calculated property:

ObjectDBX	ActiveX Automation	DXF/AutoLISP
numEntries()	Count	n/a

Merging Dictionaries

If two databases merge, a dictionary in each database may be using the same key string. To solve this problem, every dictionary has a separate group indicating what to do when databases merge.

ObjectDBX	ActiveX Automation	DXF/AutoLISP
mergeStyle()	n/a	Group 281

These are the possible values:

ObjectDBX	DXF / AutoLISP	Meaning
kDrcNotApplicable	0	Not applicable
kDrcIgnore	1	Keep the existing dictionary
kDrcReplace	2	Use the new dictionary

ObjectDBX	DXF / AutoLISP	Meaning
kDrcXrefMangleName	3	Rename the new dictionary's key string to *<database name>$<number>$<key string>*
kDrcMangleName	4	Rename the new dictionary's key string to *$<number>$<key string>*

The Minimum Contents of the Root Dictionary

Every drawing database contains a root dictionary that must contain at least four entries:

1. The key string `"ACAD_GROUP"`, which references a directory that may be empty

2. The key string `"ACAD_MLINESTYLE"`, which references a directory that contains at least one entry with the key string `"Standard"` referencing an AcDbMlineStyle object

3. The key string `"ACAD_LAYOUT"`, which references a directory that may be empty

4. The key string `"ACAD_PLOTSTYLENAME"`, which references a directory that may be empty

Dictionaries with Default

The AcDbDictionaryWithDefault object is subclassed from AcDbDictionary. This means that all properties for dictionaries, including the key/reference table, also apply to this object. Remember that in DXF you'll see the AcDbObject properties first, followed by a subclass marker (group 100), the AcDbDictionary properties, and following another subclass marker, the AcDbDictionaryWithDefault properties.

The DXF class name for this object type is `"ACDBDICTIONARYWDFLT"`. There is no DXF sequence because there is only one group code, 340, for this object.

The AcDbDictionaryWithDefault class adds only one more property to a dictionary: a default object.

ObjectDBX	ActiveX Automation	DXF/AutoLISP
defaultId()	n/a	Group 340

The default is a hard pointer (that is, this reference is deleted as soon as the referenced object is deleted) to an AcDbObject, which translates to an entity name or a handle.

Placeholder Objects

Dictionaries always contain a list of keys and object references, which creates a problem: Any object can refer only to the dictionary as a whole, not to an individual record. Therefore, if an object wants to reference another object contained in a dictionary, it has two choices: (1) it must refer to the dictionary and provide the key string, or (2) it must refer directly to the individual object.

The AcDbMline entity, for example, uses the first method and refers to the corresponding AcDbMlineStyle object. Thus, every multiline entity includes the key string of the associated style. The method for accessing the correct dictionary is hard-coded.

The AcDbRasterImage entity, on the other hand, uses the second method and refers to the corresponding AcDbRasterImageDef object. Thus, every raster image reference directly accesses the associated object, bypassing any dictionary in which it may be contained.

Now, how do you access only a key string? Any AcDbEntity object contains a *Plot Style* property. The plot style is a key string, but the corresponding style definition is *not* part of the drawing database. You could save the key string with every object (as AutoCAD does for the *Layer* and *Linetype* properties), but this would take up a lot of space and make it difficult to rename a style later.

Therefore, the AutoCAD developers introduced a dummy object, an AcDbPlaceHolder object. This placeholder has no functionality other than to point back to the directory in which it is contained. From this directory, you can then query the object's key string using the *nameAt()* function or the *GetName* method.

Although this sounds complicated at first, it offers some benefits. If Autodesk later decides to create a plot style object, you could use it instead of the placeholder while leaving the rest of the data structure intact.

The AcDbPlaceHolder object has no properties other than the AcDbObject properties. One of the AcDbObject properties is the *Owner* property, which points back to the dictionary that contained the placeholder.

The DXF class name of this object type is `"ACDBPLACEHOLDER"`.

Drawing Variables

You will remember that a drawing database contains non-objects, the global settings. While thinking about dictionaries, you might wonder, Why isn't the list of settings just a dictionary? And you'd be right. It would be possible to use a dictionary for settings if there were an object to take the setting's value. This object is called Dictionary-Variables.

The main problem with a unified object for all settings' values is that these values are of different types, which seems to be why Autodesk introduced dictionary variables with AutoCAD Release 14 but ignored them in AutoCAD 2000.

One benefit of dictionary variables is that you can easily add additional settings without changing the database file format. Autodesk did so in maintenance releases of AutoCAD Release 14.

Global Settings Saved As Variables

In AutoCAD 2000, only four settings are saved as dictionary variables:

Name	Meaning
PROJECTNAME	Defines the name of a project. Associated with this name but not in the drawing database, AutoCAD keeps the name of a directory in which AutoCAD tries to find externally referenced drawings and raster images.
INDEXCTL	Specifies whether AutoCAD should create spatial and layer indexes saved in the drawing. This is a bit-coded value with the first bit (1) set if a layer index will be created and the second bit (2) set if a spatial index will be created. (I'll discuss these indexes later in this chapter.)
SORTENTS	Specifies when AutoCAD should use an entity order defined by an AcDbSortentsTable object. The bits in this bit-coded value are as follows: the first bit (1) uses the table for object selection, the second bit (2) uses the table for object snap, the third bit (4) uses the table for redraws, the forth bit (8) uses the table for slide creation, the fifth bit (16) uses the table for drawing regeneration, the sixth bit (32) uses the table for plot output, and the seventh bit (64) uses the table for PostScript output.
XCLIPFRAME	Specifies whether AutoCAD should display the clipping border of externally referenced drawings. This is a Boolean value.

Locating the Dictionary Variables

To locate the value of a dictionary variable, you start with the root dictionary. The key string `"AcDbVariableDictionary"` refers to a second dictionary. Within this second dictionary, you'll find the variable names as key strings. Associated with each key string is a DictionaryVariables object that contains the setting's value.

DictionaryVariable Objects

The DictionaryVariables object contains only two properties. One is called *Object Schema Number*, which is always set to 0 and is undocumented.

The other property is the setting's value.

ObjectDBX	ActiveX Automation	DXF/AutoLISP
n/a	n/a	Group 1

The DXF class name for DictionaryVariables objects is `"DICTIONARYVAR"`.

Entity Groups

Geometric entities are always part of one and only one block container. This groups all entities within one container together. In addition, you might want to create smaller groups that contain only a few entities that can then be moved or manipulated together. This is the purpose of the AcDbGroup object.

An AcDbGroup object creates a logical connection between entities. The entities referenced by a group should reside in the same block container, although it is possible to group modelspace and paperspace objects together. In addition, a group has a few properties that specify certain actions on this group.

Locating a Group

To locate a certain AcDbGroup object, you start at the root dictionary. The key string `"ACAD_GROUP"` points to a directory that contains one entry for every group defined.

The key string of each entry is the group name as selected by the AutoCAD user. Groups considered *unnamed* in the AutoCAD dialog boxes use an artificial name here.

The dictionary entry then points to an AcDbGroup object that contains references to the entities enclosed in the group as well as to other properties.

The DXF class name for AcDbGroup objects is `"GROUP"`. The DXF sequence is 300, 70, 71, 340 (repeated).

AcDbGroup Objects

Groups have a name and a description. The group name is its key string from the parent dictionary and is not saved with the AcDbGroup objects. However, both ObjectDBX and ActiveX Automation provide the group name as a calculated property. The group description is an arbitrary comment string that may further explain the group's usage.

ObjectDBX	ActiveX Automation	DXF/AutoLISP
name()	Name	n/a
description()	n/a	Group 300

Groups have two Boolean flags: one flag indicates whether the group has been named by the user or was created unnamed. The other flag indicates whether selecting one group member automatically selects the whole group.

ObjectDBX	ActiveX Automation	DXF/AutoLISP
isAnonymous()	n/a	First bit (1) of group 70
isSelectable()	n/a	First bit (1) of group 71

The main part of an AcDbGroup object is the list of group members. Each member is referenced by a hard pointer.

ObjectDBX	ActiveX Automation	DXF/AutoLISP
getIndex()	Item	Group 340

The AcDbGroup object has to react whenever one of its members is deleted, selected, or changed. Therefore, a reference to the AcDbGroup object is saved in the ACAD_ REACTORS area of the member entities. A member can belong to more than one group.

ObjectDBX and ActiveX Automation provide the number of member entities in a group as a calculated property:

ObjectDBX	ActiveX Automation	DXF/AutoLISP
numEntries()	Count	n/a

 NOTE ActiveX Automation offers write-only properties such as *Layer* or *Linetype* for AcDbGroup objects. This is simply a shortcut that sets the appropriate property for all members of this group.

The Entity Order Index

The AutoCAD drawing database has an implicit order. Because each object has a handle and because handles are integers that are sequentially allocated, the handle order represents the order in which objects and entities were created.

Objects may be required to draw themselves in an order different from their creation sequence. For instance, you might want a text object to redraw and plot on top of (that is, later than) an underlying filled area. To define a specific entity order, use the AcDbSortentsTable.

The DXF class name for AcDbSortentsTable objects is "SORTENTSTABLE". The DXF sequence is 330, 331, 5 (repeat from 331). This class contains a group 5 in addition to the same number group in the AcDbObject section of this object.

Locating a Block's Entity Order Table

AcDbSortentsTable objects are not owned by the root dictionary. Instead, they are owned by their block's extension dictionary.

To locate an AcDbSortentsTable object, you start with the AcDbBlockTableRecord of the block whose entity order you want. This block's extension dictionary contains a key string of "ACAD_SORTENTS", which points to the corresponding AcDbSortentsTable object.

AcDbSortentsTable Objects

An entity order table is a list of object reference pairs. Each entity from the parent block has one entry, indexed with its AcDbObjectID. In DXF, this is the object's handle in group 331. The handles of all these objects are considered arbitrary 64-bit integers and are assigned to their objects again, however, in a different order.

The object at the bottom of the sort order, that is, the object to draw or use first, will get the smallest 64-bit integer. This means this object's reference will be associated with the smallest handle of all entities in the block. The next object in the sort order will be associated with the second smallest handle and so on. The object to be drawn on top of all others is associated with the largest of the 64-bit integers in the list.

The associated number (in DXF group 5) is in no way related to the object that has this number as its handle. The programmer simply used the only existing method to add 64-bit integers to the drawing database.

ObjectDBX	ActiveX Automation	DXF/AutoLISP
n/a	n/a	Group 331
n/a	n/a	Group 5

In addition, the AcDbSortentsTable object has a pointer back to the AcDbBlockTableRecord object with which it is associated.

ObjectDBX	ActiveX Automation	DXF/AutoLISP
n/a	n/a	Group 330

Spatial and Layer Indexes

Like every other database system, AutoCAD can maintain indexes of the database records to improve speed. To save space, these indexes are only filed out to DWG and DXF if the user explicitly requests them.

AutoCAD indexes entities according to their *Layer* property, according to their location in space, or according to both their *Layer* and their location in space. Like the entity order, indexes are specific to an AcDbBlockTableRecord object and can be found using the "ACAD_INDEX" key string in the block table record's extension dictionary. This key refers to a dictionary with artificial key strings pointing to the layer and spatial indexes.

Both AcDbLayerIndex and AcDbSpatialIndex objects are derived from a common AcDbIndex class.

The AcDbIndex Class

The AcDbIndex class is the parent class for both layer and spatial indexes. Because the AcDbIndex class is never output to DXF on its own, it has no DXF class name. AcDb-Index properties are only output as part of the subclass scheme for AcDbLayerIndex and AcDbSpatialIndex objects.

The AcDbIndex object has three properties, but only one of them is filed out using group code 40. The *Last Updated* property is of type AcDbDate, which is a real number in DXF and AutoLISP.

ObjectDBX	ActiveX Automation	DXF/AutoLISP
lastUpdatedAt()	n/a	Group 40

During an AutoCAD session, it may be important to know whether an index is still up-to-date. Therefore, ObjectDBX supplies a Boolean flag that indicates the index's currency. In DXF and DWG, the index is always up-to-date.

ObjectDBX	ActiveX Automation	DXF/AutoLISP
isUptoDate()	n/a	n/a

As a calculated property, the AcDbIndex object returns the AcDbBlockTableRecord with which it is associated.

ObjectDBX	ActiveX Automation	DXF/AutoLISP
objectBeingIndexedId()	n/a	n/a

Spatial Indexes

The spatial index of a block container is a tree structure to locate entities by their geometric extents. The format of this tree structure is not documented, which is why I can only describe how the spatial index appears in a DXF file. While working in ObjectDBX, you can use functions such as *seek()* and *next()* to traverse the index tree interactively.

The AcDbSpatialIndex class is subclassed from the AcDbIndex class, which means that the AcDbSpatialIndex object also lists all AcDbIndex properties. The object's DXF class name is "SPATIAL_INDEX".

A DXF output of a spatial index consists of six groups 40, a group 90 followed by groups 330, another group 90 followed by groups 310, and a single group 1. The six groups 40 define the transformation from 64-bit floating-point coordinates to integer coordinates used in the index tree.

The first group 90 contains the number of entities that don't have a geometric extent or whose extent is unknown to AutoCAD. The handles of these objects follow in the 330 groups.

The remainder of the AcDbSpatialIndex data is the binary dump of the index tree. It starts with a group 90 that contains the total number of bytes in the tree, followed by multiple binary chunks of group 310. The tree data ends with a group 1 that contains the string "END ACDBSPATIALINDEX BINARY DATA".

Layer Indexes

The layer index provides a fast way to access all entities associated with a specific layer. Like AcDbSpatialIndex, AcDbLayerIndex is also subclassed from AcDbIndex. And like spatial indexes, layer indexes are also used interactively inside ObjectDBX with *seek()* and *next()* functions.

The DXF class name for AcDbLayerIndex is "LAYER_INDEX". It contains a repeated list of groups 8, 360, and 90. The group 8 value is the name of a layer. There is one group 8 for every layer symbol table record.

Following the group 8 is a group 360, which is a hard owner reference to an AcDb-IdBuffer. This buffer contains a list of all entities that reference this specific layer. The final group 90 contains the number of entities listed in the AcDbIdBuffer object.

Object Lists

The AcDbIdBuffer object is simply a list of object references. Even though an AcDb-LayerIndex object contains hard ownership references to its AcDbIdBuffer objects, the *Owner* property of the AcDbIdBuffer objects is null (0).

The DXF class name for AcDbIdBuffer is "ACDBIDBUFFER". It contains repeated groups 330, each pointing to an entity.

Extension Records

The extension record object AcDbXrecord is a container for arbitrary data. It provides a more flexible way to attach application-specific information to a drawing database than xdata.

Extension records are usually associated with a specific entity in the database. To associate an entity and an xrecord, you'll add a reference to the AcDbXrecord object to the entity's extension dictionary. In ActiveX Automation, there is an *AddXRecord* method with each dictionary to do exactly this.

Since an entity's extension dictionary can reference multiple AcDbXrecord objects, it is important to use an identifying key string that describes both the application program this record belongs to and the record's contents.

Since AcDbXrecords can contain as much as 2GB of arbitrary data, they are difficult to handle in ObjectDBX and ActiveX Automation. In ObjectDBX, you use the *setFromRbChain()* and *RbChain()* functions, which operate on linked lists of result buffers. In ActiveX Automation, you use the *GetXRecordData* and *SetXRecordData* methods, which take two arrays of group codes and values as arguments. These arrays must be passed as variants.

An AcDbXrecord object can contain any groups between 1 and 369 in any sequence. The same group code can be used multiple times at different locations in the AcDbXRecord object. It's totally up to the application that created this record to understand and evaluate the groups.

Depending on the group code the corresponding group value must be:

From	To	Data Type
1	4	Text
5	5	Object handle
6	9	Text
10	17	Point or vector
38	49	Real
50	59	Angle
60	79	16-bit integer
90	99	32-bit integer
102	102	Text
105	105	Object handle
110	119	Point or vector
140	149	Real
170	179	16-bit integer

From	To	Data Type
210	219	Point or vector
270	279	16-bit integer
280	289	8-bit integer
300	309	Text
310	319	Binary chunk
320	329	Object ID
330	339	Soft pointer ID
340	349	Hard pointer ID
350	359	Soft owner ID
360	369	Hard owner ID

Groups 5 and 105 need to contain a valid handle string, and groups 320 to 369 contain object references that are a handle, an entity name, or an AcDbObjectId, depending on the environment.

Other group codes may be allowed, but their data type is undefined. In Object-DBX, you can call the *acdbGroupCodeToType()* function to convert between group codes and database types.

Merging Extension Records

The main purpose of extension records is to add application-specific data to an object by using its extension dictionary.

If two databases are merged, extension records may conflict. For example, suppose an extension dictionary is attached to the AcDbLayerTable object of a database. Within this dictionary, a key string points to an extension record. Now suppose a second database is merged into this database, which also has the same key string in the AcDbLayerTable object's extension dictionary, but a different extension record contents. Which one wins?

To solve this problem, every extension record starts with a group 280 that defines the merge strategy.

ObjectDBX	ActiveX Automation	DXF/AutoLISP
mergeStyle()	n/a	group 280

These are the possible values:

ObjectDBX	DXF/AutoLISP	Meaning
kDrcNotApplicable	0	Not applicable
kDrcIgnore	1	Keep the existing record

ObjectDBX	DXF/AutoLISP	Meaning
kDrcReplace	2	Use the new record
kDrcXrefMangleName	3	Rename the new record's key string to *\<database name\>$\<number\>$\<key string\>*
kDrcMangleName	4	Rename the new record's key string to *$\<number\>$\<key string\>*

In case you wonder how this property relates to the corresponding property of the extension dictionary, the extension record's property is designed to overwrite the dictionary's property so that application developers can individually specify what to do with their extension record.

Drawing Properties

One example for the use of extension records is the drawing properties record. If a user has added drawing properties to a database using the corresponding AutoCAD functions, this data ends up in an AcDbXRecord object.

To access the drawing properties, you use the root dictionary and access the extension record associated with the "DWGPROPS" key string. This extension record includes the following groups:

Group Code	Type	Contents
280	Integer	Generic duplicate records flag
1	String	Constant "DWGPROPS COOKIE"
2	String	Drawing title
3	String	Drawing subject
4	String	Drawing author
6	String	Drawing comment
7	String	Drawing keywords
8	String	Name of the user who last saved the drawing
9	String	Revision number (not filled by AutoCAD)
300–309	String	User-selectable drawing property 1 to 10
40	Elapsed time	Accumulated editing time in days

Group Code	Type	Contents
41	Date and time	Creation date and time (Julian date of local time zone)
42	Date and time	Date and time of last modification (Julian date of local time zone)
1	String	Hyperlink base address
90	Integer	The number of user-selectable drawing properties

The user-selectable drawing properties are saved as strings created from the property name, an equals sign (=), and the property value. If no names or values are assigned to these properties, they are still saved as a simple equals sign.

Layer Filters

Another use of an AcDbXrecord by AutoCAD is as a user-defined layer filter. This has nothing to do with the AcDbLayerFilter object. Instead, these layer filters are used to simplify the display of long layer lists within AutoCAD's user interface. Using layer lists, a user can choose to list, for example, only those layers whose names start with *Floor1*, only red layers, or all layers that have been turned off.

The user-defined layer lists are attached to the AcDbLayerTable object using an extension dictionary. Within this dictionary, you'll find a key, `"ACAD_LAYERFILTER"`, pointing to another dictionary. Within this second dictionary are the names of the user-defined layer filters. Each name is linked to an AcDbXrecord object containing the following groups:

Group Code	Type	Contents
280	Integer	Generic duplicate records flag
1	String	User-defined name (duplicated from dictionary key)
1	String	Layer name filter (regular expression)
1	String	Layer color filter (regular expression)
1	String	Layer linetype filter (regular expression)
70	16-bit integer	Layer flags filter (Boolean combination)
1	String	Layer lineweight filter (regular expression)
1	String	Layer plotstyle filter (regular expression)

A regular expression is a string according to AutoCAD's wildcard matching strategy, for example, *Floor1** or *Floor[12]-Walls* or *Hidden,Center*.

Summary

When Autodesk first designed the drawing database, it consisted of three containers: one for graphical objects, one for symbol table records, and one for drawing settings. Later, the developers at Autodesk found that there were other objects to store in a drawing database that did not fit in any of these. For instance, the drawing properties aren't graphical objects, they aren't drawing settings, and they do not fit into a symbol table either. Thus, Autodesk introduced a fourth container.

As you have seen in this chapter, this fourth container is a collection of dictionaries that in turn reference many different types of objects. Every database object that is not graphic and that is not a symbol table record goes into a dictionary.

As with symbol tables, the objects referenced by dictionaries do not create any visualization on the screen, but they may affect how entities display or how AutoCAD handles them. Examples of this are the entity sorting order and the spatial index. We will come back to nongraphical objects in later chapters in which you'll learn about other classes that directly interact with special kinds of visual entities.

The next chapter starts our discussion of the most complex type of object within the drawing database, the AcDbEntity.

CHAPTER **8**

Organization of Drawing Entities

FEATURING

Block containers 178

The block table 178

Layout blocks 181

External references 182

Block Begin and Block End objects 183

DXF representation of block containers 184

So far we have looked at the basic organization of the AutoCAD drawing database and the various ways to access it. We have looked in detail at the global settings, the symbol tables, and the objects contained in dictionaries, but you still haven't seen a single line on a drawing.

In the remainder of this book, I'll describe all the objects in a drawing database that have a visual representation. These objects are called *entities*; however, not every entity contained in a drawing database will be visible on the screen or in print. It may belong to a frozen or off layer, it may be explicitly set as invisible, or it may simply be part of an entity container that is not referenced anywhere.

This chapter deals with how you organize entities into block containers, it helps you find out which database entities are referenced.

Block Containers

Every entity belongs to one and only one block container, but a drawing database can contain any number of block containers. Block containers may be local to the drawing database or may reference a block container that is in an external drawing database. In the latter case, the block container is called an *external reference* or *xref*, for short. An external reference contains the name and filename of the external database.

A local block container is a sequential, that is, unordered, list of the drawing entities that it contains, and it can contain any number of entities. Only entities can be in a block container.

The two types of local block containers are layout and non-layout. Layout blocks are block containers that AutoCAD displays directly on the screen or on paper. Auto-CAD itself does not display non-layouts unless they are referenced by a layout block. Other software, however, can display or interact with non-layout blocks.

The Block Table

The AcDbBlockTable object owns all block containers, local or external. The block table works the same as a symbol table and identifies itself as AcDbSymbolTable, except in DXF. I'll cover the quite complex DXF representation of block containers in the last section of this chapter.

Like any other symbol table, the block table consists of symbol table records. In the block table, they are of type AcDbBlockTableRecord.

An AcDbBlockTableRecord object has a couple of properties. The primary property is the *Name* or key string.

ObjectDBX	ActiveX Automation	DXF/AutoLISP
getName()	Name	Group 2

Every block table record has an *Origin* property, which defines the origin of the local coordinate system used to define all block entities. To get the true, referenceable coordinates of a block's entity, you need to subtract the origin from the coordinates.

Origin is a historic property. All block table records created by AutoCAD Release 10 and later contain a constant point of (0,0,0).

ObjectDBX	ActiveX Automation	DXF/AutoLISP
origin()	Origin	Group 10

Usually block containers are saved to a drawing database and stay there permanently until they are explicitly deleted. In addition, there are temporary block containers.

AutoCAD uses a temporary block container, for instance, to create the entity image of a dimension object. This temporary block is automatically updated every time the dimension object changes.

Although block containers can exist whether they are referenced or not, temporary blocks are deleted automatically during a database load if they are not referenced.

Because temporary blocks aren't named by the AutoCAD user and aren't visible from the AutoCAD dialog boxes, they are called *anonymous*. Usually the block name of anonymous blocks starts with an asterisk (*).

ObjectDBX	ActiveX Automation	DXF/AutoLISP
isAnonymous()	n/a	First bit (1) of group 70

Any local, non-layout block may have a thumbnail preview image. This is a 32*32 bits device-independent bitmap (DIB) and can be used to display a rough view of the block prior to its referencing. (For more information about decoding DIBs, see Appendix A.) In DXF, the block preview image is contained in a sequence of binary chunks of group 310.

ObjectDBX	ActiveX Automation	DXF/AutoLISP
hasPreviewIcon()	n/a	n/a
getPreviewIcon()	n/a	Group 310 (repeated)

In addition to its name, a block can carry a comment string that further describes the block's usage. This is a property of the AcDbSymbolTableRecord subclass.

ObjectDBX	ActiveX Automation	DXF/AutoLISP
comment()	n/a	Group 4

In ObjectDBX, you can query the number of references to a block container using the *newBlockReferenceIdIterator()* function. In DXF and AutoLISP, you'll find the references listed as groups 331 and 332 enclosed in group 102.

ObjectDBX	ActiveX Automation	DXF/AutoLISP
newBlockReferenceIdIterator()	n/a	Groups 102, 331, 332, 102 (See the "BLOCK_RECORD Table Entries" section later in this chapter.)

A block container can include attributes, which are a kind of textual variables and are covered in detail in Chapter 16. Whenever an attributed block container is referenced, the AcDbBlockReference object contains the values for these variables. Therefore, you can query to determine whether a block container has attributes.

ObjectDBX	ActiveX Automation	DXF/AutoLISP
hasAttributeDefinitions()	n/a	Second bit (1) of group 70

Block table records in AutoCAD have some additional properties. These are attached to the AcDbBlockTableRecord object as xdata. The application name is "ACAD", and the first xdata string is "DesignCenter Data". The structure and meaning of the attached xdata is undocumented; however, the second 1070 group is the block's reference unit as taken from the following list.

ObjectDBX	ActiveX Automation	DXF/ AutoLISP	Meaning
kUnitsUndefined	acInsertUnits-Unitless	0	No unit of measurement specified
kUnitsInches	acInsertUnits-Inches	1	Inches (i.e., $2.54*10^{-2}$m)
kUnitsFeet	acInsertUnits-Feet	2	Feet (i.e., $3.048*10^{-1}$m)
kUnitsMiles	acInsertUnits-Miles	3	Statute miles (i.e., $1.609344*10^{3}$m)
kUnitsMillimeters	acInsertUnits-Millimeters	4	Millimeters (i.e. $1.0*10^{-3}$m)
kUnitsCentimeters	acInsertUnits-Centimeters	5	Centimeters (i.e., $1.0*10^{-2}$m)

ObjectDBX	ActiveX Automation	DXF/ AutoLISP	Meaning
kUnitsMeters	acInsertUnits-Meters	6	Meters (i.e., $1.0*10^0$m)
kUnitsKilometers	acInsertUnits-Kilometers	7	Kilometers (i.e., $1.0*10^3$m)
kUnitsMicroinches	acInsertUnits-Microinches	8	Microinches (i.e., $2.54*10^{-8}$m)
kUnitsMils	acInsertUnits-Mils	9	Mils (i.e., $2.54*10^{-5}$m)
kUnitsYards	acInsertUnits-Yards	10	Yards (i.e., $9.144*10^{-1}$m)
kUnitsAngstroms	acInsertUnits-Angstroms	11	Angstrom (i.e. $1.0*10^{-10}$m)
kUnitsNanometers	acInsertUnits-Nanometers	12	Nanometers (i.e., $1.0*10^{-9}$m)
kUnitsMicrons	acInsertUnits-Microns	13	Microns (i.e., $1.0*10^{-6}$m)
kUnitsDecimeters	acInsertUnits-Decimeters	14	Decimeters (i.e., $1.0*10^{-1}$m)
kUnitsDecameters	acInsertUnits-Decameters	15	Decameters (i.e., $1.0*10^1$m)
kUnitsHectometers	acInsertUnits-Hectometers	16	Hectometers (i.e. $1.0*10^2$m)
kUnitsGigameters	acInsertUnits-Gigameters	17	Gigameters (i.e., $1.0*10^9$m)
kUnitsAstronomical	acInsertUnits-AstronomicalUnits	18	Astronomical units (i.e., $1.4959787*10^{11}$m)
kUnitsLightYears	acInsertUnits-LightYears	19	Light years (i.e., $9.46053*10^{15}$m)
kUnitsParsecs	acInsertUnits-Parsecs	20	Parsecs (i.e., $3.085677*10^{16}$m)

Layout Blocks

Layout blocks are blocks that have an associated AcDbLayout object. In an AutoCAD drawing database, these blocks are named *MODEL_SPACE*, *PAPER_SPACE*, *PAPER_SPACE0*, *PAPER_SPACE1*, and so on.

You can query a block table record to determine whether it defines a layout block, and you can also query the corresponding AcDbLayout object.

ObjectDBX	ActiveX Automation	DXF/AutoLISP
isLayout()	IsLayout	n/a
getLayoutId()	Layout	Group 340

As with all other pointers, you will get the referenced object's handle, entity name, or AcDbObjectID, depending on the environment.

External References

An external reference is a block container that has no entities. Instead, it points to a block in an external database, either the external database's *MODEL_SPACE* block or any non-layout block. An external reference can have two types: attached and overlaid.

The difference between an attached reference and an overlaid reference lies in how nested external references are handled. Any xref attached to the referenced database will also become an external reference of the current database. Any xref overlaid to the referenced database is ignored.

In other words, if an xref is attached to the current database, any database referencing the current database will also see the xref. If the xref is overlaid in the current database, any database referencing the current database will not see it.

ObjectDBX	ActiveX Automation	DXF/AutoLISP
isFromExternalReference()	IsXref	Third bit (4) of group 70
isFromOverlayReference()	n/a	Fourth bit (8) of group 70

The *Name* property of xref blocks can contain a vertical bar (|).The part behind the bar is the name of the block in the external database. If the bar and block name are omitted, the block table record references the *MODEL_SPACE* block of the external database.

For location purposes, the block table record contains the complete path to the database file.

ObjectDBX	ActiveX Automation	DXF/AutoLISP
pathName()	n/a	Group 1

When working in ObjectDBX or ActiveX Automation, you can directly access the external database and operate on it.

ObjectDBX	ActiveX Automation	DXF/AutoLISP
xrefDatabase()	XRefDatabase	n/a

An xref may be temporarily unloaded from a drawing database. In this case, the AcDbBlockTableRecord remains intact, but all references to the external database are ignored.

ObjectDBX	ActiveX Automation	DXF/AutoLISP
isUnloaded()	n/a	First bit (1) of group 71

Only in ObjectDBX can you finally query the xref status using the *xrefStatus()* function. Doing so returns one of the following values:

Value		Meaning
kXrfNotAnXref	0	The queried block table record is not an xref.
kXrfResolved	1	The xref has been found and loaded.
kXrfUnloaded	2	The xref has been found and not loaded.
kXrfUnreferenced	3	The xref is not referenced.
kXrfFileNotFound	4	The xref has not been found.

Like every other symbol table that refers to an external database, ObjectDBX and DXF/AutoLISP supply two additional Boolean values for external blocks: *Dependent* is true if the block is in an external database; *Resolved* is true if the external block was found the last time AutoCAD tried to load it.

ObjectDBX	ActiveX Automation	DXF/AutoLISP
isDependent()	n/a	Fifth bit (16) of group 70
isResolved()	n/a	Sixth bit (32) of group 70

 NOTE In ObjectDBX, these two properties belong to the AcDbSymbolTableRecord subclass.

Block Begin and Block End Objects

Up to and including AutoCAD Release 12, the organization of database entities was completely different. At that time, one component of a block definition was the Block Begin bracket, which was similar to today's AcDbBlockTableRecord object.

The complete functionality of the Block Begin bracket has been taken over by the AcDbBlockTableRecord object. Therefore, the Block Begin bracket could fade into history.

Nevertheless, ObjectDBX still supports the Begin Block bracket as an AcDbBlockBegin object without any functionality. It's some kind of a virtual object, and even an ObjectDBX programmer has no way to create and/or delete objects of this class.

The only reason for the existence of this object is that in old drawings an application might have attached xdata to it. To prevent the loss of this xdata, Autodesk decided to keep this object as an entry point to the attached xdata.

Keep in mind that the AcDbBlockBegin object is a true AcDbEntity, which means that it has properties such as *Layer, Color, Linetype, Linewidth,* and *Extension Dictionary.* Some of these properties reference other objects in the drawing database and may keep them from being deleted.

To find the AcDbBlockBegin object, use the *openBlockBegin()* function of the AcDbBlockTableRecord object.

Everything I've said about the Block Begin bracket also applies to the corresponding Block End bracket, which is made available as an AcDbBlockEnd object returned by the *openBlockEnd()* function.

The DXF Representation of Block Containers

Querying the entities in a block container is simple.

- In ObjectDBX, you use the block table record's *newIterator()* function.
- In ActiveX Automation, you use the block table record's *Item* method.
- In AutoLISP, you use the *entnext* function.

In DXF, however, querying block table records and their associated entities is confusing and complicated. The information related to block table records and block containers is spread over the TABLES, BLOCKS, and ENTITIES sections of a DXF file. Let's try to sort them out.

The BLOCK_RECORD Table

Within the TABLES section of the DXF file, you'll find an additional table called "BLOCK_RECORD". The layer table starts with

```
0
TABLE
2
BLOCK_RECORD
```

which is followed by the remaining AcDbObject groups. Like the other symbol tables, this table has no owner.

The symbol table itself is of subclass AcDbSymbolTable and lists only one additional property:

```
70
<symbol table records count>
```

The value associated with group 70 is the number of records in this table.

 NOTE The record count value in symbol tables is unreliable. Iterate through the table until you find the corresponding end bracket.

The BLOCK_RECORD table ends with the following:

```
0
ENDTAB
```

BLOCK_RECORD Table Entries

Within the BLOCK_RECORD table, you'll find one entry per AcDbBlockTableRecord. This entry identifies itself as AcDbBlockTableRecord, a subclass of AcDbSymbolTableRecord. However, it contains only a few properties from the true block table record.

The DXF class name for BLOCK_RECORD table entries is "BLOCK_RECORD". Each object contains the usual AcDbObject groups, followed by both an AcDbSymbolTableRecord and an AcDbBlockTableRecord subclass marker.

Following this is a group 2 that contains the AcDbBlockTableRecord's *Name* property. Next is a group 340 that points to the corresponding AcDbLayout object. This group's value is zero for non-layout blocks.

If the block has a preview image icon, a repeated list of binary chunks follows with a group code of 310. Concatenate the chunks to get the binary thumbnail image.

Next is group 102, which contains the string "{BLKREFS", followed by the handles of all references to this block in groups 331 and 332. A block can be referenced by an AcDbBlockReference entity in another block container (group 331). Blocks from external databases are also referenced by block table records that define blocks or xrefs nested in this xref (group 332). The list of references is closed by another group 102 containing the string "}".

Following this list is any xdata attached to the AcDbBlockTableRecord object, especially the DesignCenter data.

The BLOCKS Section

As with the symbol tables, the serialized version of the drawing database (DXF) uses brackets to create containers. For historic reasons, block containers are saved in two locations in a DXF file.

All block containers except for *MODEL_SPACE* and *PAPER_SPACE*, but including all other layout and xref blocks, are saved to the BLOCKS section of a DXF file. The *MODEL_SPACE* and *PAPER_SPACE* block containers are saved to the ENTITIES section of the DXF file.

The BLOCKS section of a DXF file starts with

```
0
SECTION
2
BLOCKS
```

and ends with

```
0
ENDSEC
```

Between these brackets are all block containers except for the two listed earlier. Each block container is once again bracketed to separate it from the other containers.

The start bracket of each block container is related to the AcDbBlockBegin object I talked about earlier. It contains the remaining properties of the AcDbBlockTableRecord object and all properties of the AcDbBlockBegin object.

The Block Begin bracket uses the DXF class name "BLOCK". It starts with the usual AcDbObject groups taken from the AcDbBlockBegin object. Following this is an AcDbEntity subclass marker and the common groups for entities (see the next chapter for details). Again, the information contained in this section is taken from the AcDbBlockBegin object.

After another subclass marker of AcDbBlockBegin, several groups follow; their data is taken from the AcDbBlockTableRecord. First, a group 2 repeats the block's name. Next, a group 70 and a group 71 combine the various Boolean flags associated with the block table record. The block origin point is contained in the groups 10, 20, and 30. Next is a group 3 string, which usually repeats the block name and does not have a corresponding expression in the other environments. A group 1 contains the xref path name, if any. A final group 4 string contains an associated comment from the block table record. The object is closed by eventual xdata attached to the AcDbBlockBegin object.

Following this Block Begin bracket are all entities contained in this block container. The list ends with a Block End bracket. This bracket uses the DXF class name "ENDBLK" and contains the usual AcDbObject and AcDbEntity properties taken from the AcDbBlockEnd object. After an AcDbBlockEnd subclass marker, eventual xdata attached to the AcDbBlockEnd object closes the bracket.

Thus, an excerpt from a DXF file might look like this:

```
 0
BLOCK
<AcDbObject-related groups from AcDbBlockBegin object>
100
AcDbEntity
<AcDbEntity-related groups from AcDbBlockBegin object>
100
AcDbBlockBegin
 2
SomeBlock
 70
    0
71
    0
 10
0.0
 20
0.0
 30
0.0
 3
SomeBlock
 1

 4
SomeBlock's comment
<xdata from AcDbBlockBegin object>

... all entities contained in this block ...

 0
ENDBLK
<AcDbObject-related groups from AcDbBlockEnd object>
100
AcDbEntity
<AcDbEntity-related groups from AcDbBlockEnd object>
100
AcDbBlockEnd
<xdata from AcDbBlockEnd object>
```

The ENTITIES Section

For historic reasons and for compatibility with older versions of DXF, the contents of the *MODEL_SPACE* and *PAPER_SPACE* block containers are saved in a separate ENTITIES section.

The ENTITIES section of a DXF file starts with

```
  0
SECTION
  2
ENTITIES
```

and ends with

```
  0
ENDSEC
```

Between those brackets are all objects contained in the *MODEL_SPACE* and *PAPER _SPACE* blocks, in no particular order. The content of the two blocks is not separated with some kind of bracket or any other such symbol.

Instead, every entity in this section of a DXF file contains a special flag indicating whether this particular entity is member of the *MODEL_SPACE* block or the *PAPER _SPACE* block. This flag is saved within the AcDbEntity segment of every entity in this section. Its group code is 67. If the group 67 value is 1, the entity belongs to the *PAPER_SPACE* block container. If it's zero or if the whole group is absent, the entity belongs to the *MODEL_SPACE* container.

As an alternative approach, you could check the *Owner* property of each entity. The owner of all entities from the *MODEL_SPACE* block is the corresponding AcDbBlock-TableRecord, and all remaining enties are owned by the *PAPER_SPACE* block table record.

AutoCAD 2000 usually files out the entities from the *MODEL_SPACE* block first, followed by the entities from the *PAPER_SPACE* block. However, it's wise to use the group 67 flag or to check the block owner for each entity.

Summary

All database entities, that is, every database objects that have some kind of graphical image, are grouped into block containers. AutoCAD or any other program can display the combined visualization of such a block on the screen or on paper. In addition, blocks can reference each other, which means that the complete visualization of one block is also visible when the referencing block displays. I'll cover block insertion in detail in Chapter 16.

Any block container must have a name and an origin. It can also have a preview bitmap image, a comment, and (within the xdata of the DesignCenter application) an associated unit of measurement.

Within ObjectDBX, ActiveX Automation, and AutoLISP, access to the individual entities within a block container is easy. (See Chapter 2 if you need coding details.) Within a DXF file, the information from one single block container is spread over different locations: the TABLES, BLOCKS, and ENTITIES sections.

In the next chapter, we'll look closer at the entities contained in blocks.

CHAPTER 9

Common Properties for Entities

FEATURING

The DXF sequence for AcDbEntity   192

Layer and Color   193

Linetype   203

Linetype scale   204

Lineweight   205

Plot style   206

Visibility   207

Hyperlinks   208

Paperspace flag   208

Interactive-only properties   209

We're getting close. You have now learned how the internal structure of the AutoCAD drawing database is organized and how block containers are organized.

The objects within a block container are of type AcDbObject, as is any other object in the drawing database. But all objects in blocks are of a certain subclass of AcDbObject called AcDbEntity, which is why we call them *Entities*. Entities appear only in block containers, and every object in a block container is an entity.

Besides being objects like all the others and thus having properties, such as *Handle, Owner, Extension Dictionary*, and *Xdata*, entities have one important additional property: a visual representation. Every entity can be drawn, both on the screen and on paper. An entity can draw itself as a simple line or as a complex combination of 3D volumes, text, bitmaps, animation, and sound. In the remaining chapters of this book, we will look in detail at how entities display themselves.

In this chapter, we will look at the properties that are common to all entities. For instance, each entity has a *Layer* property that associates the entity with an AcDbLayerTableRecord object. Some other common properties are *Color, Linetype,* and *Lineweight*. All these properties are inherited from the AcDbEntity class.

The DXF Sequence for AcDbEntity

The AcDbEntity groups directly follow an AcDbEntity subclass marker (group 100), which closes the groups that belong to AcDbObject.

The first group is the *Paperspace Flag* property (group 67), which we looked at in the previous chapter. If it's omitted, the value 0 is used. The next group is the *Layer* property, which is a string associated with group code 8. It is never omitted.

The *Linetype* property uses group code 6 and defaults to `"ByBlock"` if omitted. The *Color* property is in group 62 and defaults to 256 when omitted.

Next is the *Linetype Scale* property in group 48. If it is omitted, the value 1.0 is used. The *Visibility* flag is in group 60 and defaults to 0.

The *Lineweight* property is saved in group 370. The default value for this is –1. The *Plot Style Name Type* property is in group 380, and the *Plot Style Name* property is in group 390. If both are omitted, the plot style is taken from the associated AcDbLayerTableRecord object.

NOTE   AcDbEntity objects can also contain a group 92 and multiple groups 310. You'll find these groups with so-called *custom* objects created by third-party applications. These groups define a visualization of the object using a number of AutoCAD drawing commands. This visualization can be used to display the object when the parent application is not available. See Chapter 18 for details on these groups.

Finally, the *Hyperlinks* property is saved to xdata attached to this object.

The Layer Property

An entity's *Layer* property associates the entity with one and only one AcDbLayer-TableRecord. This association has two uses. First, all entities with the same *Layer* property can be turned off, frozen, or locked by changing the corresponding property of the layer record.

Second, the entity can inherit certain properties from the layer record, thus making all entities that share a common layer look alike. Properties that can be inherited from a layer record are, for example, *Color* and *Linetype*. We'll look at these later in this chapter.

The *Layer* property is the key string of the associated AcDbLayerTableRecord object.

ObjectDBX	ActiveX Automation	DXF/AutoLISP
layer()	Layer	Group 8

Only in ObjectDBX can you also directly query the AcDbObjectID of the layer table record using the *layerId()* function.

The Color Property

The *Color* property specifies the color in which the object should display itself. Some objects, for example, AcDbMText or AcDbAlignedDimension, draw different parts in different colors. In this case, the AcDbEntity color provides the object's primary color.

Colors in ObjectDBX are objects of type AcCmColor. In ActiveX Automation, a color is an object of type ACAD_COLOR with predefined constants for the most often used colors. In DXF and AutoLISP, colors are represented by integers.

The AutoCAD Color Index

In any case, AutoCAD uses the *AutoCAD Color Index* (ACI) to define a fixed set of 255 colors. Table 9.1 lists the ACI colors and their RGB (red, green, blue) equivalents. For example, an R value of 0.65 means that for this color you use 65 percent of the maximum intensity of Red.

TABLE 9.1: THE ACI COLOR AND THEIR RGB EQUIVALENTS

ACI	R	G	B	ActiveX Automation
1	1.0	0.0	0.0	acRed
2	1.0	1.0	0.0	acYellow
3	0.0	1.0	0.0	acGreen
4	0.0	1.0	1.0	acCyan
5	0.0	0.0	1.0	acBlue
6	1.0	0.0	1.0	acMagenta
7	1.0	1.0	1.0	acWhite
8	1.0	1.0	1.0	
9	1.0	1.0	1.0	
10	1.0	0.0	0.0	
11	1.0	0.5	0.5	
12	0.65	0.0	0.0	
13	0.65	0.325	0.325	
14	0.5	0.0	0.0	
15	0.5	0.25	0.25	
16	0.3	0.0	0.0	
17	0.3	0.15	0.15	
18	0.15	0.0	0.0	
19	0.15	0.075	0.075	
20	1.0	0.25	0.0	
21	1.0	0.625	0.5	
22	0.65	0.1625	0.0	
23	0.65	0.40625	0.325	
24	0.5	0.125	0.0	
25	0.5	0.3125	0.25	
26	0.3	0.075	0.0	

ACI	R	G	B	ActiveX Automation
\multicolumn{5}{l}{**TABLE 9.1: THE ACI COLOR AND THEIR RGB EQUIVALENTS (CONTINUED)**}

ACI	R	G	B	ActiveX Automation
27	0.3	0.1875	0.15	
28	0.15	0.0375	0.0	
29	0.15	0.09375	0.075	
30	1.0	0.5	0.0	
31	1.0	0.75	0.5	
32	0.65	0.325	0.0	
33	0.65	0.4875	0.325	
34	0.5	0.25	0.0	
35	0.5	0.375	0.25	
36	0.3	0.15	0.0	
37	0.3	0.225	0.15	
38	0.15	0.075	0.0	
39	0.15	0.1125	0.075	
40	1.0	0.75	0.0	
41	1.0	0.875	0.5	
42	0.65	0.4875	0.0	
43	0.65	0.56875	0.325	
44	0.5	0.375	0.0	
45	0.5	0.4375	0.25	
46	0.3	0.225	0.0	
47	0.3	0.2625	0.15	
48	0.15	0.1125	0.0	
49	0.15	0.13125	0.075	
50	1.0	1.0	0.0	
51	1.0	1.0	0.5	
52	0.65	0.65	0.0	
53	0.65	0.65	0.325	
54	0.5	0.5	0.0	
55	0.5	0.5	0.25	
56	0.3	0.3	0.0	
57	0.3	0.3	0.15	
58	0.15	0.15	0.0	

ACI	R	G	B	ActiveX Automation
59	0.15	0.15	0.075	
60	0.75	1.0	0.0	
61	0.875	1.0	0.5	
62	0.4875	0.65	0.0	
63	0.56875	0.65	0.325	
64	0.375	0.5	0.0	
65	0.4375	0.5	0.25	
66	0.225	0.3	0.0	
67	0.2625	0.3	0.15	
68	0.1125	0.15	0.0	
69	0.13125	0.15	0.075	
70	0.5	1.0	0.0	
71	0.75	1.0	0.5	
72	0.325	0.65	0.0	
73	0.4875	0.65	0.325	
74	0.25	0.5	0.0	
75	0.375	0.5	0.25	
76	0.15	0.3	0.0	
77	0.225	0.3	0.15	
78	0.075	0.15	0.0	
79	0.1125	0.15	0.075	
80	0.25	1.0	0.0	
81	0.625	1.0	0.5	
82	0.1625	0.65	0.0	
83	0.40625	0.65	0.325	
84	0.125	0.5	0.0	
85	0.3125	0.5	0.25	
86	0.075	0.3	0.0	
87	0.1875	0.3	0.15	
88	0.0375	0.15	0.0	
89	0.09375	0.15	0.075	
90	0.0	1.0	0.0	

TABLE 9.1: THE ACI COLOR AND THEIR RGB EQUIVALENTS (CONTINUED)

TABLE 9.1: THE ACI COLOR AND THEIR RGB EQUIVALENTS (CONTINUED)

ACI	R	G	B	ActiveX Automation
91	0.5	1.0	0.5	
92	0.0	0.65	0.0	
93	0.325	0.65	0.325	
94	0.0	0.5	0.0	
95	0.25	0.5	0.25	
96	0.0	0.3	0.0	
97	0.15	0.3	0.15	
98	0.0	0.15	0.0	
99	0.075	0.15	0.075	
100	0.0	1.0	0.25	
101	0.5	1.0	0.625	
102	0.0	0.65	0.1625	
103	0.325	0.65	0.40625	
104	0.0	0.5	0.125	
105	0.25	0.5	0.3125	
106	0.0	0.3	0.075	
107	0.15	0.3	0.1875	
108	0.0	0.15	0.0375	
109	0.075	0.15	0.09375	
110	0.0	1.0	0.5	
111	0.5	1.0	0.75	
112	0.0	0.65	0.325	
113	0.325	0.65	0.4875	
114	0.0	0.5	0.25	
115	0.25	0.5	0.375	
116	0.0	0.3	0.15	
117	0.15	0.3	0.225	
118	0.0	0.15	0.075	
119	0.075	0.15	0.1125	
120	0.0	1.0	0.75	
121	0.5	1.0	0.875	
122	0.0	0.65	0.4875	

TABLE 9.1: THE ACI COLOR AND THEIR RGB EQUIVALENTS (CONTINUED)				
ACI	**R**	**G**	**B**	**ActiveX Automation**
123	0.325	0.65	0.56875	
124	0.0	0.5	0.375	
125	0.25	0.5	0.4375	
126	0.0	0.3	0.225	
127	0.15	0.3	0.2625	
128	0.0	0.15	0.1125	
129	0.075	0.15	0.13125	
130	0.0	1.0	1.0	
131	0.5	1.0	1.0	
132	0.0	0.65	0.65	
133	0.325	0.65	0.65	
134	0.0	0.5	0.5	
135	0.25	0.5	0.5	
136	0.0	0.3	0.3	
137	0.15	0.3	0.3	
138	0.0	0.15	0.15	
139	0.075	0.15	0.15	
140	0.0	0.75	1.0	
141	0.5	0.875	1.0	
142	0.0	0.4875	0.65	
143	0.325	0.56875	0.65	
144	0.0	0.375	0.5	
145	0.25	0.4375	0.5	
146	0.0	0.225	0.3	
147	0.15	0.2625	0.3	
148	0.0	0.1125	0.15	
149	0.075	0.13125	0.15	
150	0.0	0.5	1.0	
151	0.5	0.75	1.0	
152	0.0	0.325	0.65	
153	0.325	0.4875	0.65	
154	0.0	0.25	0.5	

TABLE 9.1: THE ACI COLOR AND THEIR RGB EQUIVALENTS (CONTINUED)

ACI	R	G	B	ActiveX Automation
155	0.25	0.375	0.5	
156	0.0	0.15	0.3	
157	0.15	0.225	0.3	
158	0.0	0.075	0.15	
159	0.075	0.1125	0.15	
160	0.0	0.25	1.0	
161	0.5	0.625	1.0	
162	0.0	0.1625	0.65	
163	0.325	0.40625	0.65	
164	0.0	0.125	0.5	
165	0.25	0.3125	0.5	
166	0.0	0.075	0.3	
167	0.15	0.1875	0.3	
168	0.0	0.0375	0.15	
169	0.075	0.09375	0.15	
170	0.0	0.0	1.0	
171	0.5	0.5	1.0	
172	0.0	0.0	0.65	
173	0.325	0.325	0.65	
174	0.0	0.0	0.5	
175	0.25	0.25	0.5	
176	0.0	0.0	0.3	
177	0.15	0.15	0.3	
178	0.0	0.0	0.15	
179	0.075	0.075	0.15	
180	0.25	0.0	1.0	
181	0.625	0.5	1.0	
182	0.1625	0.0	0.65	
183	0.40625	0.325	0.65	
184	0.125	0.0	0.5	
185	0.3125	0.25	0.5	
186	0.075	0.0	0.3	

TABLE 9.1: THE ACI COLOR AND THEIR RGB EQUIVALENTS (CONTINUED)

ACI	R	G	B	ActiveX Automation
187	0.1875	0.15	0.3	
188	0.0375	0.0	0.15	
189	0.09375	0.075	0.15	
190	0.5	0.0	1.0	
191	0.75	0.5	1.0	
192	0.325	0.0	0.65	
193	0.4875	0.325	0.65	
194	0.25	0.0	0.5	
195	0.375	0.25	0.5	
196	0.15	0.0	0.3	
197	0.225	0.15	0.3	
198	0.075	0.0	0.15	
199	0.1125	0.075	0.15	
200	0.75	0.0	1.0	
201	0.875	0.5	1.0	
202	0.4875	0.0	0.65	
203	0.56875	0.325	0.65	
204	0.375	0.0	0.5	
205	0.4375	0.25	0.5	
206	0.225	0.0	0.3	
207	0.2625	0.15	0.3	
208	0.1125	0.0	0.15	
209	0.13125	0.075	0.15	
210	1.0	0.0	1.0	
211	1.0	0.5	1.0	
212	0.65	0.0	0.65	
213	0.65	0.325	0.65	
214	0.5	0.0	0.5	
215	0.5	0.25	0.5	
216	0.3	0.0	0.3	
217	0.3	0.15	0.3	
218	0.15	0.0	0.15	

TABLE 9.1: THE ACI COLOR AND THEIR RGB EQUIVALENTS (CONTINUED)

ACI	R	G	B	ActiveX Automation
219	0.15	0.075	0.15	
220	1.0	0.0	0.75	
221	1.0	0.5	0.875	
222	0.65	0.0	0.4875	
223	0.65	0.325	0.56875	
224	0.5	0.0	0.375	
225	0.5	0.25	0.4375	
226	0.3	0.0	0.225	
227	0.3	0.15	0.2625	
228	0.15	0.0	0.1125	
229	0.15	0.075	0.13125	
230	1.0	0.0	0.5	
231	1.0	0.5	0.75	
232	0.65	0.0	0.325	
233	0.65	0.325	0.4875	
234	0.5	0.0	0.25	
235	0.5	0.25	0.375	
236	0.3	0.0	0.15	
237	0.3	0.15	0.225	
238	0.15	0.0	0.075	
239	0.15	0.075	0.1125	
240	1.0	0.0	0.25	
241	1.0	0.5	0.625	
242	0.65	0.0	0.1625	
243	0.65	0.325	0.40625	
244	0.5	0.0	0.125	
245	0.5	0.25	0.3125	
246	0.3	0.0	0.075	
247	0.3	0.15	0.1875	
248	0.15	0.0	0.0375	
249	0.15	0.075	0.09375	
250	0.33	0.33	0.33	

TABLE 9.1: THE ACI COLOR AND THEIR RGB EQUIVALENTS (CONTINUED)				
ACI	**R**	**G**	**B**	**ActiveX Automation**
251	0.464	0.464	0.464	
252	0.598	0.598	0.598	
253	0.732	0.732	0.732	
254	0.866	0.866	0.866	
255	1.0	1.0	1.0	

Colors 250 through 255 are shades of gray, ranging from a dark gray to a true white. In contrast, the color 7, even though named acWhite, displays white only on a black background. On a white background, color 7 displays black.

To get the color of an AcDbEntity you use:

ObjectDBX	**ActiveX Automation**	**DXF/AutoLISP**
color()	Color	group 62

In ObjectDBX, you can directly query the color's ACI if you use the entity's *colorIndex()* function.

By Block and By Layer Colors

Two special colors are not listed in the ACI table:

- acByLayer
- acByBlock

The color "acByLayer" uses the special index 256. If an entity's color is set *By Layer,* it displays using the *Color* property of its associated AcDbLayerTableRecord object.

The color "acByBlock" uses the special index 0. If an entity's *Color* property is set *By Block,* it displays in color 7, unless it is a member of a referenced block container. In this case, it uses the color of the referencing AcDbBlockReference object. This means that the same entity can display in different colors if it is referenced more than once. If the AcDbBlockReference's *Color* property is set *By Layer,* the entity displays using the *Color* property of its own layer table record, unless it is associated with the layer named "0". In this case it uses the *Color* property of the layer associated with the AcDbBlockReference object.

The Linetype Property

The *Linetype* property associates the entity with an AcDbLinetypeTableRecord object. This property contains the linetype's key string.

ObjectDBX	ActiveX Automation	DXF/AutoLISP
linetype()	Linetype	Group 6

In ObjectDBX, you can directly query the associated AcDbLinetypeTableRecord object if you use the entity's *linetypeID()* function.

Every AcDbEntity has a *Linetype* property, although some objects, such as AcDb-Text, ignore an associated linetype when they display themselves.

As with colors, two special linetypes use the key strings "ByLayer" and "ByBlock". They associate the entity with the corresponding *Linetype* property of the entity's AcDb-LayerTableRecord or AcDbBlockReference object. The strategy is exactly the same as with the special colors. If an entity uses the linetype "ByBlock" and is not referenced by an AcDbBlockReference object, it displays using the linetype "CONTINUOUS".

Linetype Mapping

The linetype definition is a property of the AcDbLinetypeTableRecord object. For non-continuous linetypes, this property defines a series of dashes, gaps, dots, and embedded symbols or strings. The linetype pattern has a fixed length that results from the length of the included dashes and gaps.

When a linetype is applied to an AcDbEntity object, the pattern length and the dash and gap lengths are scaled three times: first by the entity-specific linetype scale (discussed later in this chapter), then by the global linetype scale (see the LTSCALE global setting in Chapter 4), and eventually by the view scale (see the PSLTSCALE global setting).

This results in a true pattern length. Next, the appropriate length of the entity curve (for example, the length of a line or an arc) is divided by the true pattern length to return the number of whole pattern repetitions that can be mapped onto the entity curve.

Depending on the linetype's *ScaledToFit* property, the pattern is now mapped onto the curve: if *ScaledToFit* is false, AutoCAD draws the calculated number of repetitions, excluding the very first dash, centered on the curve. The remainder (which is at least as long as the first dash) is filled with a continuous line at the beginning and end of the curve. This guarantees that each curve begins and ends with a dash segment and that the curves' extents are clearly visible.

If *ScaledToFit* is true, AutoCAD adds one to the number of repetitions calculated, if the remaining curve length is more than half the pattern length. Next, the curve length is divided by the number of repetitions, and the linetype pattern is scaled to fit into this length. This results in a pattern that is evenly mapped onto the curve without any remainder. Since a pattern can end with a gap, however, this creates a curve display that seems to be shorter than the actual curve. AutoCAD draws a single dot at the end of a curve if the linetype pattern ends with a gap.

If a curve is shorter than the pattern length, a continuous line is drawn. Figure 9.1 shows the mapping of a linetype onto lines of different lengths. The pattern is defined by a 0.25 dash, a 0.5 gap, a dot, and a 0.25 gap, which gives a pattern length of 1.0. All scale factors are 1.0 as well. The right column uses *ScaledToFit*.

FIGURE 9.1

Linetype mapping

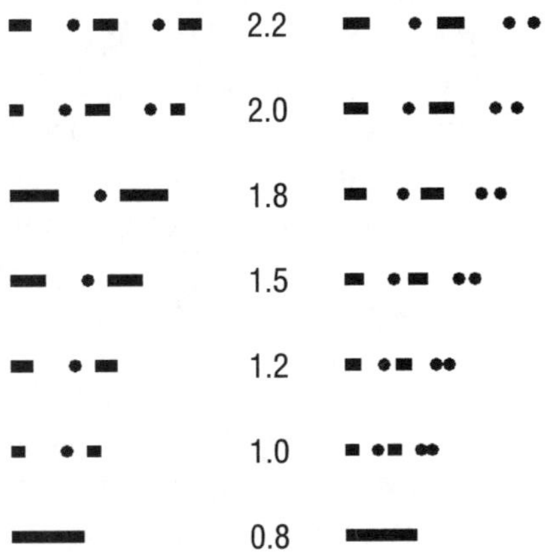

When a linetype pattern is mapped onto a closed curve, for example, a circle, the linetype is always scaled to fit, no matter how it's defined. The first pattern starts at 0°, that is, to the right. The pattern is applied counter-clockwise.

The Linetype Scale Property

The entity-specific linetype scale adds another factor to linetype scaling. Every dash or gap length in a linetype definition is multiplied by the global linetype scale (see the LTSCALE setting in Chapter 4) and eventually by the view scale (see the PSLT-SCALE setting in Chapter 4).

If the entity-specific linetype scale is different from its default of 1.0, every dash and gap length is multiplied once more, this time by the AcDbEntity's *Linetype Scale* property. The linetype scale is a 64-bit floating-point number.

ObjectDBX	ActiveX Automation	DXF/AutoLISP
linetypeScale()	LinetypeScale	Group 48

The Lineweight Property

The *Lineweight* property defines the pen width used when plotting the entity. Auto-CAD supports a fixed set of lineweights according to the typical pens used in technical drafting.

Lineweights in DXF and AutoLISP are integers associated with group code 370. In ActiveX Automation, you'll get an object of type ACAD_LWEIGHT with predefined constants for the lineweights allowed. In ObjectDBX, the lineweight is a member of the enumeration AcDb::LineWeight, for example, kAcLnWt005. The following list compares these three.

ObjectDBX	ActiveX Automation	DXF/ AutoLISP	Pen Width
kLnWt000	acLnWt000	0	Hairline, i.e., the thinnest line the output device can generate
kLnWt005	acLnWt005	5	0.05 mm
kLnWt009	acLnWt009	9	0.09 mm
kLnWt013	acLnWt013	13	0.13 mm
kLnWt015	acLnWt015	15	0.15 mm
kLnWt018	acLnWt018	18	0.18 mm
kLnWt020	acLnWt020	20	0.20 mm
kLnWt025	acLnWt025	25	0.25 mm
kLnWt030	acLnWt030	30	0.30 mm
kLnWt035	acLnWt035	35	0.35 mm
kLnWt040	acLnWt040	40	0.40 mm
kLnWt050	acLnWt050	50	0.50 mm
kLnWt053	acLnWt053	53	0.53 mm
kLnWt060	acLnWt060	60	0.60 mm
kLnWt070	acLnWt070	70	0.70 mm
kLnWt080	acLnWt080	80	0.80 mm
kLnWt090	acLnWt090	90	0.90 mm
kLnWt100	acLnWt100	100	1.00 mm

ObjectDBX	ActiveX Automation	DXF/ AutoLISP	Pen Width
kLnWt106	acLnWt106	106	1.06 mm
kLnWt120	acLnWt120	120	1.20 mm
kLnWt140	acLnWt140	140	1.40 mm
kLnWt158	acLnWt158	158	1.58 mm
kLnWt200	acLnWt200	200	2.00 mm
kLnWt211	acLnWt211	211	2.11 mm
kLnWtByLayer	acLnWtByLayer	–1	
kLnWtByBlock	acLnWtByBlock	–2	
kLnWtByLw-Default	acLnWtByLw-Default	–3	

Like the *Color* and *Linetype* properties, the *Lineweight* property can take two special values that let the entity inherit its lineweight from the associated layer table record or block reference.

A third special value, *By Lineweight Default,* is intended for use with drawings that don't use lineweight at all. In this case, the lineweight is taken from the LWDEFAULT global setting.

ObjectDBX	ActiveX Automation	DXF/AutoLISP
lineWeight()	Lineweight	Group 370

The Plot Style Property

An AcDbEntity's plot style defines the entity's outlook on paper to more detail than linetype, color, and lineweight. A plot style can overwrite an entity's color (for example, to grayscale), linetype (for example, to a device-dependent built-in linetype), or lineweight. In addition, the plot style can define how lines end, how they meet, and which pattern is to be mapped on them.

Plot styles are defined in a table; however, this table is located outside the drawing database. Inside the drawing database, you see only name references to plot styles. The plot style table filename is a property of a layout block, which allows entities to plot according to the output device.

How plot styles are used and referenced in a drawing database is a bit difficult to understand because a plot style is not simply a string. Instead, an AcDbEntity's plot style is a pointer to another object. This object could have been something like an AcDbPlotStyle object, but it isn't since the plot style definition is external to the drawing database.

Thus, the *Plot Style* property points to an AcDbPlaceHolder object. This object's owner is an AcDbDictionaryWithDefault, which you can also find by using the key string "ACAD_PLOTSTYLENAME" in the root dictionary. Within this dictionary, you can then read the plot style name associated with the AcDbPlaceHolder object. Simple, isn't it?

This complex structure misses something: the inheritance of plot styles from layer or block references to entities. This problem is solved by adding another property, the *Plot Style Name Type*. This type is one of the following:

ObjectDBX	Value	DXF
kPlotStyleNameByLayer	0	Omitted; no plot style
kPlotStyleNameByBlock	1	1, no plot style
kPlotStyleNameIsDictDefault	2	Omitted; plot style is dictionary default
kPlotStyleNameById	3	Omitted; plot style is given with entity

In ObjectDBX, the *getPlotStyleNameId()* function returns both the plot style name type and the AcDbObjectID of the AcDbPlaceHolder object.

ObjectDBX	ActiveX Automation	DXF/AutoLISP
getPlotStyleNameId(), plot style name type	n/a	Group 380
getPlotStyleNameId(), object ID	n/a	Group 390

Because getting the plot style name for an entity is quite complex, both Object-DBX and ActiveX Automation provide this name as a calculated property.

ObjectDBX	ActiveX Automation	DXF/AutoLISP
PlotStyleName()	PlotStyleName	n/a

The Visibility Property

An AcDbEntity's visibility on the screen is determined by several factors I've already mentioned: its parent block container, its layer properties, and its geometric location. But even if an object is located in the screen space, contained in a block displayed or referenced, and its layer is on and thawed, the object can still decide by itself whether it is going to display. The AcDbEntity's *Visibility* property is a Boolean flag.

ObjectDBX	ActiveX Automation	DXF/AutoLISP
visibility()	Visible	First bit (1) of group 60 negated

In DXF and AutoLISP, the group 60 value is 1 (true) if the entity is set to be invisible. If group 60 is omitted, the entity is visible.

The Hyperlinks Property

An AutoCAD 2000 entity can have an associated hyperlink pointing to any URL (Uniform Resource Locator) or local file. The hyperlink is *not* a native property of an AcDb-Entity; however, in ActiveX Automation, it looks like one. Therefore, I'll discuss it in this chapter.

In ActiveX Automation, you can query the hyperlinks collection of an entity using the *Hyperlinks* method. This returns a collection of hyperlinks, not a single one, even though each object has a maximum of one hyperlink attached. If an object is nested in a block reference, however, you can query both the entity's hyperlink and the block reference's hyperlink, if any.

Inside the drawing database, hyperlinks are saved as xdata belonging to the "PE_URL" application. When working in ObjectDBX, you can either query and evaluate this xdata or use the ActiveX Automation *getHyperlinkCollection* method.

A hyperlink is defined by the URL string, which is either a complete URL address or an address relative to the drawing's global HYPERLINKBASE setting. In addition, a hyperlink can point to a named location in the file (which for AutoCAD is a named view). Finally, a hyperlink can have additional descriptive text.

The ActiveX Automation properties in the following list are those of a virtual hyperlink object taken from the entity's *Hyperlinks* collection.

ObjectDBX	ActiveX Automation	DXF/AutoLISP
n/a	URL	First group 1000 in xdata
n/a	URLDescription	Second group 1000 in xdata
n/a	URLNamedLocation	Third group 1000 in xdata

The Paperspace Flag Property

The *Paperspace Flag* property is also *not* a native property of an AcDbEntity object. When you browse through a drawing database using DXF or AutoLISP, however, it looks like one.

This property is in group 67 and is used only to divide the elements of the DXF ENTITIES section into those that belong to the *MODEL_SPACE* block (group 67 equals zero or omitted) and those that belong to the *PAPER_SPACE* block (group 67 equals 1).

ObjectDBX	ActiveX Automation	DXF/AutoLISP
n/a	n/a	First bit (1) of group 67

You won't see this flag in the other environments because the entities are located in their corresponding block container.

Interactive-Only Properties

If you're working in ObjectDBX, you might be interested in a number of additional properties that you can query from an AcDbEntity object. None of these properties is filed to DWG or DXF, and, except for the geometric extents, none of these properties can be used in ActiveX Automation (unless you create a wrapper around the Object-DBX function that can be called in ActiveX Automation–based programs).

Any object derived from AcDbEntity must return three arrays of points to a calling application:

- The entity's grip points (where AutoCAD displays grip handles)
- The entity's osnap points for a given, supplied object snap mode
- The entity's stretch points (which AutoCAD moves during a stretch operation)

ObjectDBX	ActiveX Automation	DXF/AutoLISP
getGripPoints()	n/a	n/a
getOsnapPoints()	n/a	n/a
getStretchPoints()	n/a	n/a

Every AcDbEntity has a visual representation that takes up space in the 3D drawing volume. You can query the extents of an entity, which are the diagonal corners of the smallest box enclosing the entity. This *Bounding Box* is always aligned with the axes of the World Coordinate System. Its corners are also WCS coordinates.

ObjectDBX	ActiveX Automation	DXF/AutoLISP
getGeomExtents()	GetBoundingBox	n/a

In a two-dimensional drawing, all entities are planar (that is, flat), but also in 3D, certain objects such as a circle or text are located on a specific plane. Planar entities have an entity-specific coordinate system (ECS) aligned with the plane on which they reside. ObjectDBX provides a number of properties that you can use to query planar objects as well as their ECS.

ObjectDBX	ActiveX Automation	DXF/AutoLISP
isPlanar()	n/a	(vlax-curve-isPlanar) in AutoLISP
getPlane()	n/a	n/a
getEcs()	n/a	n/a

There are a few additional query functions for AcDbEntity objects in ObjectDBX; however, they are either duplicates of functions described in this chapter (for example, the *blockId()* function is equivalent to the *owner()* function) or are too specialized and complex for this book. For information on these functions, see the ObjectARX documentation.

Summary

The entities in a drawing database differ in the way they display and print, and they differ in their defining properties. To describe a straight line, you need properties that are different from those you use to describe a circle or an annotation.

All entities share a common set of properties, however. On one hand, they are all database objects and, as such, have properties such as *Handle* or *Owner*. On the other hand, all entities have some kind of visual representation and the properties described in this chapter. The *Layer* and *Visibility* properties affect whether the entity draws itself on the screen. *Linetype, LinetypeScale, Lineweight, PlotStyleName,* and, again, *Layer* affect *how* the object displays and prints.

This chapter ends our discussion of the database fundamentals. Next we look at some specific entities.

CHAPTER 10

Curves and Other Simple Drawing Entities

FEATURING

The properties of curves   211

Unbounded straight lines   215

Single-bounded straight lines   216

Finite straight lines   216

Circles   219

Circular arcs   220

Ellipses and elliptical arcs   222

Spline curves   224

3D faces   227

And finally you've made it. Now that you've read the first chapters of this book, you know everything needed to understand an AutoCAD line and other drawing entities. In the remaining chapters, we'll look at the graphical objects that make up an AutoCAD drawing.

I have grouped the AutoCAD drawing entities into a number of categories, and each category constitutes a chapter, such as annotation objects, bitmap images, and embedded objects. This chapter concentrates on the basic entities that make up a drawing: lines, circles, and three-dimensional faces. We'll look at the following individual objects:

AcDbXline   In 3D space, an unbounded straight line that extends to infinity in both directions

AcDbRay   A single-bounded straight line that extends to infinity in one direction

AcDbLine   A finite straight line

AcDbCircle   A planar circular curve

AcDbArc   A segment of a planar circular curve

AcDbEllipse   A planar elliptical curve

AcDbSpline   A planar or nonplanar splined curve

AcDbFace   A three- or four-sided planar or nonplanar face in 3D space

Since all entities in this chapter except for the last one are curves and, therefore, are derived from a common AcDbCurve class, we'll start by looking at the properties of curves.

The Properties of Curves

Many objects in a drawing (and almost all objects covered in this chapter) are curves. A curve is a one-dimensional object. Oops, you may say: circles are two-dimensional, and splines may even be three-dimensional. Right you are. You may need two or three dimensions to list all the points that lie on the curve, but you need only one dimension to define it.

You can put your pen at the start point of any curve and draw along the curve. Although your pen moves in only one direction (forward), it reaches all points that lie on the curve. You cannot reach every point on a planar region or in a 3D volume by moving your (infinitely thin) pen. Such objects are not curves.

Parametrical Representations of Curves

Resulting from the idea of the moving pen is the concept of parametric curves. If your pen moves 10 millimeters a second, you can tell at any time at which exact coordinates your pen is located. Thus, the time is the parameter of the curve, and every point on the curve is a function of the time.

The parametrical formulas for some curves are quite easy. Let's take, for instance, a straight line that goes from (1,2,3) to (4,6,9). If we take the difference (or vector) between start and end point, which is (3,4,6), we can define our line as follows:

```
L := (1,2,3) + u * (3,4,6)
```

with the single parameter u ranging from 0 through 1.

If u is zero, the formula calculates (1,2,3), which is our line's start point. If u equals 1, the formula calculates (4,6,9), which is the end point. Whatever value you insert into the formula, you always get a point on the straight line. The parameter must not exceed the valid range, of course.

Let's look at a circle drawn around (0,0) with a radius of 1. The parametrical formula of this circle is:

```
C := ( cos(u), sin(u), 0 )
```

with u ranging from 0° through 360°.

Again, if you try to insert various values from the parameter range into the formula, you'll always get a point on the circle. If you reduce the parameter range, perhaps by letting u range from 45° through 90° only, you shorten the curve, which in this example produces a circular arc.

When working in ObjectDBX or AutoLISP, you can directly interact with the parametrical representation of a curve in many ways. None of this information is filed out to DWG or DXF, however. If you're working with DXF files, you need to regenerate the parametrical representation of a curve from the data saved in the file.

The following list contains the various ObjectDBX functions to query parametrical curves. When working in AutoLISP, you need to add the `vlax-curve-` prefix, like this:

```
(vlax-curve-getStartParam aCurveObject)
```

ObjectDBX	Meaning
getStartParam()	Returns the parameter value of the curve's start point
getStartPoint()	Returns the point with the lowest parameter value
getEndParam()	Returns the parameter value of the curve's end point
getEndPoint()	Returns the point with the highest parameter value
getPointAtParam()	Returns the point at a given parameter value

ObjectDBX	Meaning
getParamAtPoint()	Returns the parameter value for a given point on the curve
getParamAtDist()	Returns the parameter value for a point at a given distance along the curve from the start point
getPointAtDist()	Returns the point at a given distance along the curve from the start point
getDistAtParam()	Returns the distance along the curve between a point at the given parameter and the start point
getDistAtPoint()	Returns the distance along the curve between a given point and the start point
getClosestPointTo()	Returns the point on the curve closest to a given point

A curve's parameter can have a lower and an upper limit. In this case, we call the curve *bounded*. If entering the lowest value and the highest value of the parameter range results in the same point, we call the curve *closed*. If an unbounded curve repeats itself over and over, we call the curve *periodic*.

ObjectDBX	ActiveX Automation	AutoLISP
isClosed()	n/a	(vlax-curve-isClosed)
isPeriodic()	n/a	(vlax-curve-isPeriodic)

Curve Properties

Closed planar curves enclose an area, which you can query in ObjectDBX, AutoLISP, and ActiveX Automation. Open planar curves also return an area value. This value is the area of the region built by connecting start and end points with a straight line.

ObjectDBX	ActiveX Automation	AutoLISP
getArea()	Area	(vlax-curve-getArea)

A final common property of curves is their derivative. ObjectDBX and AutoLISP provide you with the first and second derivatives of any curve at a given point.

If you keep in mind that even though our parameter representation is one-dimensional, the resulting points are in 3D space. Thus, we can write our curve as (x(u), y(u), z(u)). AutoCAD calculates the three first derivatives (x'(u), y'(u), z'(u)) and returns the three values at a given u as an AcGeVector3d. The same procedure also returns a vector of the second derivative at a given point.

In a one-dimensional case, you may see the first derivative as the grade of the curve's tangent in this point, while the second derivative is the curvature at this point.

ObjectDBX	ActiveX Automation	AutoLISP
getFirstDeriv()	n/a	(vlax-curve-getFirstDeriv)
getSecondDeriv()	n/a	(vlax-curve-getSecond-Deriv)

Finally, ObjectDBX provides a set of functions to create new objects from a given curve, including offset curves, projections, and approximations.

Curves in DXF

Even though many drawing entities are curves and therefore derived from AcDb-Curve, this class is abstract and does not produce any properties filed to DWG or DXF. Thus, in DXF you will not see an AcDbCurve subclass marker or any group codes related to curves.

Unbounded Straight Lines

The simplest drawing entity is the unbounded straight line, which is represented by the AcDbXline class. The xline entity extends indefinitely in both directions. On the screen and on paper, it runs from one edge of the drawing to the other. An xline has no extents or bounding box.

To completely define an AcDbXline object, you need to know one point located on the line and a direction vector, which tells how the line extends from the base point.

Selecting the base point on an xline is an arbitrary decision. Any point will do. Also keep in mind that flipping the direction vector creates an xline that is equivalent to the original line. Although all these xlines describe the same mathematical object, their parametrical representation is different. It is

```
X := BasePoint + u * DirectionVector
```

and u ranges from negative to positive infinity.

The base point is an arbitrary point in 3D space expressed in WCS coordinates (AcGePoint3d). The direction vector is also in WCS and normalized to a unit vector (AcGeVector3d).

ObjectDBX	ActiveX Automation	DXF/AutoLISP
basePoint()	BasePoint	Group 10
unitDir()	DirectionVector	Group 11

The DXF class name for AcDbXline is "XLINE". The sequence of AcDbXline-related groups is 10, 11. Don't forget that all points and vectors need three coordinates and three groups in DXF. Thus, the true sequence in DXF is 10, 20, 30, 11,21, 31. I abbreviate this to 10, 11 so that it compares to the AutoLISP group codes. (If you need more information about the different data types and how they appear in the various environments, see Chapter 3.)

ActiveX Automation provides an additional *SecondPoint* property, which is simply the base point plus the direction vector.

Single-Bounded Straight Lines

A variant of the xline is the AcDbRay object. This is also a straight line of infinite length, but it is bounded in one direction.

A ray has a base point and a direction vector. It extends from the base point along the direction vector to infinite length. It does not extend beyond the base point, however. Thus, in its parametrical representation, *u* ranges from zero to infinity.

As with an AcDbXline, the base point is an arbitrary 3D point in WCS coordinates, and the direction vector is a unit vector.

ObjectDBX	ActiveX Automation	DXF/AutoLISP
basePoint()	BasePoint	Group 10
unitDir()	DirectionVector	Group 11

The DXF class name for AcDbRay is "RAY". The sequence of groups in DXF is 10, 11. Again, ActiveX Automation provides a *SecondPoint* property, which is simply the base point plus the direction vector.

Finite Straight Lines

If we bound an xline in both directions, we end up with a finite straight line or just a line. A line is an object of class AcDbLine.

The parametrical representation of a line again takes a base point (now called *start point*) and a unit vector that describes the direction the line takes from the start point. The parameter range is bounded by zero (for the start point) and by the line's finite length (for the end point).

The properties of a finite line are a bit different from the definition used in xlines and rays. Again, there is a start point. Instead of a direction vector and a length, however, the line uses the end point directly. As usual, points are 3D, are in WCS, and are of type AcGePoint3d.

ObjectDBX	ActiveX Automation	DXF/AutoLISP
startPoint()	StartPoint	Group 10
endPoint()	EndPoint	Group 11

Two lines that share the same end points in opposite order are not identical. The DXF class name for AcDbLine objects is "LINE". The sequence of groups in DXF is 39, 10, 11, 210.

Lines That Have a Thickness

As you can see from the DXF groups listed in the previous section, an AcDbLine has more properties than start and end point. What are they for?

To understand the *Normal* and *Thickness* properties, we once again have to step back in history. In May 1985, Autodesk introduced 3D Level 1 as part of AutoCAD Version 2.1.

At that time, 3D in AutoCAD was far from what we know and use today. Recent versions of AutoCAD allow you to place wireframes, surfaces, and volumes at arbitrary locations and orientations in 3D space.

In 1985, AutoCAD didn't even know about Z coordinates. You could draw only in 2D. To mimic a little bit of 3D, you could elevate a line or circle onto a different Z level. The object, however, was still parallel to the X/Y plane. You couldn't assign different Z coordinates to the ends of a line.

You could, however, add a *Thickness* value to the line. (This has nothing to do with lineweights!) A thick line would extrude from its elevated position for a given Z height. This addition transforms the straight line into a surface entity, which may hide other objects when seen from a 3D direction.

AutoCAD gave up the *Elevation* property when true 3D coordinates were introduced. It kept the *Thickness* property, however. Thus, even today's AutoCAD drawing database can include lines that aren't lines but 3D surfaces.

Because there is no predefined Z direction for an arbitrary 3D line, the drawing database needs to add a direction vector (AcGeVector3d) to determine the direction into which the line extrudes. This direction is named *Normal*, although this term is not valid by today's definition of a normal. A normal vector is a vector that is perpendicular to a plane, but there is no such plane associated with a line. A better term would be *Extrusion Direction*.

The *Normal* vector can point in an arbitrary direction. If the *Thickness* value (a 64-bit real) is not zero, the line extrudes along this direction for the given thickness. Figure 10.1 shows an extruded line.

ObjectDBX	ActiveX Automation	DXF/AutoLISP
normal()	Normal	Group 210
thickness()	Thickness	Group 39

FIGURE 10.1

A line with a thickness

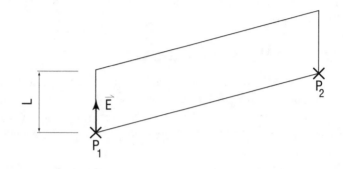

If the line's associated linetype has gaps, the surface created by extruding the line also has gaps that you can see through, as in Figure 10.2.

FIGURE 10.2

A thick line with its associated linetype

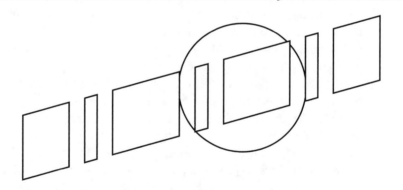

Calculated Properties for Lines

In addition to the defining properties listed in the previous section, three properties are available that are calculated from the start and end point coordinates:

- The *Length* property returns the line's length.
- The *Angle* property returns the angle between the line's direction vector and the WCS x-axis.
- The *Delta* property returns the coordinates of the vector from start to end point.

ObjectDBX	ActiveX Automation	DXF/AutoLISP
n/a	Length	n/a
n/a	Angle	n/a
n/a	Delta	n/a

Circular Curves

A circle is an object of type AcDbCircle. It is a planar curve derived from AcDbCurve with all points having a constant distance from a center point—the radius.

Like other planar entities, a circle defines its own local coordinate system. The X/Y plane of this coordinate system is parallel to the plane on which the circle is drawn. Within this local coordinate system, the parametrical representation of a circle is

```
C := Center + Radius * ( cos(u), sin(u), 0 )
```

and *u* ranges from 0° through 360° (or from 0 through 2*π when working in radians).

A Circle's Local Coordinate System

The local coordinate system of a circle or other planar entity is called the *Entity Coordinate System* (ECS). The ECS is defined as follows:

- The ECS z-axis is perpendicular to the plane in which the circle is drawn. This is also called the plane's normal and is returned by the circle's *Normal* property.
- The world origin (0,0,0) is also the ECS origin.
- The ECS x-axis is calculated from the ECS z-axis using the arbitrary axis algorithm discussed in Chapter 3.
- The ECS y-axis is simply the cross-product of ECS Z and ECS X.

The interactive environments such as ObjectDBX and AutoLISP come with a series of functions to translate points between an entity's ECS and the global WCS (and other coordinate systems). When working with DXF files, you need to use one of the various implementations of the arbitrary axis algorithm to create this transformation on your own.

The Defining Properties of a Circle

An AcDbCircle entity is defined by its *Center*, *Radius*, and *Normal* properties. Because circles can be extruded, a fourth defining property is the circle's *Thickness*. The normal vector defines both the ECS and the extrusion direction, which means that circles can only be extruded perpendicular to the plane in which they are drawn. Therefore, an extruded circle defines a true cylinder surface.

Extruded circles and other extruded curved lines are displayed in AutoCAD using tesselation lines that are parallel to the extrusion direction. The density of these lines depends on the *Detailing* (also *Arc Smoothness*) property of the viewport in which they are drawn.

As is the case with lines, an associated linetype can create gaps in the cylinder surface. The circle surface itself is always opaque in hidden line views.

The center point is a 3D point and is returned in WCS coordinates in ObjectDBX and ActiveX Automation. In AutoLISP and DXF, the center coordinates are in the circle's local coordinate system. The normal vector is, of course, always in WCS. The radius is a length, that is, positive and greater than zero.

ObjectDBX	ActiveX Automation	DXF/AutoLISP
center(), in WCS	Center, in WCS	Group 10, in ECS
radius()	Radius	Group 40
normal()	Normal	Group 210
thickness()	Thickness	Group 39

The DXF class name for an AcDbCircle object is `"CIRCLE"`. The DXF group sequence is 39, 10, 40, 210.

The Calculated Properties of a Circle

ActiveX Automation supports two additional calculated properties:

- The *Circumference* property, which returns the length of the circle's outline
- The *Diameter* property, which is simply twice the radius

ObjectDBX	ActiveX Automation	DXF/AutoLISP
n/a	Circumference	n/a
n/a	Diameter	n/a

If you are interested in the *Area* property of a circle, remember that a circle is derived from AcDbCurve and therefore supports all curve properties, including the area value.

Circular Arcs

A circular arc is a bounded circle curve. Usually, circular arcs are simply referred to as *arcs*. Don't forget that the AutoCAD drawing database also supports elliptical arcs.

A circular arc is an object of class AcDbArc, which is directly derived from AcDb-Curve and not, as one could expect, from AcDbCircle.

An arc uses all properties and the parametrical representation of a full circle. The only difference is that the value range for the parameter u is limited from a start angle to an end angle.

Arcs in an AutoCAD drawing database are always defined and drawn counter-clockwise, which means that the end parameter is always larger than the start parameter (as it is with every curve). You might be wondering how this allows you to define an arc with a start angle of 270° and an end angle of 45°. Simply use 360° + 45° for the end parameter. The end parameter can range up to 720°. The two *angles* used to define arcs in all environments are the two parameters transformed into the range from 0° through 360° (which is called a *first period* angle).

Like all elements of the arc's parameter representation, the start and end angle are expressed in the arc's local coordinate system. In other words, they are relative to the ECS x-axis. Like any other angle, these are degree values in DXF and radian values in all other environments. As with circles, an arc can be extruded to a certain thickness along its normal vector.

ObjectDBX	ActiveX Automation	DXF/AutoLISP
center(), in WCS	Center, in WCS	Group 10, in ECS
radius()	Radius	Group 40
startAngle(), in ECS	StartAngle, in ECS	Group 50, in ECS
endAngle(), in ECS	EndAngle, in ECS	Group 51, in ECS
normal()	Normal	Group 210
thickness()	Thickness	Group 39

The DXF class name of an AcDbArc object is "ARC". The DXF group sequence is 39, 10, 40, 50, 51, 210. In ActiveX Automation, you have access to several calculated arc properties, including the arc's start and end points.

 WARNING   When calculating these two points in other environments, keep in mind that an ASCII DXF file may contain a limited resolution if the AutoCAD user decided to create it that way. In this case, the offset between the calculated end point and an adjacent line may introduce serious errors that result in gaps where there should have been closed contours. Always create DXF files using maximum resolution!

Calculated properties in ActiveX Automation are the start and end points in WCS coordinates, the total (that is, included) angle, and the arc length.

ObjectDBX	ActiveX Automation	DXF/AutoLISP
n/a	StartPoint	n/a
n/a	EndPoint	n/a
n/a	TotalAngle	n/a
n/a	ArcLength	n/a

Ellipses and Elliptical Arcs

Ellipses and elliptical arcs are similar to circles and circular arcs. Because they are newer AutoCAD entities, they don't carry some of the burden of circles and arcs. For instance, they don't have a *Thickness* property since they cannot be extruded. Also, they don't need the arbitrary axis algorithm to calculate their local coordinate system.

Another benefit of ellipses and elliptical arcs is that they are both expressed by the same AcDbEllipse class that is derived from the abstract AcDbCurve class. All ellipses, whether arcs or not, have start and end parameters. With full ellipses, the start parameter is 0, and the end parameter is $2*\pi$.

An ellipse uses a local coordinate system that is calculated as follows:

- The local z-axis is perpendicular to the plane on which the ellipse is drawn. This is the ellipse's *Normal* property.
- The local x-axis is parallel to the ellipse's major axis. This is the *Major Axis Vector* property.
- Finally, the local origin is the ellipse center as returned by the *Center* property.

Within this local coordinate system, the parametrical representation of a complete ellipse is simple:

```
E := ( a * cos (u), b * sin(u), 0)
```

and *u* ranges from 0 through $2*\pi$.

In this formula a is half the ellipse's major axis length, and b is half the ellipse's minor axis length. The *major* axis is the one that defines the parameter 0 point. It is not necessarily the larger of the two axes.

In the case of an elliptical arc, the parameter range is from start parameter to end parameter, which creates an elliptical arc that goes counter-clockwise from its start point to its end point. As with circles, the end parameter may be in the range of up to $4*\pi$.

The parameter used to define an elliptical arc looks like an angle. It is *not* the angle between the major axis and maybe the start point as with a circular arc, however.

Using the parametrical representation, you can calculate ellipse angles from their parameters and vice versa. In ObjectDBX, the AcDbEllipse object provides two functions for this calculation: *angleAtParam()* and *paramAtAngle()*.

The defining parameters for the major and minor axes of an ellipse are a bit strange as well. You need one direction (of the major axis) and two lengths. The defining parameters are one vector (AcGeVector3d), which gives us both the direction and the length of (half of) the major axis, and the ratio between major and minor axes lengths.

The major axis vector must have a positive length and must be perpendicular to the ellipse's normal vector. In all environments, including DXF, all points are in WCS coordinates.

ObjectDBX	ActiveX Automation	DXF/AutoLISP
center()	Center	Group 10
majorAxis()	MajorAxis	Group 11
normal()	Normal	Group 210
radiusRatio()	RadiusRatio	Group 40
getStartParam()	StartParameter	Group 41
getEndParam()	EndParameter	Group 42

The DXF class name of an AcDbEllipse object is `"ELLIPSE"`. The DXF group sequence is 10, 11, 210, 40, 41, 42.

The AcDbEllipse object provides several calculated properties that simplify the use of ellipses. This includes calculating the start and end points and angles from the parameters and calculating the major and minor axes lengths and directions. The calculated angles are to be read in the ellipse's local coordinate system relative to the major axis. The radius returned is half the length of the corresponding axis.

ObjectDBX	ActiveX Automation	DXF/AutoLISP
n/a	StartPoint	n/a
n/a	EndPoint	n/a
startAngle()	StartAngle	n/a
endAngle()	EndAngle	n/a
n/a	MajorRadius	n/a
n/a	MinorRadius	n/a
minorAxis()	MinorAxis	n/a

Spline Curves

All the curves I have discussed so far in this chapter have a single, uniform parameter representation. This changes with spline curves. A spline curve is defined in segments. For example, there might be one formula for parameter values between zero and one, another formula for parameter values between one and two, and so on.

To create a smooth curve, adjacent segments of a spline must follow certain rules:

- The composite curve has to be continuous. In other words, you can't have a gap at the end of a segment. The first formula must calculate the exact same point from its maximum parameter value as the next segment's formula from its minimum parameter value.

- The first derivative of the composite curve must also be continuous. In other words, the composite curve has no sharp bends where the segments meet.

- Finally, the second derivative of the composite curve must be continuous. In other words, the curvature at the end of one segment must be the same as the curvature at the beginning of the next segment.

If a spline has a *degree* greater than 2, these derivatives must also be continuous. The *order* of a spline is the degree plus one, that is, a spline of order 3 or *cubic* spline is continuous up to the second derivative.

ObjectDBX	ActiveX Automation	DXF/AutoLISP
degree()	Degree	Group 71

Spline curves can be defined in several ways. AutoCAD uses a type of splines known as *nonuniform rational B-splines* (or simply *NURBS*). The term *nonuniform* refers to the parameter ranges, in which the first segment's parameter range might be smaller or larger than the second, third, and so on. The term *B-spline* refers to the basis function (formula) that describes the individual segments. The term *rational* refers to how the various segment formulas relate.

The basic functions used to define the individual spline segments are a bit more complex than what I provide here, and developing them would take a bit too much space. If you're interested in this topic, I suggest reading Daniel Olfe's book *Computer Graphics for Design–From Algorithms to AutoCAD* (Prentice Hall, 1995), which devotes 50 pages to splines. NURBS are powerful curves because they can also define analytical curves such as circles or ellipses.

In AutoCAD, the AcDbSpline entity represents two types of NURBS curves: those that know how they have been constructed and those that don't. The first set has all the information of the second set, but in addition keeps a list of defining points, two tangents, and a tolerance value.

The Fit Data of a Spline

A spline's fit data is a sequence of points used to generate the spline curve. AutoCAD remembers these until an operation directly modifies the calculated curve, for example, by moving control points or by introducing weights. In this case, the spline's fit data is lost because you cannot calculate it backward from the NURBS data.

The fit data points define a series of locations through which the spline must pass. This does not completely define the curve, because you can draw the first and last segments in multiple ways. Therefore, the spline either has additional information in the form of start and end tangent directions, or the start and end points are used more than once.

ObjectDBX	ActiveX Automation	DXF/AutoLISP
getFitPointAt()	FitPoints	Group 11
getFitTangents(), start tangent	StartTangent	Group 12
getFitTangents(), end tangent	EndTangent	Group 13

All environments, including DXF, also supply a calculated property: the number of fit points.

ObjectDBX	ActiveX Automation	DXF/AutoLISP
numFitPoints()	NumberOfFitPoints	Group 74

The spline curve passes exactly through the specified points. A user may have chosen, however, to allow the curve to pass close to the specified points.

The *Fit Tolerance* property defines how good fit points and the curve must match. It is the maximum distance between a fit point and the curve.

ObjectDBX	ActiveX Automation	DXF/AutoLISP
fitTolerance()	FitTolerance	Group 44

NURBS Data

Every AcDbSpline object, regardless of whether it has fit data, includes the information on the spline curve itself. Modifying any of this information while in AutoCAD automatically deletes the curve's fit data. In DXF, manipulating the NURBS data without deleting the fit data creates an inconsistent entity.

The definition of a spline also consists of a number of points, called *control points* or *knots*. These two are not exactly the same. With open splines, the first and last control point creates *k* identical knots (*k* is the order of the spline). The control points do not necessarily lie on the resulting curve. They simply define where the NURBS is going to be.

ObjectDBX	ActiveX Automation	DXF/AutoLISP
getControlPointAt()	ControlPoints	Group 10

Again, there is a calculated property for the set of control points:

ObjectDBX	ActiveX Automation	DXF/AutoLISP
numControlPoints()	NumberOfControlPoints	Group 73

Every pair of adjacent control points defines one segment of the spline's parametrical representation. The *Knot Values* are the parameter values at the control points.

ObjectDBX	ActiveX Automation	DXF / AutoLISP
n/a	n/a	Group 72 (number of knots)
getNurbsData(), knots	Knots	Group 40

Every control point can have an associated weight that pulls the curve toward the control point if the weight is larger than 1.0. Initially, all control points have an identical weight of 1.0.

If a spline has varying weights, it is called *rational* because a ratio of weights comes into play. You can query to determine if a spline is rational, and you can get the weights for all control points.

ObjectDBX	ActiveX Automation	DXF/AutoLISP
isRational()	IsRational	Third bit (4) of group 70
weightAt()	ControlPoints	Group 10

Finally, two tolerance values are used within the calculation of control points and knots.

ObjectDBX	ActiveX Automation	DXF/AutoLISP
getNurbsData(), control point tolerance	n/a	Group 43
getNurbsData(), knot tolerance	n/a	Group 42

The AcDbCurve Properties and Splines

I said before that AcDbCurve properties are never made available to DXF and ActiveX Automation. This is not true for NURBS; you can check a number of Boolean flags.

ObjectDBX	ActiveX Automation	DXF/AutoLISP
isClosed()	Closed	First bit (1) of group 70
isPeriodic()	IsPeriodic	Second bit (2) of group 70
isPlanar()	IsPlanar	Fourth bit (8) of group 70
n/a	n/a	Fifth bit (16) of group 70: isLinear

If a spline curve is planar, you can query the curve's plane's normal vector in AutoLISP and DXF.

ObjectDBX	ActiveX Automation	DXF/AutoLISP
n/a	n/a	Group 210

The DXF Sequence for Splines

AcDbSpline objects use the "SPLINE" DXF class name. The sequence of groups in DXF is as follows: 210, 70, 71, 72, 73, 74, 42, 43, 44, 12, 13, 40 (repeated), 41 (repeated), 10 (repeated), 11 (repeated). All coordinates are in WCS.

This concludes our initial discussion on curves. Chapter 13 will cover another type of curve, the polyline. Before we get into annotations, however, which is the topic of the next chapter, I want to discuss one more database entity.

3D Faces

The AcDbFace object describes a simple surface in 3D. An AcDbFace object is a four-sided, not necessarily planar, surface. Even though it looks like a quadrangle, this object is *not* a curve. The visible parts of the face are simply the edges of the face. The internal of the face is also part of the face. For example, it hides other objects and fills with a color in shaded views.

If the four corners of a face do not lie on a common plane, they create a nonplanar face. Unfortunately, the AcDbFace definition is based on only the four corner points. There is no information about the geometric structure of the internal of a face. Depending on your application, you may need to apply a Coons surface or a B-spline surface to the given edges. Or you can act like AutoCAD and simply divide nonplanar faces into two planar triangles when needed. Figure 10.3 shows a nonplanar 3D face with theoretical isolines.

FIGURE 10.3

A 3D face surface

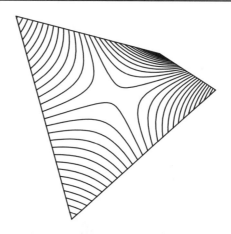

AcDbFace objects always have four corners (and therefore four edges). The Auto-CAD commands allows you to create three-sided faces, but in the database even those end up as four-sided faces with corners 3 and 4 having identical coordinates.

ObjectDBX	ActiveX Automation	DXF / AutoLISP
getVertexAt(0)	Coordinates(0)	Group 10
getVertexAt(1)	Coordinates(1)	Group 11
getVertexAt(2)	Coordinates(2)	Group 12
getVertexAt(3)	Coordinates(3)	Group 13

All coordinates are in WCS. Edge 1 connects corners 1 and 2, edge 2 connects corners 2 and 3, edge 3 connects corners 3 and 4, and edge 4 connects corners 4 and 1.

In a wireframe view, you can make individual edges of a face invisible. This is used to suppress a common edge of two adjacent faces, which then look like a multisided face. The visibility of each edge is controlled by a Boolean flag.

ObjectDBX	ActiveX Automation	DXF/AutoLISP
isEdgeVisibleAt(0)	VisibilityEdge1	First bit (1) of group 70 negated
isEdgeVisibleAt(1)	VisibilityEdge2	Second bit (2) of group 70 negated
isEdgeVisibleAt(2)	VisibilityEdge3	Third bit (4) of group 70 negated
isEdgeVisibleAt(3)	VisibilityEdge4	Fourth bit (8) of group 70 negated

In DXF, the corresponding bit is set when the edge is *not* visible. The DXF class name for an AcDbFace object is `"3DFACE"`. The sequence of groups is 10, 11, 12, 13, 70.

Summary

In this chapter, you learned about the first set of database objects: simple curves and simple faces. In theory, using only a few of them, such as lines and arcs, allows you to draw any vector image (or "drawing"). Not long ago there were drafting programs that were limited to such basic curves.

Using and understanding the curves described here is quite simple, but they provide a good starting point for the next chapters, which cover many other, often much more complex, objects. Our next topic is the annotations within a drawing.

CHAPTER **11**

Annotation Objects

FEATURING

Points	*232*
Shape symbols	*234*
Single lines of text	*235*
Paragraph text	*240*
Feature control frames	*245*
Semi-custom annotation objects	*248*

Although the basic curves and faces form the most important group of AutoCAD drawing entities, the annotation objects are a close second. Annotation objects add no geometric information to the model or part saved in a drawing. Instead, they help the human reader of such a drawing to understand and manufacture the part.

A special form of annotation is a dimension. Dimensioning is quite complex and involves a large number of cooperating objects. Therefore, I'll cover dimensioning in its own chapter, which is next. This chapter explains the following annotation objects:

AcDbPoint   A marker for a single point in 3D space

AcDbShape   A single annotation symbol

AcDbText   A single line of annotation text

AcDbMtext   A whole paragraph of annotation text

AcDbFcf   A feature control frame, which is a boxed annotation containing symbols and text

The AcDbArcAlignedText and RText annotation objects are common in AutoCAD drawing databases but not completely implemented.

All annotation objects are planar entities. Even though they may use lines and curves to display themselves, annotation objects ignore any associated linetype and always display using continuous lines. We'll start by looking at the simplest annotation object, a point marker.

Point Objects

The AcDbPoint object represents a marker that displays a single location in 3D space. In rare cases, points describe geometry on its own, but even then, the AcDbPoint object creates an annotation marker at the corresponding location.

To display point markers, AutoCAD supports a fixed set of symbols, which are shown in Figure 11.1. The selected symbol is a global setting, and all points in a drawing use the same symbol. The PDMODE global setting defines the symbol to use, and the PDSIZE global setting determines the size of the point marker. The size is absolute, or it is relative to the current view. See Chapter 4 for details.

The point location is given in world coordinates in all environments.

ObjectDBX	ActiveX Automation	DXF/AutoLISP
position()	Coordinate	Group 10

FIGURE 11.1

Available point marker symbols

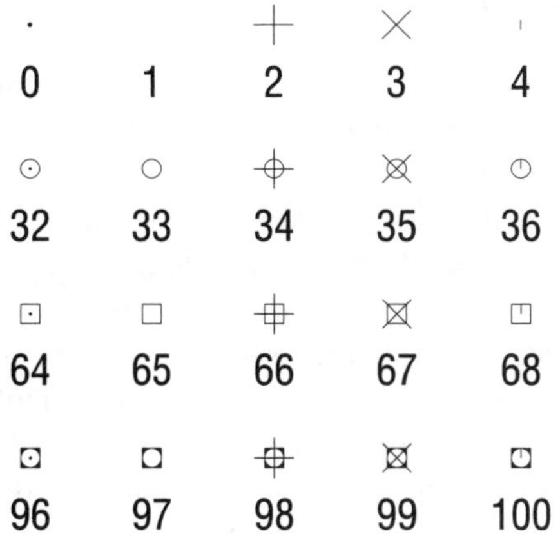

.		+	×	ı
0	1	2	3	4
⊙	○	⊕	⊗	◔
32	33	34	35	36
⊡	□	⊞	⊠	⊓
64	65	66	67	68
⊡	▢	⊕	⊠	◪
96	97	98	99	100

Because the point symbol is a planar entity, it has an originating plane that is defined by its normal direction vector.

ObjectDBX	ActiveX Automation	DXF/AutoLISP
normal()	Normal	Group 210

This direction vector defines the local coordinate system of the point marker with its origin at the point location and its x-axis calculated from the normal using the arbitrary axis algorithm.

The rotation of the symbol within this local coordinate system is the angle between the local x-axis and the horizontal of the point symbol, as shown in Figure 11.1.

ObjectDBX	ActiveX Automation	DXF/AutoLISP
ecsRotation()	n/a	Group 50

Within its local coordinate system, the point marker looks like a collection of lines and circles. For historic reasons, the point marker symbol can be extruded along its normal vector. In this case, it becomes a collection of extruded lines (faces) and extruded circles (cylinder surfaces). A single dot is extruded into a straight line. (For more on extruded lines and circles, see Chapter 10.)

ObjectDBX	ActiveX Automation	DXF/AutoLISP
thickness()	Thickness	Group 39

An AcDbPoint object uses the DXF class name "POINT". The sequence of groups in DXF is 39, 10, 210, 50.

Shape Symbols

The AcDbShape object defines a shape symbol insert, which is similar to a point marker object. The main difference is that AcDbShape objects can reference different symbols in different sizes.

The AcDbShape object does not contain any information about the geometry or shape of the symbol. Shape symbols are defined in shape symbol libraries, which are external to the drawing database. The AcDbTextStyleTable object contains the file-names of any symbol libraries attached to the current database.

Interestingly, the reference to a shape symbol is by name and does not contain any link to the corresponding AcDbTextStyleTableRecord object. It seems as if AutoCAD keeps a list of names of all shapes taken from the files referenced by the text style table. If two loaded files contain a shape of the same name, the result is undefined.

ObjectDBX	ActiveX Automation	DXF/AutoLISP
name()	Name	Group 2

Shapes are saved in files of type SHX, which are AutoCAD's compiled shape library files. Autodesk does not publish the format of compiled shape files. The shape geometry consists of 2D lines and arcs. Figure 11.2 shows a sample shape symbol.

FIGURE 11.2

A shape symbol

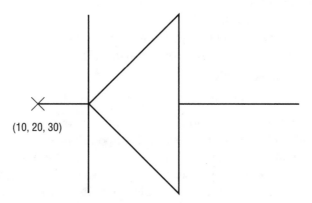

(10, 20, 30)

The shape's *Location* (start point), *Normal, Thickness,* and *Rotation* properties resemble their counterparts for the AcDbPoint object. The local coordinate system of a shape is calculated from the normal vector. As is the case with circles, the ECS origin equals the world origin. The location of the shape is returned in ECS coordinates in DXF and AutoLISP.

ObjectDBX	ActiveX Automation	DXF/AutoLISP
position(), in WCS	InsertionPoint, in WCS	Group 10, in ECS
normal()	Normal	Group 210
rotation()	Rotation	Group 50
thickness()	Thickness	Group 39

In addition, every insertion of a shape symbol can be individually scaled and transformed. Three transformations are applied:

- A general scaling applied to all coordinates from the shape definition
- A linear scaling applied only to the X coordinates in the shape definition,
- An eventual shearing of all shape components, as shown in Figure 11.3

FIGURE 11.3

The shearing of a shape symbol

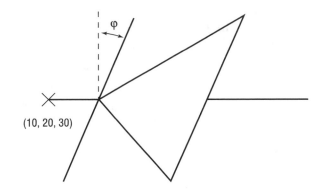

φ

(10, 20, 30)

ObjectDBX	ActiveX Automation	DXF/AutoLISP
size()	Height	Group 40
widthFactor()	ScaleFactor	Group 41
oblique()	ObliqueAngle	Group 51

The AcDbShape object's DXF class name is `"SHAPE"`. The DXF sequence is 39, 10, 40, 2, 50, 41, 51, 210.

Single Lines of Text

The individual characters of an AutoCAD vector font are not only *like* shape symbols, they *are* shape symbols. In fact, AutoCAD even uses the same file extension

(SHX) for both vector fonts and shape symbol libraries. The AcDbTextStyleTable object contains both the references to font files and those to shape libraries.

When drawing a vector font text, AutoCAD draws the shape associated with the first text character. At the end of the shape, it draws the shape associated with the second text character and so on. Even though AutoCAD can also use Windows fonts (TTF), it helps to think of text objects as a connected series of shapes.

The AcDbText object defines a single line of text, that is, a number of connected shapes. Even the space character in an AutoCAD vector font is a shape (it contains only one gap vector). The DXF class name is "TEXT", and the DXF group sequence is strange: following the usual AcDbText subclass marker (group 100) are the groups 39, 10, 40, 1, 50, 41, 51, 7, 71, 72, 11, and 210. Following this is another subclass marker, again using the string "AcDbText", and a final group 73.

Like all annotation objects, text lines are planar entities. The plane's normal defines the local coordinate system for the text. As with circles and shape symbols, the ECS origin equals the world origin, and the local x-axis is calculated from the normal using the arbitrary axis algorithm.

The following properties are exactly equal to those of an AcDbShape object:

ObjectDBX	ActiveX Automation	DXF/AutoLISP
position(), in WCS	InsertionPoint, in WCS	Group 10, in ECS
normal()	Normal	Group 210
rotation()	Rotation	Group 50
thickness()	Thickness	Group 39
size()	Height	Group 40
widthFactor()	ScaleFactor	Group 41
oblique()	ObliqueAngle	Group 51

All shape transformations, such as *Scaling, X-Scaling,* and *Shearing,* are applied to all shapes (characters) that form the text string. In addition, the AcDbText object allows two additional shape transformations:

- The *Backwards* property mirrors each shape by multiplying the shape's X coordinates by –1.

- The *Upside Down* property consequently multiplies the Y coordinates by –1.

Both create mirrored text that runs from right to left or upside down.

ObjectDBX	ActiveX Automation	DXF/AutoLISP
isMirroredInX()	Backward	Second bit (2) of group 71
isMirroredInY()	UpsideDown	Third bit (4) of group 71

Text Style and Characters

The two main properties of a single line of text are the text style and the list of characters to draw.

The *Text Style* property links the AcDbText object to an AcDbTextStyleTableRecord object. The table entry defines the font file to use with this text. With SHX fonts, it also defines which variant of the font is to be used. SHX font files can include two font definitions: one for horizontal text, and another for vertical text.

ObjectDBX	ActiveX Automation	DXF/AutoLISP
textStyle()	StyleName	Group 7

ObjectDBX returns the AcDbObjectId of the symbol table record, and the other environments return the record's key string.

You can query the list of characters to draw through the second AcDbText property:

ObjectDBX	ActiveX Automation	DXF/AutoLISP
textString()	TextString	Group 1

Like any other string in the AutoCAD drawing database, the text string is allowed to contain any Unicode character, whether in the current code page or not.

If the *Text String* property contains characters that are not available in the associated font file, AutoCAD displays a question mark.

For historic reasons (that is, from the time those characters were not included in any reasonable font), an AcDbText object exchanges some character sequences with a different character. These sequences are as follows:

Text String Content	Becomes
%%d	Degree symbol °
%%p	Tolerance symbol +/–
%%c	Diameter symbol ⌀

In addition, a double percent (%%) followed by any three-digit number references the shape or character associated with this number in the font file. In the very unlikely case that you want to draw two consecutive percent characters as ordinary text, you need to write six of them.

The caret symbol (^) reduces the ASCII value of the following letter by 64. This creates control characters, which are unlikely to be used in annotation text. It is more likely that you'll want a caret in your text. If so, use a caret followed by a space character.

If a text style references both an SHX font file and a *Big Font* file, the first character from the *Big Font* file becomes an escape character. Within a text string, the escape character's ASCII code is multiplied by 256 and added to the ASCII code of the following character. This calculation gives the *Big Font* file-internal position of the character to draw.

Text Formatting

An AcDbText object supports no individual formatting for characters in the text string. AutoCAD simply draws one character's shape following the other.

By using special shape definitions, some SHX font files allow code sequences that create a subscript or a superscript effect. You cannot determine this, however, from the character string used in the AcDbText object. This is just a property of the individual font file used.

The only way to add some kind of formatting to individual characters in a text string is to use the %%u and %%o character sequences. The %%u sequence is not drawn to the screen. Instead, this sequence starts the underlining of the text. The underlining continues to the end of the text or to the next %%u sequence, whichever comes first. The corresponding sequence, %%o, overlines the text, that is, draws a line above the characters.

If you need further formatting options, see the AcDbMtext object described next.

Text Justification

Any AcDbText object is simply a series of connected shapes or subsequent characters when visualized.

The text properties I've discussed so far completely describe this visualization. An AcDbText object, however, has a few more properties that affect the way AutoCAD later edits the object.

Even though every text entity has an insertion point where the first character shape starts, this point can be a calculated property. For instance, the text entity may have been drawn right-justified in AutoCAD. In this case, AutoCAD calculates the text insertion point from the entered justification point and the overall text length.

To visualize the text, you need only the calculated insertion point, but for later edits it is wise to also remember the justification point and the justification style.

ObjectDBX	ActiveX Automation	DXF/AutoLISP
alignmentPoint()	TextAlignmentPoint	Group 11

The text alignment point is undefined and omitted from DXF and AutoLISP if the text is justified to the insertion point (that is, to the left).

The text alignment is set by two properties, which define the horizontal and vertical justification of the text.

ObjectDBX	ActiveX Automation	DXF/AutoLISP
horizontalMode()	HorizontalAlignment	Group 72
verticalMode()	VerticalAlignment	Group 73

The horizontal alignment is taken from the following list:

ObjectDBX	ActiveX Automation	DXF/AutoLISP
kTextLeft	acHorizontalAlignmentLeft	0
kTextCenter	acHorizontalAlignmentCenter	1
kTextRight	acHorizontalAlignmentRight	2
kTextAlign	acHorizontalAlignmentAligned	3
kTextMid	acHorizontalAlignmentMiddle	4
kTextFit	acHorizontalAlignmentFit	5

The vertical alignment is taken from the following list:

ObjectDBX	ActiveX Automation	DXF/AutoLISP
kTextBase	acVerticalAlignmentBaseline	0
kTextBottom	acVerticalAlignmentBottom	1
kTextVertMid	acVerticalAlignmentMiddle	2
kTextTop	acVerticalAlignmentTop	3

The position of the justification point depends on the horizontal and vertical alignment. The maximum height of characters and the distance that descenders extend below the baseline are set in the font file. Both do not depend on the actual text string contents.

Horizontal	Vertical	Justification Point
Left	Baseline	n/a
Left	Bottom	Intersection of left border and descender line
Left	Middle	Intersection of left border and midline between baseline and maximum character height
Left	Top	Intersection of left border and maximum character height
Center	Baseline	Midpoint between left and right end of baseline

Horizontal	Vertical	Justification Point
Center	Bottom	Combines Center/Baseline and Left/Bottom
Center	Middle	Combines Center/Baseline and Left/Middle
Center	Top	Combines Center/Baseline and Left/Top
Right	Baseline	Right end of baseline
Right	Bottom	Combines Right/Baseline and Left/Bottom
Right	Middle	Combines Right/Baseline and Left/Middle
Right	Top	Combines Right/Baseline and Left/Top
Aligned	Baseline	Right end of baseline
Fit	Baseline	Right end of baseline
Middle	Baseline	Center of the bounding box of the actual text string drawn

The alignment point is the same for Right/Baseline, Aligned/Baseline, and Fit/Baseline. The three variants differ in how AutoCAD modifies the AcDbText object as soon as the alignment point moves.

At Right/Baseline, the text insertion point moves accordingly. At Aligned/Baseline, the insertion point does not move. Instead, the text height changes until the text string fills the complete baseline. At Fit/Baseline, the width factor changes so that the text string again starts at the insertion point.

Paragraph Text

AcDbText objects have certain limitations. You cannot use more than one font, one style, or one color within a single line of text, and longer text strings do not word-wrap into multiple lines. Paragraph text overcomes these limitations.

The AcDbMText object has similarities to an AcDbText object. Both use properties such as *Text Style* and *Text Height* to define the outlook of the characters to be drawn. A paragraph text, however, allows embedded formatting codes and automatically wraps long text strings into multiple lines.

Let's look at the properties common to the AcDbText and AcDbMText objects first. Both text objects are planar. A normal defines the local coordinate system, which is calculated in the same way for both. Both have a text style and a text height, although for paragraph text these properties define only the default character properties. And, finally, both have a *Rotation* property, which defines the orientation of the baseline in the local coordinate system.

ObjectDBX	ActiveX Automation	DXF/AutoLISP
normal()	Normal	Group 210
rotation()	Rotation	Group 50
textHeight()	Height	Group 40
textStyle()	StyleName	Group 7

The *Rotation* property is replicated in another property that contains the WCS direction vector and corresponds to the ECS rotation angle.

ObjectDBX	ActiveX Automation	DXF/AutoLISP
direction()	n/a	Group 11

Contrary to AcDbText objects, paragraph text makes direct use of several properties of the associated text style table record. In ObjectDBX, you can use the following functions to directly access the symbol table record: *isMirroredInX()*, *isMirroredInY()*, and *oblique()*.

MText Location and Size

An AcDbMText object fills a rectangle located in the text's local coordinate system. The rectangle is rotated to create baselines other than horizontal baselines.

Defining properties of this rectangle are an insertion point (one corner), a width, and an attachment direction. The rectangle height depends on the number of lines needed to draw the text.

ObjectDBX	ActiveX Automation	DXF/AutoLISP
location(), in WCS	InsertionPoint, in WCS	Group 10, in ECS
width()	Width	Group 41
attachment()	AttachmentPoint	Group 71

The bounding rectangle can be attached to the insertion point in nine ways:

ObjectDBX	ActiveX Automation	DXF/AutoLISP
kTopLeft	acAttachmentPointTopLeft	1
kTopCenter	acAttachmentPointTopCenter	2
kTopRight	acAttachmentPointTopRight	3
kMiddleLeft	acAttachmentPointMiddleLeft	4
kMiddleCenter	acAttachmentPointMiddleCenter	5

ObjectDBX	ActiveX Automation	DXF/AutoLISP
kMiddleRight	acAttachmentPointMiddleRight	6
kBottomLeft	acAttachmentPointBottomLeft	7
kBottomCenter	acAttachmentPointBottomCenter	8
kBottomRight	acAttachmentPointBottomRight	9

The text rectangle is drawn in such a way that the insertion point becomes the corresponding corner or midpoint of the rectangle, for example, the top-left corner or the midpoint of the left edge.

Within this rectangle, the text is drawn from left to right until it reaches the predefined width. There the text word-wraps, which means that the complete word that passes the right edge is written to the next line. If a word is longer than the rectangle width, it is not broken into two pieces. Instead, it is drawn over the right edge of the paragraph rectangle.

One property describes the text flow direction (left to right, top to bottom); however, this property is not evaluated in AutoCAD 2000.

ObjectDBX	ActiveX Automation	DXF/AutoLISP
flowDirection()	DrawingDirection	Group 72

According to the AutoCAD documentation, the plan is for this property to contain the following values. It's currently set to inherit the text flow from the text style table record.

ObjectDBX	ActiveX Automation	DXF/AutoLISP
kLtoR	acRightToLeft	1
kTtoB	acTopToBottom	3
kByStyle	acByStyle	5

Because words will be moved to the next line before they reach the right edge, the true bounding rectangle of the paragraph text is slightly narrower than the predefined maximum width. And with very long words, the bounding rectangle may be even wider. You can query both the actual width and the actual height of the bounding rectangle.

ObjectDBX	ActiveX Automation	DXF/AutoLISP
actualWidth()	n/a	Group 42
actualHeight()	n/a	Group 43

MText Contents and Formatting

The actual contents of the multiline text is a long string of characters. This string contains both the characters to draw and the eventual formatting codes.

In DXF and AutoLISP, the string is broken into chunks of 250 characters, using group code 3. The last (or only) chunk shorter than 250 characters uses group code 1.

ObjectDBX	ActiveX Automation	DXF/AutoLISP
contents()	TextString	Group 3 (repeated), group 1

If a paragraph text needs to be broken into multiple lines, the baseline of each new line is offset from the previous baseline. To determine the line spacing distance, you use two properties:

ObjectDBX	ActiveX Automation	DXF/AutoLISP
lineSpacingStyle()	LineSpacingStyle	Group 73
lineSpacingFactor()	LineSpacingFactor	Group 44

Possible values for the line-spacing style are:

ObjectDBX	ActiveX Automation	DXF/AutoLISP
kAtLeast	acLineSpacingStyleAtLeast	1
kExactly	acLineSpacingStyleExactly	2

Line spacing is determined by the default text height of the AcDbMText property. Nominal line spacing is 5/3 this height. This is multiplied by the line-spacing factor if the style is set to *exactly*. If the style is set to *at least*, nominal line spacing is 5/3 times the height of the tallest character in a line.

You can modify the height of individual characters as well as their color, font, and other attributes by embedding formatting characters into the text. A first group of formatting characters represents control codes not usually available in text strings:

Formatting Characters	Meaning
\P	Hard line break
\~	Nonbreaking space
\\	Single backslash; otherwise used as an escape character
\{	Single opening curly bracket; otherwise used as block begin
\}	Single closing curly bracket; otherwise used as block end

The remaining characters modify the formatting of the text string characters. The format change is either valid from the code position to the end of the string, or it is restricted to a block of text. In the latter case, the block is enclosed with curly brackets ({ ... }).

Some formatting codes are followed by a parameter, for example, a color number or font filename. The parameter ends with a semicolon character.

Formatting Characters	Parameter	Meaning
\A	0, 1, or 2	Change alignment to bottom, center, or top
\C	ACI color number	Change character color
\F	Font information	Change to a different font (See the comment following this list.)
\H	New height or relative height followed by an x	Change text height
\L		Start underlining
\l		End underlining
\O		Start overlining
\o		End overlining
\T	New distance or relative distance followed by an x	Change kerning, i.e., character spacing
\W	New width or relative width followed by an x	Change character width, i.e., X scaling

A new font is given either by the name of an SHX font file including the .SHX extension or by the name of a Windows font (*not* filename), followed by the Windows font properties for bold, italic, charset, pitch, and family identifier, for example, \FArial|b1|i0|c0|p34; for Arial bold.

A final formatting code is \S, which defines stacked text or fractions. The \S formatting code is followed by two text segments, separated either by a slash (/) or a caret (^). A slash generates a stacked fraction, including a fraction bar; a caret creates stacked text without a fraction bar. Usually, a height setting precedes the stack code.

DXF Representation of Paragraph Text

The DXF class name for an AcDbMText object is "MTEXT". The group codes for this entity appear in the following order: 10, 40, 41, 71, 72, 3 (repeated), 1, 7, 210, 11, 42, 43, 50, 73, 40.

Feature Control Frames

A feature control frame is a special annotation object that is usually attached to geometry by a leader arrow. The annotation describes certain tolerance issues that a manufactured part has to fulfill, for example, how parallel two faces must be or how smooth a surface is to be.

An AcDbFcf object is similar to a line of text even though it can consist of two or more lines. Like paragraph text, formatting characters are used to separate the individual elements that make up the text string. Each line of the control frame is bounded by a rectangle.

Figure 11.4 shows an example of a feature control frame. This figure doesn't illustrate any real world tolerance controls; it simply shows some of the things an AcDbFcf object can contain.

FIGURE 11.4

A feature control frame

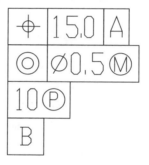

Because a feature control frame is an annotation object, it needs roughly the same data as AcDbText or AcDbMText objects. It gets this information in another way, however. Who says a historically grown data structure should be consistent?

This entity is also a planar object. It has a normal and a local coordinate system. The local coordinate system is defined differently, however. The AcDbFcf object has an insertion point, a normal, and a direction vector. The insertion point becomes the origin of the local coordinate system, the direction defines the x-axis, and the normal defines the z-axis. All these are WCS coordinates and directions.

ObjectDBX	ActiveX Automation	DXF/AutoLISP
location()	InsertionPoint	Group 10
direction()	DirectionVector	Group 11
normal()	Normal	Group 210

Within its local coordinate system, an AcDbFcf entity is always horizontal. Therefore, no rotation angle is needed.

The upper left corner of the feature control frame has a local X coordinate of zero and a local Y coordinate that is equal to the calculated text height.

The DXF class name for AcDbFcf is "TOLERANCE". The DXF group code sequence is 3, 10, 1, 210, 11.

Dimension Style-Based Data

Although an AcDbText object takes its character height from a local property, and an AcDbMText object takes the text height from its associated text style, the AcDbFcf object takes the height from a dimension style.

An AcDbFcf object does not reference a text style directly. Instead, it references an AcDbDimstyleTableRecord that in turn references a text style. This has the additional benefit for the feature control frame in that it can also use other properties of the dimension style (for example, colors) for its creation.

ObjectDBX	ActiveX Automation	DXF/AutoLISP
dimensionStyle(), object ID	StyleName, key string	Group 3, key string

Of the many properties of an AcDbDimstyleTableRecord, a feature control frame uses only the following, which are directly available in ActiveX Automation.

Dimstyle Property	ActiveX Automation	Meaning
dimclrd()	DimensionLineColor	Color of Fcf frame lines
dimclrt()	TextColor	Color of Fcf symbols and text characters
dimscale()	ScaleFactor	Overall scale factor for height calculation
dimtxsty()	TextStyle	Text style for FcF text characters
dimtxt()	TextHeight	Nominal text height

As with every dimstyle-based entity, the properties taken from the AcDbDimstyleTableRecord object can be overwritten by local settings. These settings are attached to the entity as xdata (more on this in the following chapter).

The height of text characters and symbols in a feature control frame is calculated by multiplying the text height with the overall scale factor, whereas the layout-relative scale factor described with the other dimension objects may be used.

The height of the frame boxes around each text segment is twice the calculated text height. The width is the sum of text width and text height, which generates an evenly spaced border around each frame box.

Formatting Codes

The frame contents are defined by a text string similar to the one used with AcDbM-Text objects.

ObjectDBX	ActiveX Automation	DXF/AutoLISP
text()	TextString	Group 1

The text consists of plain characters, symbols taken from a special gdt.shx font, and formatting codes.

Formatting Characters	Meaning
\n	New line; closes the current frame box and opens a new one right below the previous frame
%%v	Creates a vertical bar separating two adjacent frame boxes
{\Fgdt;a}	ANSI angularity symbol
{\Fgdt;b}	ANSI perpendicularity symbol
{\Fgdt;c}	ANSI flatness symbol
{\Fgdt;d}	ANSI profile surface symbol
{\Fgdt;e}	ANSI circularity symbol
{\Fgdt;f}	ANSI parallelism symbol
{\Fgdt;g}	ANSI cylindricity symbol
{\Fgdt;h}	ANSI circular runout symbol
{\Fgdt;i}	ISO symmetry symbol
{\Fgdt;j}	ANSI true position symbol
{\Fgdt;k}	ANSI profile line symbol
{\Fgdt;l}	ANSI least material condition symbol
{\Fgdt;m}	ANSI maximum material condition symbol
{\Fgdt;n}	ANSI diameter symbol
{\Fgdt;o}	ANSI square symbol
{\Fgdt;p}	ANSI projected tolerance symbol
{\Fgdt;q}	Centerline symbol
{\Fgdt;r}	ANSI concentricity symbol
{\Fgdt;s}	ANSI regardless of feature size symbol
{\Fgdt;t}	ANSI total runout symbol
{\Fgdt;u}	ANSI straightness symbol

Formatting Characters	Meaning
{\Fgdt;v}	ANSI counterbore symbol
{\Fgdt;w}	ANSI countersink symbol
{\Fgdt;x}	ANSI depth symbol
{\Fgdt;y}	ANSI conical taper symbol
{\Fgdt;z}	ANSI slope symbol
{\Fgdt;%%130}	ISO angularity symbol
{\Fgdt;%%131}	ISO symmetry symbol
{\Fgdt;%%132}	ANSI all around symbol

Semi-Custom Annotation Objects

In addition to the annotation objects in this chapter, AutoCAD drawing databases often contain annotation objects of type AcDbArcAlignedText and of type RText (not AcDbRText!).

These two objects are generated by so-called *Bonus* routines shipped with Auto-CAD. Autodesk does not consider them full native drawing objects, and they qualify as custom objects just like those created by any third-party developer (see Chapter 18 for details).

As *Bonus* objects, they lack a published ObjectDBX interface, and their DXF documentation is anything but complete. Therefore, all I can supply here is a handful of tips about how to decode arc-aligned and remote text objects.

Both objects have an ActiveX Automation interface, but this interface is not part of the AutoCAD type library. Each of these objects has its own type library, which is shipped with AutoCAD. The files are *axctextapp.tlb* for arc aligned text and *axrtext.tlb* for remote text.

Arc-Aligned Text

The AcDbArcAlignedText bonus object (DXF class name "ARCALIGNEDTEXT") defines a text string whose characters are distributed along a circular arc. It combines the properties of simple text and the geometric data of a circular arc.

The arc data is given by a center point (DXF group 10 in WCS), a normal (DXF group 210), and a radius (arc radius in DXF group 40 plus arc offset in DXF group 44). The start parameter is given by a start angle (DXF group 50 in radians) and a start offset (DXF group 46). The end parameters of the arc are given by an end angle (DXF group 51 in radians) and an end offset (DXF group 45). This defines the circular arc on which the base points of the characters are placed. It does not define a visible arc object. If there is an associated AcDbArc object, it is referenced as DXF group 330.

All text characters are drawn radial to the arc. The text string can be found in DXF group 1. The text properties are the text style (DXF group 7), character height (DXF group 42), and width (DXF group 41). Calculated properties are probably the font (DXF group 2) and bigfont (DXF group 3) names as well as the bold, italic, and underline flags (DXF group 74, 75, and 76), the font type (DXF group 79), and the character set, pitch, and family values (DXF groups 77 and 78).

The spacing and justification of the text along the arc are controlled by another group of properties: character spacing (DXF group 43), character order (DXF group 70), and the direction, alignment, and side flags (DXF groups 71, 72, and 73).

Value ranges, as well as the meaning of each value, are unknown. If you need to create arc-aligned text or if you need to interpret data you find in a drawing database, you have just about as good a chance of doing so as you would have with any other custom object: You can force the designer of the object to document it completely, or you can guess the meaning of the various properties.

Remote Text

Contrary to the multitude of settings for arc-aligned text, the remote text object has only a few properties. They are even more difficult to evaluate, however.

Remote text is variable text that will be evaluated at every regeneration of the drawing database. Therefore, it is powerful to combine external (or AutoCAD-internal) data with a drawing.

The two kinds of remote text are:

- Constant or variable *internal* text
- Constant or variable *external* text

In the case of external text, all the RText object provides is a link to an external text file. DXF group 1 then contains the filename. With internal text, the DXF group 1 contains the actual text string; however, the text string may contain DIESEL expressions.

DIESEL is a string-oriented programming language that is built into AutoCAD. Although the DIESEL source code is in the public domain, I know of no implementation other than the one used in AutoCAD. A DIESEL string is parsed sequentially, and expressions are enclosed by $(and). Every expression evaluates to a string that is then concatenated to the remaining characters. DIESEL expressions start with a function name that is followed by parameters. Functions exist to perform a number of useful actions, such as getting the current time, getting information about the drawing and the state of AutoCAD, and formatting and calculating numbers. Thus, an RText object can be used to display the current date and time in a drawing.

The DXF representation of an RText object (DXF class name "RTEXT") documents the text location (group 10), rotation (group 50), and normal (group 210). It also defines character height (group 40) and text style (group 7).

As I mentioned, the DXF group 1 contains either the actual text pattern to evaluate or a filename. The first bit (1) of DXF group 70 distinguishes between those two: if set, group 1 contains the actual text expression. The second bit (2) of group 70 specifies whether the text can contain paragraph text codes that are to be evaluated (if set).

As you can see, the RText object gives you a lot of control over the contents and outlook of an annotation. It has no justification or word-wrap option, however. Creating or evaluating such an object requires a lot of trial and error as well as the implementation of a complete DIESEL interpreter.

Summary

Annotation objects have a split personality. In many applications, they are completely irrelevant. If you want to pass contours to a laser cutting machine or if you want to calculate the volume of a box, you don't care if the drawing contains annotations. In other applications, annotations are important, however. If you are going to display the drawing on the laser cutting machine's terminal screen, the operator would be very unhappy if you forget to include the annotations.

Displaying annotations exactly as they appear in AutoCAD is very difficult for an external program. Some important details, such as the shape of a character, are not part of the drawing database. Also, the exact formatting and word-wrap depends on knowing the correct size of each character as it is defined external to the database.

This topic becomes even more complicated when you look at a special type of annotation, dimensioning. This is what we do next.

CHAPTER **12**

Dimensioning Objects

FEATURING

Dimensions and style   252

Dimension scaling   253

Calculating the dimension text string 254

Tolerances and alternate dimensioning 256

Dimension text, lines, and arrows   259

Positioning dimension text   263

AcDbDimension properties   267

Aligned and rotated linear dimensions 269

*Angular, diametrical, and radial
dimensions*   270

Coordinate dimensions   273

A dimension is an annotation that includes measurements taken from the drawing's geometry. In the AutoCAD drawing database, however, dimensions are *not* associated with any geometric entities. As soon as it is built, the dimension object is constant, even if the measured geometry changes.

An AcDbDimension object references locations in the drawing. You can change these references to point to other locations. When you do, a dimension object rebuilds itself and calculates new annotation text.

The visual representation of a dimension object consists of lines, block references, and text, which makes it complicated for other programs to visualize an AutoCAD dimension object exactly as AutoCAD does (if this is desired). To help these programs, every dimension object is associated with its own block container. This dimension block contains the most recent visualization of an AcDbDimension object.

AcDbDimension is a generic dimension class. No objects of this class are in the drawing database. In this chapter, we'll look at the following dimension objects derived from this class:

AcDbAlignedDimension A linear dimension with its dimension line parallel to the measured distance

AcDbRotatedDimension A linear dimension with its dimension line rotated

AcDb3PointAngularDimension An angular dimension defined by three points

AcDb2LineAngularDimension An angular dimension defined by four points

AcDbDiametricDimension A diameter dimension

AcDbRadialDimension A radius dimension

AcDbOrdinateDimension A dimension of a single coordinate

I'll start by discussing some basic dimension properties such as the dimension text and dimension scaling. Next, we'll look at the AcDbDimension properties that are common to all dimension objects. Finally, I'll discuss how the various dimension objects differ.

Dimensions and Style

To define, for example, a linear dimension, you basically need no more than three points: the two points between which the measurement takes place and one point that defines the location of the dimension line.

Unfortunately, people do not like standard dimensions. One wants a different arrowhead, a second wants a slightly modified text, a third wants the text adjusted, and so on. To accommodate all these modifications, a linear dimension needs almost 100 properties, which would make the dimension object very big in the database.

On the other hand, people want all dimension objects to look similar. To change the extension line color, they don't want to have to modify 100 dimension objects.

The solution is the AcDbDimstyleTableRecord object, which provides all the common properties of dimensions. A linear dimension and any other object derived from AcDbDimension needs to reference only a particular dimension style to access all these properties.

ObjectDBX	ActiveX Automation	DXF/AutoLISP
dimensionStyle(), object ID	StyleName, key string	Group 3, key string

Unfortunately, people aren't happy with this solution either. Although dimension styles create dimensions that are exactly the same, these dimensions aren't flexible. If you want one dimension to look exactly like all others, but with the first extension line suppressed, you would need to define a complete second style, which you don't want.

As a solution, AutoCAD allows you to overwrite any dimension style setting with a setting local to the actual dimension object. The corresponding data is saved as xdata on the object.

The xdata is assigned to the "ACAD" application. It starts with the string "DSTYLE" (group 1000), which is followed by an open bracket "{" (group 1002). Following this are pairs of dimension properties (group 1070) and their local setting (group code varies). The list ends with a closing bracket "}" (group 1002).

Each dimension property is identified by its group code number as used in the AcDbDimstyleTableRecord object. The override value needs to use a group code that corresponds to its data type: strings with code 1000, integers with code 1070, reals with code 1040. Object references such as the reference to the block name used as an arrowhead use the referenced object's handle, which is tagged with group code 1005.

To get the true value for any dimension property, you, therefore, need to check both the associated dimension style and eventual overrides. ObjectDBX and ActiveX Automation do this for you automatically.

Dimension Scaling

A large number of dimension style properties are lengths: the dimension text character size, the arrowhead size, gap and extension sizes, and more.

All these sizes are relative. Reading the text character height property will *not* return the final text height as it will appear on the drawing. To get the true text height, you need to multiply the *Text Height* property by the dimstyle-specific scale factor.

ObjectDBX	ActiveX Automation	DXF/AutoLISP
dimscale()	ScaleFactor	Group 40

 NOTE The group code number listed with this and all other dimension style properties is both the group code used in the AcDbDimstyleTableRecord object and the corresponding key used in dimension override xdata. Group codes of the dimension entity are marked appropriately.

The overall dimension scale is either a positive factor or 0.0. The special code 0.0 tells AutoCAD to calculate the overall scale factor according to the current layout viewport.

If the viewport scale, for instance, is 0.1 (that is, 1:10), an overall scale factor of 0.0 is replaced with the inverse of the viewport scale, that is, 10.0. Dimensions directly visualized in a layout use a viewport scale of 1.0.

Calculating the Dimension Text String

The main element of a dimension is the dimension text. This text basically contains the measured value; however, dimension text in AutoCAD can contain a lot more information. A large number of dimstyle properties affect the dimension text.

Let's follow AutoCAD's route from the measured value to the dimension text string. The measured value is either a length or an angle.

ObjectDBX	ActiveX Automation	DXF/AutoLISP
measurement()	Measurement	Dimension group 41

If the measured value is a length dimension, the value is multiplied by the length scale factor. This allows you to dimension drawings created in a different scale. If the length scale factor is negative, use the absolute value only for dimensions located in a layout block. Do not scale the measured value if the dimension is part of the *MODEL_SPACE* block.

ObjectDBX	ActiveX Automation	DXF/AutoLISP
dimlfac()	LinearScaleFactor	Group 144

The measured value is then rounded to the nearest multiple of the rounding value.

ObjectDBX	ActiveX Automation	DXF/AutoLISP
dimrnd()	RoundDistance	Group 45

Next, the measured, scaled and rounded value is converted to a string. For length and coordinate dimensions, this conversion is controlled by the linear units display format, the linear units precision, and the suppression of zeros. (For more information on values and ranges, see DIMDEC, LUPREC, DIMFRAC, and DIMZIN in Chapter 4.)

ObjectDBX	ActiveX Automation	DXF/AutoLISP
dimlunit()	UnitsFormat	Group 277
dimdec()	PrimaryUnitsPrecision	Group 271
dimfrac()	FractionFormat	Group 276
dimzin()	SuppressLeadingZeros, SuppressTrailingZeros, SuppressZeroFeet, SuppressZeroInches	Group 78

A corresponding set of properties exists for angular dimensions. See the global settings AUNITS, AUPREC, and DIMAZIN in Chapter 4 for values and ranges.

ObjectDBX	ActiveX Automation	DXF/AutoLISP
dimaunit()	AngleFormat	Group 275
dimadec()	n/a	Group 179
dimazin()	SuppressLeadingZeros, SuppressTrailingZeros	Group 79

For both lengths and angles, the decimal delimiter is replaced with the corresponding dimension style setting.

ObjectDBX	ActiveX Automation	DXF/AutoLISP
dimdsep()	DecimalSeparator	Group 278

This procedure creates a properly formatted text string that contains only the measured value. Depending on the type of drawing, you might want to add a unit string to this value or some comments.

Adding to the dimension string is achieved by a dimension text template, which is a string into which the formatted measured value is inserted. The template can include all the formatting characters and codes used by AcDbMText (see Chapter 11 for paragraph text formatting codes), including font changes and line breaks. Line breaks, however, are "\X" in dimensions, not "\P" as in AcDbMText. Line breaks create multiline dimension text. The individual lines are centered.

Within the dimension text template, the string "<>" is replaced with the formatted measured value. If the template does not contain this string, the template is built from a prefix, followed by the measured value, followed by the template text. The prefix is "R" for radial dimensions and a diameter symbol (∅) for diametric dimensions.

ObjectDBX	ActiveX Automation	DXF/AutoLISP
dimpost()	TextPrefix, TextSuffix	group 3

Adding Tolerances

This procedure gives us the primary dimension text. Next are any tolerance values. You can add tolerance information to a dimension in two ways:

- By measurement limits
- By tolerance differences

With measurement limits, you calculate the allowed maximum and minimum length or angle. These two values are then drawn instead of the measured value, as shown in Figure 12.1.

FIGURE 12.1

Measurement limits

When you measure tolerance differences, the allowed plus and minus difference is appended to the measured value. If the plus and minus tolerances are equal, the value is added following a plus/minus character. This is called a symmetrical tolerance (see Figure 12.2).

FIGURE 12.2

Tolerance differences

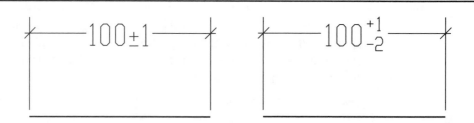

A dimension can use measurement limits or tolerance differences, but not both.

ObjectDBX	ActiveX Automation	DXF/AutoLISP
dimlim()	ToleranceDisplay = acTolLimits	Group 72
dimtol()	ToleranceDisplay = acTolSymmetrical or acTolDeviation	Group 71
dimtm()	ToleranceLowerLimit	Group 48
dimtp()	ToleranceUpperLimit	Group 47

With dimension limits, the upper limit is calculated from the scaled and rounded measurement plus the plus tolerance. The lower limit is calculated from the scaled and rounded measurement minus the minus tolerance. Each of these calculations creates two numbers, each of which runs through the same procedure. The *Symmetrical* variation differs from the *Deviation* only by using a very small value (10^{-9}) as the difference between the upper and lower limit.

The two resulting strings are stacked on top of each other (AcDbMText code \S) after their text height has been scaled down by the tolerance text factor. The stacked text is adjusted vertically to the baseline according to the values allowed for the global DIMTOLJ setting and replaces the primary dimension text.

ObjectDBX	ActiveX Automation	DXF/AutoLISP
dimtfac()	ToleranceHeightScale	Group 146
dimtolj()	ToleranceJustification	Group 283

With tolerance differences, the procedure is a little different because the primary dimension text is retained. For symmetrical tolerances, the tolerance value is run through the same formatting procedure as the measured value. This formatting includes an eventual template, but different settings for the decimal precision and the suppression of zeros.

ObjectDBX	ActiveX Automation	DXF/AutoLISP
dimtdec()	TolerancePrecision	Group 272
dimtzin()	ToleranceSuppressLeadingZeros, ToleranceSuppressTrailingZeros, ToleranceSuppressZeroFeet, ToleranceSuppressZeroInches	Group 284

The formatted tolerance value and a plus/minus character are then scaled down, vertically justified, and appended to the primary dimension text.

If plus and minus tolerance are not equal, both the plus tolerance and the negative of the minus tolerance are run through the formatting algorithm. Both resulting texts are stacked on top of each other after their text height is scaled down. This text is then justified vertically and appended to the primary dimension text.

Alternate Dimensioning

Even after all this work, we don't yet have the final dimension text as it appears on a drawing. In some countries, two systems of units are used in parallel. In this case, you have a measured value in one system of units (for example, inches) and a second value in another system of units (for example, millimeters). Alternate dimensioning is used for length and coordinate dimensions only.

ObjectDBX	ActiveX Automation	DXF/AutoLISP
dimalt()	AltUnits	Group 170

There is a constant scale factor between the units of measurement. The alternate measurement value is calculated by multiplying the primary measured value by this scale factor.

ObjectDBX	ActiveX Automation	DXF/AutoLISP
dimaltf()	AltUnitsScale	Group 143

The alternate measured value is scaled and rounded. Although the same linear length scale applies to both primary and alternate units (of course), there is a different rounding value.

ObjectDBX	ActiveX Automation	DXF/AutoLISP
dimaltrnd()	AltRoundDistance	Group 148

The calculated alternate measurement value is then formatted to a string, and tolerances are appended. The procedure is the same as for the primary value except that no template is applied at this stage. The following properties are used:

ObjectDBX	ActiveX Automation	DXF/AutoLISP
dimaltu()	AltUnitsFormat	Group 273
dimaltd()	AltUnitsPrecision	Group 171
dimaltz()	AltSuppressLeadingZeros, AltSuppressTrailingZeros, AltSuppressZeroFeet, AltSuppressZeroInches	Group 285
dimalttd()	AltTolerancePrecision	Group 274

ObjectDBX	ActiveX Automation	DXF/AutoLISP
dimalttz ()	AltToleranceSuppressLeadingZeros, AltToleranceSuppressTrailingZeros, AltToleranceSuppressZeroFeet, AltToleranceSuppressZeroInches	Group 286

Finally, the complete alternate dimension text, including any tolerances, is inserted into a template. In this template, the string " [] " is replaced with the calculated alternate dimension text. If the string is not contained in the template, the template is appended to the alternate dimension text.

ObjectDBX	ActiveX Automation	DXF/AutoLISP
dimapost()	AltTextPrefix, AltTextSuffix	Group 4

Dimension Text

Finally, the alternate dimension text is surrounded by brackets ([ ]) and appended to the primary dimension text with a single space character in between, unless the AcDbDimension object includes its own template.

If it does, this template is applied to the text. The string "<>" is replaced with the completely formatted primary dimension text (including tolerances and template), and the string " [] " is replaced with the completely formatted alternate dimension text, including brackets. Because the AutoCAD user is allowed to enter only numbers and characters into this AcDbDimension-based template and leave off the replacement strings altogether, the user can completely overwrite any measured value.

ObjectDBX	ActiveX Automation	DXF/AutoLISP
dimensionText()	TextOverride	Dimension group 1

The AcDbDimension-based template, including the replaced brackets, gives the true dimension text, which becomes an AcDbMText object in the corresponding dimension block using the text color, text height, and text style from the dimension style and the line-spacing style and factor from the AcDbDimension object.

ObjectDBX	ActiveX Automation	DXF/AutoLISP
dimclrt()	TextColor	Group 178
dimtxt()	TextHeight	Group 140
dimtxsty()	TextStyle	Group 340
textLineSpacingStyle()	n/a	Dimension group 72
textLineSpacingFactor()	n/a	Dimension group 41

Dimension Lines and Arrows

Creating the dimension lines and arrows for an AcDbDimension-based object is almost as complex as creating the dimension text. Again, a large number of properties from both the AcDbDimension object and the associated dimension style affect the final look of the dimension annotation.

Before we look at how AutoCAD generates dimension lines, I need to define a few terms. An aligned linear dimension documents the distance between two points. The *dimension line* is basically a line drawn in the dimension's plane in a predefined projection direction connecting these two points. Because it would otherwise overlay existing geometry, however, the connecting line is offset from the two points. Usually, although not necessarily, this offset is orthogonal.

Because the dimension line is offset from the two originating points, the end of the line and the corresponding point are connected by two *extension lines*. And because the dimension points are ordered, there is a first and a second extension line. Again, extension lines are usually, but not necessarily, orthogonal to the dimension line.

The intersection of the dimension line and the first extension line is a defining property of an AcDbDimension object. Among other things, this point defines the plane on which the dimension is to be drawn. This point is always in WCS.

ObjectDBX	ActiveX Automation	DXF/AutoLISP
differs depending on subclass	n/a	Dimension group 10, in WCS

In an angular dimension, the dimension line is a circular arc, and the extension lines are radial to the dimension arc. In diametric and radial dimensions, there are no extension lines, and in coordinate dimensions, there is no dimension line, only an extension line.

The color and linewidth of dimension and extension lines are properties of the individual AcDbDimension object, either inherited from the associated dimension style or through an override.

ObjectDBX	ActiveX Automation	DXF/AutoLISP
dimclrd()	DimensionLineColor	Group 176
dimlwd()	DimensionLineWeight	Group 371
dimclre()	ExtensionLineColor	Group 177
dimlwe()	ExtensionLineWeight	Group 372

At times, you don't want to see both extension lines, for example, because one extension line exactly matches a geometry line. Therefore, you can suppress either extension line. You can also suppress the first or second half of the dimension line.

The first half is the one closer to the first extension line. The word *half* is not meant mathematically, however. The division between first and second half takes place at the dimension text location.

ObjectDBX	ActiveX Automation	DXF/AutoLISP
dimse1()	ExtLine1Suppress	Group 75
dimse2()	ExtLine2Suppress	Group 76
dimsd1()	DimLine1Suppress	Group 281
dimsd2()	DimLine2Suppress	Group 282

The dimension line length and the extension line length are basically determined by the distance between the two measured points and the dimension line offset. In addition, three length values let you affect these lengths:

- The extension line offset is the distance between the measured point and the extension line start.

- The extension line extension defines how far the extension line extends beyond the dimension line.

- The dimension line extension defines how far the dimension line extends beyond the extension line.

All these are relative lengths that will be multiplied by the dimension scale value.

The dimension line extension is valid only for these arrowheads: "_ArchTick", "_Oblique", "_None", and "_Integral". With all other arrowheads, the dimension line ends short of the extension line to leave space for the arrowhead.

ObjectDBX	ActiveX Automation	DXF/AutoLISP
dimexo()	ExtensionLineOffset	Group 42
dimexe()	ExtensionLineExtend	Group 44
dimdle()	DimensionLineExtend	Group 46

At the intersection of extension and dimension line, AutoCAD inserts the arrowhead. Arrowheads are simply block containers, which means that an arrowhead can be arbitrarily complex. AutoCAD uses a predefined set of arrowheads. (For information about these arrowheads, see Chapter 4.) Users can create their own arrowheads, however. The default arrowhead is a filled triangle that is not saved or referenced as a block container.

A dimension can reference two different arrowheads:

- A first arrowhead placed at the intersection of the dimension line and the first extension line

- A second arrowhead at the intersection with the second dimension line

If there is only one arrowhead, it's referenced in a different property than if there are two arrowheads. A Boolean flag indicates the difference:

ObjectDBX	ActiveX Automation	DXF/AutoLISP
dimsah()	n/a	Group 173

The arrowheads are either referenced directly or referenced by their name.

ObjectDBX	ActiveX Automation	DXF/AutoLISP
dimblk1()	Arrowhead1Block	Group 6 (key string), group 343 (handle/entity name)
dimblk2()	Arrowhead2Block	Group 7 (key string), group 344 (handle/entity name)
dimblk()	Arrowhead1Block = Arrowhead2Block	Group 5 (key string), group 342 (handle/entity name)

The closed filled arrow is the default arrow and is *not* listed by name or handle/entity name. It uses an empty string and a null Id. When overriding the arrowhead block to get the default arrow, use a null handle.

Arrowhead blocks other than "_ArchTick", "_Oblique", "_None", and "_Integral" are supposed to use a part of the dimension line that is 1 unit wide. They are then scaled twice: first by the arrowhead size and then by the dimension scale.

The arrowheads "_ArchTick", "_Oblique, and "_Integral" use the tick size for their initial scaling. After that, the dimension scale is applied.

ObjectDBX	ActiveX Automation	DXF/AutoLISP
dimasz()	ArrowheadSize	Group 41
dimtsz()	ArrowheadSize	Group 142

Arrowheads are rotated around the intersection of the dimension and the extension line to become inline with the dimension line.

Depending on the space available between the extension lines and depending on the text placement strategy (see the global DIMATFIT setting in Chapter 4), arrowheads can be rotated to the opposite side of the extension line. In this case, an arrowhead size length line is drawn next to the arrowhead to continue the dimension line.

ObjectDBX	ActiveX Automation	DXF/AutoLISP
dimatfit()	Fit	Group 289

If the arrows are placed outside, a flag specifies whether there should be a dimension line between the extension lines.

ObjectDBX	ActiveX Automation	DXF/AutoLISP
dimtofl()	DimLineInside	Group 172

As an alternative, the user can select to suppress the arrowheads if they don't fit between the extension lines.

ObjectDBX	ActiveX Automation	DXF/AutoLISP
dimsoxd()	n/a	Group 175

Finally, if the dimension text is placed inline with the dimension line but outside the extension lines, the dimension line is lengthened up to the outer edge of the dimension text bounding box. If the dimension text is placed over one of the extension lines, the corresponding extension line is lengthened up to the outer edge of the text.

Positioning Dimension Text

By now we have a dimension text, which is comparable to a paragraph text and a collection of dimension lines, extension lines, and arrowheads. How do they fit together?

The dimension text has a bounding rectangle that is offset to create blank space around the dimension text. We call this the *dimension text box*.

ObjectDBX	ActiveX Automation	DXF/AutoLISP
dimgap()	TextGap	Group 147

If the text gap is negative, the offset is calculated as the absolute value of the *Text Gap* property. In addition, a surrounding rectangle will be drawn around the dimension text box. Figure 12.3 shows these alternatives. In some standards, the rectangle describes basic dimensioning.

FIGURE 12.3

The dimension text gap

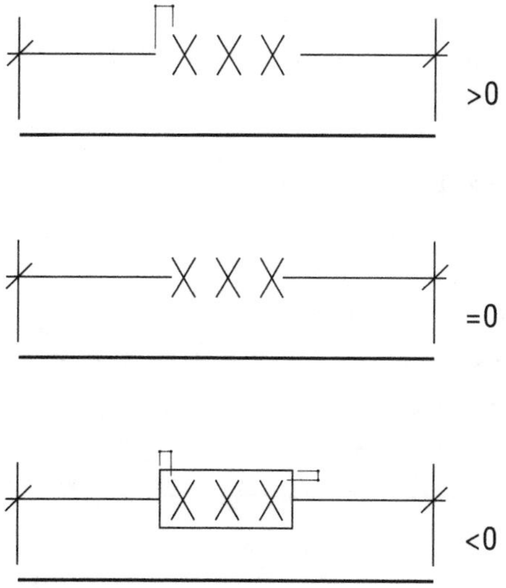

Wherever the dimension text box overlays a dimension or an extension line, the line is broken. Such a break determines the division of the dimension line into a first and second segment, both of which can be suppressed, as you've already seen.

A number of settings determine how the text box will be rotated and placed within the dimension. Let's look at the rotation first.

As is any annotation, a dimension is a planar object. Within this plane is a local coordinate system (ECS) that is defined by the world origin and the plane normal. Within this local coordinate system, a zero direction is parallel to the x-axis, as calculated through the arbitrary axis algorithm. In addition, every dimension has its own horizontal direction.

ObjectDBX	ActiveX Automation	DXF/AutoLISP
horizontalRotation()	Rotation	Dimension group 51

The horizontal rotation value is measured from the horizontal direction to the zero direction. Any text rotation is relative to the horizontal direction. The default text rotation is either horizontal to this rotation or parallel to the dimension or to an extension line, depending on two Boolean flags:

ObjectDBX	ActiveX Automation	DXF/AutoLISP
dimtih()	TextInsideAlign	Group 73
dimtoh()	TextOutsideAlign	Group 74

The following is a list of the various combinations:

Text Position	Settings	Text Rotation
Between extension lines, aligned to dimension line	DIMTIH false	Parallel to dimension line
Between extension lines, aligned to extension line	DIMTIH false	Parallel to extension line
Between extension lines	DIMTIH true	Parallel to horizontal direction
Outside extension lines, aligned to dimension line	DIMTOH false	Parallel to dimension line
Outside extension lines, aligned to extension line	DIMTOH false	Parallel to extension line
Outside extension lines	DIMTOH true	Parallel to horizontal direction

You can query the text rotation or set it to any other value using the *Text Rotation* property. This property is the angle from the dimension's horizontal direction to the text horizontal axis.

Calculating the text position is similar to calculating the text rotation. Again, there is a default text position that can be overwritten. The text position is always the center of the dimension text box even though the AcDbDimension object has a property for the text attachment that corresponds to the paragraph text attachment.

ObjectDBX	ActiveX Automation	DXF/AutoLISP
textAttachment()	n/a	Dimension group 71

The horizontal text justification defines where to put the dimension text along the dimension line. For possible values, see the DIMJUST global setting in Chapter 4.

ObjectDBX	ActiveX Automation	DXF/AutoLISP
dimjust()	HorizontalTextPosition	Group 280

This property either centers the text centered between the extension lines or places the text close to or inline with an extension line. *Close to* means that space is reserved for the dimension arrow at the correct size.

If the space between the extension lines is too small, the dimension text is placed according to the text and arrowhead positioning strategy (DIMATFIT). This may place the text outside the extension lines. A separate flag overrides this placement and forces the text within the extension lines:

ObjectDBX	ActiveX Automation	DXF/AutoLISP
dimtix()	TextInside	Group 174

Likewise, the vertical text placement is calculated. Vertical here means orthogonal to the dimension line direction. The *dimtvp()* value is ignored if *dimtad()* is non-zero. The dimension line extends beneath the text if *dimtvp()* is >0.7.

ObjectDBX	ActiveX Automation	DXF/AutoLISP
dimtad()	VerticalTextPosition	Group 77
dimtvp()	n/a	Group 145

The vertical text position can take one of four values:

ActiveX Automation	ObjectDBX/ DXF	Meaning
acVertCentered	0	Dimension text will be offset from the dimension line by the *dimtvp()* value (typically 0.0, which means that the text center is on the dimension line). Positive values offset away from the measured points.

ActiveX Automation	ObjectDBX/ DXF	Meaning
acAbove	1	Dimension text will be placed above (within the dimension's local coordinate system) the dimension line, leaving a *Text Gap* sized space in the dimension line.
acOutside	2	Dimension text will be placed on the outer side of the dimension, i.e., on the side opposite the measured points.
acJIS	3	Dimension text will be placed according to Japanese Industrial Standards (JIS), which in most cases is identical to the above placement.

Horizontal and vertical placement together create the default text position. You can query whether the dimension text is in this default position:

ObjectDBX	ActiveX Automation	DXF/AutoLISP
isUsingDefaultTextPosition()	n/a	Eighth bit (128) of dimension group 70

The calculated point is, however, simply a default position. A user can freely move the text and create the true text position.

ObjectDBX	ActiveX Automation	DXF/AutoLISP
textPosition(), in WCS	TextPosition, in WCS	Dimension group 11, in ECS

A final setting defines what should happen to text that is moved far off the corresponding dimension line.

ObjectDBX	ActiveX Automation	DXF/AutoLISP
dimtmove()	TextMovement	Group 289

The text movement is one of three values:

ActiveX Automation	ObjectDBX/ DXF	Meaning
acDimLineWithText	0	Prevents the dimension text from ever moving too far off the line. Instead, the line position follows the vertical text movement.

ActiveX Automation	ObjectDBX/ DXF	Meaning
acMoveTextAddLeader	1	Connects the center of the dimension line with a leader line to the new text position if it's moving more than the dimension text box height vertically from the dimension line.
acMoveTextNoLeader	2	Simply moves the text.

The leader that can be drawn is a straight line with a horizontal hook line of arrowhead size length. If the text is set to be above the dimension line, it will also be above this hook line, which is then lengthened to the outer edge of the text bounding box.

AcDbDimension Properties

In addition to the multiple settings that define the contents and placement of the dimension text and the placement of dimension lines, an AcDbDimension object has a few additional properties.

Like any annotation object, a dimension is a planar entity. The text, the lines, and the arrow insertion points are always within a single plane. This plane is parallel to the X/Y plane of the dimension's local coordinate system (ECS). In ObjectDBX, you can use the *elevation()* function to query the offset between the two planes. In the other environments, you need to calculate this from the available points that are on this plane, such as the text position (in ECS) or the dimension/extension line intersection (in WCS).

Every AcDbDimension object has an associated block container that carries the visualization of the dimension using AcDbMText (for the dimension text), AcDbLine (for the dimension and extension lines), and AcDbBlockReference (for the arrowheads). Within the block container, the objects are drawn on the X/Y plane. The AcDbBlockTableRecord is referenced by the dimension entity.

ObjectDBX	ActiveX Automation	DXF/AutoLISP
dimBlockId(), AcdBObjectID	n/a	Group 2, key string

The contents of this block container are recalculated with most changes of the defining properties. Because a move operation would create the exact same block container with offset coordinates, AutoCAD does not calculate a new block container. Instead, it simply moves the block insertion (or reference) point within the drawing.

ObjectDBX	ActiveX Automation	DXF/AutoLISP
dimBlockPosition(), in WCS	n/a	Group 12, in ECS

Initially, the block position is always (0, 0, block plane elevation). To translate the block entities to the drawing space, for example, when programming a DXF filter for a system that does not know about dimensions, follow the same rules that you would follow for any other block reference.

Additional objects within the dimension block are the defining points used to calculate the dimension. Although all other dimension block objects used in the visualization are on layer `"0"`, the defining points are on layer `"DefPoints"`. They are AcDbPoint objects.

The block container is flagged anonymous in the AcDbBlockTableRecord object, which means that it will be automatically deleted as soon as there is no corresponding AcDbDimension entity. The key strings (names) for dimension blocks look like `"*Dnumber"`.

Usually, every dimension block is referenced only once. Only in drawings converted from earlier AutoCAD versions can a single dimension block be referenced multiple times. In DXF, you can query this information:

ObjectDBX	ActiveX Automation	DXF/AutoLISP
n/a	n/a	Sixth bit (32) of group 70

Of the many properties of a dimension style that are common to all AcDbDimension objects, we haven't yet looked at three:

Dimstyle Setting	Meaning
dimcen()	Center mark format and size. (See the "Radial Dimensions" section later in this chapter.)
dimldrblk()	Arrowhead for leader lines. (See the next chapter.)
dimdli()	Dimension line increment. This setting does not affect the current dimension in any way. It is only used as a relative offset distance from the current dimension line to any dimension line created afterward.

In DXF and AutoLISP, the AcDbDimension groups follow a subclass marker. The sequence of groups is 2, 10, 11, 12, 70, 1, 71, 72, 41, 42, 52, 53, 54 (constant 0.0), 51, 210, 3.

DXF group 70 is a combination of several Boolean flags and a number indicating the dimension type.

First Three Bits of Group 70	Dimension Type
0	Rotated linear dimension
1	Aligned linear dimension
2	Four-point angular dimension
3	Diametric dimension
4	Radial dimension
5	Three-point angular dimension
6	Coordinate dimension

Aligned Linear Dimensions

An *aligned linear dimension* documents the distance between two measured points. The dimension line is parallel to the line between these two points. This means that, for an aligned dimension, both the horizontal direction and the dimension line direction correspond to the projection of the two points on the dimension plane.

The AcDbAlignedDimension class is derived from AcDbDimension. Therefore, an aligned dimension has all the properties discussed in this chapter. In addition, a few properties define what to dimension.

The two extension line points are the measured points, and the dimension line point is the intersection of the dimension line and the second extension line. All these are WCS points.

ObjectDBX	ActiveX Automation	DXF/AutoLISP
xLine1Point()	ExtLine1Point	Group 13
xLine2Point()	ExtLine2Point	Group 14
dimLinePoint()	n/a	Group 10 in AcDb-Dimension data

In aligned dimensions, the extension lines don't have to be orthogonal to the dimension line, that is, orthogonal to the line connecting the two measured points. The oblique angle is the angle from the dimension's horizontal direction (which, in this case, is the dimension line direction) to the extension line, mapped into 0° to 180°. The special case of 0° is handled as 90°; that is, it produces orthogonal extension lines.

ObjectDBX	ActiveX Automation	DXF/AutoLISP
oblique()	n/a	Group 52 in AcDb-Dimension data

In DXF and AutoLISP, this information is saved to the AcDbDimension part of the object. The DXF class for aligned dimensions is "DIMENSION". Following the AcDbDimension data are a subclass marker "AcDbAlignedDimension" and the groups 13 and14. The object ends with another subclass marker for "AcDbRotatedDimension".

Rotated Linear Dimensions

A *rotated linear dimension* is identical to an aligned linear dimension. The only difference is that the dimension line does not have to be parallel to the dimension's horizontal axis. Typical examples of rotated linear dimensions are vertical and horizontal dimensions.

The dimension line rotation is relative to the horizontal direction; that is, a rotation of 0° creates an aligned dimension.

ObjectDBX	ActiveX Automation	DXF/AutoLISP
rotation()	n/a	Group 50

The DXF representation of an AcDbRotatedDimension object is identical to that of an aligned dimension, including the subclass markers. Group 50 follows group 14.

Angular Dimensions: Part I

An *angular dimension* documents the included angle between the extension lines. The dimension line is a circular arc, and the extension lines are radial to this arc. The horizontal direction of an angular dimension is the arc's tangent at its midpoint.

In the AutoCAD drawing database, you'll find two kinds of angular dimensions:

- The AcDb3PointAngularDimension, which uses three points to define the extension line directions
- The AcDb2LineAngularDimension, which uses four points to define the extension line directions and is discussed in the next section

The AcDb3PointAngularDimension is derived from AcDbDimension, which includes all the properties listed so far. To define the angle to dimension, an AcDb3PointAngularDimension object uses these three points. All are in WCS.

ObjectDBX	ActiveX Automation	DXF/AutoLISP
xLine1Point()	ExtLine1EndPoint	Group 13
xLine2Point()	ExtLine2EndPoint	Group 14
centerPoint()	AngleVertex	Group 15

The distance from the angle vertex to the dimension arc is given by an arbitrary point on the arc. Again, this is a WCS point.

ObjectDBX	ActiveX Automation	DXF/AutoLISP
arcPoint()	n/a	Group 10 in AcDb-Dimension data

The DXF class name for AcDb3PointAngularDimension objects is again `"DIMENSION"`. Following the AcDbDimension groups are a subclass marker `"AcDb3PointAngularDimension"` and the groups 13, 14, and 15.

Angular Dimensions: Part II

Although three-point angular dimensions are usually related to arcs and chamfers, four-point angular dimensions typically relate to a pair of lines. The only reason for the two types of angular dimensions is that AutoCAD cannot associate a dimension with the underlying geometry. If the underlying geometry is a pair of lines, AutoCAD uses the four-point dimension so that the user can move the dimension definition points along with the line ends.

The only difference between an AcDb3PointAngularDimension object and an AcDb2LineAngularDimension object is the definition points.

ObjectDBX	ActiveX Automation	DXF/AutoLISP
xLine1Start()	ExtLine1StartPoint	Group 13
xLine2Start()	ExtLine2StartPoint	Group 10 in AcDb-Dimension data
xLine1End()	ExtLine1EndPoint	Group 14
xLine2End()	ExtLine2EndPoint	Group 15

Despite their names, the two end points are *not* the end points of the extension lines. These are the opposite end points of the virtual lines that form the angle. The extension lines are calculated as they are calculated with every other dimension: They start at the two start points (plus any offset) and then continue in the direction of the dimension line and beyond. The position of the dimension arc is once again given by a point on this arc.

ObjectDBX	ActiveX Automation	DXF/AutoLISP
arcPoint()	n/a	Group 16

The DXF definition uses the class name `"DIMENSION"` as well. Following the AcDbDimension groups are a subclass marker `"AcDb2LineAngularDimension"` and the groups 13, 14, 15, and 16.

Diametrical Dimensions

A *diametrical dimension* usually dimensions the diameter of a circle, even though an AcDbDiametricDimension object can exist on its own. Diametric dimensions don't have extension lines. The dimension line simply goes from one dimension point to the other.

ObjectDBX	ActiveX Automation	DXF/AutoLISP
chordPoint()	n/a	Group 15
farChordPoint()	n/a	Group 10 in AcDb-Dimension data

If the text is placed outside the dimension line or if no dimension line is drawn, there will be only one arrowhead on the outside of the dimension. This arrowhead is always at the chord point. The usual leader line to the dimension text may extend from this arrowhead. The leader part of the line will be inline with the dimension, while the hook line (drawn if text rotation differs from line direction) is parallel to the text. There is an obsolete *Leader Length* property with diametric and radial dimensions.

If the arrowhead is outside the two measured points, center lines can be drawn at the center of the virtual circle dimensioned, that is, at the midpoint of the two measured points. This is controlled by a property of the dimension style (which like all others can be overridden in the AcDbDiametricDimension object).

ObjectDBX	ActiveX Automation	DXF/AutoLISP
dimcen()	CenterType, CenterMarkSize	Dimension style group 141

If the center mark size is zero (CenterType = acCenterNone in ActiveX Automation), no center mark is drawn. If the center mark size is positive (acCenterMark), a small center mark is drawn. If the center mark is negative (acCenterLine), a center mark and center lines are drawn. Figure 12.4 shows which lengths are affected by the absolute value of the center mark size. The horizontal and vertical lines follow the dimension's horizontal direction.

In DXF, an AcDbDiametricDimension uses the class name `"DIMENSION"`. Following the subclass marker is only the group code 15.

Radial Dimensions

An AcDbRadialDimension is identical to an AcDbDiametricDimension. The only difference is that there won't be an arrowhead at the *Center* end of the dimension line whether or not the line is drawn. An eventual center mark is drawn at the *Center* end of the dimension line.

ObjectDBX	ActiveX Automation	DXF/AutoLISP
chordPoint()	n/a	Group 15
center()	n/a	Group 10 in AcDb-Dimension data

In DXF, the two objects differ only in their subclass marker.

Center marks and center lines

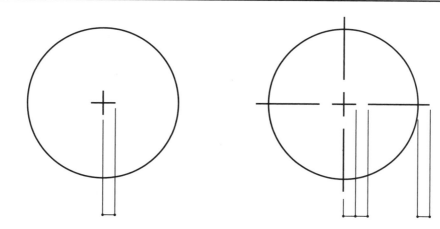

Coordinate Dimensions

Like linear dimensions, coordinate dimensions (AcDbOrdinateDimension) document a length, which is, once again, taken from two measured points.

ObjectDBX	ActiveX Automation	DXF/AutoLISP
definingPoint()	n/a	Group 13
origin()	n/a	Group 10 in AcDb-Dimension data

The length to be measured is either the horizontal or the vertical distance between the two. *Horizontal,* again, is the dimension's horizontal direction.

ObjectDBX	ActiveX Automation	DXF/AutoLISP
isUsingXAxis()	n/a	The seventh bit (64) of group 70 in AcDbDimension data is set.
isUsingYAxis()	n/a	The seventh bit (64) of group 70 in AcDbDimension data is not set.

No dimension line is drawn. An extension line connects the defining point with the end of the extension line. An extension line offset is taken into account at the defining point.

ObjectDBX	ActiveX Automation	DXF/AutoLISP
leaderEndPoint()	n/a	Group 14

If the leader end point is not horizontal (or vertical) to the defining point, a leader line will be drawn. The leader line starts at the dimension text box width, short of the so-called Leader End Point.

The DXF class name for an AcDbOrdinateDimension is `"DIMENSION"`. Following the AcDbDimension groups are a subclass marker and the groups 14 and 15.

Summary

Now you understand why AutoCAD's dimensioning functions are so complicated. The outlook of dimension annotations differs greatly between disciplines and between countries. AutoCAD is a software to be used in all countries and for all disciplines. As such, it tries to fulfill every possible standard.

The consequence is the large number of properties and settings that affect the display of dimension entities. If you try to reproduce an AutoCAD dimension in another program, you would not want to completely mimic AutoCAD's dimensioning functions. But you have two choices that create a little work. If your intention is to display only the dimension, use the dimension block already prepared by AutoCAD. If your intention is true dimensions, take the defining points from the AutoCAD dimension and build an appropriate dimension object in your own data structure.

Some of you may be wondering why I omitted the leader lines from the discussion in this chapter. Don't worry. That topic opens the next chapter.

CHAPTER **13**<u></u>

Line and Face Collections

FEATURING

Leader lines	**276**
Lightweight polylines	**279**
Heavyweight polylines	**283**
Three-dimensional polylines	**287**
Polygon meshes	**288**
Polyface meshes	**290**
Multilines	**292**

n the chapter on curves (Chapter 10), we looked at several basic drawing entities, including lines, circular arcs, splines, and faces. Although you can create most of a drawing's geometry using these simple entities, it's often advisable to create contours and other complex geometry as a whole.

The AutoCAD drawing database provides several objects that basically look like a collection of lines and/or faces. In this chapter, we'll discuss the following objects:

AcDbLeader   A continuous planar collection of several straight lines and a leader arrow. This object can also use a spline curve instead of straight lines.

AcDbPolyline   A continuous planar collection of straight lines and circular arcs. The individual segments of a polyline can have associated width settings.

AcDb2DPolyline   An older version of the AcDbPolyline entity. It uses a different, more complex definition and allows the use of spline curves.

AcDb3DPolyline   A continuous nonplanar collection of straight lines that may be splined.

AcDbPolygonMesh   A continuous collection of 3D faces; also used to describe a spline surface.

AcDbPolyFaceMesh   A noncontinuous collection of lines and faces.

AcDbMline   A planar set of parallel polylines.

Except for the last three objects, all classes are derived from AcDbCurve, which means that all curve properties described earlier in this book apply to the objects in this chapter as well.

Leader Lines

A *leader line* is a planar curve made from straight line segments. The AcDbLeader class is derived from the AcDbCurve class.

A leader can have an associated arrowhead and an associated annotation. In Auto-CAD, it looks as if the leader and the annotation form a single object; this is not the case. The annotation is completely independent from the leader that only references it. Because the associated arrowhead makes a leader line similar to a dimension, the AcDbLeader object references a dimension style to get several settings. Like the settings for any other dimension, these settings may be overridden by xdata attached to the AcDbLeader object.

ObjectDBX	ActiveX Automation	DXF/AutoLISP
DimensionStyle()	StyleName	Group 3

Properties taken from the associated dimension style are as follows:

ObjectDBX	ActiveX Automation	DXF/AutoLISP
dimasz()	ArrowheadSize	Dimension style group 41
dimclrd()	DimensionLineColor	Dimension style group 176
dimgap()	TextGap	Dimension style group 147
dimlwd()	Lineweight	Dimension style group 371
dimldrblk()	ArrowheadBlock	Dimension style group 341
dimscale()	ScaleFactor	Dimension style group 40
dimtad()	VerticalTextPosition	Dimension style group 77
dimtxsty()	n/a	Dimension style group 340
dimtxt()	n/a	Dimension style group 140

An AcDbLeader object is a planar curve. The plane it resides on is given by the normal direction and the leader's horizontal direction. The horizontal direction also defines the horizontal for the associated annotation object (if any).

ObjectDBX	ActiveX Automation	DXF/AutoLISP
normal()	Normal	Group 210
n/a	n/a	Group 211, horizontal direction

The leader curve is defined by two or more vertices.

ObjectDBX	ActiveX Automation	DXF/AutoLISP
numVertices()	Coordinates.Count	Group 76
vertexAt()	Coordinates	Group 10

Vertices are given in WCS, but must lie on the leader's plane. In ActiveX Automation, *Coordinates* returns an array containing all the vertices. There's also an indexed *Coordinate* property that you can use to retrieve a particular vertex. An associated linetype is applied on every single straight line.

Instead of a collection of straight lines, a leader can also display as a smooth curve. In this case, the vertices are used as the fit points for a spline curve.

ObjectDBX	ActiveX Automation	DXF/AutoLISP
isSplined()	Type	Group 72

A leader can be drawn with an associated arrowhead. In this case, the arrowhead block is inserted at the first vertex and rotated in the direction of the second vertex. If the distance between the two vertices is less than twice the actual arrowhead size (calculated from the relative arrowhead size and the dimension scale), no arrowhead is drawn.

ObjectDBX	ActiveX Automation	DXF/AutoLISP
hasArrowhead()	Type	Group 71

At the other end, the leader can have a hook line. A hook line is a small horizontal line from the last vertex to the annotation object. Depending on the vertical text position, this line's length is either the size of the arrowhead or the size of the arrowhead plus the text width (if the text is above the line).

ObjectDBX	ActiveX Automation	DXF/AutoLISP
hasHookLine()	n/a	Group 75.
annoWidth()	n/a	Group 41, annotation text width.
n/a	n/a	Group 74. True if hook line is in horizontal direction; false if hook line is in opposite direction.
annoHeight()	n/a	Group 40, annotation text height.

Following the hook line is the annotation. The annotation is an object on its own—an AcDbMText, an AcDbFcf, or an AcDbBlockReference.

ObjectDBX	ActiveX Automation	DXF/AutoLISP
annoType()	n/a	Group 73
annotationObjId()	Annotation	Group 340

Valid values for the annotation type are:

ObjectDBX	DXF	Meaning
kMText	0	Paragraph text annotation
kFcf	1	Feature control frame annotation
kBlockRef	2	Block reference
kNoAnno	3	No annotation

In ActiveX Automation, you can determine the annotation type by looking at the *ObjectName* property of the object associated with the *Annotation* property.

Paragraph text and block insertions are offset against the end of the leader line. You can query the vector from the last vertex to the annotation insertion point.

ObjectDBX	ActiveX Automation	DXF/AutoLISP
annotationOffset()	n/a	Group 213
n/a	n/a	Group 212, block insertion offset

The DXF class name for an AcDbLeader object is `"LEADER"`. Following the subclass marker are the groups 3, 71, 72, 73, 74, 75, 40, 41, 76, 10 (repeated), 340, 211, 210, 212, 213. Remember that the AcDbCurve class is not seen in DXF.

Lightweight Polylines

The lightweight polyline is also a planar, continuous collection of lines, derived from AcDbCurve. Although an AcDbPolyline does not have an arrowhead or an associated annotation object, it has some other unique properties.

Like a leader line, the lightweight polyline has a plane on which it is drawn. An AcDbPolyline object uses a local coordinate system (ECS). It is calculated as follows: The z-axis is parallel to the normal, the x-axis is calculated from the normal using the arbitrary axis algorithm, and the origin is the world origin plus elevation times the normal vector (that is, the drawing plane is offset by the elevation distance from the world origin).

ObjectDBX	ActiveX Automation	DXF/AutoLISP
normal()	Normal	Group 210
elevation()	Elevation	Group 38

Like circles and some other curves, a lightweight polyline can have an extrusion along the normal vector. This creates a series of faces instead of a series of lines.

ObjectDBX	ActiveX Automation	DXF/AutoLISP
thickness()	Thickness	Group 39

The main defining element of an AcDbPolyline object is the polyline vertices, which form the polyline segments.

ObjectDBX	ActiveX Automation	DXF/AutoLISP
numVerts()	Coordinates.Count	Group 90
getPointAt()	Coordinates, Coordinate()	Group 10

The ObjectDBX function *getPointAt()* can return the vertex location either as a 3D point in WCS or as a 2D point in ECS. ActiveX Automation, DXF, and AutoLISP return a 2D point in ECS. A polyline must have at least two vertices.

Like other curves, lightweight polylines can be open or closed. You can map a non-continuous linetype onto the polyline in two ways:

- By mapping the linetype onto each segment on its own
- By continuously mapping the linetype onto the complete curve

Continuous mapping can result in polylines that prevent you from visually identifying the location of the vertices. Figure 13.1 shows a polyline with segment-oriented linetype mapping (right) and continuous linetype mapping (left).

ObjectDBX	ActiveX Automation	DXF/AutoLISP
isClosed()	Closed	First bit (1) of group 70
hasPlinegen()	LinetypeGeneration	Eighth bit (128) of group 70; true for segment-oriented linetype mapping

FIGURE 13.1

Segment-oriented and continuous linetype mapping (Plinegen)

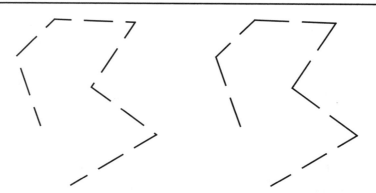

Arcs in Polylines

The vertex points divide the polyline curve into segments. Each segment can be either a straight line or a circular arc. To define arc segments, AutoCAD uses the arc's bulge (or curvature) factor.

Figure 13.2 shows an arc segment connecting segment vertex S1 with segment vertex S2. The chord length L is the distance from S1 to S2. The arc height H is the maximum distance between the arc and the chord.

FIGURE 13.2

Bulge factor
calculation

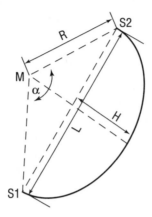

The bulge factor is calculated as 2H/L. This creates a real number that together with the two vertices completely defines the arc segment. A bulge of 0 creates a line segment; a bulge of 1 creates a semicircle. Positive bulges let the polyline turn left; negative bulges let the curve turn right. In ObjectDBX, you can use the *isOnlyLines()* function to verify that the bulges of all segments are zero.

From the bulge definition, you can easily calculate both the included angle α of the arc and the radius R:

$\alpha = 4 * \arctan(\text{Bulge})$

$R = L / (2 * \sin(\alpha/2))$

ObjectDBX	**ActiveX Automation**	**DXF/AutoLISP**
getBulgeAt()	GetBulge	Group 42

The bulge factor of a vertex always defines the segment between this vertex and the following vertex. The bulge factor associated with the last vertex defines the closing segment (if any).

Wide Polylines

The most complex property of a polyline is its width. A polyline is not just a curve; it's a series of planar regions. When extruded, each region creates a three-dimensional object.

In AutoCAD, the planar regions created from a wide polyline are seen as filled areas as long as the global FILLMODE setting is on, the view direction is perpendicular to the polyline's plane, and hidden lines are not suppressed.

Each segment of a polyline has a start and an end width. This means that at each vertex there are two widths to consider:

- The previous segment's end width
- The next segment's start width

The width is always perpendicular to the curve at any vertex. Where wide segments meet, the inner and outer edges of the region are shortened or lengthened to create a smooth connection.

Figure 13.3 shows the combination of two wide segments that meet at an angle. The first segment's start width is 3.0, and its end width is 6.0. The second segment, which starts at S2, has a start width of 9.0 and an end width of 12.0. P1 and P2 are the points where the outer edges intersect. The edges are shortened and lengthened at these points.

FIGURE 13.3

Wide linear polyline segments (FILLMODE off)

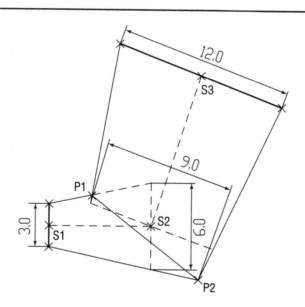

If the included angle between two adjacent wide segments is less than 28° or if the polyline has a noncontinuous linetype, the outer edges are not lengthened to their intersection. Instead, the two points perpendicular to the vertex connections are connected by a straight edge.

Of course, the arc segments of a polyline also have a width that can be different at each segment end. See Figure 13.4 for an example.

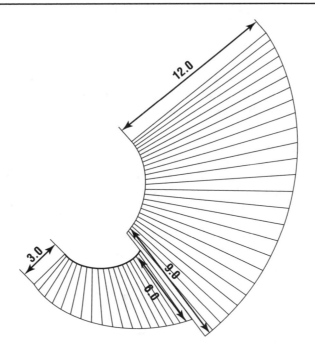

You can query the start and end widths of each segment. In addition, there is a property that contains the complete polyline's constant width, if any.

ObjectDBX	ActiveX Automation	DXF/AutoLISP
getWidthsAt()	GetWidth	Group 40, start width Group 41, end width
getConstantWidth()	ConstantWidth	Group 43

In a 3D view, wide polylines hide any objects behind them. If the polyline has a noncontinuous linetype, you can see through the areas created by the linetype gaps.

The DXF class name of an AcDbPolyline is "LWPOLYLINE". The sequence of groups following the subclass marker is 90, 70, 43, 38, 39, 10, 40, 41, 42 (repeat from 10), 210.

Heavyweight Polylines

Heavyweight polylines are an older variant of the lightweight polyline object. They are called *heavyweights* because of the more difficult and heavy data structure they need.

An AcDb2dPolyline object does not define the complete heavyweight polyline. In addition, there is a separate AcDb2dVertex object for each polyline vertex. The sequence is closed by a bracket object of type AcDbSequenceEnd.

A heavyweight polyline has the same properties and functionality as a lightweight polyline. In addition, a few properties are not available for lightweight polylines. These properties are used to generate smooth heavyweight polylines. For lightweight polylines, the corresponding functionality is created by AcDbSpline objects.

Polyline Begin

A heavyweight polyline starts with a polyline header. The AcDb2dPolyline object resembles the following properties of the lightweight polyline:

ObjectDBX	ActiveX Automation	DXF/AutoLISP
normal()	Normal	Group 210.
elevation()	Elevation	Group 10. This is the point (0, 0, *elevation*).
thickness()	Thickness	Group 39.
isClosed()	Closed	First bit (1) of group 70.
isLinetype-GenerationOn()	LinetypeGeneration	Eighth bit (128) of group 70; true for segment-oriented linetype mapping.

In addition, the heavyweight polyline header contains the following properties, which define the width values for the first segment and the polyline type for smoothed polylines.

ObjectDBX	ActiveX Automation	DXF/AutoLISP
defaultStartWidth()	GetWidth	Group 40
defaultEndWidth()	GetWidth	Group 41
polyType() == k2dFitCurvePoly	Type = acFitCurvePoly	Second bit (2) of group 70
polyType() == k2dQuadSplinePoly	Type = acQuadSplinePoly	Third bit (4) of group 70 set, group 75 = 5
polyType() == k2dCubicSplinePoly	Type = acCubicSplinePoly	Third bit (4) of group 70 set, group 75 = 6

The DXF class name for an AcDb2dPolyline object is "POLYLINE". Following the subclass marker are the groups 66 (constant 1), 10, 39, 70, 40, 41, 75, 210. The fourth (8), fifth (16), and seventh (64) bits of group 70 are not set.

Vertex Objects

Although a lightweight polyline lists all vertices within the AcDbPolyline object, a heavyweight polyline contains a separate object for each vertex. In ObjectDBX, you can use the AcDb2dPolyline *vertexIterator()* function to step through the individual vertex objects. In DXF, the AcDb2dVertex objects directly follow the polyline header.

The AcDbVertex object lists the vertex position as well as the bulge and widths of the following segment, just as a lightweight polyline does.

ObjectDBX	ActiveX Automation	DXF/AutoLISP
position()	Coordinates (in AcDb2dPolyline)	Group 10
bulge()	GetBulge	Group 42
startWidth()	GetWidth	Group 40
endWidth()	GetWidth	Group 41

The vertex position is always in the ECS of the AcDb2dPolyline object, even in ObjectDBX.

An AcDb2dVertex object has additional properties for curve-fit and splined polylines. We'll look at them later in this chapter.

The corresponding DXF class name is "VERTEX". It uses a subclass marker of "AcDb-Vertex" (an abstract group without properties), followed by the "AcDb2dVertex" subclass marker and the groups 10, 40, 41, 42, 70, 50.

 NOTE AcDbVertex is derived from AcDbEntity, which means that a vertex has a color, a linetype, and more. These must always match the corresponding polyline header.

Polyline End

The AcDbSequenceEnd object is the closing bracket for a heavyweight polyline and ends the list of vertices in DXF. In ObjectDBX, you access the sequence end using the *openSequenceEnd()* function of the AcDb2dPolyline object.

The AcDbSequenceEnd object itself does not contain any properties. Only in AutoLISP can you use the entity name in the –2 group to locate the corresponding opening bracket (AcDb2dPolyline object).

The DXF class name for AcDbSequenceEnd is "SEQEND". It contains no groups (not even a subclass marker) other than the AcDbObject and AcDbEntity groups.

Curve-Fit Polylines

A curve-fit is a simple algorithm that creates a smooth curve from a polyline. The resulting curve consists of circular arcs that meet tangentially. The resulting curve is continuous up to its first derivative.

Every vertex from the polyline is also a vertex of the curve-fit polyline. To connect two vertices with the tangent restriction intact, you must draw two circular arcs between them. Therefore, a curve-fit polyline needs additional vertices, which are included at the end of the arcs.

You can distinguish the added vertices from the original vertices by their vertex type.

ObjectDBX	ActiveX Automation	DXF/AutoLISP
vertexType() == k2dCurveFitVertex	n/a	First bit (1) in group 70

To further control the run of the curve, you can add a tangency direction with every vertex. If the tangencies are to be taken into account, the curve-fit arcs will follow their direction.

ObjectDBX	ActiveX Automation	DXF/AutoLISP
isTangentUsed()	n/a	Second bit (2) in group 70
tangent()	n/a	Group 50

The tangent direction is relative to the x-axis of the polyline's ECS. The tangents also provide the only way to recalculate the original polyline after a curve-fit has been applied.

Splined Polylines

A second way to create a smooth curve from a polyline is to calculate a spline curve that uses the polyline vertices as their control points. (See Chapter 10 for more details about splines and control points.)

An AcDb2dPolyline can describe a quadratic or cubic uniform nonrational B-spline curve. The terms *quadratic* and *cubic* refer to the spline degree, that is, the number of continuous derivations. The polyline header information specifies whether the curve is a spline and whether it's quadratic or cubic.

A splined polyline is really two curves in one: the original polyline and an approximation of the spline curve. Depending on the global SPLFRAME setting, AutoCAD will display only the approximation or both.

The original polyline defines the control points of the B-spline. In this way, it forms the exact mathematical definition for a B-spline curve. The approximation is just an aid for programs that cannot create a true B-spline curve by themselves.

The approximation of the spline curve is a polyline on its own using its individual vertices. Both polylines, however, have only one common polyline header and one common polyline sequence end.

To decide which vertices belong to the original polyline and which belong to the approximation, you look at the vertex type.

ObjectDBX	ActiveX Automation	DXF/AutoLISP
vertexType() == k2dSplineCtlVertex	n/a	Fifth bit (16) in group 70. These form the spline control points.
vertexType() == k2dSplineFitVertex	n/a	Fourth bit (8) in group 70. These form the approximation.

Three-Dimensional Polylines

An AcDb3dPolyline is similar to an AcDb2dPolyline. Again, the object is a continuous curve made from straight segments. The straight segments may, however, be oriented in space arbitrarily. Thus, a 3D polyline is an AcDbCurve, but not a planar one.

A 3D polyline has no widths and no arc segments , which makes their definition easy; however, a 3D polyline can be splined.

The AcDb3dPolyline object itself is simply a header object with very few properties.

ObjectDBX	ActiveX Automation	DXF/AutoLISP
isClosed()	Closed	First bit (1) of group 70
polyType() == k3dQuadSplinePoly	Type = acQuadSpline3DPoly	Third bit (4) of group 70 set, group 75 = 5
polyType() == k3dCubicSplinePoly	Type = acCubicSpline3DPoly	Third bit (4) of group 70 set, group 75 = 6

As with 2D polylines, the DXF class name of an AcDb3dPolyline object is "POLY-LINE". Following the subclass marker are the groups 66 (constant 1), 10 (constant 0,0,0), 70, and 75. The fourth bit (8) of group 70 is set.

The vertices of a 3D polyline are of type AcDb3dPolylineVertex. They have only the following properties:

ObjectDBX	ActiveX Automation	DXF/AutoLISP
position()	Coordinates (in AcDb3dPolyline)	Group 10.

ObjectDBX	ActiveX Automation	DXF/AutoLISP
vertexType() == k3dControlVertex	n/a	Fourth bit (16) in group 70. These form the spline control points.
vertexType() == k3dFitVertex	n/a	Third bit (16) in group 70. These form the spline approximation.

The vertex position is in WCS coordinates because a 3D polyline has no local coordinate system. If it's neither a spline control point nor a spline approximation point, it's just an ordinary vertex in an ordinary 3D polyline.

In DXF, 3D vertices use the "VERTEX" class name. Following the two subclass markers for "AcDbVertex" and "AcDb3dPolylineVertex" are the groups 10 and 70.

The AcDbSequenceEnd object is identical for 2D and 3D polylines.

Polygon Meshes

In a 3D polyline, the line segments connect two vertices. In a 3D polygon mesh, face segments connect four vertices each. An AcDbPolygonMesh object describes a rectangular, continuous, usually nonplanar surface made from quadrangular face objects. The word *rectangular* is used in a strict topological sense here. It means that you can move the vertex points into a rectangular grid without the connecting faces overlapping (except for the closing faces). Polygon meshes are not necessarily rectangular in a geometric sense.

You can order the segment vertices of a polygon mesh into M lines of N vertices each. Each line and each column look like 3D polylines. The entire mesh then contains M*N vertices and (M-1)*(N-1) faces (unless closing faces are added). A polygon mesh can be closed in M direction, in N direction, or in both directions.

The first face in the first row connects vertices 1, 2, N+1, and N+2. The second face connects vertices 2, 3, N+2, and N+3 and so on.

The AcDbPolygonMesh object has the following properties. Contrary to the objects discussed so far in this chapter, a polygon mesh, of course, is *not* a curve.

ObjectDBX	ActiveX Automation	DXF/AutoLISP
mSize()	MVertexCount	Group 71
isMClosed()	MClose	First bit (1) of group 70
nSize()	NVertexCount	Group 72
isNClosed()	NClose	Sixth bit (32) of group 70

Splined Polymesh Surfaces

As 3D polyline curves can define 3D spline curves, 3D polygon meshes can define 3D spline surfaces. Three types of splined surfaces exist. In most cases they look similar and only differ within small tolerances. Each splined surface is a smooth surface controlled by the mesh vertices. The mathematical algorithms used to generate the splined surface differ:

- Quadratic B-spline surfaces are the surface equivalent to a quadratic B-spline curve. These are uniform, nonrational B-spline surfaces that are formed from the B-spline curves created by the vertices of constant N or M.

- Cubic B-spline surfaces are the surface equivalent to a cubic B-spline curve.

- Bézier surfaces are non-uniform, nonrational B-spline surfaces, which means that their defining curves are not parallel to the vertex lines. With Bézier surfaces, you are limited to a maximum of 11 control points in both M and N directions.

Again, a splined polygon mesh is really two surfaces in one: the exact surface is defined by the surface control points, and an approximated surface is included for programs that cannot calculate a surface on their own. Depending on the SPLFRAME global setting, AutoCAD may display both.

The M and N size properties of a splined AcDbPolygonMesh refer to the number of control points in either direction. The number of vertices for the approximation is given by these additional properties:

ObjectDBX	ActiveX Automation	DXF/AutoLISP
mSurfaceDensity()	MDensity	Group 73
nSurfaceDensity()	NDensity	Group 74

To distinguish between the various surface types, you query the mesh type:

ObjectDBX	ActiveX Automation	DXF/AutoLISP
polyMeshType() == kSimpleMesh	Type = acSimpleMesh	Third bit (4) of group 70 not set
polyMeshType() == kQuadSurfaceMesh	Type = acQuadSurfaceMesh	Third bit (4) of group 70 set, group 75 = 5
polyMeshType() == kCubicSurfaceMesh	Type = acCubicSurfaceMesh	Third bit (4) of group 70 set, group 75 = 6
polyMeshType() == kBezierSurfaceMesh	Type = acBezierSurfaceMesh	Third bit (4) of group 70 set, group 75 = 8

The DXF class name used for AcDbPolygonMesh is once again "POLYLINE". Following the subclass marker are the groups 66 (constant 1), 10 (constant 0,0,0), 70, 71, 72, and 75. The fifth bit (16) of group 70 is set.

The polygon mesh vertices as well as the spline surface control points and approximating mesh vertices are of type AcDbPolygonMeshVertex. They are identical to the vertex objects used in 3D polylines except for their subclass marker and the seventh bit (64) in group 70, which is always set. Also, the sequence end bracket is identical.

Polyface Meshes

Although polygon mesh is a continuous collection of faces whose edges touch, a polyface mesh is a noncontinuous collection of faces. This means that a single AcDbPolyFaceMesh object can define faces located at arbitrary positions and not connected to one another.

A polyface mesh is based on vertices and, therefore, is similar in its definition to the polylines covered so far. Again, there is a polyline header object (AcDbPolyFaceMesh), a number of vertex objects, and a sequence end. An AcDbPolyFaceMesh has two kinds of vertex objects , however:

- The AcDbPolyFaceMeshVertex defines a vertex location, but no face.
- The AcDbFaceRecord defines a face but no location.

The two object types work together because a face record references mesh vertices.
The AcDbPolyFaceMesh header supplies only the following properties:

ObjectDBX	ActiveX Automation	DXF/AutoLISP
numVertices()	NumberOfVertices	Group 71
numFaces()	NumberOfFaces	Group 72

The DXF class name used for AcDbPolyFaceMesh is "POLYLINE" as well. Following the subclass marker are the groups 66 (constant 1), 10 (constant 0,0,0), 70, 71, and 72. The seventh bit (64) of group 70 is set.

In ObjectDBX, you will get both polyface mesh vertices and records by using the *vertexIterator()* function. You need to distinguish between the two by checking their class.

Polyface Mesh Vertices

AcDbPolyFaceMeshVertex objects are even simpler than AcDbPolygonMeshVertex objects. They have only a location, which is a WCS point.

ObjectDBX	ActiveX Automation	DXF/AutoLISP
position()	Coordinates (in AcDbPolyFaceMesh)	Group 10

In DXF, these objects use the same definition as polygon mesh vertices except for their subclass marker. The seventh and eighth bits (64 and 128) of DXF group 70 are set for objects of this type.

PolyFace Mesh Records

The polyface vertices define only locations in space; they do not create any geometry. The AcDbFaceRecord object defines faces that connect as many as four vertices. Each face record, therefore, defines a single face, which is similar to a 3D face and may have invisible edges.

A face can reference as many as four vertices. Depending on the number of faces referenced, it is one of the following:

- A single point (one vertex)
- A straight line (two vertices)
- A planar triangle (three vertices)
- A nonplanar quadrangle (four vertices)

The reference to a vertex is by an index number. Therefore, the vertices are numbered from 1 to *Number of Vertices*. This numbering is through their sequence in the drawing database only.

ObjectDBX	ActiveX Automation	DXF/AutoLISP
getVertexAt(0)	n/a	Group 71
getVertexAt(1)	n/a	Group 72
getVertexAt(2)	n/a	Group 73
getVertexAt(3)	n/a	Group 74

The vertex index can be negative or zero. A negative index means that the corresponding edge (group 71 for the edge from the first to the second vertex and so on) is invisible unless the global SPLFAME setting specifies otherwise. In ObjectDBX, you can also use the *isEdgeVisibleAt()* function.

Since face records are derived from AcDbEntity, they have their own layer, color, and plot style setting. Contrary to all other subentities used with polylines, these properties matter with face records. If one face record is red and the other is green, the first will display in red, and the second will display in green.

The DXF class name of AcDbFaceRecord is "VERTEX". A face record is not subclassed from AcDbVertex, which is why the subclass marker "AcDbFaceRecord" directly follows the AcDbEntity properties. The sequence of group codes is 10 (constant 0,0,0), 70 (constant 128), 71, 72, 73, and 74.

An AcDbPolyFaceMesh object ends with the usual sequence end bracket.

Multilines

The AcDbMline object is similar to the lightweight polyline that I described at the beginning of this chapter. It also defines a collection of lines: a series of parallel polylines.

A multiline is not a curve, and, therefore, it is not derived from AcDbCurve. It has vertices, but as in AcDbPolyline, they are part of the base object, not separated into vertex objects.

The definition of a multiline is divided into two objects:

- The AcDbMLine object defines the vertices and some additional properties that are different from multiline to multiline.

- The AcDbMlineStyle object defines the number, outlook, and spacing of the individual lines. Several AcDbMline entities can reference the same AcDbMlineStyle object.

Multiline Styles

A multiline style defines the family of lines used to draw a multiline. The multiline style itself has no visual representation and therefore is an AcDbObject.

To access an AcDbMlineStyle object, you can use the reference directly in the corresponding AcDbMline entity. As an alternative, you can use the named object dictionary, which always contains the key string "ACAD_MLINESTYLE". This key string is associated with another dictionary that contains one record per multiline style. The key string is the multiline style name, and the associated record is of type AcDbMlineStyle.

Any multiline style has a name (which is the duplicate of the key string) and a description.

ObjectDBX	ActiveX Automation	DXF/AutoLISP
name()	n/a	Group 2
description()	n/a	Group 3

The multiline style defines a series of parallel lines. Each line is offset from a virtual center line and has its own color and linetype.

ObjectDBX	ActiveX Automation	DXF/AutoLISP
numElements()	n/a	Group 71
getElementAt(), offset	n/a	Group 49
getElementAt(), color	n/a	Group 62 in elements list
getElementAt(), line-type, AcDbObjectId	n/a	Group 6, key string

The area between the leftmost (smallest offset) and the rightmost (largest offset) lines can be filled.

ObjectDBX	ActiveX Automation	DXF/AutoLISP
filled()	n/a	First bit (1) of group 70
fillColor()	n/a	Group 62 prior to elements list

Both the end and the start of a multiline sequence can have connecting lines or arcs. The ends can be cut perpendicular (the default in DXF) or under an angle. The start angle is measured against the direction from the first to the second vertex of the corresponding multiline entity. The end angle is measured against the direction from the next-to-last vertex to the last vertex.

ObjectDBX	ActiveX Automation	DXF/AutoLISP
startAngle()	n/a	Group 51
startSquareCap()	n/a	Fifth bit (16) of group 70; set when the beginnings of all lines are to be connected by a straight line
startRoundCap()	n/a	Seventh bit (64) of group 70; set when the beginnings of the leftmost and rightmost lines are to be connected by a circular arc
startInnerArcs()	n/a	Sixth bit (32) of group 70; set when the beginnings of all lines except for the leftmost, rightmost, and eventually middle lines are to be connected in pairs by circular arcs
endAngle()	n/a	Group 52

ObjectDBX	ActiveX Automation	DXF/AutoLISP
endSquareCap()	n/a	Ninth bit (256) of group 70; set when the ends of all lines are to be connected by a straight line
endRoundCap()	n/a	Eleventh bit (1024) of group 70; set when the ends of the leftmost and rightmost lines are to be connected by a circular arc
endInnerArcs()	n/a	Tenth bit (512) of group 70; set when the ends of all lines except for the leftmost, rightmost, and eventually middle lines are to be connected in pairs by circular arcs

Finally, a multiline style defines whether miter lines are to be drawn at each vertex.

ObjectDBX	ActiveX Automation	DXF/AutoLISP
showMiters()	n/a	Second bit (2) of group 70

The DXF class name of an AcDbMlineStyle object is "MLINESTYLE". The sequence of groups following the subclass marker is 2, 70, 3, 62 (fill color), 51, 52, 71, 49, 62 (line color), and 6 (repeated from 49).

Multiline Entities

An AcDbMline object defines a specific multiline entity. This object contains the vertices that create the virtual reference line parallel to which the individual lines are drawn as specified by the associated multiline style.

ObjectDBX	ActiveX Automation	DXF/AutoLISP
style(), AcDbObjectId	StyleName, key string	Group 340, handle; group 2, key string

A multiline entity is a planar object. The plane is given by the normal direction and the first vertex point. All point coordinates are in WCS. Contrary to an AcDbPolyline, a multiline has no ECS and no thickness.

ObjectDBX	ActiveX Automation	DXF/AutoLISP
normal()	n/a	Group 210

The vertices define a virtual reference line similar to a lightweight polyline. If the multiline is closed, the last vertex is connected to the first vertex. The reference line consists of straight line segments only.

ObjectDBX	ActiveX Automation	DXF/AutoLISP
numVertices()	n/a	Group 72
vertexAt()	Coordinates	Group 11
closedMline()	n/a	Second bit (2) in group 71

The various lines that are defined by the multiline style are drawn parallel to this virtual reference line. The *Justification* property defines how the AcDbMlineStyle offsets are used. Any offset is multiplied by the AcDbMline-specific scale factor.

ObjectDBX	ActiveX Automation	DXF/AutoLISP
scale()	n/a	Group 40
justification()	n/a	Group 70

The *Justification* property is one of the following:

ObjectDBX	DXF/AutoLISP	Meaning
kTop	0	The parallel line with the maximum offset is drawn at the reference line. All other lines follow to the right (when looking from the first vertex to the second).
kZero	1	The reference line matches offset zero. Positive offsets are drawn to the left; negative offsets, to the right.
kBottom	2	The parallel line with the minimum offset is drawn at the reference line. All other lines follow to the left.

Finally, the AcDbMline entity allows you to override the AcDbMlineStyle settings for connecting lines at the start and end of the multiline.

ObjectDBX	ActiveX Automation	DXF/AutoLISP
supressStartCaps()	n/a	Third bit (4) in group 70
supressEndCaps()	n/a	Fourth bit (8) in group 70

Multiline Breaks and Intersections

If one multiline overlays another or if a user decides to cut a break in a multiline, the multiline is not broken into multiple parts. Instead, it is possible to make parts of a line invisible within a segment.

The definition of breaks within a multiline segment is quite complicated, because there can be different breaks among the lines and even multiple breaks within each line.

You need to know the number of parallel lines, their direction, and their start point (calculated from the vertex along the miter with a specified distance). For each segment, the AcDbMline entity contains the following properties:

ObjectDBX	ActiveX Automation	DXF/AutoLISP
n/a, use AcDb-MlineStyle object	n/a	Group 73, number of parallel lines
axisAt()	n/a	Group 12, unit vector, direction of segment line
miterAt()	n/a	Group 13, unit vector, direction of miter
n/a	n/a	group 74, number of parameters
getParametersAt(0)	n/a	First group 41, distance along miter to virtual start point
getParametersAt(1)	n/a	Second group 41, distance along segment direction from virtual start point to true start point (zero if segment line starts at miter)

Except for the true start point (which includes an eventual break at the start point), all these values could have been calculated from the vertices and the multiline style definition.

Additional parameters define the visible and invisible parts of the line. These are given by their distance from the virtual start point. Visibility alternates; that is, the segment part starting at the true start point (from parameter 1) to the point given by parameter 2 is visible. From parameter 2 to parameter 3, it's invisible and so on.

ObjectDBX	ActiveX Automation	DXF/AutoLISP
getParametersAt(2..n)	n/a	Group 41, distance along segment direction from virtual start point

 NOTE In AutoLISP and DXF, a similar sequence of groups 75 and 42 is documented that affects the fill along a segment. This is nonfunctional in AutoCAD 2000, however.

Calculated Properties of Multilines

Even though an AcDbMline object is not a curve, in ObjectDBX, it offers both the *getPlane()* and *getClosestPointTo()* functions usually found with curves.

In DXF and AutoLISP, you'll find an additional group 10, which is a copy of the first vertex. The first bit of group 70 is always set.

The DXF class name for AcDbMline is `"MLINE"`. The sequence of groups following the subclass marker is 2, 340, 40, 70, 71, 72, 73, 10, 210, 11, 12, 13, 74, 41 (repeated), and 75 (constant 0). Repeat from 11.

Summary

Collections of lines and faces can be used as a single object in the drawing database. They are easier to handle and manipulate than a series of unrelated lines and arcs. Unfortunately, the definition of such a collection is much more complicated than a simple line.

Leader lines, lightweight and heavyweight polylines, as well as multilines are similar. However, each of these objects can perform operations that the others cannot. This includes differences in display and print.

The next chapter covers another "collection" of lines: hatches.

CHAPTER <u>14</u>

Hatches and Fills

FEATURING

The elements of a hatch definition   **300**

Contours and associations   **302**

Fills and patterns   **307**

The boundary tracer   **309**

Solids and traces   **310**

Wipeouts   **311**

A hatch is a collection of lines and thus is similar to a polyline. On the other hand, a hatch is an annotation object and thus is similar to other annotation objects. A hatch contour is a closed curve made from splines, arcs, or lines. And finally a hatch pattern is somehow related to a linetype pattern. Therefore, this chapter combines several ideas that we looked at in previous chapters.

Hatches in AutoCAD are algorithmic; that is, the properties of the AcDbHatch object are the input parameters through which AutoCAD generates hatch lines and patterns when they are needed. This is very different from bitmap fills that many other Windows programs use. And it's very different from the hatches that AutoCAD created in older versions, which were simply block containers full of hatch lines.

Contrary to the way that dimensions work, an AutoCAD hatch references the objects through which it has been created. This associativity allows AutoCAD to react to modifications and to adjust the hatch accordingly.

This chapter concentrates on the AcDbHatch object, which describes both hatched and filled areas. In addition, we'll look at AcDbSolid and AcDbTrace, which are two names for the same class of quadrangular filled regions. At the end of this chapter, we'll also take a brief look at the AcDbWipeout object, which is a sort of nonhatch you can find in many AutoCAD drawings. Unfortunately, it is also a fine example of an almost undocumented custom entity.

The Elements of a Hatch Definition

A hatch is the visualization of a specific planar region within a drawing. It is an annotation object that distinguishes this region from other regions of different material or structure.

A hatch is usually bounded by other drawing objects such as lines, polylines, circles, or splines. These curves form one or more contours that limit the hatched area; however, these curves are separate drawing objects. A hatch doesn't have to have a bounding curve because it contains the complete contour data. Hatch contours do not display.

Figure 14.1 shows a hatched region and its four bounding objects. A polyline forms the outline, and an elliptical arc and a spline form an "island," as does a text object.

A hatched region and its bounding objects are bi-directionally linked. Not only does the AcDbHatch object contain the information about which object generated a certain hatch contour, those objects also contain a link back to the AcDbHatch object. This associativity allows AutoCAD to regenerate the hatch contours and the hatch visualization as soon as any bounding object changes. Again, hatch objects may be, but do not have to be, connected to other drawing objects.

FIGURE 14.1

A hatched region

The hatch contours create one or more closed planar regions. These regions are filled with a solid color or with an arrangement of dots and lines, which is called a pattern.

The AcDbHatch object includes the complete definition of this pattern with all lines, dots, gaps, and angles. As you will see, this definition is similar to a series of linetype patterns.

Like any annotation, an AcDbHatch is a planar object. Planar objects have a normal vector that defines the plane orientation and an elevation that defines the plane offset from the world origin.

ObjectDBX	ActiveX Automation	DXF/AutoLISP
normal()	Normal	Group 210.
elevation()	Elevation	Group 10, Z coordinate. X and Y are always zero.

Normal vector and elevation define both the plane on which the hatch is drawn and the local coordinate system within this plane. The origin is the projection of the world origin along the normal vector; the x-axis is calculated from the normal vector using the arbitrary axis algorithm.

The global FILLMODE setting specifies whether hatches display. If FILLMODE is false, hatches do not display.

The DXF class name of an AcDbHatch object is "HATCH". Following the subclass marker are the groups 10, 210, 2, 70, 71, and 91. Next are the groups that describe the hatch contours, which I'll describe in the following sections in this chapter. Following the contour data are the groups 75, 76, 52, 41, and 77. Following the groups is another block of DXF groups that describe the hatch pattern that I'll cover at the end of this section. The DXF sequence of an AcDbHatch object ends with optional groups 98 and 10 (repeated), which contain information about how AutoCAD's boundary tracer created the hatch contours.

Contours and Associativity

The hatched region is bounded by a number of contours, or *loops*. Loops must be closed and may not intersect themselves or other loops. There is always at least one loop.

ObjectDBX	ActiveX Automation	DXF/AutoLISP
numLoops()	NumberOfLoops	Group 91

A loop can be associated with other database objects such as lines or circles, which are used to define the hatch loop edges. A general property tells you if there are any associated objects. The objects themselves are listed with the individual loops.

ObjectDBX	ActiveX Automation	DXF/AutoLISP
associative()	AssociativeHatch	Group 71

If a loop is completely contained within another loop, it forms an *island*. Islands may or may not be hatched, depending on the hatch style.

ObjectDBX	ActiveX Automation	DXF/AutoLISP
hatchStyle()	HatchStyle	Group 75

The hatch style is one of the following:

ObjectDBX	ActiveX Automation	DXF/ AutoLISP	Meaning
kNormal	acHatchStyleNormal	0	Hatching alternates: an island within a hatched area is not hatched; an island within an island is hatched.
kOuter	acHatchStyleOuter	1	No island is hatched.
kIgnore	acHatchStyleIgnore	2	All islands are hatched.

Loop Types

Each closed contour, or loop, consists of lines, circular or elliptical arcs, splines, or polylines. It may have been created in a number of ways:

- From external database curves (*kExternal*, 1)
- From an external database text object (*kTextbox*, 8)
- By AutoCAD's boundary tracer (*kDerived*, 4)
- By AcGePolyline2d geometry built by AutoCAD's boundary tracer or an application program (*kPolyline*,2)

The loop type is the bit-wise combination of one or more of these constants with the information about whether this particular loop is an island or an outermost loop. Contrary to the AutoCAD documentation, the *kOutermost* (16) bit is set if the loop is an island!

ObjectDBX	ActiveX Automation	DXF/AutoLISP
loopTypeAt()	n/a	Group 92

In DXF, each loop starts with the loop type (group 92) and is followed by the loop data. The loop definition ends with the list of associated objects.

Polyline-like Loops

A polyline-like loop is similar to an AcDbPolyline. It consist of an arbitrary number of vertices and optional bulge factors. All vertices are 2D points (AcGePoint2d) within the local coordinate system of the hatch.

ObjectDBX	ActiveX Automation	DXF/AutoLISP
n/a	n/a	Group 93, the number of vertices
getLoopAt(), vertices	n/a	Group 10
n/a	n/a	Group 72, has bulge factors
n/a	n/a	Group 73, is closed
getLoopAt(), bulges	n/a	Group 42

The lines and arcs connecting the vertices are calculated just as they are calculated in an AcDbPolyline. In DXF, polyline-like loops are defined using the group sequence 72, 73, 93, 10 (repeated), and 42 (repeated).

Edge-Defined Loops

If a hatch contour is not of type *kPolyline,* it is composed of a series of edges. The definition of an edge is similar to the definition of an AcDbLine, AcDbArc, AcDbEllipse, or AcDbSpline.

Edges must connect at their end points, and they may not intersect themselves or any other edge.

ObjectDBX	ActiveX Automation	DXF/AutoLISP
n/a	n/a	Group 93, number of edges

There are four types of edges:

- Lines (*kLine*, 1)
- Circular arcs (*kCirArc*, 2)
- Elliptical arcs (*kEllArc*, 3)
- Splines (*kSpline*, 4)

ObjectDBX	ActiveX Automation	DXF/AutoLISP
getLoopAt(), edgeTypes	n/a	Group 72

In ObjectDBX, the *getLoopAt()* function returns an array of pointers, each pointing to an AcGe object, which then allows you to extract the edge data. In ActiveX Automation, the *GetLoopAt* method returns an array of line, arc, ellipse, and/or spline objects. In DXF and AutoLISP, you'll find the edge data with the AcDbHatch entity: each loop starts with a group 93 followed by the appropriate number of edge definitions, which are always lead by a group 72.

Line Edges

Linear edges are of type AcGeLineSeg2d in ObjectDBX. This class offers the following properties, which are similar to the properties of the AcDbLine object I described in Chapter 10.

ObjectDBX	ActiveX Automation	DXF/AutoLISP
startPoint()	StartPoint	Group 10
endPoint()	EndPoint	Group 11

Both points are 2D points in the local coordinate system of the hatch. In DXF, a linear edge uses the group sequence 10, 11.

Circular Arc Edges

Circular curved edges are of type AcGeCircArc2d in ObjectDBX. This class offers the following properties, which are similar to the properties of the AcDbArc object I described from Chapter 10.

ObjectDBX	ActiveX Automation	DXF/AutoLISP
center()	Center	Group 10
radius()	Radius	Group 40
startAng()	StartAngle	Group 50
endAng()	EndAngle	Group 51
isClockWise()	n/a	Group 73

The center point is a 2D point in the local coordinate system of the hatch; the two angles are relative to the local x-axis. Unlike an AcDbArc (which is always counter-clockwise), an arc edge has an orientation that is expressed by the Boolean *Is Clockwise* flag.

In ObjectDBX and ActiveX Automation, there are additional calculated properties such as start point and end point. In DXF, the group code sequence for circular arc edges is 10, 40, 50, 51, 73.

Elliptical Arc Edges

Circular curved edges are of type AcGeEllipArc2d in ObjectDBX. This class offers the following properties, which are similar to the properties of the AcDbEllipse object that I described in Chapter 10.

ObjectDBX	ActiveX Automation	DXF/AutoLISP
center()	Center	Group 10
majorAxis()	MajorAxis	Group 11
majorRadius()	MajorRadius	n/a
minorAxis()	MinorAxis	n/a
minorRadius()	MinorRadius	n/a
n/a	RadiusRatio	Group 40
startAng()	StartAngle	Group 50
endAng()	EndAngle	Group 51
isClockWise()	n/a	Group 73

The center point is a 2D point in the local coordinate system of the hatch; the axes are 2D vectors relative to the center. The primary defining properties for an AcGeEllipArc2d are angles, not parameters as with AcDbEllipse. Like a circular arc edge, an elliptical arc edge has an orientation.

In ObjectDBX and ActiveX Automation, there are additional calculated properties such as start point and end point. In DXF, the group code sequence for elliptical arc edges is 10, 11, 40, 50, 51, 73.

Spline Edges

Spline-type edges are of type AcGeNurbCurve2d, which is derived from AcGeSplineEnt2d. This object is similar to the AcDbSpline object that I described in Chapter 10. It offers the following properties:

ObjectDBX	ActiveX Automation	DXF/AutoLISP
degree()	Degree	Group 94
isRational()	isRational	Group 73
isPeriodic()	isPeriodic	Group 74
numKnots()	n/a	Group 95
numControlPoints()	NumberOfControlPoints	Group 96
knotAt()	Knots	Group 40
controlPointAt()	GetControlPoint	Group 10
weightAt()	Weights	Group 42

Again, the control points are 2D points in the local coordinate system. In DXF, a spline edge is defined by this group sequence: 94, 73, 74, 95, 96, 40 (repeated), 10 (repeated), 42 (repeated).

Associated Entities

If other database entities were used to create edges of a hatch loop, these entities and the AcDbHatch object can be linked. This associativity allows AutoCAD to automatically redraw the hatch if one of the linked objects moves or changes.

Within the drawing database, this link is bi-directional. Every object associated with the hatch lists the AcDbHatch object's identification with its other reactor objects. (See Chapter 5 for information about reactors.) Whenever the object changes, it sends a notification to all objects listed in its reactor section, including the AcDb-Hatch object.

The AcDbHatch object itself lists the associated objects along with the loops they helped to create. A list of objects is associated with each loop.

ObjectDBX	ActiveX Automation	DXF/AutoLISP
n/a	n/a	Group 97, the number of objects associated with this loop
getAssocObjIdsAt()	n/a	Group 330

In ObjectDBX, the *getAssocObjIdsAt()* function returns an array of AcDbObjectId. In DXF and AutoLISP, you'll find the appropriate number of groups 330, which are either handles or entity names, depending on your environment.

Fills and Patterns

We now have the plane on which the hatch is to be drawn, and we know the area within this plane that is to be hatched. What's missing is the hatch pattern.

An AcDbHatch object supports two ways to fill the hatched area:

- A solid fill that uses the color associated with the AcDbHatch entity
- A collection of dashes and dots, which we call the hatch *pattern*

The user can define a hatch pattern in AutoCAD in multiple ways:

- By selecting one of AutoCAD's predefined patterns
- By using one of many custom patterns
- By simply drawing a pattern on the fly

The AcDbHatch object memorizes the way a hatch has been created, which allows the AutoCAD user to edit the hatch parameters later and redraw the hatch. The AcDb-Hatch object itself, however, stores only the pattern used to draw the hatch.

Predefined and custom-defined patterns have a *Name*, which is "SOLID" for a solid color fill.

ObjectDBX	ActiveX Automation	DXF/AutoLISP
patternType()	PatternType	Group 76
patternName()	PatternName	Group 2
n/a	n/a	Group 70, Boolean flag, true (1) if pattern is a solid fill

The pattern type is one of the following:

ObjectDBX	ActiveX Automation	DXF/AutoLISP
kUserDefined	acHatchPatternTypeUserDefined	0
kPreDefined	acHatchPatternTypePreDefined	1
kCustomDefined	acHatchPatternTypeCustomDefined	2

Pattern Generation Parameters

When AutoCAD generates a hatch from a predefined or custom pattern, it accesses a pattern definition stored in a separate file. This definition lists the various pattern line families for a predefined angle and scale. When the AcDbHatch object is created, this pattern definition is moved, scaled, and rotated to form the true pattern line families that are saved with the AcDbHatch object.

ObjectDBX	ActiveX Automation	DXF/AutoLISP
patternAngle()	PatternAngle	Group 52
patternScale()	PatternScale	Group 41

A user-defined pattern is generated on the fly from the current linetype according to an angle and a distance entered by the user. In addition, a user-defined pattern can be double-hatched, which means that a second set of lines is drawn and rotated 90°. As with predefined patterns, you don't have to calculate the correct line families because the AcDbHatch object already includes the rotated and scaled lines.

ObjectDBX	ActiveX Automation	DXF/AutoLISP
patternAngle()	PatternAngle	Group 52
patternSpace()	PatternSpace	Group 41, hatch line spacing
patternDouble()	PatternDouble	Group 77, true (1) for double hatching

Pattern Line Families

The hatch pattern is composed of families of parallel, but not necessarily continuous, lines. Each family extends indefinitely in all directions along the hatch plane. The hatch loops bound the regions in which the family members are visible.

There is at least one family of pattern lines.

ObjectDBX	ActiveX Automation	DXF/AutoLISP
numPatternDefinitions()	n/a	Group 78

Each family is defined by an angle and a short line segment, which is then repeated over and over both along the angle direction and perpendicular to it. The base line, that is, the first repetition of the segment, is offset against the origin of the local coordinate system, both along and perpendicular to the angle direction. The segment then repeats in this direction. The first repetition of the segment in the first parallel is again offset against the base line.

ObjectDBX	ActiveX Automation	DXF/AutoLISP
getPatternDefinitionAt(), angle	n/a	Group 53
getPatternDefinitionAt(), baseX	n/a	Group 43, offset of baseline along angle direction

ObjectDBX	ActiveX Automation	DXF/AutoLISP
getPatternDefinitionAt(), baseY	n/a	Group 44, offset of baseline perpendicular to the angle direction
getPatternDefinitionAt(), offsetX	n/a	Group 45, offset of the first parallel along the angle direction
getPatternDefinitionAt(), offsetY	n/a	Group 46, offset of the first parallel perpendicular to the angle direction
n/a	n/a	Group 79, number of dashes
getPatternDefinitionAt(), dashes	n/a	Group 49

The dashes, gaps, and dots that form the baseline segment use the exact same definition as noncontinuous linetypes: positive numbers stand for a dash of appropriate length, negative numbers define a gap length, and zero creates a dot.

If a line family contains no dash definitions, a continuous line is drawn at the given angle. In this case, the offsets along the angle direction are meaningless and, therefore, zero.

The DXF sequence for the pattern definition is 78 followed by the appropriate number of groups 53, 43, 44, 45, 46, 79, and 49 (repeated).

In ObjectDBX, you can query the total number of lines that make the hatch visualization as well as each individual line using the *numHatchLines()* and *getHatchLineDataAt()* functions.

AutoCAD's Boundary Tracer

AutoCAD includes a routine to calculate the nearest closed loop around a given *seed point*. You can use this routine to create the loops saved as an AcDbHatch object; however, you can also generate those loops in other ways.

If an AutoCAD user selected some points inside the area to be hatched and let AutoCAD's boundary tracer calculate the loops, you can later query these seed points.

ObjectDBX	ActiveX Automation	DXF/AutoLISP
n/a	n/a	Group 98, number of seed points
n/a	n/a	Group 10, seed point

The seed points are 2D points within the local coordinate system of the AcDb-Hatch entity. In DXF and AutoLISP, you'll see the group 98 followed by repeated groups 10 (and 20).

Solids and Traces

AcDbSolid and AcDbTrace are two names for the exact same thing. The only difference between the two are the class names and the DXF class names. And even the DXF subclass marker is "AcDbTrace" for both. The different names are historic and represent the commands used in AutoCAD to draw them.

A solid (not to be confused with a 3D solid volume) and a trace are quadrangular planar objects that display filled when viewed in their normal direction. If the global FILLMODE is off or if the view direction is not parallel to the object's normal, the solid and trace display like a 3D face and hide other objects.

Solids and traces are planar objects that use their own local coordinate system. Like circles and some other objects, they can be extruded along their normal.

ObjectDBX	ActiveX Automation	DXF/AutoLISP
normal()	Normal	Group 210
thickness()	Thickness	Group 39

The local coordinate system (ECS) is defined using the normal vector as the Z direction, the world origin as the ECS origin, and the x-axis calculated from the normal vector by the arbitrary axis algorithm.

A solid or a trace has four corner points, some of which may be identical. These points are WCS coordinates in ObjectDBX and ActiveX Automation; in DXF and AutoLISP, they are ECS coordinates. They are 3D points on a common plane perpendicular to the ECS X/Y plane; that is, in ECS they have the same Z value.

In clockwise order, the sequence of the four points is 0-2-3-1. It's possible to arrange the points so that the outline intersects itself, creating a bow-tie–like shape, or two filled triangles.

ObjectDBX	ActiveX Automation	DXF/AutoLISP
getPointAt(0)	Coordinates(0)	Group 10
getPointAt(1)	Coordinates(1)	Group 11
getPointAt(2)	Coordinates(2)	Group 12
getPointAt(3)	Coordinates(3)	Group 13

The DXF class name for AcDbSolid is `"SOLID"`, and the DXF class name for AcDb-Trace is `"TRACE"`. Both use the subclass marker `"AcDbTrace"` in DXF, however. The sequence of groups following the subclass marker is 10, 11, 12, 13, 39, 210.

Wipeouts

A final hatch-like object commonly found in AutoCAD drawings is the AcDbWipeout. A wipeout is like a hatch without a pattern. Instead, it uses the background color to cover any geometry that lies behind it. Wipeouts are often used in connection with text objects to allow the text to stand freely on top of other geometry.

Unfortunately, the AcDbWipeout object is not considered a *native* drawing object. It's part of the *unsupported* bonus or Express tools that are shipped with AutoCAD. In other words, Autodesk did not bother to provide a complete implementation, including ObjectDBX, ActiveX Automation, and AutoLISP access or DXF documentation.

If you find an AcDbWipeout object in a DXF file, you'll see that it lists a large number of groups. These groups are the same as those used with an AcDbRasterImage entity (described in detail in the next chapter). A wipeout entity borrows these groups because it is basically a one-pixel bitmap of minimum fade clipped to the wipeout boundary.

Using this information, you may be able to guess the meaning of most groups. As with bitmap images, the groups 10, 11, and 12 define a local, planar coordinate system, and the group 14 defines the wipeout border within this coordinate system.

The AcDbWipeout entity, along with the AcDbWipeoutVariables object, are typical examples of insufficiently implemented custom objects that are part of a drawing database. I'll cover such custom objects in detail in Chapter 18.

Summary

This chapter basically covered only one type of database object, the AcDbHatch class. You can see that a large number of properties and a complex internal structure is needed to store objects as difficult as a hatch. You also see how many pages one needs to document such a complex object. This is, of course, one of the reasons that developers of custom objects (such as AcDbWipeout) refuse to do so.

If you are familiar with hatches in other programs, you may have wondered whether the AutoCAD drawing database also allows bitmap fills. The next chapter concentrates on uses for bitmap files in AutoCAD.

CHAPTER **15**

Bitmap Images

FEATURING

Image definitions   314

Image entities   316

Image definition to entity link   319

Global settings for raster images   319

An AcDbHatch object places a collection of lines and dots on a plane. Such a hatch is an annotation object that typically describes the type of surface or material being used. Although bitmap fills are common in many drawing programs, they cannot be generated by the AcDbHatch object.

AutoCAD knows about bitmap images, however. A user can place an arbitrary bitmap image on any plane. Besides standing on their own, bitmap images can also be used to fill areas if they are arrayed and clipped.

In this chapter, I'll concentrate on bitmap images and their associated objects:

AcDbRasterImage   An AutoCAD entity. This object generates a bitmap image on the screen or on paper. It contains information about the location, orientation, and clipping, but it does not contain any information about the image itself.

AcDbRasterImageDef   Not an AutoCAD entity because by itself it creates no visual image. This object is equivalent to a block container and contains the image name and contents data. A single image definition can be referenced by several AcDbRasterImage objects if the same bitmap image is repeated at multiple locations.

AcDbRasterImageReactor   An object that creates a link between an image entity and the corresponding image definition object.

AcDbRasterVariables   An object that contains some settings that apply to all images in a drawing.

If you work with bitmap images from within ObjectDBX, AutoLISP, and DXF, you'll see the database objects as they are listed here. Within the ActiveX Automation interface these objects are combined into a single virtual *Raster* object.

Image Definitions

The AcDbRasterImageDef object forms a link between an external image file and the AutoCAD drawing database. The image itself, however, is not embedded in the database; AutoCAD saves only the image's filename.

ObjectDBX	ActiveX Automation	DXF/AutoLISP
sourceFileName()	ImageFile	Group 1

If the AutoCAD user entered a complete path, the filename contains the full path to the image. If the AutoCAD user entered the filename only, AutoCAD uses the PROJECTNAME setting from the corresponding AcDbDictionaryVar object along with its standard search strategy to find the image file.

Like block table records pointing to an external database, the external file may be loaded into the current AutoCAD session. If not found or explicitly unloaded, the image will not display through the AcDbRasterImage object.

ObjectDBX	ActiveX Automation	DXF/AutoLISP
isLoaded()	n/a	Group 280

The AcDbRasterImageDef object allows access to various properties of the attached bitmap image, such as type, color depth, and resolution.

ObjectDBX	ActiveX Automation	DXF/AutoLISP
fileType()	n/a	n/a
size()	Width, Height	Group 10
colorDepth(), bits per pixel	n/a	n/a
organization(), kAcGiPalette, kAcGiRGB, kAcGiRGBA, or kAcGiBitonal	n/a	n/a
resolutionUnits()	n/a	Group 281
resolutionMMPerPixel()	n/a	Group 11

The *Size* property is a 2D point that contains the image size in pixels (x = width, y = height). *Resolution Units* is one of the following:

ObjectDBX	DXF/AutoLISP	Meaning
kNone	0	Image has no internal unit of measurement
kCentimeters	2	Centimeters
kInch	5	Inch

The *Resolution in mm per Pixel* is, again, a 2D point, with the x coordinate describing the pixel width and the y coordinate describing the pixel height. If an image has no internal unit of measurement, this property is set to the reciprocal value of the size in pixels.

The DXF class name of an AcDbRasterImageDef object is "IMAGEDEF". The DXF sequence of groups following the subclass marker is 90 (class version: constant 0), 1, 10, 11, 280, 281.

Finding an Image Definition

To find the AcDbRasterImageDef object associated with a specific image entity, use the corresponding property of the AcDbRasterImage object (*imageDefId()*, group 340). To find all image definition objects in a database, use the value associated with the "ACAD_IMAGE_DEF" key string in the root dictionary. This value points to a dictionary that contains pointers to all raster definition objects. The key strings in this dictionary are the image filenames minus the path.

Image Entities

The AcDbRasterImageDef object itself does not generate any displayable graphics in a drawing. The AcDbRasterImage object references a raster image definition and contains the geometric properties of a bitmap display within a drawing.

A bitmap display is a planar object and uses its own internal coordinate system, which is calculated from an origin point and two vectors along the local x- and y-axes. The origin becomes the lower-left corner of the unclipped image, the x-axis points along the image width, and the y-axis points along the image height.

ObjectDBX	ActiveX Automation	DXF/AutoLISP
getOrientation(), origin	Origin	Group 10
getOrientation(), uWidth	n/a	Group 11
getOrientation(), vHeight	n/a	Group 12

The origin is given in world coordinates, and the width and height vectors are world vectors. They are not unit vectors like all other directions, however. Instead, the magnitude of the vector defines the width or the height of a single pixel along the corresponding direction. The two vectors, along with the image size, also define the scale, size, and bounding box of the unclipped image.

The implementation of the *Raster* object in ActiveX Automation overlooks the fact that a bitmap image can be oriented arbitrarily in 3D space. The *Raster* object only returns the properties *ImageWidth* (length of *Width* vector), *ImageHeight* (length of *Height* vector), and *Rotation* (from *Width* vector towards *Height* vector).

ObjectDBX	ActiveX Automation	DXF/AutoLISP
imageSize()	n/a	Group 13
scale()	ScaleFactor	n/a

The image size and all other image-related coordinates are given in the local 2D coordinate system in which one unit equals one pixel. ObjectDBX provides pixel-to-model and model-to-pixel translation functions. The *Scale* of an image reference depends on the image definition's internal unit of measurement (as described in the previous section and in the "Global Settings for Raster Images" section later in this chapter).

The image size is duplicated from the corresponding AcDbRasterImageDef object and could have been taken from there as well. In addition, the AcDbRasterImage entity contains a reference to an AcDbRasterImageDefReactor object (see the "Global Settings for Raster Images" section later in this chapter).

ObjectDBX	ActiveX Automation	DXF/AutoLISP
imageDefId()	n/a	Group 340
reactorId()	n/a	Group 360

Like all references, these properties return an AcDbObjectID, entity name, or handle, depending on the environment.

Image Manipulation

An image definition can be referenced by multiple AcDbRasterImage entities, thus creating multiple copies of the image on the screen or on paper. Each reference can use a different fade, contrast, and brightness value.

ObjectDBX	ActiveX Automation	DXF/AutoLISP
brightness()	Brightness	Group 281
contrast()	Contrast	Group 282
fade()	Fade	Group 283

Each of these settings is an integer in the range 0 through 100. A value of 50 indicates the unmodified luminance, hue, and saturation taken from the original image file. A value of 0 indicates minimum brightness, contrast, or fade, and a value of 100 indicates the corresponding maximum.

Some settings speed up image display and processing by excluding certain functionality with a specific AcDbRasterImage entity. In addition to the *Visible* property common to all entities, an AcDbRasterImage entity can be set so that only the outline frame displays, rather than the bitmap image. Because rotating an image requires additional computation, a user can also set the image reference to display the bitmap only if it is aligned with the current viewport. Clipping an image also requires processing, so an image reference can be set to ignore any clipping, as described in the next section, "Image Clipping." Finally, images that use transparency can be set to display an opaque background instead.

ObjectDBX	ActiveX Automation	DXF/AutoLISP

isSetDisplayOpt(), kShow	ImageVisisbility	First bit (1) of group 70
isSetDisplayOpt(), kShowUnaligned	ShowRotation	Second bit (2) of group 70
isSetDisplayOpt(), kClip	ClippingEnabled	Third bit (4) of group 70
isSetDisplayOpt(), kTransparent	Transparency	Fourth bit (8) of group 70

Image Clipping

When you clip an image, a smaller portion of a bitmap is displayed. Clipping is AcDbRasterImage entity-specific, which means that multiple references to the same image definition can display different parts of a bitmap.

An AcDbRasterImage can be clipped or not. If it is clipped, the boundary (or outline) is either a rectangle parallel to the local x- and y-axes (*kRect*, 1), or it's a polygon of at least three sides (*kPoly*, 2).

ObjectDBX	ActiveX Automation	DXF/AutoLISP
isClipped()	n/a	Group 280
clipBoundaryType()	n/a	Group 71

The clipping boundary is given by a set of vertices. In a rectangle, there are only two vertices: the lower-left and the upper-right corner of the clip rectangle. In a polygon, there can be an arbitrary number of vertices.

All vertices are expressed within the local coordinate system, meaning that they are pixel coordinates within the bitmap image. In ObjectDBX, you can query the model coordinates of the vertices using the *getVertices()* function. In ActiveX Automation, the *ClipBoundary* property returns a list of 2D model coordinates.

ObjectDBX	ActiveX Automation	DXF/AutoLISP
n/a	n/a	Group 91, number of vertices
ClipBoundary()	ClipBoundary	Group 14

Images in DXF

AcDbRasterImage entities use the DXF class name "IMAGE". Unlike all other *native* AutoCAD objects, a bitmap reference contains proxy graphics data within the AcDbEntity section of its DXF definition: a group 92 followed by one or more groups 310.

This proxy graphics data displays the bounding frame (whole image or clipped section) of the image on systems that don't have the AutoCAD Image Support Module (ISM) installed. For more about proxy graphics, see Chapter 18.

The DXF group sequence for image-reference entities is as follows: 90 (class version, constant 0), 10, 11, 12, 13, 340, 70, 280, 281, 282, 283, 360, 71, 91, 14 (repeated).

Image Definition to Entity Link

The AcDbRasterImage object contains a *hard reference* pointer to the corresponding AcDbRasterImageDef object. In addition, the image definition needs a pointer back to the image reference. This allows a definition object to notify all references if the attached bitmap has been changed.

In Chapter 5, you saw how reactor links work with any AcDbObject. The AcDBRasterImageDef object could have used this standard procedure to link the image definition back to the reference entities. For a reason known only to the software engineers at Autodesk, this link is implemented through an additional AcDbRasterImageDefReactor object. There is exactly one AcDbRasterImageDefReactor object for each AcDbRasterImage entity. The entity owns the object, which means that the reactor objects are not listed in a dictionary or a table.

If the bitmap definition changes, the AcDbRasterImageDef object notifies the reactor, which in turn notifies the image reference entity. Consequently, the *Reactors* property of the image definition object contains at least a pointer to the dictionary in which it is contained as well as pointers to all the AcDbRasterImageDefReactor objects linked to the references of this image.

The AcDbRasterImageDefReactor object points back to the AcDbRasterImage object, but not through its *Reactor* property. Its DXF class name is "IMAGEDEF_REACTOR". Following the subclass marker are a group 90 for the class version (constant 2) and a group 330, which once again contains the object's owner, that is, the image entity.

Global Settings for Raster Images

For the most part, the display of a bitmap image is controlled by the properties of the AcDbRasterImage object. Two global settings, however, also control the display of all bitmaps in a drawing.

Unlike other global settings, the variables for raster images are not saved in the global settings section of the drawing database or in the "AcDbVariableDictionary" dictionary. Instead, these settings are saved in a separate object of type AcDbRasterVariables.

To find the AcDbRasterVariables object, locate the key string "ACAD_IMAGE_VARS" in the root dictionary; this string points directly to the object in question.

A first setting controls the display of frames around the image entities. The frame is a rectangular or polygon continuous, no-width outline drawn along the clip boundary (or around the whole image if clipping is off). It uses the color associated with the AcDbRasterImage entity. Using the AcDbRasterVariables object, you can turn this frame off (*kImageFrameOff*, 0), draw it on top of the image (*kImageFrameAbove*, 1), or draw it below the image (*kImageFrameBelow*, 2).

ObjectDBX	ActiveX Automation	DXF/AutoLISP
imageFrame()	n/a	Group 70

For performance reasons, a second setting controls the display quality of bitmap images:

- Draft quality (*kImageQualityDraft*, 0)
- Optimum quality (*kImageQualityHigh*, 1)

The quality value affects all image entities in the drawing database. Output always uses optimum quality.

ObjectDBX	ActiveX Automation	DXF/AutoLISP
imageQuality()	n/a	Group 71

A third global setting affects the scaling of existing and new image entities. As I've mentioned, the true scale and size of a bitmap image depends on the internal unit of measurement defined in the bitmap file. This setting translates pixels to millimeters or inches. A second value is needed to further translate these values from millimeters or inches to drawing units. The *User Scale* property describes the size of AutoCAD units for the purpose of image scaling. This is not necessarily the same value as the global INSUNITS setting.

ObjectDBX	ActiveX Automation	DXF/AutoLISP
userScale()	n/a	Group 72

The *User Scale* setting is an integer that defines an AutoCAD unit in this specific drawing. The value is taken from the following list:

ObjectDBX	DXF/AutoLISP	Meaning
kNone	0	No unit of measurement specified
kMillimeter	1	Millimeters (i.e., $1.0*10^{-3}$m)
kCentimeter	2	Centimeters (i.e., $1.0*10^{-2}$m)
kMeter	3	Meters (i.e., $1.0*10^{0}$m)

ObjectDBX	DXF/AutoLISP	Meaning
kKilometer	4	Kilometers (i.e., $1.0*10^3$m)
kInch	5	Inches (i.e., $2.54*10^{-2}$m)
kFoot	6	Feet (i.e., $3.048*10^{-1}$m)
kYard	7	Yards (i.e., $9.144*10^{-1}$m)
kMile	8	Statute miles (i.e., $1.609344*10^3$m)

The DXF class name of an AcDbRasterVariables object is "RASTERVARIABLES". Following the subclass marker are the groups 90 (class version, constant 0), 70, 71, and 72.

Summary

Hybrid drawings, drawings that contain both raster and vector graphics, are a late addition to the AutoCAD list of features. The objects related to bitmap images described in this chapter are not native AutoCAD objects. Instead, they are part of an add-on application shipped with AutoCAD called the ISM (*Image Support Module*). Because of this, the image-related objects force you to spend a bit more time understanding and implementing them. As you have seen, the ObjectDBX and DXF/AutoLISP access methods do not correspond completely, and the ActiveX Automation interface is very different from the other environments.

Additionally, you should keep in mind that some implementation strategies you learned with other objects are not used with raster images. This not only includes the reactors, but also the variables storage object.

An AcDbRasterImage object references an image definition object. Multiple image objects can therefore reference the same definition and thus produce different images of the same bitmap with scale, rotatation, or clip variations. The next chapter describes how you can do the same with every AutoCAD entity.

CHAPTER **16**

Block Insertion and Attribute Objects

FEATURING

Block references   *324*

Filtered inserts   *328*

Attributes   *331*

All AutoCAD entities are organized in block containers. Although each entity has a visual representation, it does not necessarily display on the AutoCAD screen or in a printout. Only the layout blocks described in the next chapter can be viewed and plotted from within AutoCAD.

Objects within other block containers are not visible in AutoCAD unless their block container is referenced (directly or indirectly) by a layout block. Of course, other applications can freely visualize unreferenced block containers as well, and many applications, such as symbol libraries, do so.

Layout blocks can reference block containers, which, in turn, can reference other block containers. This can result in a multiple-level deep nesting of block references, or the indirect referencing of block containers that I mentioned in the previous paragraph. Of course, circular references are not allowed.

The tools to reference a block container from within an outer block container are the *AcDbBlockReference* and *AcDbMInsertBlock* objects, which we'll look at in detail in this chapter.

These two objects not only define which block container is to be referenced, they also define a transformation of the block entities. This transformation is applied to each and every object in the referenced block, which allows a scaled, rotated, and translated display of the block contents. In addition, an *AcDbSpatialFilter* can be applied to the container objects, filtering out all objects that do not fit into a given volume.

Closely related to the block reference object is the *AcDbAttribute* object, which allows you to construct different references to the same block container with different contents. Attributes are text objects associated with a block reference, not with a block container. As such, they can contain a different value with each reference.

Finally, we'll look at the *AcDbAttributeDefinition* object in this chapter. An attribute definition is included in the block container and forms the pattern for the attribute object associated with every reference of the container.

Block References

The AcDbBlockReference object is an AutoCAD entity because it has a visual representation. The visualization of a block reference object is a copy of the visualization of all objects in the referenced block container. To the user, it looks as if the complete block container contents have been inserted in the layout block (or in another block container). Consequently, the AcDbBlockReference object is also known as a block *insert*.

Looking at the visualization, multiple references to the same container create multiple copies of the contained objects. The block reference creates only a visualization, however. The user cannot modify one copy without affecting the others.

In addition to inserting a single block, a companion object to AcDbBlockReference, called AcDbMInsertBlock, can define multiple copies of the contained objects. This is often referred to as *multiple insert* or *MInsert*.

A block reference, however, does not necessarily create a one-to-one copy of the visualization of the objects contained in the block. It adds various transformations such as scales, translations, and rotations to the visualization. Thus, multiple references of the same block can look very different.

All objects from the block container will be visualized by the block reference object except for AcDbAttributeDefinition objects. These objects will undergo a special handling that I'll explain later in this chapter. In addition, some objects can change their visual appearance as they inherit properties of the AcDbBlockReference or AcDbMInsertBlock object. I'll describe this in detail in the following sections.

Any AcDbBlockReference object refers to a block container. Depending on the environment, this reference is either through the corresponding block table record's AcDbObjectId or through its key string, that is, the block name.

ObjectDBX	ActiveX Automation	DXF/AutoLISP
blockTableRecord()	n/a	n/a
n/a	Name	Group 2

Block Transformation

Each block reference defines its own local coordinate system. As is the case with circles and other objects, this is defined by a single normal vector.

ObjectDBX	ActiveX Automation	DXF/AutoLISP
normal()	Normal	Group 210

The origin of the Local Coordinate System equals the origin of the World Coordinate System. The local z-axis is parallel to the normal vector, and the local x-axis is calculated using the arbitrary axis algorithm. The local y-axis is, of course, then calculated as the cross-product of local Z and local X.

To transform a single point from the block container to this local coordinate system, you need to sequentially apply the following transformations. With an AcDb-MInsertBlock object, this creates the first copy of the block visualization.

1. Translate the original point by –1 times the block origin (see Chapter 8). For example, if you have a block container whose *Origin* property returns (10,0,0), you need to first subtract 10 from the x coordinate of every block point you want to transform. This operation transforms the point from the Local Coordinate System used inside the block container to an equivalent of the World Coordinate System.

2. Scale the point's coordinates in each direction using the scale factors of the AcDbBlockReference or AcDbMInsertBlock object. There can be a different scale factor for each coordinate direction, which means that circular objects can become distorted. Scale factors can be negative. If they are negative, a mirrored image of the visualization is created. In ObjectDBX, the *scaleFactors()* function returns an object of type *AcDbScale3d,* which then lets you access the individual scale factors.

ObjectDBX	ActiveX Automation	DXF/AutoLISP
scaleFactors()[X]	XScaleFactor	Group 41
scaleFactors()[Y]	YScaleFactor	Group 42
scaleFactors()[Z]	ZScaleFactor	Group 43

3. Rotate the point location around (0,0,0) within the X/Y plane using the *Rotation* property of the AcDbBlockReference or AcDbMInsertBlock object.

ObjectDBX	ActiveX Automation	DXF/AutoLISP
rotation()	Rotation	Group 50

4. Transform the point from the World Coordinate System to the block reference's Local Coordinate System. Because both coordinate systems share the same origin (0,0,0), this is another rotation, although now in 3D.

5. Because we are now in the block reference's Local Coordinate System, translate the point along the vector given by the insertion point of the AcDbBlockReference or AcDbMInsertBlock object.

ObjectDBX	ActiveX Automation	DXF/AutoLISP
position()	InsertionPoint	Group 10

We have been using the insertion point according to its local coordinates (ECS) as they are seen in DXF and AutoLISP. If you are working in ObjectDBX or ActiveX Automation, you'll get the insertion point in WCS coordinates. Therefore, you first need to calculate the ECS translation equivalent to the WCS coordinates of the insertion point.

When working with homogenous point coordinates, that is, four-dimensional coordinates generated as (x,y,z,1), each of the five transformations listed earlier can be expressed by a 4*4 transformation matrix T_n with the new point p' calculated as T_n*p (p and p' are column vectors). The five transformations can thus be combined into a single 4*4 transformation matrix:

$$T := T_5 * T_4 * T_3 * T_2 * T_1$$

and you'll get the transformed point $p_{reference} := T*p_{block}$. ObjectDBX allows direct access to the transformation matrix using the *blockTransform()* function.

The DXF representation of an AcDbBlockReference object uses the following group code sequence following the subclass marker: 66 (Attribute flag, see the later section on attributes in this chapter), 2, 10, 41, 42, 43, 50, 210. The DXF class name is `"INSERT"`.

Multiple Inserts

The AcDbMInsertBlock object is derived from the AcDbBlockReference object and even shares the same DXF class name, `"INSERT"`. This object, however, creates multiple copies of the block visualization. These multiple copies are arranged in a 2D rectangular fashion using *rows* and *columns*. Therefore, the AcDbMInsertBlock object has four additional properties:

ObjectDBX	ActiveX Automation	DXF/AutoLISP
columns()	Columns	Group 70
rows()	Rows	Group 71
columnSpacing()	ColumnSpacing	Group 44
rowSpacing()	RowSpacing	Group 45

The transformation algorithm described earlier creates the first copy of the block visualization (column = 1, row = 1). To create another copy, you need to add one more transformation: between steps 2 and 3 of the algorithm (that is, after the scaling but prior to the X/Y rotation), translate the point by the corresponding multitude of row and column spacing. For the copy with column index 2 and row index 3, you translate by the vector (2*column spacing, 3*row spacing, 0).

The DXF representation of an AcDbMInsertBlock object uses the following group code sequence following the subclass marker: 66 (Attribute flag, see the later section on attributes in this chapter), 2, 10, 41, 42, 43, 50, 70, 71, 44, 45, 210. The DXF class name again is `"INSERT"`. Even though the AcDbMInsertBlock object is derived from AcDbBlockReference, you cannot determine that by looking at the DXF representation.

Inherited Properties

Because a block reference (AcDbBlockReference and, consequently, AcDbMInsertBlock) is an AcDbEntity, it has an associated color, linetype, layer, lineweight, and plot style. On the other hand, every object in the referenced block container has these properties, probably using different values. Which one do you use?

In general the visualization of a block object uses the properties that it has inside the block container. However, there are exceptions to this rule:

- If the block-internal object's *Layer* property is `"0"`, the object is visualized as if its *Layer* property were equal to the layer of the AcDbBlockReference.

- If the *Color, Linetype, Lineweight,* or *Plot Style* property is set to *ByBlock*, the corresponding property of the AcDbBlockReference object is used during visualization. The ByBlock color index is zero. (For information on the other properties, see Chapter 9).

This inheritance of properties allows a user to reference the same block container multiple times and give each reference a different look. If the block reference's layer is turned off, referenced objects still display as long as their layer is visible and they don't use layer `"0"`. If the block reference's layer is frozen, no object from the block container will display, however.

Filtered Inserts

In the previous sections, we assumed that the complete contents of the referenced block container were to be displayed within the referencing block. AutoCAD, however, lets you filter the referenced block.

This filtering happens through the abstract AcDbFilter class. According to the ObjectARX documentation, there are two kinds of filters: AcDbLayerFilter and AcDbSpatialFilter. Only AcDbSpatialFilter is used in the base release of AutoCAD 2000. Consequently, layer filters can only be used by third-party applications or may not work at all. Only spatial filtering is discussed in this chapter.

Spatial Filtering

A spatial filter defines a 3D volume. This so-called clip volume is generated from a planar polygonal curve and its associated heights. Therefore, the volume is always an *n*-sided prism.

All objects from the referenced block container that lie completely inside this volume will be displayed; all that lie completely outside won't. All other objects will be split into a visible part (inside the clip volume) and an invisible part (outside the clip volume).

The AcDbSpatialFilter object is located in the extension dictionary of the block reference object. Within this extension, you'll find the `"ACAD_FILTER"` key, which points to another dictionary. In this second dictionary, you use the "SPATIAL" key to access the AcDbSpatialFilter object.

The clip volume is an extruded planar polygonal curve. Therefore, to define the volume, you need a Local Coordinate System that defines the plane of the clip polygon. This is done using the plane's normal direction along with an elevation (in ObjectDBX) or a point on the plane (in AutoLISP and DXF).

ObjectDBX	ActiveX Automation	DXF/AutoLISP
getDefinition(), normal	n/a	Group 210
getDefinition(), elevation	n/a	n/a
n/a	n/a	Group 11, the origin of the Local Coordinate System

Within this Local Coordinate System's X/Y plane is the clip polygon, which is defined through a series of two or more 2D points. If there are only two points, those points define a rectangle.

Stop! you may say. Two points define a lot of rectangles in any plane. Yes, you would need to specify at least a rotation angle or a direction to orient the rectangle. For some reason, however, AutoCAD does not record such a rotation. Instead, it records the whole transformation matrix between the coordinate system of the referencing block and the Local Coordinate System.

Transformation matrices are 4*4 matrices with which each source point is multiplied to give you the transformed point. As I mentioned earlier, to use transformation matrices, you have to work with homogenous point coordinates (x,y,z,1). For example, if the Local Coordinate System is rotated 45° around the x-axis, the translation matrix T looks like this:

0.707107	0.707107	0.0	0.0
-0.707107	0.707107	0.0	0.0
0.0	0.0	1.0	0.0
0.0	0.0	0.0	1.0

and each point is calculated as:

```
p' := T*p
```

Since the last row is always (0,0,0,1) for this kind of matrix, AutoCAD records only the upper three rows. In DXF and AutoLISP, you'll find the 12 numbers listed in the following sequence: first row from left to right, second row from left to right, third row from left to right.

ObjectDBX	ActiveX Automation	DXF/AutoLISP
n/a	n/a	Group 40, Local Coordinate System transformation matrix

Let's go back to the clip polygon. Because we now have the Local Coordinate System, the polygon is defined either by two 2D points (which create an axis-parallel rectangle) or by an arbitrary number of 2D points. In the second case, the points are connected by straight lines in sequence to form a closed polygon.

ObjectDBX	ActiveX Automation	DXF/AutoLISP
n/a	n/a	Group 70, number of points
getDefinition(), points	n/a	Group 10

Perpendicular to the clip plane, the clip volume can be bounded either in one direction or both, or it can be unbounded. Each boundary is given through a distance from the plane, measured along the normal vector.

ObjectDBX	ActiveX Automation	DXF/AutoLISP
n/a	n/a	Group 72, upper boundary exists
getDefinition(), frontClip	n/a	Group 40, upper boundary distance
n/a	n/a	Group 73, lower boundary exists
getDefinition(), backClip	n/a	Group 41, lower boundary distance

Not every block insertion is filtered, even if the extension dictionary points to an AcDbSpatialFilter object. A separate flag indicates whether the display should be clipped.

ObjectDBX	ActiveX Automation	DXF/AutoLISP
getDefinition(), enabled	n/a	Group 71

Both the clip polygon and the upper and lower boundaries reside in the coordinate system of the referencing block. Any translation, rotation, scaling, and such is already applied.

In some cases, it may be of interest to calculate the clip volume's corners as they appear in the coordinate system of the referenced block, and, in fact, this is where the filtering should take place anyway. To transform the clip volume from the referencing block back to the referenced block, you need to do the exact reverse of what you do when inserting blocks.

In mathematical terms, we need the inverse of all transformations or only the inverse of the final block transformation matrix. In DXF and AutoLISP, you'll find this inverse transformation matrix in another set of 12 group 40 values. As with the translation matrices discussed earlier, the fourth row contains only (0,0,0,1) and is therefore omitted.

ObjectDBX	ActiveX Automation	DXF/AutoLISP
n/a	n/a	Group 40, inverse block transformation matrix

The DXF class name for AcDbSpatialFilter is "SPATIAL_FILTER". Following the usual AcDbObject groups is the "AcDbFilter" subclass header. Immediately after this, you'll find the "AcDbSpatialFilter" subclass header and then the groups 70, 10 (repeated), 210, 11, 71, 72, 40 (upper boundary distance), 73, 41, 40 (Local Coordinate System transformation, repeated 12 times), and 40 (inverse block transformation, repeated 12 times).

Attribute Objects

In AutoCAD, an *attribute* is a specific kind of database object. Do not confuse this with attributes in other graphics programs in which this term is often used to describe the properties of an object.

An attribute is a text object and, as such, is similar to an AcDbText object from which it is derived. There are two flavors of attributes: constants and variables. And two objects are associated with attributes: AcDbAttribute and AcDbAttributeDefinition. But, no, they are not connected in the way it sounds.

Attribute Definitions

An attribute definition is a simple text object with a few additional properties. The AcDbAttributeDefinition object is derived from AcDbText and displays just like any other AcDbText object.

An attribute definition inherits all properties from AcDbText and uses all of them except for the text contents. Instead, the text to display depends on the condition under which the object visualizes:

Text Displayed	Condition
Tag property	The block container in which it is contained visualizes as a layout block, that is, not through a block reference object.
Text String property	The block container in which it is contained visualizes through a block reference object *and* the *Constant* property is set *and* the *Invisible* property is not set *and* the global ATTDISP setting allows attribute display.
None	The block container in which it is contained visualizes through a block reference object *and* the *Constant* property is not set.
None	The block container in which it is contained visualizes through a block reference object *and* the *Invisible* property is set.
None	The block container in which it is contained visualizes through a block reference object *and* ATTDISP is set to not display attributes.

You can see that a number of conditions result in the AcDbAttributeDefinition object not displaying. The most important condition is a non-constant attribute visualized through a block reference. This condition generates AcDbAttribute objects, the topic of the next section in this chapter.

Let's first take a look at the additional properties of an AcDbAttributeDefinition object.

I mentioned the *Tag* property earlier. Other than the *Text String* property of the underlying AcDbText object, attribute definitions have two associated text strings:

- The attribute tag
- The attribute prompt

The attribute tag distinguishes between different attribute definitions in a single block container. This information is copied into any AcDbAttribute object that is generated from this definition. When you are working in AutoCAD, you can use the tag to extract or modify certain attributes. During extraction, it functions like a field name in a database program and, therefore, must not be empty.

ObjectDBX	ActiveX Automation	DXF/AutoLISP
tag()	TagString	Group 2

The third text string associated with an AcDbAttributeDefinition object is the so-called prompt. This property defines the prompt string that is displayed when asking the user to enter a variable text string for the AcDbAttribute object generated from this definition.

ObjectDBX	ActiveX Automation	DXF/AutoLISP
prompt()	PromptString	Group 3

If the prompt string is empty, or if no corresponding attribute definition exists, attribute objects use their *Tag* property as the prompt string.

Each attribute definition has four Boolean flags. I've already mentioned two of them, *Constant* and *Invisible*. The global ATTDISP setting overwrites any visibility information associated with attributes and attribute definitions, as does the *Visibility* property of the AcDbEntity object from which both are derived.

The remaining flags are *Preset* and *Verifiable*. Like the prompt string, these two flags have no functionality with the AcDbAttributeDefinition object other than to provide defaults for any AcDbAttribute object generated from this definition.

ObjectDBX	ActiveX Automation	DXF/AutoLISP
isInvisible()	Invisible	First bit (1) of group 70
isConstant()	Constant	Second bit (2) of group 70
isVerifiable()	Verify	Third bit (4) of group 70
isPreset()	Preset	Fourth bit (8) of group 70

Since AutoCAD Release 5, attribute definitions and attributes have been documented to have a *Field Length* property. This integer was probably intended to limit the number of characters a user can enter for a variable attribute. Up to now, however, no version of AutoCAD has ever used this property.

ObjectDBX	ActiveX Automation	DXF/AutoLISP
fieldLength()	FieldLength	Group 73

Besides being of no use, the *Field Length* property created a problem when the *Vertical Alignment* property was added to the AcDbText object (and at that time DXF groups were unique within an object): DXF group 73 is supposed to be the vertical text justification. Thus, the vertical text justification of an AcDbAttributeDefinition object became group 74. For historic reasons, this is still the case today.

The DXF class name of an AcDbAttributeDefinition object is "ATTDEF". Following the "AcDbText" subclass marker are the AcDbText groups except for 73. Following the "AcDbAttributeDefinition" subclass marker are the groups 3, 2, 70, 73, and 74.

Constant Attributes

The important point about constant attributes is that they don't generate AcDb-Attribute objects. If a block container is referenced by an AcDbBlockReference or AcDbMInsertBlock object, any AcDbAttributeDefinition object within this container that has the *Constant* property set will be visualized just like an ordinary text object.

The only difference between a constant attribute and an AcDbText object is the *Invisible* property, which allows the text to become invisible without using the AcDb-Entity *Visible* property. As such, the attribute definition also reacts to the global ATTDISP setting.

Variable Attributes

With non-constant attributes, there is a completely different picture, however. If a block container is referenced by a block insert, the attribute definitions of non-constant attributes do not visualize at all.

Instead, during the initial block insertion, the attribute definitions are used as templates to generate objects of type AcDbAttribute. These attribute objects are closely linked to the corresponding AcDbBlockReference or AcDbMInsertBlock object. In fact, they are considered sub-entities of the block insertion just as vertices are sub-entities of heavyweight polylines. Like the vertices of heavyweight polylines, AcDbAttribute objects do not exist without their parent block insertion object, and like the vertices, the sequence of attributes associated with a single block insertion ends with an AcDb-SequenceEnd object.

Although AcDbAttributeDefinition objects are used to generate the AcDbAttribute object at initial block insertion, after this, the attribute and the corresponding definition are no longer connected. Even if the block container changes and AcDbAttribute-Definition objects move or even get deleted, the attributes associated with the block insertion do not change.

Once created, AcDbAttribute objects are text objects on their own. They can move independently of their definition and block insertion, and an AutoCAD user can arbitrarily alter font, size, color, and so on.

AcDbAttribute objects have the same properties as AcDbAttributeDefinition objects except for the *Prompt* property. This property is missing in an attribute object and, therefore, creates a loose link between the attribute and its definition. When you are editing attributes, AutoCAD tries to find the corresponding (that is, the same tag) AcDbAttributeDefinition object from the block container. If AutoCAD finds this object, it displays the definition's *Prompt* string to the user. If AutoCAD does not find this object, the AcDbAtrribute object uses its own *Tag* property instead.

The DXF class name of an AcDbAttribute object is "ATTRIB". Following the "AcDb-Text" subclass marker are the AcDbText groups except for 73. Following the "AcDbAttribute" subclass marker are the groups 2, 70, 73, and 74.

 NOTE Among the various interactive ways to extract attribute data from an AutoCAD drawing is the *Attribute Extraction to DXF* option. This creates an output file that looks like DXF but that contains only the block insertion objects, the attribute objects, the sequence end objects, and an EOF marker. This DXX file also differs from a standard DXF file in that constant attributes are output just like non-constant attributes.

Finding Variable Attributes

A block insertion (AcDbBlockReference or AcDbMInsertBlock) may or may not have AcDbAttribute sub-entities. Therefore, the block reference object has an additional flag that you can query:

ObjectDBX	ActiveX Automation	DXF/AutoLISP
n/a	HasAttributes	First bit (1) of group 66

In ObjectDBX, you can use the *attributeIterator()* function to get to the sub-entities of an AcDbBlockReference object. In ActiveX Automation, the *GetAttribute* method returns an array of attribute objects. (There is also a *GetConstantAttributes* method.) In AutoLISP, you'll use the *entnext* function with the entity name of the block insertion object to find the first variable attribute. In DXF, the AcDbAttribute objects directly follow the block reference object.

Although AcDbMInsertBlock supports attributes (since it is derived from AcDb-BlockReference), it does not create multiple copies of each attribute. Instead, there is only a single AcDbAttribute object that is visualized the required number of times. If you modify the attribute, all copies change accordingly. If you extract the attributes from within AutoCAD, it lists the attributes multiple times.

The AcDbSequenceEnd object is the closing bracket for a block insertion and ends the list of variable attributes in AutoLISP and DXF. In ObjectDBX, you access the sequence end using the *openSequenceEnd()* function of the AcDbBlockReference object.

The AcDbSequenceEnd object itself does not contain any properties. Only in AutoLISP can you use the entity name in the –2 group to locate the corresponding opening bracket (AcDbBlockReference object).

The DXF class name for AcDbSequenceEnd is "SEQEND". It contains no groups (nor does it contain a subclass marker) other than the AcDbObject and AcDbEntity groups.

Summary

The ability to reference block containers is a very powerful feature. It allows you to combine a series of AutoCAD entities into a block and reuse this block many times within a drawing. You only need one single AcDbBlockReference object each time, and a single change of the block container automatically changes the visualization of each of the inserts.

Implementing block references, in a drawing viewer for instance, is quite complex. Not only do you need to transform the original object multiple times until you reach the final position of the referenced points, but you also need to take into account that objects are often distorted during these transformations and cut off during clipping. What was a circle in the original block may become two or more elliptical arcs in the AcDbBlockReference visualization.

The next chapter looks at a special type of block containers: the layout blocks.

CHAPTER 17

Layout Objects

FEATURING

Plot settings	*338*
Layouts	*346*
Abstract views	*351*
Viewport-specific drawing aids	*356*
Viewports to modelspace	*357*

Although AutoCAD can use any block container both for referencing and to be referenced and although other programs can display or print any block container in a drawing database, AutoCAD itself displays and prints only those block containers whose *IsLayout* property is set.

Any block container that is a layout is linked to an additional AcDbLayout object. This object defines which part of the block container is to be printed and how.

Closely related to the AcDbLayout object is the AcDbPlotSettings class, and, in fact, the AcDbLayout object is derived from the AcDbPlotSettings class. AcDbPlotSettings objects, however, can also appear in the drawing database on their own if the user defined a set of named plot settings for later recall and use when printing layouts.

Two flavors of layout blocks exist:

- Modelspace
- Paperspace

The main difference between the two is how they display in AutoCAD. Paperspace layouts display like a sheet of paper and look like a print preview in other programs. The modelspace layout displays full screen.

A drawing database can contain an arbitrary number of paperspace layouts, but it can contain only one modelspace layout. Each drawing database must have a model-space layout.

In this chapter, we'll look at the objects related to layout blocks: the AcDbPlotSettings object and the AcDbLayout object. In addition, I'll discuss the AcDbViewport entity, which references a view into modelspace from within a paperspace layout. The AcDbViewport entity is similar to a block reference, but it defines a view instead of a block transformation. Such a view, for example, may have any hidden lines turned off. Because the definition of a view is quite complex, this chapter also includes a detailed discussion on abstract views.

Plot Settings

The AcDbPlotSettings object contains information about the output device to be used for the plot, about paper size, and about which part of the layout block is to be output.

Plot settings appear in two places in a drawing database:

- In a list of named, predefined plot settings that a user can recall and use during print
- Inside any AcDbLayout object, because this class is derived from the AcDbPlot-Settings object (Layouts are covered in the "Layout Object" section in this chapter.)

To find the list of predefined plot settings, use the `"ACAD_PLOTSETTINGS"` key in the named objects dictionary. This key points to another dictionary, in which the keys are the user-selected names of the predefined plot settings. Each key points to an AcDbPlotSettings object. In addition, the AcDbPlotSettings object itself contains its key string:

ObjectDBX	ActiveX Automation	DXF/AutoLISP
getPlotSettingsName()	Name	Group 1

If an AcDbPlotSettings object is used inside an AcDbLayout object, the *Name* property may be empty.

Plot Devices

Each plot setting is for a specific type of output device. An output device can be a printer or a fax machine from the installed Windows printer drivers, a plotter or a PostScript device using dedicated AutoCAD drivers, or an electronic plot to Autodesk's Drawing Web Format (DWF) or to a bitmap file.

AutoCAD-specific devices and electronic plots use plotter configuration files. These files allow you to define different plotters using the same driver, for example, to create a BMP file or a TIFF (Tagged Image File Format) file. Plotter configuration files are saved in AutoCAD's plotter directory and have the .PC3 extension.

The AcDbPlotSettings object carries the information about which plot device it was created for and which is valid. The plot device is either the name of a Windows printer driver as returned by Windows or the name of a .PC3 file (without the path).

ObjectDBX	ActiveX Automation	DXF/AutoLISP
getPlotCfgName()	ConfigName	Group 2

Both ActiveX Automation and ObjectARX provide methods to query the list of available plot devices.

Plot Media

Most printers and plotters can use different paper sizes. Plot settings are only valid for a specific size of a medium.

The AcDbPlotSettings object records both the name of the paper size and the corresponding sizes such as height, width, and margins. In ActiveX Automation this object is called *AcadPlotConfiguration*. The paper size name is taken from the Windows printer driver or .PC3 file. For Windows drivers, the nonlocalized paper size name is saved. The localized name of the medium can be retrieved in ObjectARX using the *AcDbPlotSettingsValidator::getLocaleMediaName()* function and in ActiveX Automation using the *GetLocaleMediaName* method.

ObjectDBX	ActiveX Automation	DXF/AutoLISP
getCanonicalMediaName()	CanonicalMediaName	Group 4

Each medium uses a different unit of measurement: although paper is typically measured in either inches or millimeters, electronic raster plots are measured in pixels.

ObjectDBX	ActiveX Automation	DXF/AutoLISP
plotPaperUnits()	PaperUnits	Group 72

The available paper units are as follows:

ObjectDBX	ActiveX Automation	DXF/AutoLISP	Meaning
kInches	acInches	0	Inches
kMillimeters	acMillimeters	1	Millimeters
kPixels	acPixels	2	Pixels

The size of the medium is given by the *Height* and *Width* properties. In addition, the AcDbPlotSettings object contains the margins for the medium, that is, the paper border in which the output device cannot print. All values are measured in paper units if you work in ObjectDBX or ActiveX Automation. In AutoLISP and DXF, you'll always get millimeters. AutoLISP and DXF provide the right and top margins, but ObjectDBX and ActiveX Automation provide the upper-right corner of the printable area, that is, the paper size minus the margin.

ObjectDBX	ActiveX Automation	DXF/AutoLISP
getPlotPaperSize(), paperWidth	GetPaperSize	Group 44
getPlotPaperSize(), paperHeight	GetPaperSize	Group 45
getPlotPaperMargins(), printableXmin	GetPaperMargins	Group 40, left margin
getPlotPaperMargins(), printableYmin	GetPaperMargins	Group 41, bottom margin
getPlotPaperMargins(), printableXmax	GetPaperMargins	Group 42, right margin
getPlotPaperMargins(), printableYmax	GetPaperMargins	Group 43, top margin

Usually, the lower-left corner of the printable area is also the plot origin, that is, the lower-left corner of the plot. The user may decide to move the plot origin to a different place, however. Typically, the plot origin is moved to center the plot on the page.

ObjectDBX	ActiveX Automation	DXF/AutoLISP
plotOrigin(), x	PlotOrigin	Group 46
plotOrigin(), y	PlotOrigin	Group 47

Another Boolean flag indicates whether the user decided to center the plot on the page:

ObjectDBX	ActiveX Automation	DXF/AutoLISP
plotCentered()	CenterPlot	Third bit (4) of group 70

Plot Rotation

The *Plot Rotation* property defines which axis of the layout conforms to which border of the plotted page.

ObjectDBX	ActiveX Automation	DXF/AutoLISP
plotRotation()	PlotRotation	Group 73

There are four possible rotations:

ObjectDBX	ActiveX Automation	DXF/AutoLISP	Meaning
k0degrees	ac0degrees	0	No rotation, i.e., the x-axis runs from left to right along paper width
k90degrees	ac90degrees	1	Rotated 90° counter-clockwise, i.e., the x-axis runs from bottom to top along paper height
k180degrees	ac180degrees	2	Rotated 180°, i.e., image appears upside down
k270degrees	ac270degrees	3	Rotated 90° clockwise

What to Plot

The AcDbPlotSettings object not only contains the information about where to plot the drawing, it also contains information about what to plot. Of course, this information is not a list of drawing entities. It is a description of the area in the layout that is to be plotted and a definition of the plot scale to use.

ObjectDBX	ActiveX Automation	DXF/AutoLISP
plotType()	PlotType	Group 74

The *Plot Type* property defines which segment or view of the current layout is to be output. Possible values and their meaning are as follows:

ObjectDBX	ActiveX Automation	DXF/ AutoLISP	Meaning
kDisplay	acDisplay	0	Plot what's currently visible onscreen
kExtents	acExtents	1	Plot the complete drawing
kLimits	acLimits	2	Plot the area defined by the current layout's limits (see the discussion of the AcDbLayout object in a later section of this chapter)
kView	acView	3	Plot a named view (see the section following this list)
kWindow	acWindow	4	Plot a window specified by two diagonal corners (see the section following this list)
kLayout	acLayout	5	Plot the paper area of the current layout (see the section following this list)

As noted in this list, some plot types need additional information to fully define the area and view to plot.

When plotting a named view, you also need to provide the name of the view to plot. This is the key string of the corresponding AcDbViewTableRecord object. A view table record defines a complete view, including perspective, camera location, and so on.

ObjectDBX	ActiveX Automation	DXF/AutoLISP
getPlotViewName()	ViewToPlot	Group 6

When plotting a window, you need to specify the diagonal corners of the area to plot. The two points lie in the X/Y plane of the display coordinate system (see the "Abstract Views" section later in this chapter).

ObjectDBX	ActiveX Automation	DXF/AutoLISP
getPlotWindowArea(), xmin	GetWindowToPlot	Group 48
getPlotWindowArea(), ymin	GetWindowToPlot	Group 49
getPlotWindowArea(), xmax	GetWindowToPlot	Group 140
getPlotWindowArea(), ymax	GetWindowToPlot	Group 141

When plotting a layout, you need to know the lower-left corner of the layout's "paper." As long as the plot origin hasn't moved, this is the negative of the left and bottom margins.

ObjectDBX	ActiveX Automation	DXF/AutoLISP
n/a	n/a	Group 148, x coordinate of lower-left corner of paper
n/a	n/a	Group 149, y coordinate of lower-left corner of paper

This last plot option is only valid if the layout has an associated "paper," of course. The modelspace layout does not have such a "paper". A Boolean flag indicates whether the plot settings have been created for a modelspace layout.

ObjectDBX	ActiveX Automation	DXF/AutoLISP
modelType()	ModelType	Eleventh bit (1024) of group 70

Plot Scales

I have now defined the plot origin (that is, the lower-left corner of the plot) and the area to plot, but to completely describe what to plot, you need some more information: the plot scale. Depending on the selected scale, the plot can fill only a small portion of the paper size, or it can extend beyond the margins into an area that the output device cannot reach.

Most plots use standard scale factors such as 1:20 or 1"=1'. Another typical scale factor is *scale to fit*, that is, the maximum scale in which the whole area to plot will still fit on the page. AutoCAD considers both this special scale and 31 predefined scales as standard scale factors.

ObjectDBX	ActiveX Automation	DXF/AutoLISP
useStandardScale()	UseStandardScale	Fifth bit (16) of group 70
stdScaleType()	StandardScale	Group 75

The standard scale is one of the following values.

ObjectDBX	ActiveX Automation	DXF/ AutoLISP	Meaning	Scale Factor
kScaleToFit	acScaleToFit	0	Maximum scale	Varies
k1_1	ac1_1	2	1:1	1.0
k1_2	ac1_2	3	1:2	0.5
k1_4	ac1_4	4	1:4	0.25
k1_8	ac1_8	5	1:8	0.125
k1_10	ac1_10	6	1:10	0.1
k1_16	ac1_16	7	1:16	0.0625
k1_20	ac1_20	8	1:20	0.05
k1_30	ac1_30	9	1:30	0.0333
k1_40	ac1_40	10	1:40	0.025
k1_50	ac1_50	11	1:50	0.02
k1_100	ac1_100	12	1:100	0.01
k2_1	ac2_1	13	2:1	2.0
k4_1	ac4_1	14	4:1	4.0
k8_1	ac8_1	15	8:1	8.0
k10_1	ac10_1	16	10:1	10.0
k100_1	ac100_1	17	100:1	100.0
k1_128in_1ft	ac1_128in_1ft	18	1/128"=1'	0.000651
k1_64in_1ft	ac1_64in_1ft	19	1/64"=1'	0.0013
k1_32in_1ft	ac1_32in_1ft	20	1/32"=1'	0.0026
k1_16in_1ft	ac1_16in_1ft	21	1/16"=1'	0.0052
k3_32in_1ft	ac3_32in_1ft	22	3/32"=1'	0.0078
k1_8in_1ft	ac1_8in_1ft	23	1/8"=1'	0.0104
k3_16in_1ft	ac3_16in_1ft	24	3/16"=1'	0.0156
k1_4in_1ft	ac1_4in_1ft	25	1/4"=1'	0.0208
k3_8in_1ft	ac3_8in_1ft	26	3/8"=1'	0.03125
k1_2in_1ft	ac1_2in_1ft	27	1/2"=1'	0.04167
k3_4in_1ft	ac3_4in_1ft	28	3/4"=1'	0.0625
k1in_1ft	ac1in_1ft	29	1"=1'	0.0833
k3in_1ft	ac3in_1ft	30	3"=1'	0.25
k6in_1ft	ac6in_1ft	31	6"=1'	0.5
k1ft_1ft	ac1ft_1ft	32	1'=1'	1.0

In all environments except ActiveX Automation, the scale factor resulting from a standard scale is available as a calculated property:

ObjectDBX	ActiveX Automation	DXF/AutoLISP
getStdScale()	n/a	Group 147

To get a nonstandard scale (or a scale not listed as *standard*), the user can provide both numerator and denominator of the scale factor. The numerator is measured in drawing units, and the denominator is measured in paper units.

ObjectDBX	ActiveX Automation	DXF/AutoLISP
getCustomPrintScale(), numerator	GetCustomScale	Group 142
getCustomPrintScale(), denominator	GetCustomScale	Group 143

There is no calculated property for the resulting custom scale or the effective (that is, standard or custom) scale.

Fine-Tuning the Plot

The AcDbPlotSettings object contains a number of flags that let the user decide whether specific objects or object properties should be plotted. These flags affect the output of hidden lines (lines in 3D that lie beyond an opaque surface), lineweights, and plot styles.

This Boolean flag determines whether hidden lines are to be suppressed. This setting affects only the objects visible in the layout itself, not those visible through an AcDbViewport entity (those have an individual property for removing hidden lines).

ObjectDBX	ActiveX Automation	DXF/AutoLISP
plotHidden()	PlotHidden	Fourth bit (8) of group 70

Each AcDbEntity has an associated lineweight; however, the plot settings determine whether this lineweight is to be used during plot. There may be plot settings in which the user prefers to see all lines as hairlines (that is, the smallest width that the output device can produce).

ObjectDBX	ActiveX Automation	DXF/AutoLISP
printLineweights()	PlotWithLineweights	Eighth bit (128) of group 70

If lineweights are to be plotted, a second question arises. Because lineweights are set up in millimeters, do you want to scale them along with the drawing? If lineweight scaling is on and a scale factor of 0.1 is chosen, a 0.5 mm wide line will be plotted that is just 0.05 mm wide.

ObjectDBX	ActiveX Automation	DXF/AutoLISP
scaleLineweights()	ScaleLineweights	Seventh bit (64) of group 70

In addition to a lineweight, every AcDbEntity can have an associated plot style. Plot styles are assigned by names, or they are chosen by using the entity's *Color* property. A plot style allows dithering, screening, or differing line ends or fills, depending on the capabilities of the output device.

Plot styles are external to the drawing database. If plot styles are to be used during layout display or plot output, AutoCAD needs an external plot style table (or style sheet). Plot style tables reside in AutoCAD's Plot Styles directory. The AcDbPlotSettings object lists only the filename (without the path). Two Boolean flags determine whether plot styles are to be used for display and output.

ObjectDBX	ActiveX Automation	DXF/AutoLISP
showPlotStyles()	ShowPlotStyles	Second bit (2) of group 70
plotPlotStyles()	PlotWithPlotStyles	Sixth bit (32) of group 70
GetCurrentStyleSheet()	StyleSheet	Group 7

If a layout contains viewports into model space (that is, AcDbViewport objects), two settings determine whether the viewport borders are to be output and whether the contents of these viewports are to be plotted first (in which case, layout objects can be drawn on top of the modelspace entities).

ObjectDBX	ActiveX Automation	DXF/AutoLISP
plotViewportBorders()	PlotViewportBorders	First bit (1) of group 70
drawViewportsFirst()	PlotViewportsFirst	Tenth bit (512) of group 70

Plot Settings in DXF

The DXF class name for an AcDbPlotSettings object is `"PLOTSETTINGS"`. Following the subclass marker are the groups 1, 2, 4, 6, 40, 41, 42, 43, 44, 45, 46, 47, 48, 49, 140, 141, 142, 143, 70, 72, 73, 74, 7, 75, 147, 148, and 149.

Layout Objects

An AutoCAD layout is the display of a layout block container within the AutoCAD user interface. Therefore, it forms the *drawing* in which a user works. For the paperspace layouts, this display also includes the outline and margins of the physical page on which the drawing is to be output.

The AcDbLayout class is derived from the AcDbPlotSettings object. Therefore, a layout has all the properties described earlier in this chapter and a few more.

Layouts are closely linked to layout blocks. They describe where and how a specific layout block is to be displayed and output in AutoCAD. Each layout block has exactly one corresponding layout object, which can be found using the *Layout* property of the AcDbBlockTableRecord object. In addition, each layout object has a pointer back to its block table record.

ObjectDBX	ActiveX Automation	DXF/AutoLISP
getBlockTableRecordId()	Block	Group 330

Layouts are named objects and are therefore accessible through a dictionary. To find all layout objects, use the `"ACAD_LAYOUT"` key in the named object dictionary. This key points to a second dictionary that lists all AcDbLayout objects by name.

ObjectDBX	ActiveX Automation	DXF/AutoLISP
getLayoutName()	Name	Group 1

The name of the modelspace layout is always `"Model"`.

Layout Tabs

When working in the AutoCAD user interface, the user switches between layouts by using tabs at the bottom of the drawing area. Each tab displays the layout name.

The leftmost tab is always the modelspace tab, that is, the tab for the AcDbLayout object whose *ModelType* property is true. The remaining layouts are shown from left to right using their tab order, which is an integer. The modelspace layout has the tab order zero; all other layouts have a unique tab order greater than zero. AutoCAD will display them from left to right in ascending order.

ObjectDBX	ActiveX Automation	DXF/AutoLISP
getTabOrder()	TabOrder	Group 71

While you are working interactively in AutoCAD, only one layout is current, and it is the one in which newly drawn objects appear. The global CTAB setting contains the tab order code of the current layout.

Layout-Specific Coordinates

Every layout has its own coordinate system that is current when new entities are added to the layout block. This coordinate system is given through its origin point and two unit vectors (x-axis and y-axis).

ObjectDBX	ActiveX Automation	DXF/AutoLISP
n/a	n/a	Group 13, recent coordinate system origin
n/a	n/a	Group 16, recent coordinate system x-axis direction
n/a	n/a	Group 17, recent coordinate system y-axis direction

Because mouse and digitizer input is usually two-dimensional, each layout also keeps track of a default z coordinate for any point input.

ObjectDBX	ActiveX Automation	DXF/AutoLISP
n/a	n/a	Group 146, elevation, i.e., z coordinate for point input

The current coordinate system of a layout is independent of any other coordinate system used in the drawing. It may, however, have been created using a named coordinate system from an AcDbUCSTableRecord or by selecting an orthographic variant of a named coordinate system. The layout records the source of the coordinate system.

ObjectDBX	ActiveX Automation	DXF/AutoLISP
n/a	n/a	Group 345, handle/entity name of corresponding AcDbUCSTableRecord (if named UCS)
n/a	n/a	Group 346, handle/entity name of base AcDbUCSTableRecord (if orthographic variant of named UCS)
n/a	n/a	Group 76, orthographic variant code

A null handle indicates that the World Coordinate System is the base coordinate system. The orthographic variant code is zero for named coordinate systems and for any coordinate system that is not orthogonal to a base-named system. If the coordinate system is an orthogonal variant of a base coordinate system, the code is taken from the following list.

Value	DXF/AutoLISP	X-axis	Y-axis
top	-1	UCS X	UCS Y
bottom	-2	UCS –X	UCS Y
front	-3	UCS X	UCS Y
back	-4	UCS –X	UCS Y
left	-5	UCS –Y	UCS Z
right	-6	UCS Y	UCS Z

Layout-Specific Settings

Some settings that were global in previous versions of AutoCAD (and still exist within the global settings of a drawing database) are now layout-specific. These settings are the drawing limits, the drawing extents, the insertion base, and the cross-viewport scaling of linetypes.

The drawing limits define the 2D area in which a drawing is supposed to fit. The drawing limits are used within AutoCAD during three operations:

- Zoom and plot commands use the drawing limits if they are requested to draw *all* of the drawing.
- An eventual grid is displayed only within the drawing limits.
- Point input is refused for coordinates outside the drawing limits if the limits check is on. The limit corners are 2D points.

ObjectDBX	ActiveX Automation	DXF/AutoLISP
n/a	n/a	Group 10, lower left-corner of the drawing limits
n/a	n/a	Group 11, upper-right corner of the drawing limits
n/a	n/a	Second bit (2) of group 70, limits check

In ObjectDBX and ActiveX Automation, you can query the drawing limits by making the layout current and checking the LIMMIN, LIMMAX, and LIMCHECK global settings. In early releases of AutoCAD 2000, the information returned by the layout object was unreliable, and changed values were not recognized.

The drawing extents are two 3D points that define a bounding box for the complete visible contents of the layout block. This information is used during plot and zoom operations. Because AutoCAD recalculates these values only when necessary, they shouldn't be trusted unless such a recalculation (*regeneration*) has been forced.

ObjectDBX	ActiveX Automation	DXF/AutoLISP
n/a	n/a	Group 14, minimum coordinates of bounding box
n/a	n/a	Group 15, maximum coordinates of bounding box

If the layout is current, the drawing extents are also available through the EXTMIN and EXTMAX global settings.

Each layout defines an insertion base point for the elements in the corresponding block. This base point is used whenever the layout is copied into a different database or block container. The insertion base point corresponds to the *Origin* property of the layout block table record. It is a 3D point.

ObjectDBX	ActiveX Automation	DXF/AutoLISP
n/a	n/a	Group 12, insertion base point

The insertion base point of the current layout is also available through the INS-BASE global setting.

A final layout-specific setting that is also available as a global setting is PSLTSCALE. This setting affects only noncontinuous lines in *MODEL_SPACE* or noncontinuous lines that are referenced by *MODEL_SPACE* and seen through a paperspace viewport (AcDbViewport) of the current layout. If PSLTSCALE is set, the dashes and gaps of these noncontinuous lines will be scaled by the scale factor of the viewport in which they appear. Thus, noncontinuous lines in two viewports display the same-length dashes even though the viewports use a different display scale.

ObjectDBX	ActiveX Automation	DXF/AutoLISP
n/a	n/a	First bit (1) of group 70, apply viewport scale to linetypes

Layouts in DXF

The DXF class name of AcDbLayout is `"LAYOUT"`. Because AcDbLayout is derived from the AcDbPlotSettings object, following the AcDbObject groups is a subclass marker for

"AcDbPlotSettings". Following the plot settings groups are another subclass marker "AcDbLayout" and the groups 1, 70, 71, 10, 11, 12, 14, 15, 345, 146, 13, 16, 17, 346, 76, 330, and 331.

Abstract Views

Although any layout block can contain any AutoCAD entity, a special kind of entity is significant to layouts—the AcDbViewport entity. Like any other entity, a viewport has a graphical representation; however, the graphical representation of a viewport is two-fold. On one hand, a viewport has a border, which, like any other entity, has a layer, color, and so on.

On the other hand, the graphical representation of the viewport is a view into the modelspace of the drawing (that is, the *MODEL_SPACE* block container). Viewports thus allow you to place different views into the modelspace on a single layout. Views can be different in view direction, scale, or perspective or even in the selection of layers they display.

Let's start by looking at views in general. Abstract views define the graphical representation of an AcDbViewport entity. However, you also find abstract views in AcDb-ViewTableRecord objects (that is, named views) and AcDbViewportTableRecord objects (that is, named modelspace viewport configurations). Both are derived from a common AcDbAbstractViewTableRecord class. Group codes and function names differ slightly among these three objects; however, the contents are always the same.

Defining an Abstract View

The most important property of an abstract view is the line of sight. Usually, the line of sight is given by two points. One point is called the eye, or *camera*; the other is the point you look at, which is called the *target*. The line of sight goes through the camera and target points.

ObjectDBX and DXF/AutoLISP save the target point and the vector from target to camera. This vector defines both the direction of the view and the view distance. Even though ObjectDBX calls this the viewDirection, it is not the direction in which you view. It's the opposite.

ObjectDBX	ActiveX Automation	DXF/AutoLISP
AcDbAbstractView-TableRecord::target() AcDbViewport::viewTarget()	Target	AcDbAbstractView-TableRecord: group 12 AcDbViewport: group 17

ObjectDBX	ActiveX Automation	DXF/AutoLISP
viewDirection()	Direction	AcDbAbstractView-TableRecord: group 11 AcDbViewport: group 16

A view is either a parallel projection of objects onto a display plane or a perspective projection. In the first case, you'll get a box in 3D space that contains the entities to show; in the second case, you'll get a pyramid.

ObjectDBX	ActiveX Automation	DXF/AutoLISP
AcDbAbstractViewTable-Record::perspectiveEnabled() AcDbViewport::isPerspectiveOn()	n/a	First bit (1) of group 71 (AcDbAbstractViewTable-Record) respectively group 90 (AcDbViewport)

The view target and direction create a display coordinate system (DCS). The Z direction equals the direction from target to camera, thus pointing toward the viewer. The DCS X direction is calculated as the cross product of (0,0,1) and view direction. If the view direction is parallel to (0,0,1), the X direction is (1,0,0). The DCS origin is the target point.

In the parallel projection, the view may be offset from the line of sight, that is, the target point may be off the screen. Therefore, a view needs additional data in order to define the DCS rectangle that will be displayed. The rectangle's center is a 2D point (AcGePoint2d), because it is located on the DCS X/Y plane. The rectangle size is given by its height and width; its rotation around its center is given by the twist angle.

ObjectDBX	ActiveX Automation	DXF/AutoLISP
AcDbAbstractViewTable-Record::centerPoint() AcDbViewport::viewCenter()	Center	AcDbAbstractViewTable-Record: group 10 AcDb-Viewport: group 12
AcDbAbstractViewTable-Record::height() AcDbViewport::viewHeight()	Height	AcDbAbstractViewTable-Record: group 40 AcDb-Viewport: group 45
AcDbAbstractViewTable-Record::width()	Width	Group 41 (AcDbAbstract-ViewTableRecord only)
AcDbAbstractViewTable-Record::viewTwist() AcDbViewport::twistAngle()	n/a	AcDbAbstractViewTable-Record: group 50 AcDb-Viewport: group 51

The view width of an AcDbViewport is determined by the view height and the ratio of viewport width and height (see the "Viewports to Modelspace" section later in this chapter.).

In the perspective, the DCS rectangle is always centered around (0,0), which is the target point. Its size is taken from the view's lens length, which works like a real camera: you start with a rectangle of 42 units diagonal length located at lens length distance from the camera point.

By dividing 42 times the view distance by the lens length, you'll get the diagonal length of the DCS rectangle. Next, select a rectangle that has the same proportions as the view's width and height, and rotate this by the view twist angle.

ObjectDBX	ActiveX Automation	DXF/AutoLISP
lensLength()	n/a	Group 42

Clipping a View

Any view can be clipped. Clipping deletes objects that are too close to the camera or too far away. Both the front and back clipping distances are measured along the view direction, starting from the target point. In other words, these are DCS Z coordinates.

A special and quite common case is to place the front clip plane at camera distance. Doing so automatically excludes all objects that are behind your eye, as in the real world. Three Booleans indicate whether clip planes are used.

ObjectDBX	ActiveX Automation	DXF/AutoLISP
frontClipDistance()	n/a	Group 43
AcDbAbstractViewTableRecord::frontClipEnabled() AcDbViewport::isFrontClipOn()	n/a	Second bit (2) of group 71 (AcDbAbstractViewTableRecord) respectively group 90 (AcDbViewport)
AcDbAbstractViewTableRecord::frontClipAtEye() AcDbViewport::isFrontClipAtEyeOn()	n/a	AcDbAbstractViewTableRecord: inverse of fifth bit (16) of group 71 AcDbViewport: fifth bit (16) of group 90
backClipDistance()	n/a	Group 44
AcDbAbstractViewTableRecord::backClipEnabled() AcDbViewport::isBackClipOn()	n/a	Third bit (3) of group 71 (AcDbAbstractViewTableRecord) respectively group 90 (AcDbViewport)

Render Modes

A final display property of abstract views is the rendering mode. AutoCAD can display 3D objects in hidden line views, flat shaded, Gouraud shaded, and other modes. The following rendering modes exist:

ObjectDBX	DXF	Meaning
k2DOptimized	0	2D UCS icon, 2D grid in DCS plane. Raster and OLE entities, linetypes and linewidth are shown.
kWireframe	1	3D UCS icon, 2D grid in current X/Y plane. Listed objects and properties aren't visible.
kHiddenLine	2	Same as kWireframe but hidden lines removed.
kFlatShaded	3	Flat shaded.
KGouraudShaded	4	Gouraud shaded.
kFlatShadedWith-Wireframe	5	Overlap of kFlatShaded and kWireframe display.
kGouraudShaded-WithWireframe	6	Overlap of kGouraudShaded and kWireframe display.

The rendering mode is an 8-bit integer. In ObjectDBX, you can use the constants in the preceding list; in DXF, you use the appropriate numbers.

ObjectDBX	ActiveX Automation	DXF/AutoLISP
renderMode()	n/a	Group 281

View-Specific Coordinate Systems

In addition to display properties, abstract views can have an associated coordinate system that is automatically activated when the view becomes active.

ObjectDBX	ActiveX Automation	DXF/AutoLISP
AcDbAbstractViewTable-Record::isUcsAssociated-ToView() AcDbViewport::isUcs-SavedWithViewport()	UCSPerViewport (AcDbViewport only)	AcDbAbstractViewTable-Record: first bit (1) of group 72 AcDbViewport: group 71

As with layouts, the associated coordinate system may be a named UCS from the AcDbUCSTable, it may be a coordinate system orthogonal to an AcDbUCSTable-Record, it may be orthogonal to the World Coordinate System, or to none at all.

If the associated UCS is a named system or an orthographic variant of a named system, the pointer to the corresponding AcDbUSCTableRecord is available. A null pointer indicates that the World Coordinate System is being used.

ObjectDBX	ActiveX Automation	DXF/AutoLISP
ucsName()	n/a	Group 345 (if named UCS) group 346 (if orthogonal to named UCS)

Because the *UCS Name* defines a set of orthogonal coordinate systems, you need to know which one. The *isUcsOrthographic()* function returns a Boolean value for each orthographic orientation you supply as an argument. Possible values are as follows:

Orientation	ObjectDBX	DXF
top	kTopView	1
bottom	kBottomView	2
front	kFrontView	3
back	kBackView	4
left	kLeftView	5
right	kRightView	6

In DXF you'll find the orientation in group 79.

ObjectDBX	ActiveX Automation	DXF/AutoLISP
isUcsOrthographic()	n/a	Group 79

Even if no named UCS is associated with the abstract view, you can query the definition of the associated UCS. The *getUcs()* function returns all three vectors.

ObjectDBX	ActiveX Automation	DXF/AutoLISP
getUcs(), origin	n/a	Group 110
getUcs(), xAxis	n/a	Group 111
getUcs(), yAxis	n/a	Group 112

Within this UCS, the user may have chosen an elevation, which is an offset of the UCS X/Y plane. The *Elevation* property defines this offset and is the z coordinate of the workplane.

ObjectDBX	ActiveX Automation	DXF/AutoLISP
elevation()	n/a	Group 146

Viewport-Specific Drawing Aids

An AcDbViewportTableRecord object has more properties than an AcDbViewTable-Record object has. These additional properties define visual drawing aids that become active with the corresponding viewport. An AcDbViewport entity also has these additional properties, although their names and group codes vary slightly.

First, the viewport can be set to automatically follow any UCS changes applied. If this flag is set, the viewport always displays the plan (or top) view of the current UCS.

ObjectDBX	ActiveX Automation	DXF/AutoLISP
isUcsFollowModeOn()	n/a	Fourth bit (8) of group 90

The *Fast Zoom* and *Circle Sides* properties work as they do with an AcDbViewport-TableRecord object.

ObjectDBX	ActiveX Automation	DXF/AutoLISP
isFfastZoomOn()	n/a	Eighth bit (128) of group 90
circleSides()	ArcSmoothness	Group 72

Each AcDbViewport can display the UCS icon, which helps the user to understand the current orientation of the coordinate system. As an additional aid, this UCS icon can be set to display itself at the UCS origin, as long as the origin is within the viewport.

ObjectDBX	ActiveX Automation	DXF/AutoLISP
isUcsIconVisible()	UCSIconOn	Sixth bit (32) of group 90
isUcsIconAtOrigin()	UCSIconAtOrigin	Seventh bit (64) of group 90

Another visual construction aid is the drawing grid, which is an array of dots with different spacing in X and Y directions. The grid spacing is a 2D point in ObjectDBX and DXF/AutoLISP. The grid can be turned on and off.

The grid is always shown in the current X/Y plane; however, it does not cover the whole plane. The grid is limited to the rectangle bounded by the LIMMIN and LIMMAX global settings. The grid rows follow the orientation set by the snap angle and start at the snap origin (discussed next).

ObjectDBX	ActiveX Automation	DXF/AutoLISP
isGridOn()	GridOn	Tenth bit (512) of group 90
gridIncrement()	GetGridSpacing	Group 15

The grid dots are simply a visual aid. They do not affect any coordinate input. A second setting called *snap* is used to limit coordinate input. If a snap grid is active, coordinate input with the mouse is possible only in specific increments.

The snap grid starts at the snap origin, a 2D point relative to the current UCS. Snap rows follow the orientation set by the snap angle. The *Snap Spacing* property contains the spacing of snap points along the rows and columns of the snap grid.

Snap grids can be orthographic or isometric. The horizontal rows and vertical columns follow certain orientations that allow the user to draw easily within the specified isometric plane. The following planes (or isometric pairs) exist:

Isometric Plane	Code	Horizontal	Vertical
Left	0	30°	90°
Top	1	30°	150°
Right	2	150°	90°

ObjectDBX and DXF/AutoLISP use the following codes.

ObjectDBX	ActiveX Automation	DXF/AutoLISP
isSnapOn()	SnapOn	Ninth bit (256) of group 90
snapIncrement()	GetSnapSpacing	Group 14
snapBasePoint()	SnapBasePoint	Group 13
snapAngle()	SnapRotationAngle	Group 50
isSnapIsometric()	n/a	Eleventh bit (1024) of group 90
snapIsoPair()	n/a	Thirteenth bit (4096) and fourteenth bit (8192) of group 90

Viewports to Modelspace

An AcDbViewport entity is an abstract view into a layout block, placed on a layout. The viewport is an entity contained in the corresponding layout block. It has coordinates and lengths that define its placement and size relative to the other entities in this block. And it has color, layer, and the other properties of an AcDbEntity.

The location of the viewport on the layout is given by its center point, which is where the *View Center* will appear in the layout.

ObjectDBX	ActiveX Automation	DXF/AutoLISP
centerPoint()	Center	Group 10

The viewport border is a rectangle of specified height and width centered around the center point.

ObjectDBX	ActiveX Automation	DXF/AutoLISP
width()	Width	Group 40
height()	Height	Group 41

The viewport rectangle is displayed using the AcDbEntity color. Linetype, lineweight, and plotstyle are ignored. The rectangle is visible if its associated layer is on and thawed and if no clipping object is used (see the discussion on viewport clipping later in this chapter). The view within the rectangle is visible even if the rectangle is not; however, the view may be turned off.

ObjectDBX	ActiveX Automation	DXF/AutoLISP
n/a	ViewportOn	Group 68

The 68 group is an integer. When this integer is positive, the viewport contents are visible. When this integer is zero, the viewport has been turned off by the user, and when it is –1, the viewport has been turned off by AutoCAD, either because the viewport is fully off the screen or because the maximum number of viewports (MAX-ACTVP) has been exceeded.

Viewport Scale

Viewport height and view height define the scale of the displayed modelspace entities. ObjectDBX and ActiveX Automation allow you to also specify a standard scale.

ObjectDBX	ActiveX Automation	DXF/AutoLISP
standardScale()	StandardScale	n/a

The standard scale is similar to the standard scales in plot settings. The following are the valid options:

ObjectDBX	ActiveX Automation	Meaning	Scale Factor
kCustomScale	acVpCustomScale	Nonstandard scale	n/a
k1_1	ac1_1	1:1	1.0
k1_2	ac1_2	1:2	0.5
k1_4	ac1_4	1:4	0.5
k1_8	ac1_8	1:8	0.125

ObjectDBX	ActiveX Automation	Meaning	Scale Factor
k1_10	ac1_10	1:10	0.1
k1_16	ac1_16	1:16	0.0625
k1_20	ac1_20	1:20	0.05
k1_30	ac1_30	1:30	0.0333
k1_40	ac1_40	1:40	0.025
k1_50	ac1_50	1:50	0.02
k1_100	ac1_100	1:100	0.01
k2_1	ac2_1	2:1	2.0
k4_1	ac4_1	4:1	4.0
k8_1	ac8_1	8:1	8.0
k10_1	ac10_1	10:1	10.0
k100_1	ac100_1	100:1	100.0
k1000_1	ac1000_1	1000:1	1000.0
k1_128in_1ft	ac1_128in_1ft	1/128"=1'	0.000651
k1_64in_1ft	ac1_64in_1ft	1/64"=1'	0.0013
k1_32in_1ft	ac1_32in_1ft	1/32"=1'	0.0026
k1_16in_1ft	ac1_16in_1ft	1/16"=1'	0.0052
k3_32in_1ft	ac3_32in_1ft	3/32"=1'	0.0078
k1_8in_1ft	ac1_8in_1ft	1/8"=1'	0.0104
k3_16in_1ft	ac3_16in_1ft	3/16"=1'	0.0156
k1_4in_1ft	ac1_4in_1ft	1/4"=1'	0.0208
k3_8in_1ft	ac3_8in_1ft	3/8"=1'	0.03125
k1_2in_1ft	ac1_2in_1ft	1/2"=1'	0.04167
k3_4in_1ft	ac3_4in_1ft	3/4"=1'	0.0625
k1in_1ft	ac1in_1ft	1"=1'	0.0833
k3in_1ft	ac3in_1ft	3"=1'	0.25
k6in_1ft	ac6in_1ft	6"=1'	0.5
k1ft_1ft	ac1ft_1ft	1'=1'	1.0

If a non-standard scale is selected, you can query the scale factor:

ObjectDBX	ActiveX Automation	DXF/AutoLISP
customScale()	CustomScale	n/a

A Boolean flag can be set to lock the viewport scale. If the viewport scale is locked, the standard AutoCAD zoom commands will not change the view scale.

ObjectDBX	ActiveX Automation	DXF/AutoLISP
isLocked()	DisplayLocked	Fifteenth bit (16384) of group 90

Clipped Viewports

Viewports are limited to rectangular shape. To create differently shaped viewports, you can use a clipping entity, which is projected onto the view DCS plane. Only those parts of the view that fall into the projected area are displayed.

The clipping entity is one of the following:

- AcDbCircle
- AcDbPolyline
- AcDb2dPolyline
- AcDb3dPolyline
- AcDbEllipse
- AcDbRegion
- AcDbSpline
- AcDbFace

It must be an element of the same layout block as the AcDbViewport object.

ObjectDBX	ActiveX Automation	DXF/AutoLISP
isNonRectClipOn()	n/a	Seventeenth bit (65536) of group 90
nonRectClipEntityId()	n/a	Group 340

If a clipping entity exists, the viewport rectangle will not display. The clipping entity itself displays according to its *Layer* property. If the corresponding layer is off, the entity doesn't display but still clips the viewport. If the layer is frozen, the viewport displays unclipped, but without a rectangle.

Hiding Lines and Layers

Each viewport has its own property for removing hidden lines. As I discussed earlier, hidden lines are lines in 3D that lie behind an opaque surface when seen using the current view direction.

The removal of hidden lines is independent of the same property in the corresponding AcDbLayout object. Although the property of the layout affects the plot of objects from the layout block container, the property of the viewport controls the removal of hidden lines in the modelspace view it creates.

ObjectDBX	ActiveX Automation	DXF/AutoLISP
hiddenLinesRemoved()	RemoveHiddenLines	Twelfth bit (2048) of group 90

Independent of their position in 3D, each viewport can prevent arbitrary objects from being displayed. To do so, each viewport contains a list of layers to freeze only in this viewport. Objects on these layers do not display, even if their layer is globally thawed (that is, by their AcDbLayerTableRecord). Although this allows you to exclude certain layers from the display, the opposite is not possible; that is, you cannot display layers that are globally off or frozen.

ObjectDBX	ActiveX Automation	DXF/AutoLISP
getFrozenLayerList()	n/a	Group 341

In ObjectDBX, you'll get an array of AcDbObjectId. In DXF, multiple groups 341 contain the AcDbLayerTableRecord objects' handles, and in AutoLISP, you'll get the corresponding entity names.

Plot Styles within a Viewport

During the discussion of plot settings, you learned that each plot setting has an associated plot style table a.k.a. style sheet. This plot style table defines how to plot the elements of a layout block. When using AcDbViewport objects to add views of the modelspace to a layout, you can overwrite the layout-specific style sheet with a viewport-specific table.

ObjectDBX	ActiveX Automation	DXF/AutoLISP
plotStyleSheet()	n/a	Group 1

As is the case with plot settings, this property contains the filename of the plot style table without a path.

The Paperspace Viewport

The last property of an AcDbViewport is the viewport sequence number, which creates a unique index to each AcDbViewport within one layout.

ObjectDBX	ActiveX Automation	DXF/AutoLISP
number()	n/a	Group 69

Each layout has at least one viewport that uses the sequence number 1. This viewport does *not* create a view into modelspace. Instead, this AcDbViewport object describes the view of the layout block entities themselves, for example, snap spacing, grid, view direction, view twist, and so on. All other viewports display a view of the modelspace block.

Viewports in DXF and AutoLISP

The DXF class name of an AcDbViewport object is "VIEWPORT". Following the subclass marker, you'll find the following groups: 10, 40, 41, 68, 69, 12, 13, 14, 15, 16, 17, 42, 43, 44, 45, 50, 51, 72, 341 (repeated), 90, 340, 1, 281, 71, 74, 110, 111, 112, 345, 346, 79, and 146.

For compatibility with previous versions of AutoCAD, the AcDbViewport object presents several of its groups twice if you work in AutoLISP: once using the groups in the previous list, and a second time as xdata belonging to the "ACAD" application. This is how previous versions of AutoCAD saved viewport data.

The following list contains the xdata groups and their meaning.

Xdata Group Code	Corresponding New Group Code	Meaning
1000		Constant string "MVIEW"
1002		Open bracket "{"
1070		Version number 16
1010	17	View target
1010	16	View direction
1040	51	View twist angle
1040	45	View height
1040	12	View center x coordinate
1040	22	View center y coordinate
1040	42	Lens length
1040	43	Front clip distance
1040	44	Back clip distance
1070	90 (first five bits only)	Various flags
1070	72	Detailing
1070	90 (eighth bit)	Fast zoom
1070	90 (sixth bit)	UCS icon visibility
1070	90 (ninth bit)	Snap on
1070	90 (tenth bit)	Grid on

Xdata Group Code	Corresponding New Group Code	Meaning
1070	90 (eleventh bit)	Snap isometric
1070	90 (bits 13 and 14)	Isometric snap pair
1040	50	Snap angle
1040	13	Snap base x coordinate
1040	23	Snap base y coordinate
1040	14	Snap spacing in x
1040	24	Snap spacing in y
1040	15	Grid spacing in x
1040	25	Grid spacing in y
1070	90 (twelfth bit)	Plot without hidden lines
1002		Open bracket " { "
1003 (layer name)	341 (entity name)	Layer frozen in viewport
1002		Closing bracket " } "
1002		Closing bracket " } "

Viewports in ModelSpace

Except for the paper space viewport (sequence number 1), an AcDbViewport object displays a view of the modelspace block. Consequently, AcDbViewport objects that are contained in the modelspace block itself do not display anything except their border rectangle.

AcDbViewport objects can be part of any block container. When they are referenced by an AcDbBlockReference object, however, they do not display any view, just their outline.

To view multiple details or faces of the modelspace block while working in the modelspace layout, you do not use AcDbViewport objects. Instead, the "*ACTIVE" configuration of the AcDbViewportTable creates multiple views of the model. Other than AcDbViewport objects, AcDbViewportTableRecord objects must be tiled and fill the screen completely.

Summary

The objects discussed in previous chapters don't declare whether they will be displayed or how they may appear on a printout. Objects form abstract models that have many uses. You can use the object model to calculate rendered images or animations programmatically, and you can control machines using the object model contours or geometry. Creating an image on the screen or on paper is only one of many uses for objects in their many abstract forms.

The objects discussed in this chapter do not deal with this abstract model. They are used for realizing the visual model on a screen or on a plot. If an application is to work with the model, it can be easily programmed to ignore the objects associated with layouts. It's okay to work only with the modelspace block contents. But if an application is to display a drawing exactly as AutoCAD does, it has to take the AcDb-Viewport objects and the layout settings into account.

This chapter ends my presentation of the native database objects in AutoCAD. There may be many more object classes in a drawing database, because every application developer (and even an AutoCAD user) is able to define their own custom objects. The next chapter concentrates on those.

CHAPTER **18**

Custom Objects

FEATURING

The ideal custom object   **368**

Proxies and zombies   **368**

Classes in DXF   **370**

Proxy objects and entities   **371**

Proxy graphics   **374**

I f you think back to the initial discussion of the AutoCAD drawing database in Chapter 1, you will remember that the database is a collection of arbitrary objects. You now know that you'll find many different kinds of objects in a drawing database. Some of them are quite common, such as AcDbLine or AcDb-Circle, and some are even required, for example, one AcDbLayerTableRecord or several AcDbDictionary objects.

Other object types such as AcDbRasterImage are seldom used, but the quantity of the various objects depends completely on the types of drawings a user creates. Some users may need many raster images in their drawings.

So far we have looked at the main AutoCAD objects, the objects that compose most drawings. There are other object types, however, and there may be many of them. In Chapter 19 we'll look briefly at some additional objects, but for many other object types, the only documentation available is the internal documentation of the object's developer.

The drawing database is a container for arbitrary objects. Some of these objects are defined by Autodesk, and many others are defined by third-party developers. Various application programs working on top of AutoCAD, including Autodesk products such as Mechanical Desktop or Architectural Desktop, create their own objects. These are commonly referred to as *custom objects*, even though there's nothing custom about them. Custom objects work exactly the same as any other database objects.

The division between *native* and *custom* objects is arbitrary. You can say that every object created by the base AutoCAD program is a native object and that every object you need to get third-party software for is a custom object. In that case, you'd expect all native objects to come with a complete ObjectDBX, ActiveX Automation, AutoLISP, and DXF interface and complete documentation.

Even with AutoCAD itself, however, there are commands which create objects that don't have documented programming interfaces or even documentation. Examples are the AcDbWipeout, AcDbArcAlignedText, and RText objects created by the corresponding Express Tools bonus commands. An even worse example is the AcDbPlant object created by AutoCAD's built-in render module, which is completely undocumented.

In this chapter, we'll take a look at custom objects and how you can use them.

The Basic Problem

Custom objects look and act just like any of the objects I've discussed so far. A user working inside AutoCAD places and modifies them just like he or she places lines or circles.

If a user places an AcDbPlant object in a drawing, it displays itself (in this case, as a combination of text and faces). The user can move the object around, scale it, rotate it, or even query its definition. To most AutoCAD commands, the object looks like a line, text, or a dimension.

Some AutoCAD commands, however, know how to use plant objects. AutoCAD's render module, for instance, aligns a bitmap and a transparency map with the plant face during rendering. This process is used to place flowers, trees, people, or other flat images at specific locations in a 3D scene.

Although the plant object acts like a built-in object, the AutoCAD core program has absolutely no idea how it works. If the object is to be displayed, AutoCAD tells the object to display itself. If the object is to be moved, AutoCAD tells the object to move itself. The same is true with all actions, even filing the object into a DWG or DXF file.

The entire display and database logic of a custom object is hidden in a set of routines that the creator of the object supplies. The display logic describes how the object displays itself. This logic may be quite complex, as is the case of a door object from Architectural Desktop, which displays differently in 2D and 3D. The database logic describes how the object exposes itself to database access functions and how it files itself into DWG and DXF files.

In previous versions of AutoCAD, these routines were part of the ObjectARX program, which also included the complete application logic. AutoCAD 2000 allows a third-party developer to separate the database logic of custom objects from the application logic. The database part, which contains the display and filing logic, supplies the ObjectDBX functionality and should reside in a file of type DBX. The application logic, which includes a user interface to create custom objects, remains in the ObjectARX application, that is, the file of type ARX.

Whether the database logic is in a DBX file or an ARX file, however, the main problem is, what happens if the database logic is *not available*?

The database and display logic of a custom object is part of a third-party application. This application is not available on each and every AutoCAD workstation. Thus, a drawing that contains such objects can be loaded into an AutoCAD workstation where the needed DBX or ARX file is not available (and where the user refuses to pay the extra money for the third-party application).

As more and more programs read AutoCAD drawings, this problem becomes even more serious. Some programs, such as AutoCAD LT, are not allowed to run ARX programs and refuse to load them. Other programs that run on non-Intel machines cannot execute ARX programs because the compiled code won't run on their CPUs.

Without their display and database logic, custom objects cannot display, won't move, and even don't know how to export themselves to DWG and DXF files or to database access interfaces such as AutoLISP or ObjectDBX.

The Ideal Custom Object

From an end user's or a programmer's point of view, a custom object should behave exactly like any other drawing object. This means that it should do the following:

- React to arbitrary AutoCAD commands in the same way that any native object reacts
- Provide a documented and complete DXF representation (also to be used from within AutoLISP)
- Provide a documented and complete ActiveX Automation interface
- Provide a documented and complete ObjectDBX interface

Therefore, the creator of the custom object needs to separate the object logic from the application logic. As soon as the DBX file contains only the display and database logic of the custom object, in most cases, the creator can provide this file for free, for example, by providing a download site from which a user can obtain the DBX file, the documentation, and the ActiveX Automation type library. A first step in this direction is the Autodesk AEC Object Enabler module, which provides access to the custom objects of Autodesk Architectural Desktop and Autodesk Land Development Desktop and is available free of charge from the Autodesk Web site.

Because the user interface to create such objects as well as the complete application logic remain in the ARX files, you would still have to buy the third-party application to make use of the custom objects. But at least they would display and file correctly to DWG and DXF files.

Supplying a DBX file for each custom object does not solve the problem of using this file on workstations that won't run Intel code or with programs that don't know how to use a DBX file. At least AutoCAD itself, however, would be able to display and use the custom object. According to Autodesk, future versions of programs running on the AutoCAD OEM kernel (for example, AutoCAD LT) should also be able to execute DBX files.

Of Proxies and Zombies

Today there are no ideal custom objects. This is true even for objects that come with the base AutoCAD product: RText has an undocumented ActiveX Automation interface and a documented DXF representation, AcDbWipeout only comes with a DXF documentation, and AcDbPlant has neither.

Also, at the time of this writing, there were no external DBX files that users could download to at least partially work with the custom objects they encounter in their drawings.

If AutoCAD opens a drawing that contains custom objects, it tries to load the corresponding DBX or ARX application (if not already loaded). To do so, the application must be available, and AutoCAD must know which application to load. This information comes with the DWG or DXF file. In a DXF file, the place to look is the CLASSES section, which is described in the next section in this chapter.

If the application is found and loaded, AutoCAD passes all display and database operations on the custom objects to the application. This includes filing it back to a DWG or DXF file.

If the application is not available, AutoCAD reads in the object's data, but it has no idea what to do with it. Without the parent application, AutoCAD cannot display the object or modify it in any way. AutoCAD preserves the object definition, however, and writes it back when the drawing is later saved to DWG.

The object is *dead* as long as the parent application is not loaded. It comes back to life, however, as soon as the user loads the application or as soon as the saved drawing is read in at a workstation that has the application loaded. Because of its intermediate *dead* state, such objects were known as *Zombies* (AcDbZombieObject, AcDbZombie-Entity) in former versions of AutoCAD (and they still identify themselves as AcDb-ZombieEntity through the ActiveX Automation interface).

Later versions of AutoCAD use a more correct naming convention. Because the object is unavailable, a proxy for this object is used as long as the real object misses its application. An AcDbProxyObject or AcDbProxyEntity (which is the proxy for an object derived from AcDbEntity, that is, an object that has a visual representation such as a layer or a linetype) exposes a limited functionality to AutoCAD and the AutoCAD user.

For instance, the custom object may allow its *Layer* property to be changed even while it's in proxy state. AutoCAD records this layer change back to the DWG file when the drawing is saved. As soon as the application is available again, the object notes its new layer and behaves correctly (we hope).

Because AutoCAD preserves the original object data, proxy objects exist only as long as the drawing database is loaded in AutoCAD. Only if a drawing that contains custom objects is saved to DXF is an AcDbProxyObject (or AcDbProxyEntity) and not the original object written to the DXF file. This is because only the object itself knows how to export itself to DXF; that is, it knows which groups to use and how to fill them. As long as the object is dead, it cannot do so.

Even if the object became an AcDbProxyObject in the DXF file, however, the complete object data still goes with it. Once the DXF file is read back into an AutoCAD file that has access to the parent application, the proxy object reverts to a custom object, for example, an AcDbPlant.

Classes in DXF

A drawing file, whether in DWG or DXF format, needs to carry some information about the custom objects it contains. This information includes the parent application and some flags about which operations are allowed with this object while it's in proxy state.

In DXF, the information about custom object classes is found in a separate CLASSES section of the DXF file. The CLASSES section directly follows the HEADER section and precedes the TABLES section.

DXF Sequence for the Class Definitions

As I've discussed earlier in this book, the serialized version of the drawing database (DXF) uses brackets to create containers. The CLASSES section of a DXF file starts with

```
  0
SECTION
  2
CLASSES
```

and ends with

```
  0
ENDSEC
```

Within this section, you'll find a sequential list of all custom object classes used in the DXF file. The definition of *custom class* may seem a bit odd, because some objects that are internal to AutoCAD, such as AcDbPlaceHolder, AcDbLayout, and AcDbDictionary-WithDefault (but not AcDbDictionary), are also listed here. In addition, the objects that are defined by AutoCAD's built-in Image Support Module (ISM), such as AcDb-RasterImage, are listed in the CLASSES section.

Each class definition starts with a group 0 of value "CLASS". The sequence of classes in a DXF file is important because AcDbProxyObject and AcDbProxyEntity reference the class they stand for using an index to the CLASSES section.

Six groups go with each class definition. A first flag in group 281 determines whether the objects of this class are derived from AcDbObject (that is, they don't have a visual representation) or AcDbEntity (that is, they do have a visual representation). Group 281 is 0 for AcDbObject-derived classes and is 1 for AcDbEntity-derived classes.

A second flag (stored in group 280) indicates whether the parent application for this class was present at the time the DXF file was created. If it was (0), the objects of this class appear in the DXF file using their DXF class name. If it wasn't (1), they appear as AcDbProxyObject or AcDbProxyEntity.

Each class definition contains three text fields:

- Group 1 is the DXF class name used for objects of this class.

- Group 2 is the class name as it appears inside the C++ code of the application. This class name forms the link between the object and its parent application's code.

- Group 3 contains textual information about the object and its application. AutoCAD displays this information in a warning that informs the user about missing applications. For instance, the RText object uses the following group 3 string. The vertical bar is used to divide the string into multiple lines of text.

```
RText|AutoCAD Express Tool|expresstools@autodesk.com
```

The group 90 is a combination of various Boolean flags that describe how the custom object will act on certain operations if it is in proxy state. For instance, one flag indicates whether changing the *Layer* property of this object is allowed when a proxy. The flags are also available to ObjectDBX when working with the corresponding AcDbProxyObject or AcDbProxyEntity object. I'll discuss them together with these two object classes in the next section.

The sequence of groups for each class definition is as follows: 0 (constant "CLASS"), 1, 2, 3, 90, 280, and 281.

Proxy Objects and Entities

If the parent application is not available, a custom object is seen through its proxy when you are working in the various development environments. If a DXF file is written while the parent application is not available, the proxy object is even written out to the DXF file.

The AcDbProxyObject is a proxy for any object derived from AcDbObject. In turn, the AcDbProxyEntity is a proxy for all objects derived from AcDbEntity. As you know, an AcDbEntity always has a visual representation and a set of common properties such as layer and linetype. The difference between AcDbProxyObject and AcDbProxyEntity is that the latter is derived from AcDbEntity as well and, as such, also has the common properties and a visual representation.

You can use the AcDbProxyObject and AcDbProxyEntity to query about the missing application.

ObjectDBX	ActiveX Automation/ AutoLISP	DXF
OriginalClassName()	n/a	CLASSES section: group 2
OriginalDxfName()	n/a	CLASSES section: group 1
ApplicationDescription()	n/a	CLASSES section: group 3

In a DXF file, you can use the proxy object's or entity's group 91 to retrieve the corresponding record of the CLASSES section. Group 91 is an integer calculated as 500 plus the zero-based index of the object's class in the CLASSES section. Thus, all proxy objects that are created from the very first class use the number 500 in group 91; those objects that are created from the second class use number 501, and so on.

The creator of a custom object decides which operations are allowed while the object is in proxy state, that is, while the parent application is not available to control this operation.

ObjectDBX	ActiveX Automation/ AutoLISP	DXF
proxyFlags()	n/a	CLASSES section: group 90

The *Proxy Flags* property is an integer that contains a combination of Boolean flags. For an AcDbProxy*Object,* the following flags are meaningful:

ObjectDBX	DXF	Meaning
kEraseAllowed	First bit (1)	If set, the object can be erased.
kCloningAllowed	Eighth bit (128)	If set, the object can be copied (also between databases).

For an AcDbProxy*Entity,* there is a different set of flags:

ObjectDBX	DXF	Meaning
kEraseAllowed	First bit (1)	If set, the object can be erased.
KTransformAllowed	Second bit (2)	If set, the object can be moved, scaled, or rotated.
KColorChangeAllowed	Third bit (4)	If set, the object color can change.
KLayerChangeAllowed	Fourth bit (8)	If set, the object layer can change.
KLinetypeChangeAllowed	Fifth bit (16)	If set, the object linetype can change.

ObjectDBX	DXF	Meaning
KLinetypeScaleChange-Allowed	Sixth bit (32)	If set, the object linetype scale can change.
KVisibilityChangeAllowed	Seventh bit (64)	If set, the object visibility can change.
kCloningAllowed	Eighth bit (128)	If set, the object can be copied (also between databases).
KLineWeightChange-Allowed	Ninth bit (256)	If set, the object lineweight can change.
KPlotStyleNameChange-Allowed	Tenth bit (512)	If set, the object plot style can change.

If an ObjectARX application tries an operation on the custom object that is not allowed, it gets an error code (*Acad::eNotAllowedForThisProxy*).

Any change to the proxy entity's properties is recorded either in the AcDbEntity-based database properties (such as *Color, Layer,* and so on) or as binary information along with the AcDbProxyEntity (in the case of a transformation). If the application is loaded again, the custom object will be changed and transformed accordingly.

Even if a custom object is in proxy state, it may still affect other database objects. For instance, it may own another custom object. To maintain the relationship between objects even if the parent application is not available, each proxy object (or entity) has a list of references. In ObjectDBX, the *getReferences()* function returns both a list of AcDbObjectIds and a list of link types. Each link type can be one of the following:

ObjectDBX	DXF
kDxfSoftPointerId	330
kDxfHardPointerId	340
kDxfSoftOwnershipId	350
kDxfHardOwnershipId	360

For information about the various methods you can use to link objects, see Chapter 1. In DXF, you'll find a list of handles that use the group codes in the above list. For a reason that is not clear, the list ends with a group 94 of value zero.

 NOTE Both AutoLISP and ActiveX Automation provide access only to the AcDbObject and AcDbEntity properties of a proxy object using the DCOM interface to these classes.

Original Object Data

A DXF file needs to store the original data of the custom object so that it can be reconstructed later. Because AutoCAD has no idea how to interpret the data from the custom object it reads from a DWG file and because the application to create a usable DXF group code structure from this isn't there, the DXF file contains only a binary image of the original data.

The group 93 of an AcDbProxyObject or AcDbProxyEntity contains the number of bits (!) saved for the custom object. Following this are various groups 310 that contain the binary data. If group 70 is set to zero, this is an exact image of what the parent application saved to the DWG file. If group 70 is set to one, even the binary information has been retrieved from a DXF file.

Because the original object data is binary, AutoCAD saves in group 95 a number that indicates the drawing file format that was used to create this binary data.

For an AcDbProxyEntity, the groups 92 (length in bytes) and 310 (binary data) contain an image used to represent the proxy entity on the screen and in print. For more on proxy graphics, see the "Proxy Graphics" section later in this chapter.

The DXF Sequence for Proxy Objects

If a custom object is written to DXF while the object's parent application is not available, it is written to the DXF file as an AcDbProxyObject or AcDbProxyEntity (depending on whether it has associated graphics).

The DXF class name for an AcDbProxyObject is "ACAD_PROXY_OBJECT". It contains the usual AcDbObject groups followed by the "AcDbProxyObject" subclass marker. Next is a group 90, constant set to 499, followed by groups 91, 95, 70, 93, 310 (binary object data, repeated), 330 (repeated), 340 (repeated), 350 (repeated), 360 (repeated), and 94.

The DXF format of an AcDbProxyEntity is similar. The DXF class name is "ACAD_PROXY _ENTITY". Following the AcDbObject groups is a subclass marker for "AcDb-Entity" and the usual AcDbEntity groups. Next is a subclass marker "AcDbProxy-Entity" and a group 90, which is always 498. Following this are the groups 91, 95, 70, 92, 310 (binary graphics data, repeated), 93, 310 (binary object data, repeated), 330 (repeated), 340 (repeated), 350 (repeated), 360 (repeated), and 94.

Proxy Graphics

Custom objects derived from AcDbEntity have a visual representation. When AutoCAD is supposed to draw this representation, however, the application that knows how to draw the object may not be present.

Instead of leaving a blank spot on the drawing where the custom entity is supposed to appear, AutoCAD remembers a visualization with each custom entity. This is just *a* visualization, not necessarily *the* visualization. On the one hand, the parent application specifies whether AutoCAD should record the last visualization used or only the bounding box of this visualization. On the other hand, the visualization of a custom entity may depend on circumstances.

The AcDbPlant object, for instance, uses a different visualization for each view direction: the plant name is always perpendicular to the view direction. Thus, whichever visualization AutoCAD remembers is *wrong* as soon as the user changes the view direction and the application updating the AcDbPlant object is not present.

The visualization helps AutoCAD or other programs that use the AutoCAD OEM engine (such as AutoCAD LT) to display at least some kind of image for the custom object, even if it's not completely correct.

All custom objects and some of the other objects described so far save a visualization with each instance. This visualization, also known as *proxy graphics*, is saved in the AcDbEntity section of the custom object's DXF representation. For proxy entities, the visualization is part of the AcDbProxyEntity section. In both cases, a group 92 contains the length of the graphics data in bytes, and multiple groups 310 contain the visualization itself.

The visualization is saved as a set of drawing commands for the AutoCAD graphics engine. This is similar to a WMF file, which contains drawing commands for the Windows graphics engine, although the drawing commands of the two engines differ.

The drawing commands for the AutoCAD graphics engine (and, therefore, the format of the proxy graphics) create a graphical language on their own. In the following sections, I'll discuss the drawing commands and describe how they appear in a drawing database.

The Structure of Proxy Graphics

The proxy graphics information in a DXF file consists of a header followed by an arbitrary number of drawing commands. The header is made of two 32-bit integers. The first integer contains the overall number of bytes that describe the proxy graphics. The second integer contains the overall number of drawing commands that define the visualization of this object.

Following this header are the drawing commands. Each command is composed of two 32-bit integers and an arbitrary number of varying-length command arguments. The first integer contains the number of bytes in this command definition. The second integer is a code that identifies the drawing command (for example, circle, polygon, or mesh). The type and number of command arguments depend on this integer code.

The Proxy Graphics Drawing Commands

Following is a description of the various drawing commands you might encounter in a custom object's visualization. For more information about these commands and their arguments, see the ObjectARX Developer's Guide.

Floating point numbers (*real*) are always 64-bit integers, and counts are usually 32-bit (unless noted). Strings are zero-terminated and are always a multiple of 4 bytes. Points and vectors are composed of three 64-bit floating-point numbers.

Command Code 0 (kAcGiOpBad)   Indicates an invalid drawing command. You should not encounter this command in a drawing file. It takes no arguments.

Command Code 1 (kAcGiOpSetExtents)   Defines the geometric extents of the proxy graphics visualization. This command takes two AcGePoint3d (that is, three 64-bit floating-point values each) arguments: the lower-left corner and the upper-right corner of the bounding box.

Command Code 2 (kAcGiOpCircle1)   Draws a circle that is defined by the center, radius, and normal vector. The corresponding AcGiGeometry function is *circle()*. Arguments are the center point (AcGePoint3d), the radius (64-bit floating point value), and the normal vector (AcGeVector3d).

Command Code 3 (kAcGiOpCircle2)   Draws a circle, but uses three points on the perimeter to define it. This command uses the alternative parameters to the AcGiGeometry *circle()* function. Arguments are three AcGePoint3d points.

Command Code 4 (kAcGiOpCircularArc1)   Defines a circular arc. Like the first circle command, arguments are the center point, radius, and normal vector. Additional arguments are the start vector, the sweep angle, and the arc type. The start vector points from the center to the start point of the arc.

The sweep angle defines the included angle of the arc. Positive angles are drawn counter-clockwise from the start point. The arc type is a 32-bit integer and one of the following:

Arc Type	Value	Meaning
KAcGiArcSimple	0	Draws only the arc.
KAcGiArcSector	1	Draws the arc and two lines connecting the endpoints and the center. This closed segment may be filled.
KAcGiArcChord	2	Draws the arc and one line connecting the two endpoints. This again forms a fillable area.

The corresponding AcGiGeometry function is called *circularArc()*.

Command Code 5 (kAcGiOpCircularArc2)   Displays an arc that is defined by two endpoints and a point between them on the arc's curve. This corresponds to the second method to call *AcGiGeometry::circularArc()*. Arguments are the start point, the point on the arc, the end point, and the arc type.

Command Code 6 (kAcGiOpPolyline)   Displays an open, no-width polyline made from straight segments. The corresponding AcGiGeometry function is *polyline()*. Arguments are one integer indicating the number of vertices followed by the sequence of AcGePoint3d coordinates.

Command Code 7 (kAcGiOpPolygon)   Equivalent to the previous command, but displays a closed polyline by connecting the first and last vertex as well. The AcGiGeometry function is called *polygon()*.

Command Code 8 (kAcGiOpMesh)   Draws a mesh of connected, four-sided faces oriented (topologically) in rows and columns. Besides the list of vertices, the command also provides methods to control the edges, faces, and vertices of the mesh. It corresponds to the *AcGiGeometry::mesh()* function.

This command can take many arguments. First is the number of rows and the number of columns, each a 32-bit integer. Next is the list of AcGePoint3d coordinates that form the vertices.

Following the list of vertices are five lists of edge control data, five lists of face control data, and two lists of vertex control data. Each list starts with an integer code indicating the list contents:

- ACGI_COLORS (1) defines colors of edges or faces.
- ACGI_LAYER_IDS (256) defines the layer associations of edges or faces.
- ACGI_LINETYPE_IDS (512) defines the linetypes of edges.
- ACGI_MARKERS (32) defines markers (identifications) of edges or faces.
- ACGI_VIS_DATA (64) defines the visibility of edges or faces.
- ACGI_NORMALS (128) defines the normal vectors of faces of vertices.
- ACGI_ORIENTATION (1024) defines the orientation of vertices.

Each list contains the corresponding number of repetitions of the associated data type. Edges are listed in row-first order. That is, if you number the first row of vertices from 1 to n, the second row from $n+1$ to $2n$ and so on, the first edge is the one connecting vertices 1 and 2, the second edge is made from vertices 2 and 3, and so on. The same goes for the faces. The first face is the one made from vertices 1, 2, $n+1$, and $n+2$, the second face is made from vertices 2, 3, $n+2$, and $n+3$ and so on.

The list of colors contains one 16-bit integer (the AutoCAD color index) per face or edge. Layers and linetypes use the handles (or ObjectIds) of their AcDbSymbolTableRecord. Markers are 32-bit integers; normals are AcGeVector3d objects. For visibility flags, 8-bit integers are used, whereas in addition to kAcGiInvisible (0) and kAcGiVisible (1), a third value kAcGiSilhouette (2) may be used for invisible edges that become visible under certain conditions. The orientation of vertices indicates the direction that the vertices appear to follow when viewed while looking down the normal axis toward any given vertex. A 32-bit integer is used per vertex, which is kAcGiClockWise (1), kAcGiCounterClockWise (-1), or kAcGiNoOrientation (0).

Command Code 9 (kAcGiOpShell)   Draws a shell created from (not necessarily connected) faces. The corresponding AcGiGeometry function is *shell()*. The arguments are the same as for a mesh. The only difference is the additional list of faces between the vertex list and the first edge data list.

The face list starts with an integer containing the number of faces. Then for each face there is an integer containing the number of vertices that this face references and the corresponding number of vertex indices. Negative indices define holes in a face. The edge sequence that is relevant for the edge control lists follows the sequence in which the edges are defined by the faces.

Command Code 10 (kAcGiOpText1)   Displays a text string. This command corresponds to the first variant of *AcGiGeometry::text()*. Arguments are the start point (AcGePoint3d), the normal vector (AcGeVector3d), the text horizontal direction (AcGeVector3d), the text height (real), the width factor (real), the obliquing angle (real), and the message to display (string). A simple vector font is used.

Command Code 11 (kAcGiOpText2)   Displays a text string. This command corresponds to the second variant of *AcGiGeometry::text()*. Instead of the simple vector font used by the previous command, this command allows you to specify the font and font properties.

Arguments are the start point (AcGePoint3d), the normal vector (AcGeVector3d), and the text horizontal direction (AcGeVector3d). Next is the text string followed by a length indicator (integer, −1 if text string is zero-terminated). A Boolean flag (but 32-bit integer) indicates whether control codes such as %%d are to be interpreted (0) or not (1). Following this are text height (real), width factor (real), and obliquing angle (real).

Next is a spacing factor (real) applied to the individual characters in the string, followed by Boolean flags (integers) for backward, upside down, vertical, underlined, and overlined. Last are two strings: the font name and a bigfont name.

Command Code 12 (kAcGiOpXLine)   Draws an unbounded line passing through two points. The corresponding function is *AcGiGeometry::xline()*, and arguments are the two AcGePoint3d coordinates.

Command Code 13 (kAcGiOpRay)   Draws a single bounded line starting at one point and passing through another. The corresponding function is *AcGiGeometry::ray()*. The first argument is the start point; the second argument is the point through which the ray passes.

Command Code 14 (kAcGiOpColor)   Sets the color of any subsequently drawn object. This command corresponds to *AcGiSubEntityTraits::setColor()*. As an argument, it takes the AutoCAD color index value, which is an integer.

Command Code 15 (kAcGiOpLayerName)   Sets the layer of any subsequently drawn object. This command corresponds to *AcGiSubEntityTraits::setLayer()*. It takes the layer name as an argument.

Command Code 16 (kAcGiOpLayerIndex)   Also sets the layer of subsequently drawn objects. Here the argument is the corresponding handle/AcDbObjectId of the AcDbLayerTableRecord.

Command Code 17 (kAcGiOpLineTypeName)   Sets the linetype of any subsequently drawn object. This command corresponds to *AcGiSubEntityTraits::setLineType()*. The argument is the linetype name.

Command Code 18 (kAcGiOpLineTypeIndex)   Also sets the linetype of subsequently drawn objects. As with layers, the argument is the corresponding handle/AcDbObjectId of the AcDbLinetypeTableRecord.

Command Code 19 (kAcGiOpSelectionMarker)   Sets the selection marker (identification) of any subsequently drawn object. This command corresponds to *AcGiSubEntityTraits::setSelectionMarker()*. The marker is an integer.

Command Code 20 (kAcGiOpFillType)   Also sets the fill mode of subsequently drawn objects according to *AcGiSubEntityTraits::setFillType()*. The argument is an integer that can have two possible values: kAcGiFillAlways (1) and kAcGiFillNever (2). Only closed objects are filled. The global FILLMODE setting is to be honored.

Command Code 21 (kAcGiOpBoundingBoxSave)   A note that the bounding box of the graphics display is to be saved. This command takes no arguments.

Command Code 22 (kAcGiOpTrueColor)   Sets the true color of any subsequently drawn object. This command corresponds to *AcGiSubEntityTraits::setTrueColor()*. The argument is of type AcCmEntityColor.

Command Code 23 (kAcGiOpLineWeight)   Sets the lineweight of any subsequently drawn object. This command corresponds to *AcGiSubEntityTraits::setLineWeight()*. The argument is the lineweight index (integer).

Command Code 24 (kAcGiOpLineTypeScale)   Sets the linetype scale of any subsequently drawn object. This command corresponds to *AcGiSubEntityTraits::setLineTypeScale()*. Its only argument is the scale (real).

Command Code 25 (kAcGiOpThickness)   Sets the thickness (that is, the Z extrusion) of subsequently drawn objects. This command corresponds to *AcGiSubEntityTraits::setThickness()*. The thickness (real) is passed as the argument.

Command Code 26 (kAcGiOpPlotStyleName)   Sets the plot style name of any subsequently drawn object. This command corresponds to *AcGiSubEntityTraits::setPlotStyleName()*. Two arguments follow: the plot style name type (integer) and the plot style name index (integer).

Command Code 27 (kAcGiOpPushClipBoundary)   Defines a clipping boundary for all subsequently drawn objects. Any previous clip boundary is saved and restored when the current boundary is popped off the stack. The corresponding AcGiGeometry function is called *PushClipBoundary()*.

   This command takes a large number of arguments. (See the discussion of spatial filters in Chapter 16 for details.) The arguments are the normal direction (AcGeVector3d), the target point (AcGePoint3d), an array of 2D points defining the clip outline, two AcGeMatrix3d that describe the transformations from object coordinate system to clip space and the inverse of the block transformation matrix, two flags (integers) for front and back clipping, two reals describing the front and back clip plane distances, and a final flag indicating whether the clip outline is to be drawn.

Command Code 28 (kAcGiOpPopClipBoundary)   Deletes the current clip boundary from the stack and restores any previous boundary, which is then applied to subsequently drawn objects. The corresponding function is *AcGiGeometry::popClipBoundary()*. This command takes no arguments.

Command Code 29 (kAcGiOpPushTransformM)   Adds another transformation to all subsequently drawn objects. The transformation matrix (AcGeMatrix3d) is passed as an argument.

Command Code 30 (kAcGiOpPushTransformV)   Similar to the previous command, but applies to view transformations.

Command Code 31 (kAcGiOpPopTransform)   Deletes the latest transformation from the stack and restores any transformations previously applied. This command takes no arguments.

Command Code 32 (kAcGiOpPlineNormal)   Draws an open polyline. This command is similar to the code 6 command, but in addition specifies a normal vector for the polyline. It corresponds to *AcGiViewportGeometry::polylineEye()*. Arguments are the number of vertices (integer), the vertices (AcGePoint3d), and the normal vector (AcGeVector3d).

Command Code 33 (kAcGiOpMaxOpCodes)   This command should not occur.

Why Bother?

Keeping in mind that the proxy graphics may even contain a meaningless visualization. It may not be worth bothering with this information unless you have to develop a different CAD program and you try to produce the exact same display as AutoCAD would.

Summary

The concept of an extensible drawing database first introduced with AutoCAD Release 13 offers huge benefits for the AutoCAD user. No longer do you need to draw a door using four lines and an arc. No longer do you need to put your door lines into a block and add attributes for material and manufacturer. Now you can have a door object that knows by itself how to draw in 2D or 3D and that has all the specifications needed for design, purchasing, and facilities management.

But this concept also introduces severe problems. With many third-party developers introducing their own custom objects, the drawing database is reduced to a container of objects that even AutoCAD has no knowledge of. As long as the parent application is not available, the wonderful door object is even less useful than the lines and arcs used earlier. To allow AutoCAD users to work with door objects the same as they work with every other drawing object, the application developer needs to guarantee that the application code is available on every AutoCAD workstation and to every database access program.

Although custom objects are external to the native AutoCAD code, they are still AutoCAD objects. The next chapter discusses external data that is just embedded in a drawing database.

CHAPTER 19

Embedded Objects

FEATURING

Bodies, solids, and regions	**385**
ACIS data	**386**
OLE data	**389**
VBA projects	**392**

Some of you may have noticed that although I've discussed most of the native drawing entities in AutoCAD and have even described how to interact with other, non-native objects, I haven't mentioned a single word about AutoCAD's built-in solid models, about spheres and cylinders, boxes and tori, or even regions. The reason for this is simple: These objects aren't native drawing entities, and they aren't custom objects either. They are something altogether different.

As most of you know, at some time in the development of AutoCAD, Autodesk ceased to develop its own solid-modeling kernel and joined many other CAD companies in licensing the ACIS solid-modeling kernel developed by Spatial Technology. Consequently, AutoCAD doesn't care about the internals of a solid model. AutoCAD simply provides a user interface to the ACIS solid-modeling kernel. The task of handling data (which is what this book is about) no longer falls to AutoCAD and is the province of the ACIS kernel.

The ACIS-internal data structure is saved to a container inside the AutoCAD database, which, to all environments, looks like an AcDbEntity. AutoCAD itself provides very limited access to the data ACIS records inside the database.

In the first part of this chapter, we'll look at the various ACIS objects found in a drawing database and at the functionality these objects leave to an application that is accessing the database. In the case of embedded ACIS objects, AutoCAD provides only storage for the internal ACIS data that describes the object. AutoCAD itself has absolutely no knowledge of the structure and contents of the embedded information.

The concept of embedding foreign information into a document is quite common in the Windows world and is known as OLE (Object Linking and Embedding). Although AutoCAD does not use OLE to store ACIS data in the drawing database, the storage is analogous. In addition, like many other Windows programs, AutoCAD can embed arbitrary foreign objects inside an AutoCAD drawing,

As is the case with ACIS objects, the drawing database provides a container into which the external application saves its internal data.

In the second part of this chapter, I'll discuss the AcDbOle2Frame object, which is used as a container for external objects.

In addition to embedding objects such as ACIS solids or Word documents, an AutoCAD database can also embed *code*. As you can do in Microsoft Word or other Office products that include Microsoft's Visual Basic for Applications module, an AutoCAD user can save VBA modules external to the documents but also along with a document file, which in our case is a DWG or DXF file.

At the end of this chapter, I'll briefly discuss the AcDbVbaProject object, which is used as a container for embedded VBA projects. Despite its capabilities, this database-resident object itself is quite simple.

Bodies, Solids, and Regions

When working interactively in AutoCAD, a user can create spheres and wedges, solid boxes and tori, and extruded and revolved areas. To ACIS, however, these objects are all the same.

The ACIS data structure knows only a single type of model, which is called a *body*. A body has no idea how it was created. All it knows is how it looks. This is why you cannot query a sphere in AutoCAD about its radius or query a box about its lengths.

The internal data structure of ACIS defines each body by a number of points that form vertices, edges, loops, faces, shells, and bodies. Because the ACIS data defines the shell or boundary of the solid volume, this is called a *boundary representation*.

To ACIS all bodies are alike. There are no spheres or tori, boxes, or wedges. Once the solid object is created, it is recorded as an ACIS body. AutoCAD, however, divides ACIS bodies into three groups:

- Regions (AcDbRegion)
- 3D solids (AcDb3dSolid)
- Bodies (AcDbBody)

An AcDbRegion describes a planar (that is, two-dimensional) body made from closed, non-intersecting loops. If a loop is enclosed in another loop, it forms an island or inner boundary of the region. A single region may be created from multiple unconnected outer loops. In short, you can say that a region is any planar body from which you can calculate the surface area. A typical example of a region is the planar section through an arbitrary solid model.

An AcDb3dSolid describes a single three-dimensional body created from closed, non-intersecting shells. Like regions, shells can be enclosed in each other, thus forming a cavity inside a solid volume. And just like regions, a single 3D solid can be created from multiple unconnected shells. A 3D solid is everything for which you can calculate the volume.

 NOTE Do not confuse 3D solids (AcDb3dSolid) with 2D solids (AcDbSolid). The latter (described in the discussion of hatches and fills in Chapter 14) is a quadrangular planar filled area and has nothing to do with ACIS.

An AcDbBody is used for all ACIS bodies that are not regions or 3D solids. This may be a single vertex, loop or face, a combination of nonplanar regions, two intersecting shells, or any other data structures that should not appear in a "real world model." From within the AutoCAD user interface, you cannot create bodies that are not regions or 3D solids. Third-party applications running inside AutoCAD can create such objects, however. Also, you can import ACIS solids developed in other CAD programs into AutoCAD, which also allows you to create AcDbBody objects.

ACIS Data

Depending on the environment, you can access the ACIS data embedded in the drawing database. To work with this data, you usually need the ACIS libraries and a license from Spatial Technology.

If you are working in ObjectARX, the *AcDbBody::body(), AcDb3dSolid::body(),* and *AcDbRegion::body()* functions return a pointer to the internal ACIS data. You can use this pointer to access the ACIS body from within the ACIS libraries.

ObjectARX developers also have access to the *BREP API* inside AutoCAD. This API (application programming interface) allows you to query and extract vertices, curves, loops, or faces from an ACIS object. Objects and functions from the Boundary Representation library are prefixed by *AcBr*. (For more information, see the ObjectARX Developer's Guide.) Common functions such as extracting a face or an edge or extruding, removing, or offsetting faces are also available from the AcDb3dSolid object directly.

Programmers working in ActiveX Automation have no access to the embedded ACIS data.

If you are working in AutoLISP or DXF, you have access to the complete ACIS-internal data because it is filed with the drawing database. Using this data, however, requires (a) a small trick to decipher the ACIS data and (b) access to the ACIS libraries or another ACIS-enabled program to use and manipulate the data you find.

If you're looking at an ACIS body from within AutoLISP or by traversing a DXF file, you will find something that looks like this:

```
(1 . "koo ml n o       ")
(1 . "h J1410(1 nl ^\\VL kqoqm QK mk R01 R>& mk noeooenf nfff ")
(1 . "rn fqffffffffffffffffj:rooh n:rono ")
(1 . "=0;& {rn {n {rn {rn |")
(1 . "3*2/ {rn {m {l {o |")
(1 . "3*2/ {rn {rn {k {o |")
(1 . ",7:33 {rn {rn {rn {j {rn {n |")
(1 . ",7:33 {rn {rn {rn {i {rn {m |")
(1 . "9><: {h {rn {rn {l {rn {g 90-(>-; ,6183: |")
```

and so on.

This is a sequence of encrypted strings that contain the complete ACIS-internal data. Deciphering this information is easy as soon as you look at a second way to export ACIS data from within AutoCAD.

Like any other program using the ACIS kernel, AutoCAD can export any ACIS body to an SAT file. The SAT file format is defined by Spatial Technology and is used to interchange ACIS bodies between application programs. Documentation about the structure and contents of an SAT file is available from Spatial Technology at http://www.spatial.com.

This is the SAT file that corresponds to the ACIS solid listed earlier:

```
400 23 1 0
7 Unknown 13 ACIS 4.0.2 NT 24 Mon May 24 09:59:18 1999
-1 9.9999999999999995e-007 1e-010
body $-1 $1 $-1 $-1 #
lump $-1 $2 $3 $0 #
lump $-1 $-1 $4 $0 #
shell $-1 $-1 $-1 $5 $-1 $1 #
shell $-1 $-1 $-1 $6 $-1 $2 #
face $7 $-1 $-1 $3 $-1 $8 forward single #
```

and so on.

Comparing the two, you'll immediately see that spaces in the SAT file are found as spaces in the AutoLISP (or DXF) strings. The AutoLISP data is equivalent to the SAT version 4.0 data written by ACIS. The encryption is a simple character-to-character conversion: 9 becomes f, 8 becomes g, 7 becomes h, 6 becomes i, .. l becomes 3, m becomes 2, n becomes 1, and so on. Simply take the encrypted character and subtract its ASCII value from 159 to get the ASCII value of the character in the SAT file. (And don't decrypt the spaces.)

Modifying the embedded ACIS data is not recommended; you may render it in such a way that ACIS cannot interpret it later. If you have the ACIS libraries, use the ObjectARX *body()* function and operate on the ACIS data directly. If you need to work with an external program on the data embedded in a DXF file, keep in mind that you can also extract the ACIS data directly to an SAT file.

The DXF class names for the three ACIS objects are "BODY", "REGION", and "3DSOLID". With each object, you'll get the usual AcDbEntity groups, followed by a subclass marker. All three objects use the same subclass marker: "AcDbModelerGeometry". Following this are a group 70 (constant 1) and one group 1 for each line in the corresponding SAT file.

Querying Volume and Area

Although you cannot access the embedded ACIS data from a program using the ActiveX Automation interface to the drawing database, you can query some properties from both a 3D solid and a region. These properties include the center of the region or solid, the area, the volume, and other geometric data.

For an AcDb3dSolid object, the list of properties is as follows:

ObjectDBX	ActiveX Automation	DXF/AutoLISP
getMassProp(), volume	Volume	n/a
getMassProp(), centroid	Centroid	n/a
getMassProp(), monInertia	MomentOfInertia	n/a
getMassProp(),prodInertia	ProductOfInertia	n/a
getMassProp(),prinMoments	PrincipalMoments	n/a
getMassProp(),prinAxes	PrincipalDirections	n/a
getMassProp(),radiiGyration	RadiiOfGyration	n/a
getArea()	n/a	n/a

The *Area* property returns the combined surface area of all faces that form the shell of the 3D solid. The *Volume* property is measured in cubic drawing units. The center, or *Centroid,* is a 3D world point. Moments and product of inertia and radii of gyration are returned as three numbers, one for each of the world x-, y-, and z-axes. The principal moments (three reals) are measured along the principal axes (three vectors).

The list of properties available for an AcDbRegion object is a bit different. Because regions are planar entities, you can also query the plane's normal direction (and in ObjectARX also the plane itself). To find the base plane of the region in ActiveX Automation, use the centroid. Note, however, that ActiveX Automation access to AcDbRegion objects was defunct in early releases of AutoCAD 2000.

ObjectDBX	ActiveX Automation	DXF/AutoLISP
getArea()	Area	n/a
getPerimeter()	Perimeter	n/a
getNormal()	Normal	n/a
getPlane()	n/a	n/a
getAreaProp(), origin	n/a	n/a
getAreaProp(), xAxis	n/a	n/a
getAreaProp(), yAxis	n/a	n/a
getAreaProp(), centroid	Centroid	n/a
getAreaProp(), monInertia	MomentOfInertia	n/a
getAreaProp(), prodInertia	ProductOfInertia	n/a
getAreaProp(), prinMoments	PrincipalMoments	n/a
getAreaProp(), prinAxes	PrincipalDirections	n/a
getAreaProp(), radiiGyration	RadiiOfGyration	n/a

The *Origin*, *xAxis,* and *yAxis* properties define a Local Coordinate System within the plane of the region. *Centroid* and all remaining properties are 2D points and vectors within this Local Coordinate System.

 NOTE Because these properties are not available to the AutoLISP *entget* function, you need to use the ActiveX Automation interface from AutoLISP to AutoCAD if you want to query a solid's volume or area.

OLE Data

You have seen that AutoCAD provides only storage for the internal ACIS data that describes the object. AutoCAD itself has absolutely no knowledge of the structure and contents of the embedded information.

This concept, the embedding of foreign information into a document, is quite common in the Windows world, where it is known as OLE (Object Linking and Embedding). Many Windows programs can embed foreign objects in their documents. For instance, you can embed an Excel worksheet in a Word document, or you can embed an AutoCAD drawing into an Access table. Similarly, you can embed objects such as sounds, animations, and documents into an AutoCAD drawing.

Using OLE involves two application programs. The OLE *server* application is responsible for the embedded data and knows how to display and print it. The OLE *client* application simply provides storage and screen space.

AutoCAD can work both as an OLE server and as an OLE client. In this book, we will look only at the OLE client side, because this is where the drawing database is involved. When working as an OLE client, AutoCAD needs to provide storage and screen space to the OLE server, for example, the Microsoft Equation editor.

To support a large range of client applications, OLE servers usually supply an image of the embedded information to the client using various formats, for example, a bitmap, formatted text, unformatted text, and WMF vector graphics.

The AcDbOle2Frame object acts as a container for the embedded information. This object is used for OLE version 2 data interchange. AutoCAD can read OLE version 1 data from older AutoCAD versions (AcDbOleFrame), but it will save OLE version 2 data only and convert AcDbOleFrame objects to AcDbOle2Frame objects internally.

ObjectDBX	ActiveX Automation	DXF/AutoLISP
n/a	n/a	Group 70, OLE version number (constant 2)

When working in ObjectDBX, you can retrieve the embedded information using the OLE frame's *getOleObject()* function. As with ACIS, this gives you a pointer to the embedded object.

As the OLE object becomes part of the drawing database, it is filed out to DWG and DXF. In a DXF file, you will find the binary data as a list of groups 310. This list is preceded by a group 90 that contains the length of the OLE data in bytes. The list ends with a group 1 that contains the constant string "OLE". The binary OLE data in DXF contains not only the external OLE object, but also AutoCAD-internal information such as location, size, and link reference.

AutoLISP and ActiveX Automation do not provide any access to the embedded data.

The OLE Source and Type

AutoCAD not only remembers the internal data, but it also records some additional information about the object, such as the type of server application, the external file name and target, and the way the object is linked to an external file (if at all).

You can embed an OLE object into an AutoCAD drawing in three ways:

- OT_LINK (1) links the OLE object to an external file of the server application.
- OT_EMBEDDED (2) copies the complete external file into the AcDbOle2Frame object and deletes the information about where it came from.
- OT_STATIC (3) embeds only an image of the external file, for example, a bitmap or a metafile.

ObjectDBX	ActiveX Automation	DXF/AutoLISP
getType()	n/a	Group 71

If the object is linked to an external file, you can query the path to this file from within ObjectDBX. If the link goes only to a portion of this file, for example, a range of cells or a bookmark, you can also query the complete link name, including the linked item.

ObjectDBX	ActiveX Automation	DXF/AutoLISP
getLinkPath()	n/a	n/a
getLinkName()	n/a	n/a

Of course, the link path and link name are saved to DXF as well, but they are buried inside the binary OLE data.

What you can get in DXF and AutoLISP as well is the *User Type*. This is a string that identifies the type of embedded data, for example, a Microsoft Excel worksheet, a Microsoft Equation Editor equation, a Paintbrush bitmap, and so on. The user type is provided by the OLE server application and typically uses a localized description.

ObjectDBX	ActiveX Automation	DXF/AutoLISP
getUserType()	n/a	group 3

Location, Orientation, and Size

OLE objects always display perpendicular to the view direction and are aligned with the x- and y-axis of the display coordinate system; that is, they always display parallel to the screen edges.

The location and size of an OLE object is given in world coordinates. This allows a user to place the OLE object in relationship to other objects in the drawing database.

ObjectDBX	ActiveX Automation	DXF/AutoLISP
getLocation()	n/a	group 10

The location is always the upper-left corner of the OLE object. The lower-left corner is calculated using the *position()* function in ObjectDBX or the group 11 in AutoLISP or DXF.

The *position()* function returns a rectangle of all four corners either in world coordinates or in GDI coordinates. DXF group 11 contains the world position of the lower-right corner of the OLE display rectangle. The binary OLE data in DXF, however, contain all four corners.

 NOTE You cannot modify the location or size of an OLE frame using AutoLISP or DXF. The data is saved along with the binary OLE object and always restored from there.

Group 73 in AutoLISP and DXF additionally provides information about whether the object was inserted onto a layout (1) or directly into modelspace (0). This paper-space flag is repeated in the binary OLE date as well.

OLE Data in DXF

The DXF class name for an AcDbOle2Frame object is "OLE2FRAME". The sequence of groups following the subclass marker is 70, 3, 10, 11, 71, 72, 90, 310 (repeated), and 1.

The groups 310 contain the following information about the OLE object:

Bytes	Type	Meaning
2	Signature	Constant 5580h.
1	8-bit integer	1 if object was embedded into paper-space; 0 otherwise.

Bytes	Type	Meaning
3*8	AcGePoint3d	Upper-left corner.
3*8	AcGePoint3D	Upper-right corner.
3*8	AcGePoint3d	Lower-right corner.
3*8	AcGePoint3D	Lower-left corner.
4	32-bit integer	Constant 0.
4	32-bit integer	Value of TILEMODE setting during embedding (0 or 1); Release 13 compatibility only.
...	OLE object	Serialization of the OLE object as provided by the parent application.

VBA Projects

AutoCAD includes the complete VBA module from Microsoft. Like the embedded objects described so far, this module is fairly independent of AutoCAD. All AutoCAD provides is a user interface to start and use the VBA module itself or any VBA-created macros. VBA projects can be saved to an external file, but like Excel, AutoCAD also provides a storage container for VBA macros inside a drawing file.

If a drawing file contains VBA macros, a user can directly access them without having to load additional files or the VBA development environment. If an embedded VBA project contains an embedded autoexecuting macro, automatic tasks can be performed as soon as the drawing loads into AutoCAD. I don't think I need to explain how this opens the door for misbehaving code such as a drawing virus.

The Location of VBA Projects in a Drawing

To find the embedded VBA project in a drawing database, use the key string "ACAD_VBA" in the drawing's root dictionary. This string points to another dictionary that contains the key string "VBAProject". Following this link, you'll get to the AcDbVbaProject object.

VBA Project Data

The AcDbVbaProject object contains no less and no more than the corresponding DVB file used to store the project outside a drawing file. It is just a copy of this binary file.

The DXF class name of an AcDbVbaProject is "VBA_PROJECT". Following the common AcDbObject groups is a group 90 that contains the length of the binary data in bytes. Following this are multiple groups 310 that contains binary chunks of the VBA project.

And in the End...

This chapter closes our tour of the AutoCAD drawing database. We looked at Auto-CAD objects in general and at most of the specific entities you will find in a drawing database.

I covered the various ways you can access and use the properties of the various objects, but I could not discuss everything you can do with AutoCAD objects. For instance, although we looked at the properties of each object, I did not cover all the methods that each object provides. Those methods are not part of the drawing database as it is written to a DWG or DXF file.

The information in this book should help you to develop your own applications that work with AutoCAD data. While doing so, you will probably discover new objects or new procedures. If you do and you think that others could also benefit from them, drop me a note at dietmar@crlf.de.

Thank you for reading this book to its end. And don't overlook the appendices.

APPENDIX **A**

The Drawing Preview Image

AutoCAD drawing files contain a small bitmap with the last screen contents. External programs and AutoCAD's Open File dialog box can read this bitmap and display it as a preview image, which helps a user select the correct drawing.

AutoCAD drawing files exist in either DWG or DXF format. Both variants can contain a drawing preview image; however, this image only exists if the user set AutoCAD to generate and save the preview image. Earlier versions of AutoCAD created previews in either bitmap or vector graphics formats. Recent versions only use bitmaps.

This appendix describes how to extract the preview image from a drawing file.

Previewing DWG

A DWG file is a binary file. You need to find the correct spot in the DWG file to extract and display the preview image.

If you are working in ObjectARX, you can use the *acdbDisplayPreviewFromDwg()* function to display the preview from any DWG file into a preview window (which you need to provide). In this case, AutoCAD does everything for you.

If you're not working in ObjectARX, but in ObjectDBX (or if you want to directly access the bitmap), you can use the *AcDbDatabase::thumbnailBitmap()* function, which returns a pointer to the bitmap image.

Finally, if you are working with an external program, you can find the preview image by following these steps:

1. Open the DWG file and look at bytes 14 to 17. This is the absolute address of the preview area of the DWG file (as usual, the least significant byte is first).

2. Go to the address you located in step 1. Skip 16 bytes, which form a sentinel string.

3. Next are 4 bytes that contain the overall size of the preview area.

4. A single byte contains the number of preview images included in this file.

5. Following this is a table of preview image addresses. Each entry contains a code byte, the 4-byte start absolute address of the preview image, and the 4-byte length of the preview image. There are as many entries as the number from step 4 indicates.

Starting with AutoCAD Release 13, there are three types of preview images in DWG files: Code 1, Code 2, and Code 3. AutoCAD 2000 only creates two of them: Codes 1 and 2. Code 1 indicates a textual preview. The start address then points to a zero-terminated string. (No, this is not the comment string that AutoCAD requests when you are saving drawing templates, and there is no functionality to set this textual preview.)

Code 2 indicates a bitmap preview. The start address points to the first byte of the bitmap preview. Code 3 indicates a WMF preview (from Release 13 or 14). In this case, the preview is a Windows metafile with 22 byte Aldus header.

Previewing DXF

In a DXF file, the preview information (if any) can be found in a separate THUMBNAIL-IMAGE section, the last section following the OBJECTS section.

Unlike a DWG file, a DXF file does not provide you with a direct pointer to the bitmap image. You need to read through the complete file to find the start of the THUMBNAILIMAGE section, which looks like this:

```
  0
SECTION
  2
THUMBNAILIMAGE
```

Like any other section, this section ends with

```
  0
ENDSEC
```

Within the THUMBNAILIMAGE section, you'll find a single group 90 that contains the length of the preview image data in bytes.

Following this are multiple groups 310 that contain the binary preview bitmap data.

The Preview Bitmap

Whether you used the ObjectDBX functions, code 2 in the algorithm, or the THUMB-NAILIMAGE section of a DXF file to find the bitmap preview, you'll end up with binary data that describes the preview bitmap.

The preview image is a device independent bitmap (DIB) as defined by Windows. You can directly pass the binary data to the Windows API functions that draw a DIB to the screen.

A DIB is made from three sections. First comes a bitmap header (BITMAPINFO-HEADER) that documents the bitmap width and height, color depth, compression, and resolution. AutoCAD preview images are always uncompressed and use a color depth of 8 bits, that is, 256 colors.

The size of the preview image depends on the side length ratio of the drawing editor window used to create the thumbnail. It is always 256 * 188 pixels or less. A typical width is 180 pixels; a typical height is 100 pixels.

Following the bitmap header (whose first 4 bytes contain its length) is the color palette that is used. The color palette of an AutoCAD preview image consists of 256 color definitions. Each color definition (RGBQUAD) is 4 bytes; the first 3 bytes contain the Blue, Green, and Red intensity of the color, and the fourth byte is unused.

Finally, there is the pixel data, which is a sequential list of the bitmap pixels. In an AutoCAD preview image, there is always 1 byte per pixel that points to the corresponding color from the palette. The bitmap starts with the upper-left corner and then follows the first row, the second row, and so on.

APPENDIX <u>B</u>

Additional Sources

Large parts of this book are the result of my long-term study of the AutoCAD drawing database format. Some of this information is based on other books and articles, which often add more details or present alternative viewpoints.

Some of these titles are out of print, and some of them have not been translated into English or published in the United States. Nonetheless, they contain valuable information that is not available elsewhere. You can find and order many of them by searching the Web. Libraries and used-book stores are also excellent sources for both out-of-print and foreign-language titles.

Computer Graphics Tutorials

Brugger, Ralf. *3D-Computergrafik und animation* (Bonn: Addison-Wesley, 1993).

Earle, James. *Graphics for Engineers* (Reading, Mass: Addison-Wesley, 1992).

Foley, James et al. *Computer Graphics—Principles and Practice* (Reading, Mass: Addison-Wesley, 1990).

Hoschek, Lasser. *Grundlagen der geometrischen Datenverarbeitung* (Stuttgart: Verlag Teubner, 1992).

Computer Graphics Reference Books and Material

Grabowski, Ralph. "Upfront eZine"; available from `http://users.uniserve.com/ ~ralphg`, published weekly.

Holtz, W. Bradley. "The CAD Rating Guide"; available from `http://www.wbh.com`.

AutoCAD Tutorials

Frey, David. *AutoCAD 14: No Experience Required* (San Francisco: Sybex Inc., 1998).

Frey, David. *AutoCAD 2000: No Experience Required* (San Francisco: Sybex Inc., 1998).

Leigh, Ronald. *Solid Modeling with AutoCAD* (Chapel Hill, N.C.: Ventana Press, 1992).

Omura, George. *Mastering AutoCAD 14* (San Francisco: Sybex Inc., 1997).

Omura, George. *Mastering AutoCAD 2000* (San Francisco: Sybex Inc., 1999).

Omura, George, and Steven Keith. *Mastering AutoCAD 2000 for Mechanical Engineers* (San Francisco: Sybex Inc., 1998).

Omura, George. *Mastering AutoCAD 2000 Premium Edition* (San Francisco: Sybex Inc., 1999).

Omura, George. *Mastering AutoCAD 3D* (San Francisco: Sybex Inc., 1996).

Pitzer, David et al. *Inside AutoCAD* (Indianapolis: New Riders Publishing, 1996).

Raker, Daniel, and Harbert Rice. *INSIDE AutoCAD* (Thousand Oaks, Calif.: New Riders Publishing, 1989).

Shumaker, Terence, and David Madsen. *AutoCAD and Its Applications* (Tinley Park, Ill.: Goodheart-Willcox, 1996).

Zirbel, Jay, and Steven Combs. *Using AutoCAD* (Indianapolis: QUE, 1995).

AutoCAD Reference Books

Autodesk, Inc. *AutoCAD 2000 Command Reference.*

Autodesk, Inc. *AutoCAD 2000 User's Guide.*

Autodesk, Inc. *AutoCAD 2000 Customization Guide.*

Autodesk, Inc. *AutoCAD Express Tools.*

Grabowski, Ralph. *The AutoCAD Technical Reference* (Albany, N.Y.: Delmar Publishers, 1992).

Günther, Karin Susann. *Das AutoCAD-Lexikon* (Munich: Rossipaul-Verlag, 1991).

Hampe, Kurt et al. *Killer AutoCAD Utilities* (Indianapolis: New Riders Publishing, 1993).

Head, George. *The AutoCAD Productivity Book* (Chapel Hill, N.C.: Ventana Press, 1995).

Omura, George, and B. Robert Callori. *AutoCAD 14 Instant Reference* (San Francisco: Sybex Inc., 1997).

Omura, George, and B. Robert Callori. *AutoCAD 2000 Instant Reference* (San Francisco: Sybex Inc., 1999).

Walker, John. *The Autodesk File* (Thousand Oaks, Calif.: New Riders Publishing, 1989).

————. *The Autodesk File, Bits of History, Words of Experience*; available from `http://www.fourmilab.ch`.

AutoCAD Application Development

Fehr, Beat. *Die AutoCAD Applikationen* (Munich: Rossipaul-Verlag, 1993).

AutoCAD Programming

ADGE. *Proceedings of the CAMP ADGE*, conference reports (Basel, Switzerland: Auto-CAD Developers Group Europe, published twice yearly).

Gesner, Rusty, and Joseph Smith. *Maximizing AutoCAD Release 12* (Carmel, Ind.: New Riders Publishing, 1992).

————. *Maximizing AutoLISP* (Carmel, Ind.: New Riders Publishing, 1992).

Hampe, Kurt. *The AutoCAD Professional's API Toolkit* (Carmel, Ind.: New Riders Publishing, 1993).

Jump, Dennis. *AutoCAD Programming* (New York: TAB Books, McGraw-Hill, 1991).

Rudolph, Dietmar. *Die AutoCAD Programmierung* (Munich: Rossipaul Medien, 1991).

Tammik, Jeremy. *10,000 Minutes of ADS Talks* (Basel, Switzerland: AutoCAD Developers Group Europe, 1994).

————. *ADGE ADS++ Workgroup Minutes* (Basel, Switzerland: AutoCAD Developers Group Europe, published every second month).

————. *Das AutoCAD Development System ADS* (Munich: Rossipaul Medien, 1993).

Tickoo, Sham. *Customizing AutoCAD* (Albany, N.Y.: Delmar Publishers, 1994).

Smith, Joseph, and Rusty Gesner. *Customizing AutoCAD* (Thousand Oaks, Calif.: New Riders Publishing, 1989).

AutoLISP Programming

Autodesk, Inc. *AutoCAD 2000 AutoLISP Reference*.

Autodesk, Inc. *Visual LISP Developer's Guide*.

Friedman, Daniel, and Matthias Felleisen. *The Little LISPer* (Cambridge, Mass.: MIT Press, 1987).

Head, George. *AutoLISP in Plain English* (Chapel Hill, N.C.: Ventana Press, 1995).

Kreiker, Phil. *The CAD Cookbook Collection* (Cleveland, Ohio: Advanstar Communications, 1993).

Oliver, William. *Illustrated AutoLISP* (Plano, Tex.: Wordware Publishing, 1990).

Rawls, Rod, and Mark Hagen. *AutoLISP Programming* (South Holland, Ill.: Goodheart-Willcox, 1994).

Rudolph, Dietmar. "Vital LISP: The Return of the AutoLISP Compiler," *CAD++ Newsletter* (June 1995).

Rudolph, Dietmar. *AutoLISP—Die Programmiersprache in AutoCAD* (Munich: te-wi Verlag, 1988).

Winston, Patrick, and Berthold Horn. *LISP* (Bonn: Addison-Wesley, 1987).

AutoCAD ActiveX Programming

Autodesk, Inc. *AutoCAD 2000 ActiveX and VBA Developer's Guide*

Autodesk, Inc. *AutoCAD 2000 ActiveX and VBA Reference*

ObjectARX and ObjectDBX

Autodesk, Inc. *ObjectARX Developer's Guide*

Autodesk, Inc. *ObjectARX Migration Guide*

Autodesk, Inc. *ObjectARX Reference*

AutoCAD Database Objects

Adkison, Bill. "AutoCAD Perspective View Transformation Formula," internal memo, Autodesk, Inc.

Autodesk, Inc. *Autodesk Device Interface/ADI Driver Development ToolKit Version 4.2, Appendix A: Color Assignments*.

Autodesk, Inc. *AutoShade Version 2 with Autodesk Renderman User Guide, Appendix B: Color Lists*.

Jones, Frederik, and Lloyd Martin. *The AutoCAD Database Book* (Chapel Hill, N.C.: Ventana Press, 1991).

Olfe, Daniel. *Computer Graphics for Design—From Algorithms to AutoCAD* (Englewood Cliffs, N.J.: Prentice Hall, 1995).

DWG

The OpenDWG Alliance. "AutoCAD R13/R14 DWG File Specification"; available from http://www.opendwg.org.

Rudolph, Dietmar. "How Autodesk Gave Up Control Over its DWG and DXF File Formats," *CAD++ Newsletter* (December 1994).

DXF

Autodesk, Inc. *AutoCAD 2000 DXF Reference.*

Morrison, Dan. "Things to check if DXF conversions will not work," internal memorandum, Autodesk, Inc.

National Economic Development Council (NEDC). *Subset of DXF for the Exchange of 2D CAD Drawings* (London: National Economic Development Office, 1992).

———. *Subset of DXF for the Exchange of Unstructured 2D CAD Drawings* (London: National Economic Development Office, 1991).

Rudolph, Dietmar et al. *DXF intern* (Essen: CR/LF GmbH, 1998).

Rudolph, Dietmar et al. *Der DXF-Standard* (Munich: Rossipaul Medien, 1993).

Rudolph, Dietmar. "DXF—Can You Get There From Here?" *CADENCE* (March 1995).

Rudolph, Dietmar. "DXF—Mythos und Wirklichkeit," *PC-Professionell* (March 1992).

Rudolph, Dietmar. "First Aid for R13 DXF Translation," *CAD++ Newsletter* (March 1995).

Weber, Dave. "DXF Made Easy." O.V.O. BLUEPRINT CO. LTD. Memorandum.

Spline Curves and Surfaces

Beach, Robert. *An Introduction to Curves and Surfaces in Computer Aided Design* (New York: Van Nostrand Reinhold, 1991).

De Boor, Carl. *A Practical Guide to Splines* (Berlin: Springer Verlag, 1978).

Olfe, Daniel. *Computer Graphics for Design—From Algorithms to AutoCAD* (Englewood Cliffs, N.J.: Prentice Hall, 1995).

ACIS

Spatial Technology, Inc. "ACIS Geometric Modeler, Format Manual, Version 2.1"; available from `http://www.spatial.com`.

DIESEL

Autodesk, Inc. "Status line configuration and DIESEL string expression language," *AutoCAD Customization Guide and AutoCAD LT Manuals*

Fehr, Beat. "The Power of Turbo DIESEL," *Proceedings of the CAMP ADGE, May 1994* (Basel, Switzerland: AutoCAD Developers Group Europe, 1994).

Gesner, Rusty, and Joseph Smith. "Running on DIESEL," *Maximizing AutoCAD Release 12* (Carmel, Ind.: New Riders Publishing, 1992).

Rudolph, Dietmar. "D-I-E-S-E-L"; available from `http://www.crlf.de`.

Tammik, Jeremy. "DIESEL," *Das AutoCAD Development System ADS* (Munich: Rossipaul Medien, 1993).

ActiveX Programming

Chappell, David, and David Linthicum. "ActiveX Demystified," *BYTE* (September 1997).

Hart-Davis, Guy. *Mastering VBA 6* (San Francisco: Sybex Inc., 2000).

Windows API

Simon, Richard J. *Windows NT Win32 API Superbible* (Corte Madera, Calif.: Waite Group Press, 1997).

INDEX

Note to Reader: In this index, **boldfaced** page numbers refer to primary discussions of the topic; *italics* page numbers refer to figures.

Symbols & Numbers

%% (double percent), for font file characters, 237
+/- (tolerance symbol), characters replaced by, 237
^ (caret symbol), for font file characters, 237
2D solids, 385
3D faces, **227–228**, *228*
3D polylines, **287–288**
3D solids, querying properties from, 387
3D volume, spatial filter to define, 328
16-bit integer, signed, 54, **55–56**
32-bit integer, signed, **56–57**
64-bit floating-point numbers, 61

A

abstract views, **351–355**
    defining, **351–353**
    rendering mode, **354**
ACAD_COLOR object, 59
ACAD_FILTER key, 328–329
ACAD_GROUP, 41, 163
ACAD_LAYOUT key string, 163, 347
ACAD_LWEIGHT object, 59, 205
ACAD_MLINESTYLE key string, 163, 292
ACAD_PLOTSETTINGS key, 339
ACAD_PLOTSTYLENAME key string, 163, 207
ACAD_PROXY_OBJECT, 374
ACAD_VBA key string, 392
AcadDocument, 38
AcadLine object, 41
ACADMAINTVER (AutoCAD database maintenance version number), **80**
AcadPlotConfiguration, 339
ACADVER (AutoCAD database version number), 7, 76, **79**
acByBlock color, 202
acByLayer color, 202
AcDb library, xix
AcDb2dPolyline object, 276, 284, 286
    FILLMODE and, 82
    settings for display, 87
AcDb2dVertex object, 284

AcDb2LineAngularDimension object, 252, 270, 271
AcDb3DPolyline object, 276, 287
AcDb3dSolid object, 385
    properties, 388
AcDb3PointAngularDimension object, 252, 270–271
AcDbAlignedDimension object, 252, 269
    color for, 193
AcDbArc object, 212, 221
AcDbArcAlignedText object, 248–249, 366
AcDbAttribute object, 80, 324, 331
    AcDbAttributeDefinition object relation to, 334
    Boolean flags in, 60
    properties, 334
AcDbAttributeDefinition object, 80, 324, 331–333
    visibility, 332
AcDbBlockBegin object, 47
    xdata attached to, 184
AcDbBlockEnd object, 47
AcDbBlockReference object, 267, 324, **324–328**
    Linetype property of, 203
    using color of, 202
AcDbBlockTable object, **178–181**
AcDbBlockTableRecord object, 178, 183–184
    newBlockReferenceIdIterator() function, 47
    newIterator() function, 47
AcDbBody object, 385
AcDbCircle object, 212, 219
AcDbCurve object, properties and spline curves, **226–227**
AcDbDatabase object, constructor for, 43
AcDbDiametric Dimension object, 252
AcDbDictionaryWithDefault object, **163**
AcDbDimension object, 252
    properties, **267–269**
AcDbDimStyleRecord object, 246
AcDbDimStyleTable symbol table, **144–150**
AcDbDimStyleTableRecord object, 120, 253
acdbDisplayPreviewFromDwg() function, 396
AcDbEllipse object, 212, 222
    calculated properties, 223
AcDbEntity class, 192
    sequencing in DXF file, **192–193**

AcDbFace object, 212, 227–228, *228*
    settings for display, 87
AcDbFaceRecord object, 290, 291
AcDbFcf object, 232, 245
AcDbFilter class, 328
acdbGetAdsName() function, 121
AcDbGroup object, locating, 166
acdbGroupCodeToType() function, 172
AcDbHandle class, 65
AcDbHatch object, 300
    FILLMODE and, 82
acdbHostApplicationServices, workingDatabase()
    function, 43
AcDbIdBuffer object, 170
AcDbIndex class, **169**
AcDb::kDwgBChunk, 72
AcDb::kDwgHandle object handle, 65
AcDbLayerFilter object, 328
AcDbLayerIndex object, 169, 170
AcDbLayerTable object, 174
AcDbLayerTable symbol table, **134–138**
AcDbLayerTableRecord object
    Color property of, 202
    Linetype property of, 203
AcDbLayout object, 182, 347
    block containers linked to, 338
AcDbLeader object, **276–279**
AcDbLine object, 41, 212, 216, 267
AcDbLinetypeSymbolRecord object, 83
AcDbLinetypeTable symbol table, **138–141**
AcDbLinetypeTableRecord object, 203
AcDbMInsertBlock object, 324, 325, **327**, 335
AcDbMline object, 164, 276, 292, **292–297**
    FILLMODE and, 82
AcDbMlineStyle object, 292
AcDbMText object, 232, 240, 267
    color for, 193
    location and size, **241–242**
AcDbObject class, 10, 120
    extensionDictionary() function, 124
    reactors() function, 123
AcDbOle2Frame object, 389–390
acdbOpenAcDbEntity() function, 45
acdbOpenAcDbObject() function, 45
acdbOpenObject() function, 44–45
AcDbOrdinateDimension object, 252, **273–274**
AcDbPlaceHolder object, 164, 207
AcDbPlant object, 367
AcDbPlotSettings object, 338
    information about plot contents, **341–343**
    and output device, 339
AcDbPlotSettingsValidator::getLocaleMediaName()
    function, 339
AcDbPoint object, 84, 85, **232–233**

AcDbPolyFaceMesh object, 276, 290
AcDbPolyFaceMeshVertex object, 290
AcDbPolygonMesh object, 276
    settings for display, 87
AcDbPolyline object, 276, **279–283**
    FILLMODE and, 82
AcDbProxyEntity, 369, 371
    Proxy Flags property, 372–373
AcDbProxyObject, 369, 371
    Proxy Flags property, 372
AcDbRadialDimension object, 252
AcDbRasterImage object, 314, 316
    color, 320
    hard reference pointer in, 319
AcDbRasterImageDef object, 314
AcDbRasterImageDefReactor object, 319
AcDbRasterImageReactor object, 314
AcDbRasterVariables object, 314, 320
AcDbRay object, 212, 216
AcDbRegAppTable symbol table, **158**
AcDbRegion object, 385
    properties, 388
AcDbRotatedDimension object, 252, 270
AcDbSequenceEnd object, 285, 335
AcDbShape object, 232, *234*, **234–235**
AcDbSolid object, 310–311, 385
    FILLMODE and, 82
AcDbSortentsTable object, **168**
    to define entity order, 165, 167–168
    ownership by extension dictionary, 168
AcDbSpatialFilter object, 324, **328–331**
    in extension dictionary, 328–329
AcDbSpatialIndex object, 169, 170
AcDbSpline object, 212, 224
    settings for display, 87
AcDbText object, 232, 236, 240
AcDbTextStyleTable object, 234, 236
AcDbTextStyleTable symbol table, **141–144**
AcDbTextStyleTableRecord object, 234
AcDbTrace object, 310–311
    FILLMODE and, 82
    width setting for, 105
AcDbUCSTable symbol table, **151–152**
AcDbVertex object, 285
AcDbViewport entity, 351
AcDbViewportTable symbol table, **154–157**
AcDbViewportTableRecord object, to define visual
    drawing aids, 356
AcDbViewTable symbol table, **152–153**
AcDbWipeout object, 311, 366
AcDbXline object, 212, 215
AcDbXrecord object, **171–174**
AcDBZombieEntity, 369
AcDbZombieObject, 369

acedGetVar() function, 50
acedSetVar() function, 50
AcGeCircArc2d, 304
AcGeEllpArc2d, 305
AcGeLineSeg2d, 304
AcGeNurbCurve2d, 305
AcGePoint3d data type, 66, 215
AcGeVector3D data type, 215
AcGiOpCircle1 (drawing command), 376
ACIS data structure, 385, **386–389**
ACIS solid-modeling kernel, 384
AcRxClass object, naming function, 121
ActiveX Automation, 18, **36–42**
    to access database, xx
    to access entities, **39–40**
    binary chunks in, 73
    class determination in, 121
    to create entities, **40**
    custom objects in, **41–42**
    disadvantages, 50
    double data type, 61
    integers in, 56, 57
    non-objects in, 42
    to obtain UCSORG setting, 77
    opening communication with AutoCAD, 37
    points in, 67
    retrieving of xdata, 128
    string objects, 64
    to work with dictionaries, **41**
add methods, 40
addbGetObjectID() function, 121
AddObject method, 41
AddXRecord method, 171
ads_real data type, 61
aligned linear dimensions, **269–270**
alignment of text styles, 244
alternate dimensions, **258–259**
ambient light, settings for, 103
ANGBASE, 90
ANGDIR, 90
Angle property, for line, 218
angleAtParam() function, 223
angles
    settings for, 90
    values as real numbers, 61
angular dimensions, 145, **270–271**
    precision for, 146
annotation objects, 232. *See also* text
    feature control frames, *245*, **245–248**
    hatch as, 300
    leaders with, 276, **278–279**
    semi-custom, **248–250**
anonymous blocks, 179
appendAcDbEntity() function, 48

applications, information for custom objects, 369
arbitrary axis algorithm, **70–72**
arbitrary link, group codes, 126
arc-aligned text, **248–249**
Arc Smoothness property, of viewports, 220
Architectural Desktop, 366
arcs
    circular, **220–222**
    elliptical, **222–223**
    in polylines, **280–281**
Area property
    of 3D solid, 388
    of circle, 220
arrowheads, 268
    for dimension lines, **261–263**
    leaders with, 276, 278
    settings, 146, 147, 148
ARX file type, 367
ASCII DXF file, **22–23**
    binary chunks, 72
    end-of-file information, 24
    group code in, 59
    real numbers, 62
    resolution, 221
    signed 16-bit integer in, 55
    signed 32-bit integer in, 56
    signed 8-bit integer, 57
assoc function, 29
attached reference, vs. overlaid reference, 182
ATTDISP, 76, 333
ATTMODE (attribute display mode), **80**
attribute definition, 324
attribute objects, **331–335**
attribute tag, 332
attributeIterator() function, 335
attributes, 12, 324
    constant, **334**
    text string visibility, 80
    variable, **334–335**
AUNITS, 90, 108
AUPREC, 90, 108
AutoCAD
    accessing objects, xviii–xxii
    database class hierarchy, 9–10, *10*, *11*
    drawing file contents, xvii
    drawings vs. models, **3**
    embedding OLE object in, 390
    Release 13, 13
    versions, xxii–xxiii
AutoCAD 2000
    custom objects routines, 367
    version number, 79
AutoCAD Color Index, 137, **194–202**

AutoCAD database maintenance version number (ACADMAINTVER), **80**
AutoCAD database version number (ACADVER), 7, 76, **79**
AutoCAD LT, xxii
   and ARX programs, 367
Autodesk AEC Object Enabler module, 368
Autodesk Architectural Desktop, 368
Autodesk Land Development Desktop, 368
AutoLISP, xix, 18, **26–36**
   16-bit integer in, 56
   to access ACIS internal data, 386–387
   binary chunks, 72
   database access from, **28–29**
   dictionary access in, **32–34**
   disadvantages, 50
   modifying and making objects in, **34–35**
   object identification by, 8
   points in, 67
   reading and writing drawing settings, **35–36**
   real numbers in, 61
   retrieving entities with, **30–32**
   signed 32-bit integer in, 57
   signed 8-bit integer, 57
   string objects, 64
   viewports in, **362–363**
automation client, xx
automation server, xx
axctextapp.tlb type library, 248
axes of UCS (User Coordinate System), 151
axrtext.tlb type library, 248

B

B-spline, 224
background of bitmap, transparency of, 317
backslash, in MText object, 243
Backwards property
   of text string, 236
   of text styles, 143
base point, on xline, 215
baseline dimensions, spacing of, 147
Bézier surfaces, 289
Big Font file, 237–238
binary chunks, 22–23, 72
binary data, in drawing database, **72–73**
binary DXF file, **22–23**
   binary chunks, 72–73
   end-of-file information, 24
   group code in, 59
   real numbers in, 61
   signed 16-bit integer in, 55
   signed 32-bit integer in, 57

signed 8-bit integer, 57
   strings in, 64
binary thumbnail image, 185
bitmap images, 314
   clipping, **318**
   definitions, **314–316**
   display quality, 320
   in DXF file, **318–319**
   entities, **316–319**
   manipulation, **317–318**
block begin objects, **183–184**
block containers, **178**
   AcDbViewport objects as part of, 363
   in ActiveX Automation, 40
   adding object to, 48
   attributes in, 180
   DXF representation, **184–188**
   filtered inserts, **328–331**
   inherited properties, **327–328**
   linking to AcDbLayout object, 338
   multiple inserts, **327**
   query of number of references to, 180
   references, **324–328**
   spatial index for, **170**
   temporary, 179
   visibility, 324
block end objects, **183–184**
block insert, 324
block table, **178–181**
block table records, properties, 180–181
BLOCK_RECORD table, **184–185**
   entries, **185**
blockId() function, 48
blocks, 6
Blocks collection, 39
BLOCKS section in DXF file, 24
blockTransform() function, 327
bodies, **385–386**
body() function, 387
bonus objects, 248
Boolean data type
   16-bit integer to represent, 58
   as integers, **60**
border, of viewports, 358
boundary representation, 385
boundary tracer, **309–310**
bounded curve, 214
bounded line, drawing command for, 379
bounding box
   defining for visible contents of layout block, 349–350
   for entities, 209
   for text, 242
brackets in DXF file, 21

breaks in multilines, 295–296
BREP API, 386
bulge factor calculation, 280–281, *281*
byte order, 55

C

calculated properties, 12
    for handle, 120–121
    for lines, **218–219**
    for multilines, **297**
camera
    in abstract view, 351
    placing front clip pane at, 353
car function, 28–29
caret symbol (^), for font file characters, 237
Cartesian coordinate systems, 68
cdr function, 28
CECOLOR, 90
CELTSCALE, 90
CELTYPE, 90
CELWEIGHT, 90
center marks
    format and size, 268
    settings, 147
center point, of viewports, 357
Center property
    of circle, 219–220
    of ellipse, 222
CEPSNTYPE, 90
chamfer, settings for, 91
CHAMFERA, 91
CHAMFERB, 91
CHAMFERC, 91
CHAMFERD, 91
character definition, 13
character range, **65**
character sets, **64–65**
    setting to define, 81
Circle objects, 36
Circle Sides property, for viewport, 356
circles
    coordinate systems for, **219**
    defining properties, **219–220**
    dimensions of diameter, 272
    in proxy graphics visualization, 376
circular arc edges, **304–305**
circular arcs, **220–222**
circular curves, **219–220**
Circumference property, of circle, 220
classes, **9–10**
    name vs. DXF name, 121
    of objects, **121–122**

CLASSES section in DXF file, 24, **370–371**
CLAYER, 91
client application for OLE, 389
clip volume, 328–329
    boundaries, 330
clipping
    viewports, **360**
    views, **353**
clipping boundary, drawing command for, 380
clipping image, 317, **318**
closed curve, 214
closed polyline, drawing command for, 377
closing objects, **44–45**
CMLJUST, 91
CMLSCALE, 91
CMLSTYLE, 91
code pages, 64, 81
collection in Visual Basic, 38
color
    of characters, 244
    of dimension and extension lines, 147, 260
    drawing command for, 379
    signed 16-bit integer for, 59
Color property
    of AcDbLayerTableRecord object, 202
    for entities, 192, **193–202**
    of layer, 136–137
colorIndex() function, 202
COM Automation. *See* ActiveX Automation
comments
    in ASCII DXF files, 22, 23
    for blocks, 179
composite curve. *See* spline curves
compression value, for text styles, 144
constant attributes, **334**
constants, predefined, 58
containers, 2. *See also* block containers
    ObjectARX to iterate through, **45–47**
    for objects with graphical representation, 6
    parsing into objects, 25
control points, of spline, 225–226
coordinate dimensions, **273–274**
Coordinate property, for leaders, 277
coordinate systems, **68–69**
    for AcDbFcf object, 245
    for AcDbPolyline object, 279
    for bitmap, 316
    for block reference, 325–326
    for circles, **219**
    display, for viewport, 352
    for ellipse, 222
    for layout, **347–349**
    for solids and traces, 310–311
    for views, **354–355**

coordinates, xviii
    for points, 66
    as real numbers, 61
core objects, 14
Count property, of collections, 38
cubic B-spline surfaces, 289
curly brackets, in MText object, 243
cursor movement, settings for, 101
curve-fit polylines, **286**
curved 3D solids, setting for, 80–81
curves
    circular, **219–220**
    leaders as, 277
    parametrical representations, **213–214**
    properties, **212–215**
    spline, **224–227**
custom objects, 193, 366
    basics, **366–367**
    departure from ideal, **368–369**
    ideal, **368**
    storage of original data, **374**

D

database records, indexes of, 169
database settings, ObjectDBX shortcuts to, **49–50**
date and time, of drawing creation, 104
date values, **63**
DCOM (Distributed Component Object Model), xx
defining points, for dimension calculation, 268
defining properties, 12, 54
degree symbol, characters replaced by, 237
Delphi, xx
    code for database access, 36
Delta property, for line, 218
Dependent property, of layer, 138
derivative of curves, 214
DesignCenter application, 63
Detailing property, of viewports, 156, 220
device independent bitmap (DIB), for preview
    image, 397–398
diameter dimensions, 145, **272**
Diameter property, of circle, 220
diameter symbol, characters replaced by, 237
DIB (device independent bitmap), for preview
    image, 397–398
dictadd function, 35
dictionaries, **5**, **161–163**. *See also* root dictionary
    access in AutoLISP, **32–34**
    ActiveX Automation to work with, **41**
    contents, **161–162**
    creating, 35
    with default, **163**

extension, 33
global settings as variables, **165**
layouts accessed through, 347
locating variable values, **165–166**
merging, **162–163**
placeholder objects, **164**
reactor links used with, 124
DictionaryVariables object, **164–166**
    properties, **166**
dictnext function, 33
dictremove function, 35
dictrename function, 35
dictsearch function, 32–33
DIESEL programming language, 249
DIMADEC, 91, 146
DIMALT, 91, 146
DIMALTD, 91, 146
DIMALTF, 92, 146
DIMALTRND, 92, 146
DIMALTTD, 92, 146
DIMALTTZ, 92, 146
DIMALTU, 92, 146
DIMALTZ, 92, 146
DIMAPOST, 92, 146
DIMASO, 92
DIMASZ, 92, 146
DIMATFIT, 93, 109, 146, 265
DIMAUNIT, 93, 146
DIMAZIN, 93, 109, 146
DIMBLK, 93, 109–110, 147
DIMBLK1, 93, 147
DIMBLK2, 93, 147
DIMCEN, 93, 147
DIMCLRD, 93, 147
DIMCLRE, 94, 147
DIMCLRT, 94, 147
DIMDEC, 94, 147
DIMDLE, 94, 147
DIMDLI, 94, 147
DIMDSEP, 94, 147
dimension style table, 4
dimensions, 232, 252
    aligned linear, **269–270**
    alternate, **258–259**
    angular, **270–271**
    arrowheads, **261–263**
    coordinate, **273–274**
    diametrical, **272**
    lines, **260–261**
    radius, **272–273**
    rotated linear, **270**
    scaling, **253–254**
    settings for, 91–98
    styles, 132, **144–150**, **252–253**

families, **145**
properties, **145–150**
text, **259**
placement, 149–150, **263–267**
string calculation, **254–256**
template, 255–256
tolerances, *256*, **256–258**
DIMEXE, 94, 147
DIMEXO, 94, 148
DIMFRAC, 94, 110, 148
DIMGAP, 94, 148
DIMJUST, 94, 111, 148
DIMLDRBLK, 95, 148
DIMLFAC, 95, 148
DIMLIM, 95, 148
DIMLUNIT, 95, 111, 148
DIMLWD, 95, 148
DIMLWE, 95, 148
DIMPOST, 95, 148
DIMRND, 95, 149
DIMSAH, 96, 149
DIMSCALE, 96, 149
DIMSD1, 96, 149
DIMSD2, 96, 149
DIMSE1, 96, 149
DIMSE2, 96, 149
DIMSHO, 96
DIMSOXD, 96, 149
DIMSTYLE, 96
DIMTAD, 96, 111–112, 149
DIMTDEC, 97, 149
DIMTFAC, 97, 149
DIMTIH, 97, 149
DIMTIX, 97, 150
DIMTM, 97, 150
DIMTMOVE, 97, 112, 150
DIMTOFL, 97, 150
DIMTOH, 97, 150
DIMTOL, 97, 150
DIMTOLJ, 97, 112, 150
DIMTP, 97, 150
DIMTSZ, 98, 150
DIMTVP, 98, 150
DIMTXSTY, 98, 150
DIMTXT, 98, 150
DIMTZIN, 98, 150
DIMUPT, 98
DIMZIN, 98, 112–113, 150
direction vector, for 3D line, 217
disguised integers, **57–60**
display precision, settings for, 91
DISPSLH (show silhouette lines for 3D solids), **80–81**
Distributed Component Object Model (DCOM), xx

document object, Layers property of, 38
Documents collection, 37
documents in AutoCAD ActiveX interface, 37–38
drawing aids, for viewport, **356–357**
drawing database, xvii, xxiii, 3. *See also* DXF (Drawing Interchange Format)
ActiveX Automation to access, xx, **36–42**
AutoLISP and Visual LISP to access, xix, **26–36**
binary data in, **72–73**
containers, 132
handles in, **65**
integers, **54–57**
as multidimensional object, 21
non-objects in, **7**
object hierarchy, 38
ObjectARX to access, xix–xx, **42–50**
objects in, **161**
other access options, **50–51**
plot settings in, 338
points in, **66–72**
real numbers, **61–63**
strings, **64–65**
drawing extents, for layout, 349
drawing grid, 356
in viewport, 157
Drawing Interchange File. *See* DXF (Drawing Interchange Format)
drawing limits for layout, 349
drawing properties record, as extension record, **173–174**
drawings
contents, **2–3**
vs. models, **3**
DWF file format, xxii
DWG file format
previewing, **396–397**
as trade secret, 51
DWGCODEPAGE (drawing character set), **81–82**
DXF (Drawing Interchange Format), xxi–xxii, **18–26**
16-bit integer in, 55
to access ACIS internal data, 386–387
ASCII and binary, **22–23**
vs. AutoLISP, 27
block containers representation, **184–188**
CLASSES section, **370–371**
criticisms, **20**
disadvantages, 50
ENTITIES section, **188**
HEADER section, 24, 76
images in, **318–319**
layer table sequence in, **134**
layouts in, **350–351**
myths, **19–20**

name vs. class name, 121
objects in, **161**
to obtain UCSORG setting, 77–78
OLE data in, **391–392**
point storage in, 67
preview images, **397**
properties omitted, 26
sequence for proxy objects, **374**
sequence for spline curves, **227**
sequence for symbol tables, **133**
sequencing for AcDbEntity, **192–193**
serializing drawing data, **21**
settings sequence in, **115–117**
structure, **23–25**
viewports in, **362–363**
dxfName() function, 121

E

ECS (Entity Coordinate System), 69
edge-defined loops in hatched areas, **303–304**
ELEVATION, 98
elevation() function, 267
Elevation property, 217
    for viewport, 355
ellipses, **222–223**
elliptical arc edges, **305**
elliptical arcs, **222–223**
embedded objects, **9**
    group code to start, 25
end-of-file information, in DXF file, 24
end point, 216
end-section bracket, in DXF file, 24
ENDBLK object, 35
ENDCAPS, 98
entdel function, 34
entget function, 28, 29, 31, 126
entities, **6**, 120, 132, 178, 192
    ActiveX Automation to access, **39–40**
    ActiveX Automation to create, **40**
    bitmap images, **316–319**
    Color property for, **193–202**
    color settings for, 90
    functions to access database-resident data, 48
    handling in ObjectDBX, **47–48**
    Hyperlinks property, **208**
    interactive-only properties, **209–210**
    Layer property for, **193**
    Linetype property, **203–204**
    Linetype Scale property, **204–205**
    Lineweight property, **205–206**
    name calculation, 120–121
    Paperspace Flag property for, **208–209**

Plot Style Name Type property, 207
Plot Style property, **206–207**
retrieving with AutoLISP, **30–32**
Visibility property, **207–208**
ENTITIES section in DXF file, 24–25, **188**
entity association list, 28
Entity Coordinate System (ECS), 69
entity groups, **166–167**
entity interchange file, 19
entity names
    in AutoLISP, 27
    of dictionary, 33
    retrieving, **29–30**
entity order index, **167–168**
entmake function, 34, 35
entmakex function, 34, 35
entmod function, 34
entnext function, 31
entsel function, 28
enumerations, as integers, **58**
extended object data (xdata), **126–129**. *See also*
    xdata (extended object data)
extension dictionary, 33
    AcDbSortentsTable object ownership by, 168
    AcDbSpatialFilter object in, **328–329**
    for layer table, **135**
    links, **124–125**
extension lines
    for dimensions, 260
    lineweights, 148
    settings, 147
extension records, **171–174**
    merging, **172–173**
extensionDictionary() function, 49
external applications, to extract preview image,
    396
external databases, references to blocks from, 185
external images, AcDbRasterImage object to link
    to, 314
external layers, **137–138**
external references, 178, **182–183**
external text, RText object to link to, 249
EXTMAX, 99, 350
EXTMIN, 99, 350
EXTNAMES, 99
extracting objects, xxii
extruded circles, 220
Extrusion Direction, 217
extrusion, of lightweight polyline, 279

F

Fast Zoom property, for viewport, 356

feature control frames, *245*, **245–248**
  dimension style-based data, **246**
  formatting codes, **247–248**
Field Length property, of attribute definitions, 333
FILLETRAD, 99
FILLMODE (fill display mode), **82**, 281
  and hatch display, 301
fills, for hatched areas, **307–309**
filtered inserts, in block containers, **328–331**
FINGERPRINTGUID, 99
finite straight lines, **216–219**
first period angle, 221
Fit Tolerance property, of spline curves, 225
flags. *See* Boolean data type
floating viewports, 88
font() function, 143
fonts, 244
  early AutoCAD definition for, 141
foreign objects, embedding in AutoCAD drawing, 384
formatting single lines of text, **238**
fractions, displaying in dimensions, 148
frames, display around image entities, 320
Frozen property, of layer, 135–136

G

getAssocObjIdsAt() function, 306
getAt() function, 45–46
GetAttribute method, 335
getBlockTable() function, 45
getClosestPointTo() function, 297
GetConstantAttributes method, 335
getDimstyleChildId() function, 145
getDimstyleParentId() function, 145
GetExtensionDictionary method, 41, 124
getGripPoints() function, 48
getHatchLineDataAt() function, 309
getHyperlinkCollection method, 208
getIntoAsciiBuffer() funciton, for representation of handle, 65
getLoopAt() function, 304
getNamedObjectsDictionary() function, 49
getOleObject() function, 390
getPlane() function, 297
getPlotStyleNameID() function, 207
getPointAt() function, 280
getRecord() function, 46
getReferences() function, 373
getUcs() function, 355
getvar function, 35–36
GetVariable method, 42
getVertices() function, 318

GetXData method, 128
GetXRecordData method, 171
global scale factor, settings, 148
globally unique identifier (GUID), 99, 107
grip points
  of entities, 209
  querying object's, 48
group codes, 21, **59**
  to describe setting value in DXF, 78
  for xdata, **128–129**
groups, entity, **166–167**
GUID (globally unique identifier), 99, 107

H

hairline, 83
handles
  in drawing database, **65**
  for objects, 7, 8, **120–121**
    order, 167
  settings for, 99
HANDSEED, 99
hard line break, in MText object, 243
hard owner, 9, 161–162
  group codes, 126
hard pointer, 8
  group codes, 126
HasExtensionDictionary property, 124
hatched areas, 300, *301*
  associated entities, **306**
  contours and associativity, **302–306**
  elements of definition, **300–301**
  fills and patterns, **307–309**
  pattern line families, **308–309**
  settings for, 82
  solids and traces, **310–311**
HEADER section in DXF file, 24, 76
heavyweight polylines, **283–287**
  end, **285**
  header, **284**
  vertex objects, **285**
height of text, 244
Height property
  for plot media, 340
  of text styles, 143–144
hidden lines, suppression in plot, 345
hook lines, leaders with, 278
horizontal alignment of text, 239
horizontal rotation of dimension text, 264
HYPERLINKBASE, 99, 208
Hyperlinks property, for entities, 193, **208**

I

IEEE (Institute of Electrical and Electronics Engineers), 62
images. *See also* bitmap images
    global settings, **319–321**
implicit links, 9
INBASE, 99
increment, for dimension lines, 268
INDEXCTL dictionary variable, 165
indexes
    of database records, 169
    entity order, **167–168**
inheritance, 10
insertion point, for text entity, 238
instantiating object, 43
Institute of Electrical and Electronics Engineers (IEEE), 62
INSUNITS drawing setting, 63, 99, 113–114
integers, **54–57**
    Boolean data type as, **60**
    disguised, **57–60**
    enumerations as, **58**
    signed 16-bit, 54, **55–56**
    signed 32-bit, **56–57**
    signed 8-bit, **57**
interface, 41–42
International Organization for Standardization (ISO), 82
intersections, in multilines, 295–296
isA() function, 121
isEdgeVisibleAt() function, 291
island in hatches, 302
IsLayout property, and printing block container, 338
ISO (International Organization for Standardization), 82
isTreatElementsAsHard() function, 162
isUcsOrthographic() function, 355
italic text, 144

J

Java code for database access, 36
JOINSTYLE, 99
Julian dates, 63
justification
    of dimension text, 265
    for single lines of text, **238–240**
Justification property, 295

K

kAcGiOpBad (drawing command), 376
kAcGiOpCircle2 (drawing command), 376
kAcGiOpCircularArc1 (drawing command), 376
kAcGiOpCircularArc2 (drawing command), 377
kAcGiOpColor (drawing command), 379
kAcGiOpLayerIndex (drawing command), 379
kAcGiOpLayerName (drawing command), 379
kAcGiOpLineTypeIndex (drawing command), 379
kAcGiOpLineTypeName (drawing command), 379
kAcGiOpLineTypeScale (drawing command), 380
kAcGiOpMaxOpCodes (drawing command, 381
kAcGiOpMesh (drawing command), 377
kAcGiOpOpBoundingBoxSave (drawing command), 379
kAcGiOpOpFillType (drawing command), 379
kAcGiOpOpLineWeight (drawing command), 379
kAcGiOpOpTrueColor (drawing command), 379
kAcGiOpPlineNormal (drawing command), 380
kAcGiOpPlotStyleName (drawing command), 380
kAcGiOpPolygon (drawing command), 377
kAcGiOpPolyline (drawing command), 377
kAcGiOpPopClipBoundary (drawing command), 380
kAcGiOpPopTransform (drawing command), 380
kAcGiOpPushClipBoundary (drawing command), 380
kAcGiOpPushTransformM (drawing command), 380
kAcGiOpPushTransformV (drawing command), 380
kAcGiOpRay (drawing command), 379
kAcGiOpSelectionMarker (drawing command), 379
kAcGiOpSetExtents (drawing command), 376
kAcGiOpShell (drawing command), 378
kAcGiOpText1 (drawing command), 378
kAcGiOpText2 (drawing command), 378
kAcGiOpThickness (drawing command), 380
kAcGiOpXLine (drawing command), 378
key string
    in dictionary, 161
    of symbol record, 30
keys, 4–5
    listing for dictionary, 33
knots, of spline, 225–226

L

Last Updated property, of AcDbIndex object, 169
layer filters, as extension record, **174**
layer index, **170**
    setting for, 165

Layer property
    of block-internal object, 328
    for entities, 192, **193**
    indexing entities by, 169
layer record, properties, **135–137**
layerID() function, 193
LayerOn property, of layer, 136
layers
    drawing command for, 379
    external, **137–138**
    hiding in viewports, 360–361
    settings for, 91
Layers property, of document object, 38
layers table, 4, **134–138**
layout blocks, 35, 178, **182**
    coordinate systems, **347–349**
    in DXF file, **350–351**
    plotting, 343
    settings, **349–350**
    tabs to switch between, 347
layout objects, **346–351**
Leader Length property, 272
leaders, 145, **276–279**
Length property, for line, 218
lengths
    as real numbers, 61
    units, **63**
libraries, of symbol shapes, 141, 234
lightweight polylines, **279–283**
LIMCHECK, 99
LIMMAX, 100, 356
LIMMIN, 100, 356
line breaks, in dimension text, 255
line edges for hatches, **304**
line feeds, in ASCII DXF files, 22
line of sight, in abstract view, 351
line spacing, distance for MText object, 243
linear dimensions
    aligned, **269–270**
    display format, 148
    labels for, 146
    precision of, 147
    rotated, **270**
lines
    calculated properties for, **218–219**
    finite straight, **216–219**
    hiding in viewports, **360–361**
    multilines, **292–297**
    with thickness, **217–218**, *218*
Linetype property
    for entities, 192, **203–204**
    of layer, 136–137
Linetype Scale property, for entities, 192, **204–205**
linetype symbol table record, 83

linetype table, **4**
linetypeID() function, 203
linetypes
    definitions, **139–141**
    drawing command for, 379, 380
    mapping noncontinuous to polyline, 280
    predefined, **138–139**
    properties of, **139**
    settings for, 90
Linetypes table, *132*, **138–141**
Lineweight property
    for entities, 192, **205–206**
    of layer, 136–137
lineweights
    drawing command for, 379
    plot settings for, 345
    settings for, 90
    signed 16-bit integer for, 59
linewidth, of dimension and extension lines, 260
linking objects, **8–9**
links
    from AcDbRasterImageDef object to external
        image, 314
    extension dictionary, **124–125**
    object pointers for, 66
    reactor links, **123–124**
Linowes, Jonathan, 51
LISP, xix
local block container, 178
Location property, of shape, 234
Locked property, of layer, 136
logic, objects vs. application, 368
loops in hatched areas, 302–303
    edge-defined, **303–304**
    polyline-like, **303**
LTSCALE (global linetype scale factor), **83**, 203
LUNITS, 58, 100, 114
LUPREC, 100
LWDEFAULT, 206
LWDISPLAY (linewidths display), **83–84**

M

Major Axis Vector property, of ellipse, 222
mantissa, 61
mapping linetypes, **203–204**, *204*
MAXACTVP, 100
MEASUREMENT, 100, 115
measurement units, 63
    alternate dimensions for multiple, 258–259
    limits for tolerances, *256*
Mechanical Desktop, 366
member variables, 12

MENUNAME, 100
merging
    dictionaries, **162–163**
    extension records, **172–173**
meshes
    drawing command for, 377–378
    polyface, **290–292**
    polygon, **288–290**
methods, 11
MicroCAD, 19
Microsoft Visual C++, for ObjectDBX, 43
MInsert, 325
MIRRTEXT, 100
*MODEL_SPACE block, 6, 182
    AutoLISP and, 30–31
    bounding box, settings for, 99
    in DXF file ENTITIES section, 185, **188**
    layout, 347
    plot settings, 343
    PSLTSCALE and, 86
    TILEMODE setting and, 87
    viewports to, 351, **357–363**
ModelType property, of AcDbLayout object, 347
MText objects, contents and formatting, **243–244**
multilines, **292–297**
    breaks and intersections, **295–296**
    calculated properties, **297**
    entities, **294–295**
    styles, 91, **292–294**
multiple insert, 325

N

name field, for records in symbol table, 4
Name property
    of AcDbBlockTableRecord object, 178
    of layer, 135
    of linetypes, 139
    of text styles, 142
    of UCS (User Coordinate System), 151
    of viewports, 154
    of views, 153
    of xref blocks, 182
named objects dictionary, 34, 161
named views, **152–153**
    plotting, 342
namedobjdict function, 34
negative numbers, 56
nesting block references, 324
newBlockReferenceIdIterator() function, 180
newIterator() function, 46, 47
    for dictionaries, 49
non-entities, 159

non-layout blocks, 178
nonbreaking space, in MText object, 243
nonuniform rational B-splines (NURBS), 224,
    225–226
normal, 70–71
Normal property
    of circle, 219–220
    of ellipse, 222
    of lines, 217
    of shape, 234
normal vector, 70, 217
normalized vector, 67
notification, opening object for, 44
null handle, 348
numbers. *See also* integers
    real, **61–63**
numHatchLines() function, 309
NURBS (nonuniform rational B-splines), 224,
    225–226

O

Object Coordinate System (OCS), 69
Object DXF. *See* DXF (Drawing Interchange Format)
object pointers, **66**
Object Schema Number property, of DictionaryVariables object, 166
ObjectARX, xix–xx, 8, 18, **42–50**, 386
    to access AutoCAD database, **43**
    iterating through containers, **45–47**
ObjectDBX, 42–43, 44
    16-bit integer in, 56
    to access drawing database, xxi
    ads_real data type, 61
    binary chunks in, 73
    char data type, 64
    for dictionaries, **49**
    disadvantages, 50
    entity handling in, **47–48**
    functions to query parametrical curves, 213–214
    to obtain UCSORG setting, 77
    points in, 66
    shortcuts to database settings, **49–50**
    signed 32-bit integer in, 57
    signed 8-bit integer, 57
    vectors in, 68
ObjectID, 8
    calculation from handle, 120–121
ObjectName property, of objects, 121
objects, 2, 3, **25–26**
    adding to block container, 48
    class of, **121–122**

custom, in ActiveX Automation, **41–42**
database contents associated with, 28
deleting, 34
in DXF file, **161**
embedding, **9**
extension dictionary link, **124–125**
handle for, **120–121**
identifying, **7–9**
inclusion in book, 14
instantiating, 43
linking, **8–9**
making and modifying in AutoLISP, **34–35**
opening and closing, **44–45**
other pointers, **125–126**
owner of, **122**
properties, **11–13**
reactor links, **123–124**
OBJECTS section in DXF file, 25
obliquing angle, for text objects, 144
OCS (Object Coordinate System), 69
Off property, of layer, 135–136
OLE (Object Linking and Embedding), 384,
  389–392
object location, orientation and size, **391**
source and type, **390–391**
OLE Automation. *See* ActiveX Automation
OLESTARTUP, 100
openBlockBegin() function, 48, 184
openBlockEnd() function, 48, 184
OpenDWG alliance, xvii, 51
opening objects, **44–45**
order of spline, 224
ordinate dimensions, 145
origin of UCS (User Coordinate System), 151
Origin property, of AcDbBlockTableRecord object,
  179
ORTHOMODE, 101
osnap points of entities, 209
output devices, plot settings for, 339
overlaid reference, attached reference vs., 182
overlined text, 238, 244
owner of objects, **122**
Owner property of entities, 188

P

paper sizes, and plot settings, 339–340
*PAPER_SPACE block, 6, 182
  AutoLISP and, 30–31
  in DXF file ENTITIES section, 185, **188**
  settings for, 101, 103
  TILEMODE setting and, 87
Paperspace Flag property, for entities, 192, **208–209**

paperspace viewport, **361–362**
  PSLTSCALE and, 86
paragraph text, **240–244**
  DXF representation, **244**
parallel polylines, 292
parallel projection for view, 352
paramAtAngle() function, 223
parameters, passing points as, 66
parsing, container into objects, 25
patterns, for hatched areas, 301, **307–309**
.PC3 file extension, 339
PDMODE (point display mode), 76, **84**, 232
  reading and writing, 35–36
PDSIZE (point display size), *85*, **85**, 232
PE_URL application, 208
PELEVATION, 101
pen width, 205
percent symbol doubled (%%), for font file characters, 237
periodic curve, 214
persistent links, 123
PEXTMAX, 101
PEXTMIN, 101
PINSBASE, 101
placeholder objects, in dictionaries, **164**
planar entity, 70, 209–210
  dimension as, 267
  text line as, 236
PLIMCHECK, 101
PLIMMAX, 101
PLIMMIN, 101
PLINEGEN, 101
PLINEWID, 101
Plot Rotation property, 341
plot settings, **338–346**
  fine-tuning, **345–346**
  for layout, 343
  media and, **339–341**
  for output devices, 339
  rotation, **341**
  scale, **343–345**
Plot Style Name property, for entities, 192
Plot Style Name Type property, for entities, 192,
  207
Plot Style property
  for AcDbEntity object, 164
  for entities, **206–207**
plot style, settings for, 90
plot styles
  for AcDbEntity object, 346
  within viewport, **361**
Plot Type property, 342
PlotConfigurations collection, 41
Plotstyle property, of layer, 136–137

Plottable property, of layer, 136
plotter configuration files, 339
plotting named views, 342
point objects, xviii, **232–233**
pointers, **125–126**
points
    in drawing database, **66–72**
    symbols for display, 84–85, *85*, *233*
polyface mesh records, **291–292**
polyface mesh vertices, **290–291**
polyface meshes, **290–292**
polygon meshes, **288–290**
    settings for, 104
polyline-like loops, **303**
polylines
    arcs in, **280–281**
    curve-fit, **286**
    drawing command for, 377
    heavyweight, **283–287**
        header, **284**
        vertex objects, **285**
    lightweight, **279–283**
    settings for, 101
    splined, **286–287**
    three-dimensional, **287–288**
    wide, **281–283**, *282*, *283*
polymesh surfaces, splined, **289–290**
position() function, 391
precision of numbers, 61
    in ASCII DXF files, 62
predefined constants, 58
preview images
    extracting and displaying, 396
    in Open File dialog box, 392
    types in DWG file, 396
PROJECTNAME dictionary variable, 165
prompt property, of AcDbAttributeDefinition
    object, 333
properties
    of AcDbDimension object, **267–269**
    ActiveX Automation to access, 39–40
    of curves, **212–215**
    defined vs. calculated, **12**
    of dimension styles, **145–150**
    inherited, for block containers, **327–328**
    of layer record, **135–137**
    of linetypes, **139**
    missing, **12–13**
    of objects, **11–13**
    of text styles, **142–144**
    of UCS (User Coordinate System), **151–152**
    of viewports, 154
    of views, **153**
proxy entities, **371–374**

Proxy Flags property, 372
proxy graphics, **374–381**
    drawing commands, **376–381**
    structure, **375**
proxy objects, 369, **371–374**
    DXF sequence, **374**
PROXYGRAPHICS, 101
PSLTSCALE (paperspace linetype scaling), 83, **86**, 203
    and layouts, 350
PSVPSCALE, 102
PUCSBASE, 102
PUCSNAME, 102
PUCSORBACK, 102
PUCSORG, 102
PUCSORGBOTTOM, 102
PUCSORGFRONT, 102
PUCSORGLEFT, 102
PUCSORGRIGHT, 103
PUCSORGTOP, 103
PUCSORTHOREF, 103
PUCSORTHOVIEW, 103
PUCSXDIR, 103
PUCSYDIR, 103

Q

QTEXTMODE (quick text display), **86–87**
quadratic B-spline surfaces, 289
query of object's grip points, 48

R

radius dimensions, 145, **272–273**
Radius property, of circle, 219–220
Raster object, 316
rational spline, 226
ray, 216
RbChain() function, 171
reactor links, **123–124**
Reactors property, of image definition object, 319
read-only objects, 44, 45
real numbers, **61–63**
records
    in dictionaries, 5
    in drawing database, 3
    extension, **171–174**
    polyface mesh, **291–292**
    in symbol tables, 4
references
    external, **182–183**
    for proxy object, 373
regenerating drawing, settings for, 103

REGENMODE, 103
regions, **385**
    querying properties from, 387
registered applications symbol table, **158**
relative hyperlinks, settings for, 99
remote text, **249–250**
rendered images, normal direction and, 71
rendering mode, for abstract views, **354**
resolution units, 315
Resolved property, of layer, 138
Richards, Matt, 51
right-hand rule, 68
Rohrbaugh, Gary, 51
root dictionary, 5, 161
    minimum contents, **163**
    owner query and, 122
rotated linear dimensions, **270**
rotating image, 317
Rotation property
    of shape, 234
    of text, 241
rounding for dimensions, 149
routines for display and logic, for custom objects, 367
RText object, 248, 366, 368

S

safearray, binary chunk as, 73
SAT file format, 387
scale to fit, 343
ScaledToFit property, of linetypes, 139, 203–204
scaleFactors() function, 326
scaling
    dimensions, **253–254**
    plots, **343–345**
    viewports, **358–360**
Scaling property, of text string, 236
Screen Coordinate System (SCS), 69
screen coordinates, for viewport, 156
SecondPoint property, for ray, 216
seed point, 309–310
seek() function, 46
segments in linetype, 139
sequencing in DXF file, 21
serialization of multidimensional data structure, 21
server application for OLE, 389
setAt() function, 49
setFromRbChain() function, 171
settings
    ACADMAINTVER (AutoCAD database mainte-
        nance version number), **80**

ACADVER (AutoCAD database version number), 7, 76, **79**
    access to, **77–78**
    additional, **89–115**
    ATTMODE (attribute display mode), **80**
    for AutoCAD for state, 76
    dimension-related, 109
    DISPSLH (show silhouette lines for 3D solids), **80–81**
    DWGCODEPAGE (drawing character set), **81–82**
    FILLMODE (fill display mode), **82**, 281, 301
    LTSCALE (global linetype scale factor), **83**, 203
    LWDISPLAY (linewidths display), **83–84**
    PDMODE (point display mode), 35–36, 76, **84**, 232
    PDSIZE (point display size), *85*, **85**, 232
    PSLTSCALE (paperspace linetype scaling), 83, **86**, 203, 350
    QTEXTMODE (quick text display), **86–87**
    saved in drawing file, 7
    sequencing in DXF file, **115–117**
    SPLFRAME (spline frame display), **87**, 286, 289
    TILEMODE (modelspace display), **87–88**
    VISRETAIN (retain visibility settings), **88–89**
setUscorg() function, 77
setvar function, 35–36
SetVariable method, 42
SetXRecordData method, 171
SHADEDGE, 103, 115
SHADEDIF, 103
Shape Number property, of linetypes, 140
shape symbols, *234*, **234–235**
shapeNumberAt() function, 140
shapeStyleAt() function, 140
shearing of symbol shapes, *235*
Shearing property, of text string, 236
SHX file type, 13, 141, 142, 236
    for fonts, 237
sign bit, for 16-bit integer, 56
signed 16-bit integer, 54, **55–56**
signed 32-bit integer, **56–57**
signed 8-bit integer, **57**
silhouette outline, 81
single-bounded straight lines, **216**
Size property, of AcDbRasterImageDef object, 315
SKETCHINC, 103
SKPOLY, 103
snap grid, 357
snap setting, 157
Snap Spacing property, of viewports, 157, 357
soft owner, 8, 162
    group codes, 126
soft pointer, 8
    group codes, 126

SoftSource libraries, 51
solid models, 384, 385
solids for hatched areas, **310–311**
SORTENTS dictionary variable, 165
spacial filtering, **328–331**
spacing, around dimension text, 263
spatial index
    of block container, **170**
    setting for, 165
Spatial Technology, 384
    Web site, 387
SPLFAME, 291
SPLFRAME (spline frame display), **87**, 286, 289
spline curves, **224–227**
    AcDbCurve properties and, **226–227**
    DXF sequence, **227**
    fit data of, **225**
    NURBS (nonuniform rational B-splines),
        225–226
    settings for display, 87
spline edges, **305–306**
splined polylines, **286–287**
splined polymesh surfaces, **289–290**
SPLINESEGS, 104
SPLINETYPE, 104
ssget function, 28
stacked text, 244
start point, 216
start-section bracet, in DXF file, 24
step() function, 46
straight lines, finite, **216–219**
stretch points, of entities, 209
string values, **64–65**
    in binary DXF file, 22
STYLESHEET, 104
subscript, 238
superscript, 238
surfaces, splined polymesh, **289–290**
SURFTAB1, 104
SURFTAB2, 104
SURFTYPE, 104
SURFU, 104
SURFV, 104
symbol record, key string of, 30
symbol shapes, libraries of, 141
symbol tables, **4–5**, **132–133**
    AcDbDimStyleTable, **144–150**
    AcDbLayerTable, **134–138**
    AcDbLinetypeTable, **138–141**
    AcDbRegAppTable, **158**
    AcDbTextStyleTable, **141–144**
    AcDbUCSTable, **151–152**
    AcDbViewportTable, **154–157**
    AcDbViewTable, **152–153**

collections for, 38
in DXF file, 24, **133**
fixed records in, 5
interator object for, 46
for linetypes, 83
owner query and, 122
record count value in, 134
VISRETAIN and, 88–89
symbols
    for point display, 84, *85*, *233*
    shearing, *235*
symmetrical tolerance, 256
SYSCODEPAGE global setting, 65
system variables, ObjectDBX access to, 50
SYSVAR command, 76

T

table of registered applications, 4
tables. *See also* symbol tables
    to define plot styles, 206
TABLES section in DXF file, 24
Tag property, of attribute definitions, 332
tagging in DXF file, 21
tangency direction, for curve-fit polylines, 286
target for line of sight, 351
tblnext function, 30, 31
tblobjname function, 29–30
    to access block container, 31
TDCREATE, 104
TDINDWG, 63, 104
TDUCREATE, 104
TDUPDATE, 105
TDUSRTIMER, 105
TDUUPDATE, 105
templates, for AcDbDimension object, 259
temporary block containers, 179
terminology, 2
text
    for dimensions, **259**
        positioning, **263–267**
    paragraph, **240–244**
    remote, **249–250**
    single lines, **235–240**
        formatting, **238**
        justification, **238–240**
        styles and characters, **237**
    string values, 22, **64–65**
text box, for dimensions, 263
Text Height property, for dimensions, 254
text objects
    attribute as, 331
    display setting, 86

Text property, of linetypes, 140
text string
    calculation for dimensions, **254–256**
    drawing command for, 378
    visibility of attribute, 80
Text Style property, 237
text style symbol table, 132, **141–144**
text style table, 4
textAt() function, 140
TEXTSIZE, 105
TEXTSTYLE, 105
THICKNESS, 105
thickness
    drawing command for, 380
    lines with, **217–218**, *218*
Thickness property
    of lines, 217
    of shape, 234
third-party objects, 14, 366
    database and display logic, 367
three-dimensional. *See 3D at beginning of index*
thumbnail image
    binary, 185
    preview for non-layout block, 179
THUMBNAILIMAGE section in DXF file, 25, 397
tiled viewports, 88, 154
TILEMODE (modelspace display), **87–88**
time values, **63**
timer, user-defined, settings for, 105
tolerance symbol (+/-), characters replaced by, 237
tolerances in dimensions, 150, *256*, **256–258**
total editing time, for drawing database, 104
traces for hatched areas, **310–311**
TRACEWID, 105
transformation matrices, 329
transparency of bitmap background, 317
TREEDEPTH, 105
True Type fonts, 141
TTF file type, 13
type library, 18, 36

U

UCS icon, displaying, 156, 356
UCS (User Coordinate System), 68–69, **151–152**
    settings, 114–115
UCSBASE, 105
ucsBaseOrigin() function, 152
UCSNAME, 105
UCSORG, 77, 106
UCSORGBACK, 106
UCSORGBOTTOM, 106
UCSORGFRONT, 106

UCSORGLEFT, 106
UCSORGRIGHT, 106
UCSORGTOP, 106
UCSORTHO, 114
UCSORTHOREF, 106
UCSORTHOVIEW, 106, 114
UCSXDIR, 107
UCSYDIR, 107
unbounded straight lines, **215–216**
underlined text, 238, 244
Unicode character set, 64
    and text strings, 237
unit vector, 67
UNITMODE, 107
units of measurement, 63
    alternate dimensions for multiple, 258–259
    limits for tolerances, *256*
Upside Down property
    of text string, 236
    of text styles, 143
user coordinate system table, 4
User Coordinate System (UCS), 68–69, **151–152**
    settings, 102, 114–115
user-defined layer filters, 135
user-defined pattern, for hatched areas, 308
user-defined timer, settings for, 105
User Scale property, for images, 320–321
USERI*n*, 107
USERR*n*, 107
USRTIMER, 107

V

variable attributes, **334–335**
VBA (Visual Basic for Applications), 36–37
vector, **67–68**
VERSIONGUID, 107
vertex objects, **285**
vertexIterator() function, 285, 290
vertical alignment of text, 239
Vertical Alignment property, of AcDbText object, 333
Vertical property, of text styles, 143
vertices
    of 3D polyline, 287–288
    polyface mesh, **290–291**
view table, 4
viewport borders, in output, 346
viewport configuration, 154
viewport sequence number, 361
viewports, 88, 351
    Arc Smoothness property of, 220
    clipped, **360**

Detailing property of, 220
drawing aids, **356–357**
in DXF file, **362–363**
hiding lines and layers, **360–361**
to MODELSPACE, **357–363**
paperspace, **361–362**
plot styles within, **361**
scale, **358–360**
scale and dimensions, 254
settings for, 100, 102
viewports table, 4, **154–157**
views
abstract, **351–355**
clipping, **353**
coordinate systems, **354–355**
named, **152–153**
visibility
of block containers, 324
of face edges, 228
layers and, 134
Visibility property
for entities, 192, **207–208**
of object, 60
Visible property, for AcDbRasterImage entity, 317
VisiCalc, 19
VISRETAIN (retain visibility settings), **88–89**
Visual Basic, xx
code for database access, 36
Visual Basic for Applications (VBA), xx, 36–37, 384
projects, **392**
Visual C++, 50
Visual LISP, xix, 27
code for database access, 36
visual representation for entity, 192
visualization of block, 6
visualization, of custom entity, 375
Volume property, of 3D solid, 388

W

Walker, John, 19
Web sites
OpenDWG alliance, 51
Spatial Technology, 387
wide polylines, **281–283**, *282*, *283*
width of view, 353
Width property, for plot media, 340
Windows 95/98, character sets, 64
Windows fonts, 141
Windows NT, character sets, 64
wipeouts, **311**
wire frame, 80–81
face edges in, 228

word wrap, 242
World Coordinate System (WCS), 68
for entity bounding box, 209
for OLE object, 391
WORLDVIEW, 107

X

X-Scaling property, of text string, 236
XCLIPFRAME, 165
xdata (extended object data), **126–129**
attached to AcDbBlockBegin object, 184
dimension style setting as, 253
group codes and values, **128–129**
reading and writing, **127–128**
selecting, **126**
shortcuts to associate with owner, 158
XEDIT, 107
xline entity, 215
XREF command, 88
xref (external reference), 178, **182–183**
xrefStatus() function, 183

Z

Z coordinate, 217
settings for, 98, 101
Zombies, 369

ABOUT THE AUTHOR

Dietmar Rudolph lives in Essen, a city of some 600,000 people, in the western part of Germany. He studied mathematics, computer science, and operations research and received an M.Sc. in Mathematics from the Ruhr-Universität Bochum.

After working for several years as a programmer and consultant, in 1986 he founded CR/LF Corp., an independent consulting company specializing in CAD/CAM and technical documentation.

As president of CR/LF, Rudolph is responsible for a number of large-scale CAD/CAM projects, including huge client-specific AutoCAD applications, data exchange, and integration of many software components and machinery. In a second area of business, CR/LF localizes and authors software and documentation for several well-known companies such as Autodesk, ICEM Technologies, CAD Distribution, Design Pacifica, and Basis Software. For more on CR/LF services, visit `http://www.crlf.de`.

In addition to his work at CR/LF, Rudolph has written, translated, edited, and published more than 60 computer books and several hundred articles for magazines such as *Cadence, CAD User,* and *AutoCAD-Magazin*, in both German and English.

In 1997, Rudolph joined the well-known AutoCAD experts Owen Wengerd, Steve Johnson, and Paul Kohut as a manager of CADLock, Inc., a company specializing in data security solutions. As vice-president of CADLock, Rudolph takes part in the development of AutoCAD add-ons for secure drawing exchange. CADLocked drawings include unmodifyable owner information, are password protected, and refuse all AutoCAD operations the owner decided to lock. Visit `http://www.cadlock.com` for details.

Rudolph actively participates in ADGE (AutoCAD Developers Group Europe—and beyond), the independent association of AutoCAD third-party developers. He is a Registered Autodesk Consultant and DXF Threadmaster of the AutoCAD forum on Compuserve (GO ACAD) and of the Autodesk newsgroups.

Comments and additions to this book are welcome at `dietmar@crlf.de`.